Politics and Society in Great Yarmouth 1660–1722

PERRY GAUCI

CLARENDON PRESS · OXFORD

1996

Oxford University Press, Walton Street, Oxford OX2 6DP

Oxford New York
Athens Auckland Bangkok Bombay
Calcutta Cape Town Dar es Salaam Delhi
Florence Hong Kong Istanbul Karachi
Kuala Lumpur Madras Madrid Melbourne
Mexico City Nairobi Paris Singapore
Taipei Tokyo Toronto
and associated companies in
Berlin Ibadan

Oxford is a trade mark of Oxford University Press

Published in the United States
by Oxford University Press Inc., New York

British Library Cataloguing in Publication Data
Data available

Library of Congress Cataloging in Publication Data
Gauci, Perry,
Politics and society in Great Yarmouth, 1660–1722 / Perry Gauci.
p. cm. — (Oxford historical monographs)
Includes bibliographical references and index.
1. Great Yarmouth (England)—Politics and government. 2. Great
Yarmouth (England)—Social conditions. 3. Great Yarmouth (England)—
Economic conditions. 4. Local government—England—History.
I. Title. II. Series.
JS3425.G744G38 1996
942.6′18066—dc20 95–30137
ISBN 0–19–820605–4

1 3 5 7 9 10 8 6 4 2

Typeset by Graphicraft Typesetters Ltd., Hong Kong

Printed in Great Britain
on acid-free paper by
Bookcraft Ltd.,
Midsomer Norton, Avon

PREFACE

EVEN though a relative newcomer to historical research, I am already heavily indebted to a host of supportive friends and associates. My principal academic obligation lies with my supervisor and sub-editor, Dr Clive Holmes. It was he who first suggested that the Great Yarmouth archive might be a rich source to mine, and ever since he has been an avuncular mentor for my first forays into the archives. His constructive criticisms, accessibility, and infectious enthusiasm for the subject are the source of any value that might accrue from this piece of work. Prior to Clive, I had been especially fortunate to benefit from the sagacious and inspiring counsel of many tutors, and due thanks from a truly grateful pupil are accorded to Robert Parry, Peter Anthony, Alan Beatson, Vivian Green, Susan Brigden, Paul Langford, and John Spurr. In addition, Paul Langford and Peter Borsay, the examiners of the doctoral thesis upon which this publication is based, merit great thanks for their perceptive critique of my work, and for reading earlier drafts of this book.

During my research I was funded by grants from the British Academy and the Fiddian Scholarship Fund at Brasenose College, Oxford. Both organizations were quick to answer my cries for financial help, particularly when I requested additional funds for study away from home. All the staffs of the various record repositories which I have visited on my travels deserve recognition and thanks for handling my requests with patience and efficiency, but I would like to single out Paul Rutledge and the rest of the staff at the Norfolk Record Office as especially generous in sparing me their time and expertise. They were also instrumental in my gaining access to the Townshend papers at Raynham, and I would like to thank The Marquess Townshend for allowing me to cite materials from his family archive. I would also like to acknowledge Dr A. R. Michel for use of one of his tables, and the British Library for the illustration in this work. The History of Parliament Trust in London have kindly given me permission to use their unpublished biographies and constituency articles for the forthcoming volumes on the 1690–1715 period, and I would like to thank all my colleagues there for their support. In particular, David Hayton, Mark Knights, and Stuart Handley showed exemplary patience by reading large sections of this book in draft, and have ensured that I avoided many pitfalls.

Friends who have helped me maintain a sense of perspective on my researches must also be mentioned. Jerry Chubb, Gareth Parry, and the brothers Loffhagen have been unstinting in their support of my labours when lodging with them in London, as has James McHugo. Beyond them, it would be invidious to single out individuals, but sincerest thanks nevertheless to all the boys and girls from Monmouth, Lincoln, and Brasenose.

My last, and greatest, wish of gratitude must go to my family, who have backed me so whole-heartedly through the perilous world of modern graduate studies. This book is dedicated to them. The contribution of Christina Harper, its newest member, is, and will remain, incalculable.

Author's Note

All dates are given in Old Style, but with the year taken to have started on 1 January. Spelling has been modernized where it is possible to do so without affecting the meaning of the quotation.

CONTENTS

List of Tables   ix

List of Illustrations   x

Abbreviations   xi

Introduction   1

1. Oligarchy and Community: The Corporate Institution   15
    i.   The Corporate Assembly   19
    ii.   The Freemen   40
    iii. The Outsiders   48

2. Oligarchy and Community: The Corporate Personnel   57
    i.   Recruitment and the Civic Career   60
    ii.   The Corporate Family   68
    iii. The Corporation, Trade, and Wealth   78
    iv.   The Corporation and the Religious Divide   88
    v.   Region and Realm   91

3. The Challenge of the Restoration: 1660–74   100

4. The Challenge Met: 1675–81   129

5. Regulation and Revolution: 1681–88   151

6. Uncertainty and Unity: 1689–1702   174

7. The Townshend Triumph: 1702–22   211

Conclusion   255

Appendices   265
    1. Survey of Yarmouth Corporate Finances: 1660–1720   265
    2. Distribution of Wealth through the Ward System:
        1660–1720   268

3. *Admission of Freemen by Yarmouth Corporation:*
   1620–1740   269
4. *A Mercantile Élite: The England Dynasty*   270
5. *An Assembly Network: The Wakeman Dynasty*   272

Bibliography   275

Index   293

LIST OF TABLES

2.1	Average time taken for freemen to enter the assembly	62
2.2	Office tenure of assemblymen (in years)	64
2.3	Executors and supervisors chosen by assemblymen	76
2.4	Occupational structure of the assembly and the town	79
2.5	Corporate influence on local mercantile activity	82
2.6	Wealth distribution at Yarmouth, 1660–61	85

LIST OF ILLUSTRATIONS

Figures

1. Genealogical table showing the England dynasty   271
2. Genealogical table showing the Wakeman dynasty   273

Map

Map showing Great Yarmouth in 1725   *xii*

ABBREVIATIONS

Add. mss	Additional Manuscripts, British Library
BIHR	Bulletin of the Institute of Historical Research
BL	British Library
Bodl.	Bodleian Library, Oxford
CJ	Journal of the House of Commons
CSPD	Calendar of the State Papers, Domestic
CTB	Calendar of Treasury Books
CUL	Cambridge University Library
EHR	English Historical Review
Henning, *House of Commons, 1660–90*	B. D. Henning (ed.), *The History of Parliament: The House of Commons, 1660–90* (London, 1983), 3 vols.
HJ	Historical Journal
HMC	Historical Manuscripts Commission
JBS	Journal of British Studies
LJ	Journal of the House of Lords
NAC	Norwich Archdeaconry Court
NCC	Norwich Consistory Court
NNAS	Norfolk and Norwich Archaeological Society
NRO	Norfolk Record Office
NRS	Norfolk Record Society
Palmer, *History of Great Yarmouth*	C. J. Palmer, *A History of Great Yarmouth, Designed as a Continuation of Manship's History of that Town* (Great Yarmouth, 1856).
PCC	Prerogative Court of Canterbury
PL	Paston Letters, Bradfer Lawrence mss Ic
PRO	Public Record Office, Chancery Lane
Sedgwick, *House of Commons 1715–54*	R. Sedgwick ed. *The History of Parliament: The House of Commons, 1715–54* (London, 1970), 2 vols.
Swinden, *History of Great Yarmouth*	H. Swinden, *The History and Antiquities of the Ancient Burgh of Great Yarmouth* (Norwich, 1772).
TRHS	Transactions of the Royal Historical Society
UEA	University of East Anglia
VCH	Victoria County History

Great Yarmouth in 1725

INTRODUCTION

TUESDAY, 28 September 1675 was not a date destined to go down in the annals of British history. Even the student of Restoration politics would be hard pressed to attach any particular significance to it. King Charles II was at Whitehall, attending to the day-to-day business of government, a chore with which he famously had little patience. Parliament was not sitting, Charles having prorogued it several months before after another stormy session. The country's domestic news was certainly of little moment, for the *London Gazette* was more concerned with the great European issue of the day, the conflict of France against the Dutch, on which England had looked for over two years as a mere passive spectator. More memorably, Sir Christopher Wren was currently supervising the construction of Greenwich Observatory, but there was little else for succeeding generations to commemorate.[1]

However, away from the metropolis, for one Norfolk peer *en route* to Great Yarmouth it was a red-letter day indeed. Having recently received an invitation from the port's ruling corporation, Robert, Lord Paston was about to make his first official visit to the town which nine months before had elected him as its high steward, the most prestigious office in its power to bestow. This appointment reflected his growing prominence both in the county and at court, his peerage of May 1673 the latest of a series of royal favours gained in return for his conspicuous loyalty to the Crown. Despite these honours, Paston knew that he faced a major test as he travelled towards Yarmouth, perceiving it to be a highlight of an unofficial progress through the county whose leadership he coveted. His own entourage, consisting of an attendance of some 40 horse, had been primed to gauge the response of the townsmen, as well as warned not to jeopardize his reputation by an untimely bout of ill-behaviour. As one observer wryly commented, 'the eyes and hearts' of the region were on him, and he could not afford to fail his hosts on this occasion. In the parlance of modern historiography, Paston well understood that that day would see the meeting of centre and locality.

By late afternoon Paston had arrived at the hamlet of Caister, two miles to the north of Yarmouth, where, despite the rain, his entourage was

[1] *CSPD* 1675–6, pp. 173, 322; *London Gazette*, 27–30 Sept. 1675; *Wren Society*, xix. 113–15.

greeted by a magnificent welcoming committee of some 300 horse. After
a toast to the high steward, the cavalcade acted as an escort into the inner
sanctum of the town, guns booming out their welcome as Paston passed
through the gates. Loud huzzas from the packed streets greeted him as he
finally alighted from his coach, and would continue to ring in his ears
over the next two days as he was plunged into a round of civic festivities.
The members of the town's ruling council, the assembly, were keenest to
fête their nominal leader, granting him the freedom of the borough, and
lavishly entertaining him at a 'magnificent dinner' attended by over 300
of the local well-to-do. Paston's departure on the Thursday saw a repeat
of the celebrations which had accompanied his arrival, the townsmen
singing 'loath to depart' when taking leave of their visitors at Caister.
Most importantly for the relationship between the town and its patron,
'there seemed in all a general satisfaction, they mightily pleased with their
high steward, and he as well with them'.[2]

Such events have rarely cluttered the pages of conventional histories.
Only in the last few decades have the proponents of the study of local
history banished the ghost of antiquarianism which had relegated their
work to cursory glances, or, as one researcher acidly put it, to the status
of 'providing footnotes for somebody else's History of England'.[3] However, there has been a growing awareness among historians that the significance of such episodes as Paston's state visit merit closer study, in
recognition of their intrinsic importance as well as for the insights which
they bring to general themes and problems. For certain, the long-term
implications of Paston's sojourn were not lost on Yarmouth's leaders,
who were well aware that in the person of Lord Paston lay the economic,
religious, and political future of the port. It may have been a routine day
elsewhere, but at Yarmouth Paston's arrival directly impinged upon the
livelihoods and beliefs of 10,000 local inhabitants. What greater importance could a single event have had for the local populace? Moreover,
an examination of the underlying tensions masked by the pomp of his
entrance can illuminate the strains of early modern government, as well
as the specific difficulties of political leaders after the Restoration. What
more could the historian desire of his subject? A primary concern of this
study of Yarmouth's political development between 1660 and 1722 is to
show that the local case study, when securely set in a general context, can
be of much wider interest.

    [2] PL, R. Flynt to Lady Yarmouth, 8 Oct. 1675; J. Fisher to same, 29 Sept. 1675, 1 Oct.
1675; J. Gough to same, 1 Oct. 1675.
    [3] H. P. R. Finberg, *Local History in the University* (Leicester, 1964), 14.

Recognition of the potential significance of local studies has been one of the most important developments in British historiography since the Second World War. While fears have been expressed for the manner in which the study of history has fractured into a myriad of sub-disciplines, local history has gone from strength to strength, questioning the over-riding importance of 'traditional' political history, principally written from the standpoint of Whitehall, Westminster, and the City. Guided by several path-finding scholars, the study of the localities has rapidly matured as an academic discipline, gaining converts and university departments on its way. For analysts of English political history in the early modern period, the locality has become a familiar hunting-ground, challenging perceptions of major events such as the Reformation and the Civil War. In particular, the importance of the interplay of centre and locality has been identified as a key theme for understanding the impact of such turning-points in our history. For most of the intervening three centuries even Norfolk historians seemed more excited by the arrival of the King at Yarmouth in 1671, rather than with Paston's visit of 1675, but the significance of the latter occasion would now be readily recognized by students of Restoration politics and society.[4]

The main beneficiary of this wave of interest in the localities has been the early Stuart period. By the mid-1960s debate surrounding the causes of the English Civil War, that hoariest of historiographic chestnuts, was in danger of a stifling attack of ideological overkill, as a scholarly battle was fought to ascertain the gentry's contribution to the outbreak of hostilities. However, the publication in 1966 of Alan Everitt's seminal work, *The Community of Kent and the Great Rebellion, 1640–60*, shifted the 'gentry controversy' away from socio-economic analysis towards a more nuanced and constructive methodology. His argument for a 'county community' consciousness, which necessarily conditioned the impact of national developments on the locality, had an immediate impact on a younger generation of scholars, leading to a flood of county studies which has yet to ebb completely. Even though many of these studies have seriously questioned the typicality of Kent as a semi-autonomous state within a state, his achievement in awakening an awareness of contemporary horizons will remain a lasting one.[5]

Everitt's influence was soon translated to students of the early modern

---

[4] See, for example, F. Heal, *Hospitality in Early Modern England* (Oxford, 1990), 311–12.
[5] A. Everitt, *The Community of Kent and the Great Rebellion*, 1640–60 (Leicester, 1966). For a critique of the county community model, see C. Holmes, 'The County Community in Stuart Historiography', in *JBS* 19 (1980), 54–73.

English town. Several excellent works on urban politics prior to the Civil
War had already appeared before 1966, most notably those of Wallace
MacCaffrey and Valerie Pearl, but Everitt gave even further momentum
to research in this field.[6] As a result, analysts of the townsmen of Newcastle, Norwich, and Bristol have raised many issues concerning the
provincial response to the outbreak of Civil War, and the most recent
studies have reflected the increasing sophistication of local history, concerned as they are to delineate the interaction of the townsmen with their
county neighbours, as well as with the organs of central government. Thus,
even though this book examines the consequences, rather than the causes,
of England's mid-century upheavals, it still looks to the scholarship of
the early Stuart period for its inspiration.[7]

While our understanding of the early Stuart town has been significantly advanced over the last twenty years, few monographs have examined provincial urban politics after 1660.[8] It is a surprising historiographic
omission, for general accounts of the late Stuart period have credited the
towns with a central role in the upheavals of the age. Historians have
accorded an increasing importance to the widespread municipal purges
of Charles II and James II, regarding royal policy towards the corporations as a significant cause of the Glorious Revolution. Moreover, the
fact that over three-quarters of the House of Commons was returned
by the boroughs has directed analysts of the 'rage of party' under William and Anne to investigate the political organization of the provincial
towns. As yet, however, there remains a dearth of urban case studies to
test the general themes identified by such work, particularly for the
period from the Restoration through to the advent of the Hanoverian age.
Therefore this study of Yarmouth seeks to explore an era of significant

---

[6] W. T. MacCaffrey, *Exeter, 1540–1640* (Cambridge, Mass. 1958); V. Pearl, *London and
the Outbreak of the Puritan Revolution* (Oxford, 1961).

[7] For the most comprehensive monographs of seventeenth-century provincial towns, see
R. Howell, *Newcastle-upon-Tyne and the Puritan Revolution* (Oxford, 1967); J. T. Evans,
Seventeenth-Century Norwich (Oxford, 1979); D. H. Sacks, *Trade, Society and Politics in
Bristol 1540–1640* (New York, 1985), 2 vols. For an important collection of recent urban
studies, see R. C. Richardson (ed.), *Town and Countryside in the English Revolution* (Man-
chester, 1992).

[8] Evans, *Seventeenth-Century Norwich*, remains the most important work on the politics
of the post-Restoration provincial town. However, although politics was not their primary
interest, encouragement for further research into the period comes from D. H. Sacks, *The
Widening Gate: Bristol and the Atlantic Economy, 1450–1700* (Berkeley, 1991); and D. Hey,
The Fiery Blades of Hallamshire: Sheffield and its Neighbourhood, 1660–1740 (Leicester,
1991). London, as befitting its size and importance, has continued to attract scholars—
T. Harris, *London Crowds in the Reign of Charles II* (Cambridge, 1987); G. S. De Krey,
A Fractured Society: The Politics of London in the First Age of Party (Oxford, 1985).

political development from an under-explored, but clearly important, perspective.

In the absence of intensive studies of the late Stuart town, our under-standing of urban political development in the period has been most significantly advanced by social and economic historians. Since the late 1950s the pioneering work of W. G. Hoskins and H. J. Dyos has provided the greatest stimulus to research into the urban environment, their writ-ings continuing to spark new historiographic initiatives. Hoskins also served as a most effective advocate of local history by demonstrating how the smallest community could bring insights into the workings of the state as a whole, an achievement shared for other periods by his academic colleagues at Leicester University.[9] As early as 1963 the *Urban History Newsletter* had appeared to provide a focus for growing interest in the subject, a role now ably filled by its successors, the *Urban History Year-book* and *Urban History*. Most significantly, the work of Peter Clark, Paul Slack, and Charles Phythian-Adams has cleared much of the ground for future research by tackling theoretical problems, clarifying objectives, and assessing the sources available.[10]

However, even though the primary interests of these scholars lay with the workings of urban society and its economy, their contribution to the study of early modern politics must be acknowledged. Demography and migration may not seem issues of immediate interest to the parliamentary analyst, but several of the broader themes addressed by social and eco-nomic historians have directly advanced the study of urban politics. Since the early 1970s the most important focus for general research concerned 'crisis and order' in English towns between 1500 and 1700, a lively debate centring on the demographic and economic challenges facing urban lead-ers. In order to assess the response of the towns to such recurrent diffi-culties urban historians conducted a thorough review of the workings of the early modern town, thereby gaining an understanding of its capacity

[9] In particular, see W. G. Hoskins, *Local History in England* (London, 1959), and id., *Provincial England* (London, 1963). For a review of the work of H. J. Dyos, the doyen of English urban historians, see S. Mandlebaum, 'H. J. Dyos and British Urban History', in *Economic History Review*, 2nd ser. 37 (1985), 437–47.

[10] The formidable historiography of the early modern town is most ably summarized by the editors of collected articles, see P. Clark and P. Slack (eds.), *Crisis and Order in English Towns, 1500–1700* (London, 1972); eid., *English Towns in Transition* (London, 1976); A. Everitt (ed.), *Perspectives in English Urban History* (London, 1973); P. Clark (ed.), *Country Towns in Pre-industrial England* (Leicester, 1981); id. (ed.), *The Transformation of English Provincial Towns* (London, 1984); J. Barry (ed.), *The Tudor and Stuart Town: A Reader in English Urban History, 1530–1688* (London, 1990); P. Borsay (ed.), *The Eighteenth-Century Town: A Reader in English Urban History, 1688–1820* (London, 1990).

to weather the effects of demographic crisis and trade cycle. Although agreement on general patterns of urban development has remained elusive, the historians participating in that debate have significantly advanced our knowledge of the complex structures of town life. Moreover, their economic interests naturally directed them to consider the interrelationship of the towns with their hinterlands, thereby highlighting the wider impact of urban developments.[11]

Similar lessons have been learnt from the pursuit of a related theme, the role of oligarchy as a structural foundation of the early modern town. Identified as the dominant feature of English urban government and society, the rule of the few was an integral study for students of 'crisis and order', particularly as it had been credited as a general force for stability. Several prosopographic studies provided insights into the social background of urban provincial leaders, and gave rise to a controversy concerning the propensity of urban oligarchies either to decrease or increase in the course of the sixteenth and seventeenth centuries. The bewildering diversity of English towns has once again defeated an academic consensus, even though most incorporated boroughs were ruled by a small group of self-elected councillors throughout the early modern period. The arguments still rage but the debate has already had a significant impact, reminding all researchers to acknowledge the capacity of traditional urban structures to accommodate change.[12]

However, perhaps the most significant aspect of the oligarchy debate was the attempt made to delineate the relationship of the political process with social and economic forces. The methodologies of urban historians, who generally retained a holistic approach to the study of the early modern town, have clearly had an important influence, particularly by highlighting the shortcomings of too strict a thematic approach, which may minimize the interaction of urban affairs. As H. J. Dyos observed, one has to study 'the city as such, the whole interlocking apparatus without which urban life could not function, the generations of buildings and generations of men'. When focusing on the corporate assemblies,

---

[11] For a summary of the debate, see Barry (ed.), *The Tudor and Stuart Town*, 6–7.

[12] Doubts concerning the pervasiveness of oligarchy in provincial towns have been aired by J. T. Evans, 'The Decline of Oligarchy in Seventeenth-Century Norwich', in *JBS* 14 (1974), 44–76; and Hey, *Fiery Blades of Hallamshire*, 197–249. However, for trenchant criticism of Evans's thesis, see R. O'Day, 'The Triumph of Civic Oligarchy in the Seventeenth Century', in R. O'Day *et al.* (eds.), *The Traditional Community under Stress* (Milton Keynes, 1978), 103–36. Again, for a summary of the debate, see Barry (ed.), *The Tudor and Stuart Town*, 24–8. For a welcome European perspective, see A. Cowan, 'Urban Elites in Early Modern Europe: An Endangered Species?', in *BIHR* 64 (1991), 121–37.

scholars had to abandon an overly thematic approach, for the study of local government only served to illuminate the complex interplay of town life. Most significantly, as a channel for social, economic, and political change, and as a broker for the dialogue between centre and locality, the corporation appeared a fine vantage-point from which to chart general urban development. Not surprisingly, a growing chorus of political analysts have recognized the rewards to be gained from corporate prosopography, and have heralded provincial town government as an area requiring urgent investigation.[13]

The most recent work on the late Stuart town has fully endorsed the value of a more comprehensive approach to the study of urban society and its politics. Jonathan Barry's work on Bristol, for instance, has furthered our understanding of religious divisions by exploring the impact of 'community' within a large borough. More generally, Peter Borsay's analysis of an 'urban renaissance' in Augustan England has demonstrated how town élites could decisively shape their local environment, while also highlighting their susceptibility to external influences. Moreover, having completed several short studies of the provincial reaction to the challenges of the post-Restoration period, a band of self-styled revisionists has identified the need for 'a social history of politics' to address the causes of late seventeenth-century conflict. Such works have revitalized interest in the late Stuart town, placing its study high on the agenda of many scholars.[14]

From these various lines of academic inquiry the form of this study of Great Yarmouth has evolved, seeking as it does to approach the late Stuart period with a broader conception of the urban political process. My initial concern was to find an archive which would reveal a comprehensive picture of the concerns of urban politicians, in order to gauge their response to an age of obvious upheaval. As one of the largest and wealthiest provincial towns in Restoration England, it was evident that Yarmouth would act as a very sensitive barometer of the tensions of the late Stuart period. More importantly, Yarmouth's considerable civic archive not only permitted a more ambitious study of provincial urban

---

[13] H. J. Dyos, 'Urbanity and Suburbanity', in D. Cannadine and D. Reeder (eds.), *Exploring the Urban Past* (Cambridge, 1982); L. Glassey, 'Local Government', in C. Jones (ed.), *Britain in the First Age of Party, 1680–1750* (London, 1987), 151–72; Borsay (ed.), *The Eighteenth-Century Town*, 22–4.

[14] Barry, 'The Parish in Civic Life: Bristol and its Churches, 1640–1750', in S. Wright (ed.), *Parish, Church, and People* (London, 1988), 152–78; P. Borsay, *The English Urban Renaissance* (Oxford, 1989); T. Harris, P. Seaward, and M. Goldie (eds.), *The Politics of Religion in Restoration England* (Oxford, 1990).

affairs, but also suggested that the corporate assembly would have to be the pivotal study of the port's society and politics. Ever since their demise at the hands of the municipal reformers in the 1830s, the corporations have rarely been portrayed in a favourable light, and their lack of accountability has been generally perceived as a licence for indolence and corruption. Perhaps the most damning criticism came from Sidney and Beatrice Webb, who concluded from their comprehensive survey of corporate rule that 'already at the [Glorious] Revolution the constitution was in decay, and its spirit departed'.[15] However, even though Yarmouth was dominated by a merchant oligarchy, from the outset of my researches the town assembly appeared at the very centre of local life, playing a vital role on account of its wide-ranging responsibilities. Indeed, corporate records credit the borough's governors with a vitality, flexibility, and breadth of vision which invalidates any crude dismissal of their capacity for ruling the Yarmouth populace. It soon became apparent that there was a great deal of work to be completed on the role of urban government in late Stuart politics and society.

In order to assess the impact of the corporation, the first two chapters are devoted to a study of its structure and personnel. As the most regular forum for local leaders to meet to discuss town affairs, the political significance of the assembly was immediately apparent, but its importance was further consolidated by a study of the responsibilities of local government. In a period in which local offices were mercilessly used for the pursuit of political ends, it is easy to dismiss their practical importance, and to overlook the onus which such posts placed upon their incumbents. However, the experience of corporate office must be acknowledged as a significant influence on the outlook of the local élite. An extensive analysis of the assembly's routine concerns, when combined with an examination of its relationship with local townsmen and external authorities, provides a more realistic impression of the priorities of an urban hierarchy. In particular, especial attention has to be given to the corporation's role as guardian of the town's rights and privileges, a theme which underlines the symbiotic relationship of the town and corporation.

Moreover, a study of the assembly's personnel reveals their little-appreciated commitment to the locality, which has to be recognized as an enduring agent for local stability in times of crisis. By analysing a wide range of possible influences on the corporator, from his household to his

---

[15] S. and B. Webb, *English Local Government: The Manor and the Borough* (London, 1924, 2nd edn.), 403. For a more modern, and sympathetic, account, see B. Keith-Lucas, *The Unreformed Local Government System* (London, 1980), 15–40.

workplace, and from his wealth to his religion, the corporation's role as a centripetal force within urban society was clearly established. It might not have been elected along democratic principles, and such groups as the Dissenters might have been excluded from its counsels by law, but its membership did reflect its oft-stated commitment to serve the general interest of the town. Far from appearing a closed shop of like-minded men, the Yarmouth councillors were susceptible to external forces of division, as well as to agencies of change. Taken together, the first two chapters portray an understudied political culture which has to be recognized as a critical factor in determining a major borough's response to the challenges of the late Stuart period.

In order to develop the themes raised by this opening section, there follows a series of narrative chapters, the parameters of each seeking to reflect moments of local significance. The decision to structure most of this work in narrative form reflects a desire to ascertain the *pace* of the local political process, to delineate the exact influence, where possible, of the various groups involved and of the issues they promoted. The lack of detailed monographs has allowed general works to neglect local self-determination and to gloss over the provincial response to political change. Therefore, the interplay of urban, county, and central authorities is represented at length here in the hope that Yarmouth's example will encourage others to pursue themes whose importance became immediately apparent in the course of my research, such as the concern of the local electorate for economic issues, or the apolitical responsibilities of the parliamentary member. Such considerations broaden the scope of general narratives by highlighting the importance of developments which lack the dramatic significance of parliamentary elections or municipal purges. It is a telling reflection on the priorities of previous political researchers that although much work has been completed on the rage of party politics after 1689, few analysts have sought to explain the significance of a contemporaneous rise in the number of urban improvement acts produced by an annually sitting Parliament.[16]

The necessity for such in-depth work on the late Stuart town is only

---

[16] However, note E. L. Jones and M. E. Falkus, 'Urban Improvement and the English Economy in the Seventeenth and Eighteenth Centuries', in Borsay (ed.), *The Eighteenth-Century Town*, 116–58; S. Handley, 'Local Legislative Initiatives for Economic and Social Development in Lancashire, 1689–1731', in *Parliamentary History*, 9 (1990), 14–37; L. Davison, T. Hitchcock, T. Keirn, and R. Shoemaker (eds.), *Stilling The Grumbling Hive: The Response to Social and Economic Problems in England, 1689–1750* (Stroud, 1992). On the growth of parliamentary lobbying, see J. Brewer, *The Sinews of Power: Money and the State, 1688–1783* (London, 1989), 231–49.

too obvious to the period specialist. Post-Restoration politics suffers from great neglect when compared to the early Stuart age, and researchers have continued to comment upon the absence of local studies to further our understanding of an era of significant development.[17] Although recent work on the counties has begun to examine events after 1660, there has been generally little interest in the provincial towns, which in appearance remain a most promising subject for research. Indeed, such is the importance of the boroughs to any account of political upheaval under the later Stuarts, that our understanding of an age of regulation and revolution has been limited by our ignorance of the reaction of the corporations.[18]

More specifically, urban studies are required to address one of the most important themes identified by general works on late seventeenth- and early eighteenth-century Britain, the growth of political stability from the ruins of the Interregnum state. Such formidable scholars as Holmes, Plumb, Speck, and Horwitz have wrestled with the development of the central institutions of government during that period, and their work has influenced all general accounts of English politics in that age.[19] However, despite the interest shown by historians in such key events as the borough regulation of the 1680s, or in such important areas as urban psephology, there has been little effort to examine the internal workings of the English provincial town. Resting content with the view that the urban world was securely ruled by an oligarchy of the local well-to-do, whose members increasingly accepted the patronage and protection of their gentrified or noble neighbours, scholars have only credited the provincial towns with a passive contribution towards the political stability of the Georgian period. By analysing the period from the understudied perspective of the local governor, however, a very different impression of urban politics emerges, forcing a reconsideration of some of the key

[17] S. K. Roberts, 'Public or Private? Revenge and Recovery at the Restoration of Charles II', in *BIHR* 59 (1986), 173; P. J. Norrey, 'Restoration Regime in Action: the Relationship between Central and Local Government in Dorset, Somerset, and Wiltshire 1660–78', in *HJ* 31 (1988), 789.

[18] P. Jenkins, *The Making of a Ruling Class: The Glamorgan Gentry, 1640–1790* (Cambridge, 1983); A. Coleby, *Central Government and the Localities: Hampshire, 1649–89* (Cambridge, 1987). For some time general works have being calling for urban monographs—J. R. Jones, *The Revolution of 1688 in England* (London, 1972), 142–3; and J. H. Plumb, *The Growth of Political Stability in England, 1675–1715* (London, 1967), 94–6.

[19] For the major works on the period, see Plumb, *Growth of Political Stability in England*; G. S. Holmes, *British Politics in the Age of Anne* (London, 1967); W. Speck, *Tory and Whig: The Struggle in the Constituencies, 1701–15* (London, 1970); H. Horwitz, *Parliament, Politics, and Policy in the Reign of William III* (Manchester, 1977). For the most recent surveys of the Augustan period, see G. S. Holmes, *The Making of a Great Power* (London, 1993); T. Harris, *Politics under the Later Stuarts* (London, 1993).

themes identified by such work. In particular, the relationship between borough and patron demands closer study, as does the manner in which party issues affected the local electorate. Just as Stuart politicians regarded the response of local governors as a critical consideration when imposing their policies on the nation, so the researcher should strive to delineate the provincial response to political change.

The passivity of the Yarmouth leadership when faced by purges of its government or by the predatory advances of the borough-monger clearly cannot be taken for granted, and in this regard I was particularly fortunate to find a wealth of correspondence between the town and its patrons, the Lords Paston and Townshend. Yarmouth could very easily be dismissed as the pawn of the Pastons, and subsequently the Townshends, by a cursory analysis of its political development, but the problems which these patrons encountered should warn against over-hasty assumptions concerning the ease of aristocratic dominance. The corporation never courted a patron without an assurance that he could prove useful for the furtherance of its own ambitions, and even as powerful a figure such as the second Viscount Townshend found the establishment of his 'interest' an extremely difficult process. The 'triumph of the gentry' may have been trumpeted for the late seventeenth century, but only in the absence of any real analysis of the contemporary influence of the towns. Clearly, there is a need for detailed work on the political relationship between urban and rural society.[20]

Most significantly, Yarmouth testifies to the influence of the party issues which are held to have increasingly divided English society from the 1680s onwards. Despite its introspective image, the corporation was ever anxious for news of major political developments, and there can be no pretence that national events failed to excite the Norfolk port. The presence of a large Dissenting congregation was an enduring source of tension, forcing Yarmouth's leaders to confront one of the most contentious political issues of the late Stuart period. However, the religious problem did not exist in a social vacuum, and the local perspective can aid our understanding of the resonance of such bitter divisions. The impact of religiously motivated purges, or of the imposition of penal statutes on fellow townsmen, only really becomes apparent when the social dimension of such policies are considered. More generally, the town's upheavals under the later Stuarts reveal that local leaders did not mindlessly follow the party line, for their own experiences would remain the most critical

[20] R. Hutton, *The Restoration: A Political and Religious History of England and Wales, 1658–1667* (Oxford, 1985); A. Fletcher, *Reform in the Provinces* (New Haven, 1986).

influence in determining their response to the great issues of the day. An intensive local study also enables the development of political views to be charted from one generation to the next, a perspective which challenges the significance of such historiographic watersheds as 1660, 1688, or 1714.

The immediate question raised by the individual town study is, of course, typicality, for although it may achieve merit for unpicking the intricacies of a complex society, it demands to be set in the more general context of urban development. Throughout the work I have endeavoured to incorporate the experience of other towns where possible, if only to contrast it with Yarmouth's response to the challenges of the period. However, even this approach is open to charges of atypicality, and runs the risk of misrepresenting the peculiar development of other towns by too facile a comparison. It would be easy to claim, as a Yarmouth historian of the early seventeenth century did, that the port was 'the very quintessence' of English coastal towns, but it would be unwise to do so in the absence of an intensive comparative survey.[21] Emphasis has therefore been laid upon Yarmouth's *structural* similarities with other corporate towns, and an attempt had been made to outline the common experience it shared with other urban centres under the later Stuarts. When studying economic development historians have hitherto attempted to group towns typographically, seeking for the purposes of comparison to ascertain a town's predominant commercial function. Political considerations do not lend themselves to such easy categorization, but the identification of key components of Yarmouth's political mechanism can illuminate the workings of many other boroughs.

For my principal concern, urban government, there is little doubt that Yarmouth shared the response of other urban governors during the uncertainties of the post-Restoration period. By 1660 most of the nation's 200 incorporated boroughs were ruled by a small council of co-opted members, thus broadly mirroring Yarmouth's political structure. Just as importantly, after 1660 all the country's corporations faced up to the task of implementing the same controversial statutes, and they all had to address similar challenges, most notably the onset of sustained warfare after 1689. Moreover, although Yarmouth's interests were peculiar to its situation, the manner in which its leaders sought to defend them could be espied in the political processes of other towns, just as eager to defend treasured rights and privileges. Thus, the study of Yarmouth retains an

---

[21] T. Manship, *History of Great Yarmouth*, ed. C. J. Palmer (Great Yarmouth, 1854), 118.

importance in its own right, for even while recognizing its uniqueness, insights can be gained which throw much light on the politics of urban England at that dramatic time.

Yarmouth, of course, cannot provide all the answers. For all the wealth of its archive, it stubbornly refused to yield any significant information concerning certain aspects of local political life. For instance, no Yarmouth poll book survives for the period under review; evidence concerning the influence of women in urban government remains elusive; and, perhaps most frustratingly, a more rigorous analysis of the role of the masses is precluded by a lack of sources. However, despite the obvious attraction of the corporate records, I have endeavoured to pay a due regard for all urban influences, whatever their source. That the assembly emerges at the very centre of this account of Yarmouth's development simply reflects the fact that the responsibilities of self-government planted it firmly at the helm of urban society, irrespective of the demands of class or gender. Most significantly, its primacy was attested by townsmen outside of the corporation, as well as by authorities beyond Yarmouth. No study of the politics of the urban *polis* can ignore the decisive influence of local government as a centripetal force within the locality, and as one of its surest bridges to the outside world. Even as stubborn a foe of urban independence as Robert, Lord Paston could not begrudge the corporations their overdue share of the historiographic spotlight.

The achievements of county and urban scholars in the last forty years have pointed the way forward for students of the early modern period, continuing as they do to assert their corrective perspectives for both local and national historians. The doubters still remain, a fact witnessed as recently as 1975 when one of the leading scholars of urban history alluded to the 'somewhat pedestrian, even amateur, taint' associated with the study of the individual town. However, local history today can certainly be counted among the most flourishing of academic disciplines, imbued with an optimism perhaps best expressed by John Ives, a Yarmouth antiquarian who confidently asserted in 1772 that his fellow local historians

are no longer represented as men of uncultivated minds, fit only to pore over musty records, or grovel amongst ruined walls; and their accounts are no longer considered the dull effusions of pedantry of the verbose disquisitions of folly.

Two centuries on, with the battle for respectability won, the study of the provinces still promises a rich harvest of exciting and challenging work.[22]

[22] C. Phythian-Adams, *Desolation of a City: Coventry and the Urban Crisis of the Late Middle Ages* (Cambridge, 1979), 1; Swinden, *History of Great Yarmouth*, preface.

I

Oligarchy and Community:
The Corporate Institution

Another infirmity of a commonwealth, is the immoderate greatness of a town . . . as also the great number of corporations, which are as it were many lesser commonwealths in the bowels of a greater, like worms in the entrails of a natural man.

HOBBES's censure of the seventeenth-century corporation has set the tone for nearly all commentaries on the unreformed government of English towns.[1] From the denunciations of the borough regulators of the 1680s to the criticisms of the municipal reformers in the 1830s, this image of autonomy and isolation has coloured national policy and historical opinion. Moreover, when the history of the early modern corporation came to be written by Sidney and Beatrice Webb in Edwardian times, this impression was largely upheld.[2] Ever since their magisterial work, historians have tended to shy away from the study of the corporations, and few analysts have tried to come to terms with the actual workings of these local institutions, reflecting a generally held belief that such research could contribute little to our understanding of the nation's politics and society. Even post-war studies of the seventeenth-century town have endorsed this negative stereotype, portraying the typical corporation as a small body of rich neighbours, usually pursuing the same trade and often closely interrelated. Perpetuating their supremacy under the authority of a royal charter, the assemblymen are held to have shut off the vast

[1] T. Hobbes, *Leviathan*, ed. C. McPherson (Harmondsworth, 1968), 374–5.
[2] For Lord Chief Justice Saunders's condemnation of municipal independence during the trial of the London charter in 1683, see W. C. Costin and J. S. Watson (eds.), *The Law and Working of the Constitution* (London, 1961), i. 255. For a survey of the findings of the Royal Commission on Municipal Corporations, see A. J. E. Cockburn, *The Corporations of England and Wales* (London, 1835). While paying tribute to the variety of the constitutions they had studied, the Webbs concluded that their most unifying theme was the corporations' struggle for independence from local and county rivals—S. and B. Webb, *English Local Government: The Manor and the Borough* (London, 1924, 2nd edn.), 381–3. B. Keith-Lucas noted that the average size of the early nineteenth-century town council ranged between only ten and thirty members—*The Unreformed Local Government System* (London, 1980), 15–40.

majority of the local community from their counsels, thereby allowing themselves free rein to seek personal advantage. Until recently, little work had been produced to suggest that the corporations were anything other than a cause for embarrassment in the otherwise glorious evolution of England's revered constitution.[3]

However, there have been signs that Hobbes's worm may be turning. Sparked by the growth of interest in the problems facing early modern governors, studies have been produced which show an obvious dissatisfaction with the sterile and over-generalized concept of oligarchic corporate rule. Clark's work on Gloucester and Kirby's study of Leeds are but two examples of the rewards to be reaped from an approach which tries to understand how the government of the few actually worked, rather than concentrating exclusively on the potentially corrupt, or archaic, features of the corporate constitution.[4] Such renewed interest in the subject has led to an important reshaping of ideas on the nature of early modern urban government, particularly concerning its structural foundations.[5] Recognition that oligarchy is too static a concept to portray corporate development has been brought about by Evans's work on Norwich, which provocatively suggested that oligarchy, after its heyday in the fifteenth century, might have been in decline in the early modern period. This observation has been seriously questioned by subsequent research, but it has served to make historians more aware of the complexities of urban government.[6] Most importantly, recent studies of the corporation have tried to understand the institution as the creation of local circumstances, rather than dismissing it as the superimposed invention of Machiavellian

[3] J. T. Evans, *Seventeenth-Century Norwich* (Oxford, 1979), 319. Perhaps the most frustrating example of current disinterest towards the corporations came with A. Fletcher's *Reform in the Provinces* (New Haven, 1986), a valuable survey of seventeenth-century local government which chose not to investigate the running of the provincial towns.

[4] See P. Clark, 'The Civic Leaders of Gloucester, 1580–1800' in Clark (ed.), *The Transformation of English Provincial Towns* (London, 1984), 311–46; J. Kirby, 'Restoration Leeds and the Aldermen of the Corporation 1661–1700', in *Northern History*, 22 (1986), 123–74.

[5] However, our understanding of the medieval corporation remains more advanced, see S. Reynolds, *An Introduction to the History of English Medieval Towns* (Oxford, 1977), chs. 5 and 6. Moreover, see S. Rigby, 'Urban Oligarchy in late Medieval England', in J. A. F. Thomson, *Towns and Townspeople in the Fifteenth Century* (Gloucester, 1988), 62–86, for a very important update of J. Tait's classic survey of 'The Common Council of the Borough', in *EHR* 46 (1931), 1–29. A significant step forwards in our knowledge of the corporations after 1660 would be taken if a successor was produced to M. Weinbaum, *British Borough Charters, 1307–1660* (Cambridge, 1943).

[6] Evans's thesis is developed in 'The Decline of Oligarchy in Seventeenth-Century Norwich', in *JBS* 14 (1974), 46–77. For a critique of its shortcomings, see R. O'Day, 'The Triumph of Civic Oligarchy in Seventeenth-Century England', in O'Day *et al. The Traditional Community Under Stress* (Milton Keynes, 1977), 103–36.

figures at court or in the provinces. Indeed, a recent study of the pre-1640 corporation has suggested that the oligarchic rule might have been an 'effective and arguably even appropriate form of local government'.[7] The corporations, just as much as the individuals which comprised them, cannot be divorced from the societies that they led, even if in appearance they stood aloof by dint of their authority. The adoption of this open-minded approach is one of the most significant advances of the recent historiography of English local government.

Yet, in spite of this healthy change in attitude towards the corporations, there is still much more work to be done if the institution is to be accorded its proper place within the structure of early modern English society. Even though the daunting variety of the nation's 200 borough constitutions have been sufficient to intimidate most from embarking on as comprehensive a survey of the institution as the Webbs, individual case studies have shown that their work failed to address key areas of corporate life.[8] For instance, their overwhelming interest in the urban justice of the peace precluded an in-depth study of the workings of the assemblies, despite the fact that those bodies bore widespread responsibilities. Most importantly, an attempt has to be made to integrate corporate activity within the greater spheres of county and national government. The contemporary importance of the corporations in Whitehall and Westminster was signalled by the concern of Cromwell and the later Stuarts to regulate them, and their study should reflect the true extent of such influence.[9] The gulf which still exists between 'local' and 'national' histories has not helped to reveal the complex relationships which existed between town leaders and the 'foreigners' with whom they came into contact. It is an omission as serious as the failure to understand the corporation's constant interaction with its own locality; an exchange that could not have

[7] R. Tittler, *Architecture and Power: The Town Hall and the English Urban Community, c.1500–1640* (Oxford, 1991), 98–100.

[8] Note the recent view of P. Langford, who described the Webbs's approach as 'that of the Fabian archaeologist disinterring a bizarre and irrational structure, rather than the historian recapturing the spirit of a once flourishing organism'—*Public Life and the Propertied Englishman, 1689–1798* (Oxford, 1991), p. viii. He provides the most comprehensive analysis of English local government in the eighteenth century, and must be read in tandem with P. Corfield's survey of corporate government—*The Impact of English Towns, 1700–1800* (Oxford, 1982), 146–67. The student of the late seventeenth-century corporation relies heavily on the articles of P. Clark for guidance, most notably his introduction to the *Transformation of English Provincial Towns*, 1–49.

[9] See B. Henderson, 'The Commonwealth Charters', in *TRHS* 3rd ser. 6 (1912), 129–62; R. Pickavance, 'English Boroughs and the King's Government: A Study of the Tory Reaction, 1681–5', Oxford D.Phil. 1976.

functioned along the formal constitutional lines which have been for so long the main interest of corporate historians. This present study undertakes to analyse one corporate society from a variety of perspectives in order to assess the role of this institution in its own right.

The choice of case study has largely been determined to examine one of England's classic merchant oligarchies, whose surviving records might permit a realistic impression of its activities to be formed. Great Yarmouth in Norfolk, where a corporation of 24 aldermen and 48 common councillors ruled over a population of some 7,000 in 1660, presents a fine example of the cooptative government so loathed by later reformers.[10] The aldermen and common councillors congregated as a single body to run local affairs, leaving the vast bulk of the local population with no official right of consultation. Entrance to this charmed circle of local government was reserved exclusively for those who had gained the freedom of the borough, a privileged status which could only be achieved with the assembly's consent. The freemen numbered only some 600 local residents at the Restoration, a figure suggesting a probable ratio of only one freeman to every three households.[11] Moreover, in the course of the early modern period the Yarmouth corporation became even more oligarchic in form by its decision of 1703 to cut its number of assemblymen from 72 to 54. In every way the Yarmouth corporation fulfils the traditional oligarchic image, and its structure certainly mirrored that of other major provincial towns. At the time of the Restoration the Leicester assembly, the institution most savagely criticized by the municipal reformers and by the Webbs, convened as a body of 24 aldermen and 48 common councillors. However, Yarmouth's cooptative recruitment system also bracketed it with one of few corporations to receive some praise from the reformers, its rival port of King's Lynn. Such contrasting reputations recommend caution when assessing the workability of an essentially undemocratic system of local rule. For certain, Yarmouth's corporate infrastructure will

[10] For an analysis of Yarmouth's demographic development, see A. Michel, 'The Port and Town of Great Yarmouth . . . 1550–1714', Cambridge Ph.D. 1978, pp. 14–27. E. Wrigley places the town as the ninth largest provincial centre in *c.*1670 with a population of 8,000, and the sixth most populous in 1700 with 10,000 inhabitants—see *Journal of Interdisciplinary History*, 15 (1984–5), 686. Other surveys suggest that Yarmouth's population was even larger, with some 10,000 inhabitants in the 1660s and 11,000 in 1700—G. Holmes, *The Making of a Great Power* (London, 1993), 686.

[11] My estimate of the freeman-to-household ratio assumes the average size of the household to have been 4.25 persons, following the example of A. O. Whiteman in her edition of *The Compton Census* (Oxford, 1986), p. lxvii. The freeman figure comes from Henning, *House of Commons, 1660–1690*, i. 324–7. For a comparison with other towns, see D. Hirst, *The Representative of the People?* (Cambridge, 1975), 94.

serve to question the wisdom of approaching local institutions with ahistorical notions of the criteria for 'good' government.[12]

When attempting to convey the workings of an institution as complex as the corporation, it is a difficult, though necessary, task to break away from the mundane recitation of constitutional relationships established by charter and local ordinance. Their study remains of fundamental importance, but it should be greatly extended by an awareness of the flexibility of the corporate system. The existence of less formalized channels of influence, both within the ruling assembly and connecting it to authorities outside, will be missed by an overemphasis on its prescribed modes of procedure. When acting as a corporate body, the assembly had to react to any demand placed upon it, forcing it to adapt its general powers to the needs of a particular moment. The detailed political narratives in Chapters 3 to 7 will show the bewildering variety of such duties, and they form the bulk of this work in order that the corporation may be understood as a constantly evolving and dynamic institution, rather than the monolith which it has been for so long portrayed. Moreover, the following analysis of the Yarmouth corporation will be divided into three subsections in order to probe both the 'efficient' and 'dignified' structures of its constitution.[13] Most interest will centre on the internal workings of the assembly, but this section will be followed by a consideration of its relationship with the freeman body, and then by an examination of its connections with authorities beyond its fine town walls. Developments across the 1660–1720 period will be discussed as they impinged on the assembly's position, but with the historic development of the corporation's authority very much in mind. It is often a complex picture, but the very attempt at clarification will reveal the full extent of the corporation's responsibilities and problems, many of which have been previously obscured by indifference or misunderstanding.

i. THE CORPORATE ASSEMBLY

The most comprehensive guide to the rule of the corporation remains the charter. Although earning a reputation as political footballs under the

---

[12] See Keith-Lucas, *Unreformed Local Government System*, 18, 27; also R. Greaves, *The Corporation of Leicester, 1689–1836* (Leicester, 1970, 2nd edn.). The Commissioners of 1835 did not publish any report on the Yarmouth corporation. However, an independent, and similarly condemnatory, survey survives in the form of H. Barrett, *The Great Yarmouth Corporation* (London, 1834).

[13] See Walter Bagehot, *The English Constitution* (Harmondsworth, 1963). Its mid-Victorian insights will stimulate constitutional thinkers of all periods for many generations to come.

later Stuarts, suffering merciless abuse at the hands of the royal authority
in whose name they were granted, the charters were enduring symbols of
the aims and identity of the corporations. The most authoritative account
of their development alluded to the 'essential sameness' of the privileges
and immunities granted by the crown by the mid-seventeenth century,
but that should not lead us to dismiss their importance in delineating the
particular form of each urban society.[14] Moreover, while the emphasis on
the autonomy of jurisdiction contained within them might reflect a desire
amongst local leaders for self-regulation, it is vital to see that such independence was not won without cost. The charter must be regarded as the
result of the crown's dependence on the 'natural' governors of the towns
to run their own localities, and such service had to be rewarded with
special privileges. Of course, such royal licence did not extend indefin-
itely, as the proceedings of *quo warranto* proved, but the series of charters
gained by each corporation permitted its leaders to influence the form
and character of its own government. With the establishment of their
local control, however, came a concomitant responsibility on the corporators
to rule their community in an equitable and just way, which constituted
a heavy burden on the individual councillor and the collective body of the
assembly alike. Therefore, a key theme for the study of oligarchic rule
remains the methods evolved by the assembly to ensure that all its
membership responded effectively to their administrative burdens in exchange for the honour and perquisites of office. Struggling to fulfil its
allotted responsibilities under the pressure of a demanding local community and against the intrusion of external authorities, the assembly
cannot be simply dismissed as an unresponsive bastion of privilege. The
corporation's historic development, its internal tensions, and its interaction with the local community are all necessary areas for study to achieve
a balanced perspective of the corporation.

Ever since its first grant of 1208, Yarmouth had enjoyed continued
royal favour with a series of confirmations and extensions of what it came
to regard as its 'ancient' rights and immunities.[15] In the eyes of the crown,
the town had long been a vital port and training-ground for mariners, a
significance symbolized by the award of a court of admiralty in 1559. The
charters would always pay eloquent testimony to this bond of utility
between centre and locality, and the Yarmouth corporation was never

---

[14] Weinbaum, *British Borough Charters, 1307–1660*, pp. xi–xiii.
[15] Yarmouth, in common with other boroughs, claimed its rights as prescriptive, i.e. pre-
dating any specific royal grant. For a transcription of all of Yarmouth's charters, see Y/
C18/4; for a synopsis of their contents, see Palmer, *History of Great Yarmouth*, 1–42.

slow to remind national authorities of their historic contribution to the nation. In return, the crown acknowledged its debt to the 'laudable services' of the port, but reminded the town authorities of their responsibility to ensure 'the keeping of the peace, and the good rule and government of the same'.[16] The original recipient of the charter had been the Guild of Merchants, and there had been little change in the nature of the local economy to challenge its mercantile successors as the natural leadership of the community. The Guild itself had fallen into decline in the course of the sixteenth century until it only retained its fraternal role as a dining club, thereby leaving the way clear for the bicameral corporation to supplant its role in local government. However, until the early seventeenth century the 'Guild-hall' remained the corporation's sole meeting-place, and reminders of the corporation's mercantile origins were perpetuated long after the Guild's demise.[17] Newcomers to the assembly in 1660 still had to 'heyne the Guild' by paying an entry fine, as well as swear the corporator's oath 'to be one of our Brotherhood or Merchant Guild of this town and to keep the old use and custom thereof'.[18] While the dockside continued to predominate, there would be no doubt that the corporation embodied mercantile opinion, even though it might contain a wide selection of trades amongst its membership. Whatever the structure of local government, commercial interests would always be represented in corporate affairs, and this economic reality, rather than the insidious influence of corruption or nepotism, established the particular character of Yarmouth's governing hierarchy.

While the charter remained the ultimate sanction of corporate authority, the constitutional structure erected to execute its powers had been determined by a series of ordinances passed by the assembly itself. Since

---

[16] Yarmouth's maritime history has been well covered, most authoritatively by N. J. Williams, *The Maritime Trade of the East Anglian Ports, 1550–1590* (Oxford, 1988). Unpublished surveys include Michel, 'Port and Trade of Great Yarmouth . . . 1550–1714', Cambridge Ph.D. 1978; and J. D. Murphy, 'The Town and Trade of Great Yarmouth, 1740–1850', UEA Ph.D. 1979.

[17] See P. Rutledge, 'Great Yarmouth Assembly Minutes, 1538–45', in *NRS* 39 (1970), 8. The history of Yarmouth's guilds is very obscure until Henry Manship's Jacobean account of their past activities, a fact lamented by A. R. Saul in 'Great Yarmouth in the Fourteenth Century: A Study in Trade, Politics, and Society', Oxford D.Phil. 1975, pp. 12–14. The corporation only chose to move its routine meetings from the Guildhall to the town's justice hall (the Tolhouse) in 1622—Y/C18/3, p. 253.

[18] For all civic oaths, see Y/C18/2. Other studies which highlight the survival of Guild customs into seventeenth-century corporate life include Evans, *Seventeenth-Century Norwich*, 52; R. Howell, *Newcastle-upon-Tyne and the Puritan Revolution* (Oxford, 1967), 39, 48–9; G. Metters, 'The Rulers and Merchants of King's Lynn in the Early Seventeenth Century', UEA Ph.D. 1982, pp. 19, 377.

the early fifteenth century the presidency of the corporation had been entrusted to two bailiffs, both elected in late August from the ranks of the aldermen. The 24-strong aldermanic bench had evolved from the late thirteenth-century 'jurats' who had administered the town's original four leets. The aldermen were recruited from the assembly's junior legislative body, the 48-strong common council, whose existence can be traced to the late fifteenth century.[19] Furthermore, the assembly's control of the town's executive and its legislature mirrored its domination of the local judiciary. Ever since the grant of a separate commission of the peace in 1494, Yarmouth's JPs had been largely drawn from the ranks of the assembly's highest office-holders, a practice which could only magnify the importance of the corporate élite.[20] As a result, there was little which escaped the assembly's jurisdiction in Yarmouth, and such omnipotence in local affairs could be interpreted as a licence for arbitrary action on the part of its membership. However, this assumption would ignore an impressive range of assembly ordinances which show a less than confident faith in its supremacy. The comprehensiveness of their local authority lumbered the corporation's members with a workload of fearsome proportions, and its leaders could not rely on the status of office to ensure the efficient service of every corporator. Moreover, the very success of amalgamating all local authority into its hands made the assembly extremely sensitive over challenges to its control, however slight they may have been. The ordinances thus reveal the tensions existing within the corporation, for even its air of impregnability was designed to conceal many inherent weaknesses.

By the rules which it imposed on its own membership, the corporation sought to champion the virtues of order, efficiency, and independence as the essential principles of its governance. These ordinances cannot be dismissed as mere rhetoric, or as an apology for oligarchic rule, for they were directed exclusively at a corporate audience. As a priority, assembly members were constantly reminded of the need to demonstrate their personal fitness for the role of local governor, in order that the corporate body would appear as the town's natural leadership. Practical considerations dictated that the assembly's recruitment was limited to local men

[19] See Rutledge, in *NRS* 39 (1970), 5–22.

[20] In accordance with the charter of 1494, Yarmouth had 8 JPs—the 2 bailiffs, 4 burgesses (usually 2 aldermen chosen by the bailiffs together with the 2 retiring bailiffs), and 2 lawyers (usually the town clerk and the recorder). The reforms of the 1703 charter, which increased their number to 11, would not alter this corporate influence, for the mayor, high steward, recorder, understeward and the 7 most senior aldermen all became *ex officio* justices—Palmer, *History of Great Yarmouth*, 26, 42.

who would have the time and financial resources to make a substantial commitment to the demands of corporate business. This inevitably led them to choose from the upper ranks of local society, for only wealth could bring the leisure-time required of the efficient corporator. The greater merchants could also be reasonably expected to have a closer identification of interest with the advancement of the town's economy, and they constituted a source of credit on which the assembly was often forced to call. However, even local notables required constant reminders of their responsibilities in office when the demands of civic life were potentially so great.

Most significantly, the sumptuary ordinances enforced by the assembly reflected the corporation's constant need to assert and justify its control over the locality, and this objective could be achieved most directly by the personal distinction of the individuals who staffed its offices. One of the corporation's first moves to restore order after the social and political upheavals of the Interregnum was to insist that its members wear their black and red gowns to church and on other civic occasions. As the ordinance observed, the assembly had to have 'men of the best rank and gravity and so to be distinguished from the inferior sort of people by their habit, especially on solemn occasions'.[21] Concern for sumptuary distinction might seem a matter which fits perfectly with the pompous image which has been traditionally applied to municipal councils, but such anxiety pinpoints the pressure on the corporation to find prospective councillors of the right calibre. Other corporations gave gown-wearing a similar priority, the assembly of Aldeburgh in Suffolk regarding civic apparel to have made a general contribution to 'the more credit of the town'. Pontefract's aldermen valued the distinction of their gowns so much that they voted in 1657 not to wear them should 'it be rain or snow'. Local government had to be supported by the propriety of its membership, or else, as in the times of the Interregnum, fears would be raised that the whole fabric of the social order was under threat of collapse.[22]

In order to maintain the supremacy of the local élite, an outward show of corporate unanimity to local and outsider alike was deemed essential. Disunity was a major obstacle to the efficient execution of official

---

[21] Y/C19/7, f. 370—assembly order 31 Dec. 1660.

[22] *HMC Various Collections*, iv. 286; R. Holmes (ed.), *The Book of Fines of the Pontefract Corporation, 1653–1726* (Pontefract, 1882), 35. For the York corporation's attempt to preserve unity by enforcing such fines, see R. C. Richardson (ed.), *Town and Countryside in the English Revolution* (Manchester, 1992), 55–6.

business and was likely to make the corporation more vulnerable to the unwelcome intrusion of rival authorities eager to take advantage of its temporary weakness. The Restoration provides another good example of the determination of the corporation to re-establish its affairs after bitter years of intra-assembly dissension, when orders were issued for the orderly rotation of speakers in debates, for the levying of fines to stop 'any manner of indecent or uncomely railing', and for the use of the ballot in disputed motions.[23] The corresponding ordinance of the New Windsor corporation was more explicit in its intention, calling upon its members to 'reverentially and orderly debate, reason, and declare their wisdoms and knowledge in the matters provided'. Other assemblies attempted to maintain order by controlling the agenda for debate, with the Liverpool corporation ruling in 1685 that motions had to be submitted two days before a meeting so that its proposers 'may be more perfectly known'. There was no pretence that the corporation always resembled the picture of harmony which it aspired to be, but the strenuous attempts made to curtail internal strife indicated the seriousness with which local governors approached their duties.[24]

Mark Kishlansky has recently emphasized the consensual nature of the early modern English polity, particularly for the pre-Civil War period, but it is important to see that such contingencies as the Yarmouth election quest (which he uses to illustrate his thesis) were introduced to combat the very real prospect of damaging division.[25] The quest, used exclusively for municipal elections after 1660, was a twelve-man selection committee chosen by a complex procedure which aimed to ensure a fair electoral process. A child, standing on a table for all to see, would select three names from each of four hats, all of which contained the names of nine common councillors. This body of twelve corporators would then choose the corporation's officers for the coming year in the sanctuary of a locked room, having sworn an oath to do so without 'fear, fraud, collusion, affection, or favour for any person'.[26] Kishlansky brings out the

[23] Y/C18/3—rotation of speakers (1615), f. 193; the ballot (1624), f. 269; indecent words (1516), f. 75. The town's divisive seventeenth-century history was to see the anti-swearing ordinance continually invoked, most notably in March 1645, November 1650, and again in November 1651—Y/C19/7, ff. 62v, 176, 211.

[24] S. Bond (ed.), *The First Hall Book of the Borough of New Windsor* (Windsor, 1968), p. xix; J. A. Picton (ed.), *The City of Liverpool: Selections from the Municipal Archives and Records from the Thirteenth to Seventeenth Centuries* (Liverpool, 1883), 265.

[25] M. Kishlansky, *Parliamentary Selection* (Cambridge, 1986), 36. He notes the similarity of Yarmouth's quest to the election methods practised at York and Cambridge.

[26] Y/C18/1, f. 3. In order to expedite the process, no food or drink was allowed to be taken into the room.

anti-factional aspects of this system well, but such elaborate ritual did not prevent internecine struggle within the corporation from the 1620s right through to the 1650s and beyond.[27] The repeated assertion of the need for order in debate indicated the great pressure on the assembly to keep the passions of its own members in check, mindful as it was of its susceptibility to faction and the worrying inertia which division could bring in its wake.

The most interesting of the assembly's attempts to curb internal disunity was the use of the ballot, for it serves to identify one of the points of potential friction within the constitution: the delicate balance of power between the aldermen and the common councillors. Until the Restoration the two houses had voted separately on balloted issues, thereby allowing either of them to sabotage a motion should opposition be effectively mobilized. Although the ordinance reviving the ballot in 1660 did not make any reference to a change in this practice, from that time onwards divisions were settled by a straight vote of the whole assembly.[28] This new procedure probably resulted from increased demands for assembly unity after the dislocations of the recent past, and it certainly had the effect of neutralizing one source of tension inherent in the corporation's structure. Only in the early eighteenth century would contention surround the issue of the ballot again, when assembly business all but ground to a halt for six months in the course of 1719. The aldermen were then claiming the right of veto over the wishes of the lower house, and the common councillors stubbornly opposed this direct attack on their role in assembly affairs. Their intransigence won the day to preserve their place within the corporate constitution, but the episode serves as a reminder of the delicate relationship between the two houses.[29] There was no evidence to suggest

[27] For a critique of Kishlansky's argument, see R. Cust, 'Parliamentary Elections in the 1620s: The Case of Great Yarmouth', in *Parliamentary History*, 11 (1992), 179–91. Moreover, even as complex a system as the quest was not immune to the influence of faction, as witnessed by the 'long time' that its members always took in deliberation. In August 1663, in the bitter aftermath of a recent corporate purge, the quest took 21 hours to make its choices—Y/C19/8, f. 22.

[28] The assembly books record only a few instances of balloted motions before 1660, and the last mention of the corporation voting in separate houses came in August 1650 when a common councillor was reported to have arrived at the Tolhouse: 'while the aldermen were in voting'—Y/C19/7, f. 170v.

[29] For the circumstances of this dispute, see Ch. 7. The methods used by the common councillors to force aldermanic candidates on to the upper house should warn against any dismissal of their influence in this apparently top-heavy system—see Palmer, *The Perlustration of Great Yarmouth* (Great Yarmouth, 1872–5), i. 73–4. They were certainly in a better position than their Newcastle counterparts, who could be easily thwarted by the high aldermanic quorum required for the passage of by-laws—Howell, *Newcastle-upon-Tyne*, 50–2.

that the common councillors were asserting the rights of the Yarmouth populace against the threat of an over-mighty aldermanic bench, for it was a dispute taking place *within* the élite, not on its fringes. Other towns experienced the same constitutional difficulties. For instance, at Warwick the balance of power tipped decisively against the assistants at the end of the seventeenth century, while divisions between the two houses of the Northampton corporation caused many problems from the 1740s to the end of the eighteenth century. For the sake of ordered rule an image of corporate harmony had to be kept up, but the ballot at least permitted an expression of discord within the assembly. The Leicester corporation even catered for a three-way ballot, evidently perceiving it to be in its interest for a wider variety of local opinion to be expressed. At Yarmouth the assembly books themselves bear witness to this governmental priority of order with their frustratingly brief references to intra-assembly dissension.[30]

The corporation's attempts to control the unpredictable occurrence of faction frequently put its leadership under intense short-term pressure, but beyond the destructive influence of division there were other enervating problems of a less dramatic, but equally worrying nature. While the councillors were apt to disagree over important issues, they were much more likely to threaten the completion of assembly business by their absence from its counsels. The pervasiveness of assembly influence through all spheres of local life meant that its meetings were under great pressure to complete business swiftly and efficiently, even when convened as often as once a month.[31] Fines for absenteeism, for late arrival, or for early departure indicated that civic duties were heavy and that the corporation found it difficult to discipline the activities of its members when they had competing demands on their time from the workplace or home. In 1660 non-attendance fines were doubled on the argument that the bad example

---

[30] P. Styles, *The Corporation of Warwick, 1660–1835* (Oxford, 1938), 40–3; J. C. Cox (ed.), *The Records of the Borough of Northampton* (London, 1898), ii. 22; G. A. Chinnery (ed.), *The Records of the Borough of Leicester, 1689–1835* (Leicester, 1965), v. 53, 69. Tait concluded that the wave of new common councils in the fifteenth century had come in direct response to the disturbances caused by popular involvement in civic elections, with Parliament giving its blessing to their establishment at Northampton and Leicester in 1489—*EHR* 46 (1931), 2.

[31] Rutledge notes that the Yarmouth assembly had met, on average, thirty-one times each year in the mid-sixteenth century—*NRS* 39 (1970), 13. This is more in line with Newcastle's governors who met once every week—Howell, *Newcastle-upon-Tyne*, 50. Similarly, the Hull corporation attempted to establish weekly meetings in the sixteenth century but had to settle for bi-weekly councils in the succeeding century—*VCH Yorkshire: E. Riding* (London, 1969), i. 124.

set by several notorious absentees caused 'inconveniences and disorders', and the corporation would continue to maintain its pressure on such wayward members.[32] Thirty years later two councillors were actually disenfranchised for their reluctance to appear at the assembly, and by 1712 the fines for early departure had risen to a level 120 times greater than those levied at the Restoration.[33] The fundamental importance which the assembly attached to the diligence of its membership was testified by the fact that in the 1660–1720 period non-attendance accounted for most of the non-political dismissals of councillors.

Moreover, the most dramatic of the changes ushered in by the 1703 charter, the decision to cut corporate membership by a quarter, was a direct result of the assembly's difficulty in forcing councillors to fulfil their duties. As the petition for the new charter asserted: 'there are not resident in the said burgh [of Yarmouth] persons of sufficient ability, qualified by law, to support their current constitution.' In very much the same vein, the Shrewsbury assembly had sought a similar reduction in personnel in 1684, fearing that its rule would 'become liable to be exposed to the contempt of disorderly men'.[34] The keeping of 'breeds' which recorded each councillor's attendance also bore witness to the importance which Yarmouth's leaders attached to this issue, and they show that the assembly's reforms could prove effective in matters of self-regulation. The great plague of 1665–6 was a particular threat to assembly discipline, for many councillors fled to their country retreats to escape the pestilence, thereby causing a series of six inquorate assemblies which disrupted assembly business for 14 months. However, the confirmation of assembly fines in October 1666 had the desired effect with average attendance climbing from 39 to 50 in the course of the civic years 1665–6/ 1666–7. As the essential problem of a state which expected long and loyal service from its unpaid local magistrates, attendance to duty would remain a constant worry for both the local and national executive. The fundamental importance of this issue was emphatically highlighted by the Nottingham assembly's ordinance of 1707, which justified an increase in fines by reasoning that 'the burgesses of this town . . . have entrusted us . . . (as their representatives) to transact all matters . . . for the public

[32] Y/C19/7, f. 369v. The Norwich corporation regarded absenteeism in a similar light— Evans, *Seventeenth-Century Norwich*, 43. Reynolds noted that the problem of absenteeism had become a major concern for town rulers in Lincoln, York, and Worcester as early as the fifteenth century—*English Medieval Towns*, 180–1.

[33] Y/C19/9, ff. 203v, 216v; Y/C19/10, ff. 229–30—by the ordinances of 1712, a councillor could be fined 40s. for each absence after his third offence.

[34] Swinden, *History of Great Yarmouth*, 769; Styles, *Corporation of Warwick*, 26–7.

weal and advantage of this town, and the same can't be performed without public meeting at the Hall'.[35]

The onerous demands made upon the individual councillor are sufficient to explain why many dragged their feet or refused outright to fulfil the tasks allotted to them. Turning up at the assembly meetings was just the basic requirement of assembly duty, and an analysis of the corporation's officers and committees serves to emphasize the commitment needed to bear such responsibilities. At the top of the corporate tree the two bailiffs experienced pressures commensurate with their exalted status within the locality, handling all of the assembly's urgent business and representing the institution in its customary dealings with external authorities. However, their routine tasks were sufficient to break the enthusiasm of the keenest official. They were on daily call to hear any town matter brought to them at the town's Tolhouse, and exercised widespread judicial powers ranging from the presidency of the weekly borough court to the role of justice at the town's own court of quarter-session. Such was the pressure of work in these offices that fines for refusal had to be raised to a level of £100 to deter recalcitrant councillors from shirking their duties.[36] The bailiffs' allowance remained at £90 p.a. throughout our period, even though such a sum hardly covered the hospitality which was expected of them at the town's sessions and on other civic occasions. As one incumbent reflected wearily on his bailiwick in 1696–7, 'the execution of that office was always looked upon as burdensome and expensive and several have been ruined and impaired thereby'.[37] The switch to a mayoralty in 1703 was made after the assembly had struggled to find two candidates willing to take up these posts, even from an aldermanic bench which, in general, showed itself ready to make considerable sacrifices for the corporate cause. The honour attached to the mayoralty, symbolized by the award of a swordbearer, was an incentive

---

[35] For the breeds, see Y/C20/1; *Records of the Borough of Nottingham* (London, 1900), v. 38–9. Unexcused absenteeism halted abruptly after the assembly followed up its ordinance with the expulsion of two leading offenders in 1668—Y/C19/8, ff. 74, 103. The corporation set its quorum at half of the membership of each house—Y/C36/4.

[36] After fining an alderman £40 for failing to give a 'satisfactory' reason for his refusal to serve as bailiff in September 1669, the assembly proceeded to set a table of fines to dissuade future recalcitrance on the part of its councillors—common councillor £25, alderman £50, bailiff £100—Y/C19/8 ff. 122, 130v. These were generous in comparison to those set by the Hull corporation, which levied a £500 fine for a refusal to serve as mayor and a £300 penalty for locals declining an aldermanic seat—*VCH: East Riding*, i. 123–5.

[37] *CJ*, xiv. 512. However, unlike London, the Yarmouth corporation saw no need to set a wealth qualification for the tenure of its highest offices—Corfield, *The Impact of English Towns*, 154.

calculated to overcome such reluctance through the powerful agency of personal pride. The actual powers of the mayoralty did not extend much beyond those of the senior bailiff which the new office had superseded, and thus this reform can be seen as an attempt to increase administrative efficiency, rather than as a means to harden the hierarchical distinctions of its upper élite. Yarmouth was not alone in taking measures to enforce service from its officials. The Leicester assembly raised its penalty for recalcitrant common councillors to 100 marks in 1691, deeming that a refusal to serve was a 'great hindrance' to the government of the town. The following year Pontefract's corporation increased its fines for reluctant aldermen from £30 to £40, arguing that it needed 'good, sufficient, and discreet men' to staff the assembly. Other corporations, however, took steps to ease their officers' burden in recognition of the burgeoning of civic responsibilities during the Augustan period. For instance, the Warwick assembly trebled the mayor's allowance between 1694 and 1727, while at Reading the corporation sought to compensate for a cut in mayoral income by taking upon itself the cost of the mayor's feast.[38]

The Yarmouth assembly's recruitment problems were not so acute with the two chamberlains, who were the civic officials ranking immediately below the bailiffs in the order of officers chosen each St John's day.[39] However, their responsibility for administering the town's finances was no less daunting in scale, for Yarmouth had one of the largest corporate turnovers in the provinces as a result of its income from harbour tolls and fish customs, and its massive expenditure on a silting havenmouth. The town's founding charter clearly evoked this financial tie to the sea, and the liability of ensuring the safe passage of ships into the port put the corporation under constant strain. Despite the achievement of a series of parliamentary acts which helped to subsidize the assembly's haven schemes after 1670, corporate finance was a constant source of anxiety and its

[38] Chinnery (ed.), *Leicester Records* v. 10–11; Holmes (ed.), *Book of Entries of Pontefract*, 193–4; Styles, *Corporation of Warwick*, 66; *HMC 11th Report VII*, 203. For an illustration of the mayor's burden, see the eighteenth-century pandactula listing his round of civic duties through the year—Palmer, *History of Great Yarmouth*, 59–65. A previous attempt to introduce a mayoralty had been made in 1673 after a brace of aldermen had refused to become bailiffs for the second time in four years—Y/C19/8, f. 192. The paucity of mayoral candidates was to be a major concern at King's Lynn after 1660 as well—Metters, 'The Merchants and Rulers of King's Lynn', 33–4.

[39] The chamberlains owed their origin to the reforms of 1426 when the number of bailiffs was cut from four to two—Rutledge, in *NRS* 39 (1970), 6. A survey of their accounts, and the town's general finances, can be found in Appendix 1. For the most authoritative discussion of corporate finances, see E. J. Dawson, 'Finance and the Unreformed Borough', Hull Ph.D. 1978.

organization reflected this. In response to a particular cash-flow crisis in March 1657 the assembly created a salaried chamberlain's post with an annual stipend of £30, but this short-lived experiment shared the limited success enjoyed by other financial initiatives before 1700.[40] The assembly was content to continue with its unpaid chamberlains, annually electing a board of four auditors to monitor their accounts. An audit would be held each spring on what was termed 'Black Friday', when all the town's officers reported on their respective areas of corporate responsibility. This meeting permitted the assembly to make a thorough assessment of its overall fiscal stability, enabling it to enact necessary reforms on the basis of the information gathered. The audit was actually designated a 'grand assembly', and attendance was more strictly regulated than usual as a reflection of the importance of the occasion. As the crucial moment when the assembly took stock of its affairs, the audit serves to illustrate the scope and burden of the corporation's self-appointed tasks.[41]

Two muragers reported on the expenses incurred in the maintenance and repair of the town's mile-long wall and its eighteen towers. Two half-dole collectors were responsible for the town's dues from the catches of fish taken up by vessels using Yarmouth's port facilities.[42] Two church-wardens administered the parish's expenditure on religious observance, particularly the costly maintenance of St Nicholas's, one of the largest parish churches in the country. More lucratively, the ballastmaster recorded the profits from the sale of sand and earth to unladen ships. However, the most important source of income was the local custom levied on the herring catch, the direct responsibility of the chamberlains themselves. 'Heyning' dues proved unpredictable in yield, but the annual appointment of sixteen herring-tellers earmarked the importance which the corporation attached to this toll. Their number also reflected the assembly's difficulty in collecting a levy which was even criticized by some of its own councillors, but the demands of the corporation's coffers meant that the assembly had to burden a large number of its members with the collection

[40] Y/C19/7, f. 290. The salary was meant to allow the chamberlain to bestow 'most of his time' to the management of the town's finances.

[41] Palmer, *History of Great Yarmouth*, 6. The St John's Day election meeting was the only other assembly to be ruled a grand assembly. An ancient ordinance required the auditors to begin their task on 8 December, thereby allowing them some three or four months in which to prepare their accounts—Y/C18/3, pp. 23–5.

[42] Half-doles were levied on all catches greater than two lasts (2,400 fish). After the voyage expenses had been met, the profits of the catch would be split into doles (shares) between the crew, the boat owners, and the town. The town's dole would be further divided between the corporation and the church.

of this imposition.[43] Finance was the key agent of the corporation's continued stability, for it powered the services which both maintained and justified its control of local society. Most significantly, the repeated selection of certain councillors to the posts of auditor or chamberlain remained the only discernible pattern in corporate office-holding. The assembly needed experience in these demanding and important positions, since these personnel could have a direct influence on the overall stability of corporate rule. Particularly after 1700, the assembly regarded fiscal reform as the catalyst for improvement throughout Yarmouth society.[44]

These individual offices were an infrequent liability for most councillors, particularly for those below the aldermanic bench, but all were likely to be called up for perennial duty on one of the town's standing or *ad hoc* committees. The former included the 'assistance' which acted as an emergency assembly of councillors ready to advise the bailiffs at a moment's notice.[45] The other permanent bodies were more specific in their brief, such as the haven committee which supervised the maintenance of the harbour, and the hutch committee which was responsible for the administration of the civic archive. Their constant vigilance over corporate affairs revealed the jealousy with which the assembly guarded any advantage it might enjoy, whether derived from nature or by law. The annually elected Kirkley Road committee also illustrated this corporate resolve, monitoring coastal waters seven miles to the south of Yarmouth to prevent the sale of herring during the annual fish fair. This body was actually enforcing a privilege confirmed by the crown in 1386, and the fines levied for non-attendance to this duty again bespeak an irksome, though valued, corporate obligation. *Ad hoc* committees would back up the work of the assembly in a myriad of different tasks, ranging from the inspection of local guttering to the composition of a petition to the monarch. After 1660 the assembly

---

[43] Michel, 'The Port and Town of Yarmouth . . . 1550–1714', p. 255, observed that the unpredictable nature of corporate fishing dues hindered the assembly's plans for the long-term reform of its finances. The heyning toll was calculated by the difference between the wholesale price of herring at the quayside and its value at the auction chamber, with the corporation again taking a share of the profits. A. Saul underlined the importance of this custom by noting that the medieval corporation had always chosen affluent men as herring-wardens since their creation in 1413—'Great Yarmouth in the Fourteenth Century', 26.

[44] There was no *cursus honorum* to structure the civic career of Yarmouth's corporators. Chamberlains would be expected to serve for two consecutive years in order to ensure that one of them had previous experience in that office. Some councillors served for as many as six years in a row as auditor—e.g. Benjamin England 1678–84, Anthony Ellys 1712–18.

[45] The assistance was convened on fifty-two occasions between 1660 and 1720, and its decisions were subject to the ratification of the next full assembly. The level of attendance at its meetings ranged between ten and twenty councillors.

entrusted corporate affairs to a rising number of standing committees, mainly in response to the increasing sophistication and volume of its business.[46] The surviving records of the standing committees give evidence of sterling service, but the value of the *ad hoc* bodies cannot be disputed, for they continued to provide vital flexibility within the rigid confines of the corporate constitution.

The corporation did not make all these demands on its membership without any sensitivity to their onerousness. Occasional pardons from corporate service were granted to councillors on petition, and the practice of rotating offices ensured that their burden was more equitably spread through the assembly's membership.[47] Yet such leniency could not be extended too widely when there were so many pressing matters demanding attention, and thus the assembly had to find ways of inspiring commitment in its personnel. Heavy fines have already been noted as a direct means of enforcing service, but a more permanent loyalty to the corporate cause was sought through a deliberate aggrandizement of the status of the councillor, both as a figure of note within his own community and as part of the body with ultimate responsibility for the general welfare of the locality. The clannishness of urban oligarchies has remained one of the most potent images of their rule, but this impression has to be partially understood as a consequence of the corporation's desperate need to ensure the cooperation of its unpaid membership. The elaborate ritual associated with the corporation was not simply a pompous manifestation of its local power, but rather an integral part of its campaign to cultivate the loyalty of its councillors. Peter Borsay's recent work on civic ceremonial emphasizes its survival into the eighteenth century as a counterpoint to the supposed decline in élite customary activity, and its preservation can be seen as a response to corporate needs.[48] The councillor would have

[46] Standing committees were usually appointed at the first assembly meeting of the civic year in October. In 1660 there were three—the assistance, the hutch, and the haven committees. The following bodies were then created during the assembly's periodic reforming drives: town debts (1676); workhouse (1676); admiralty jurisdiction (1700); waterbailiff's investments (1701); Fisherman's Hospital (1703).

[47] One of the rare instances of dismissal from office without penalty, other than in respect of a councillor's ill health, came in April 1670 when two corporators were allowed to step down after they had sustained 'great losses' in their trade—Y/C19/8, f. 134v.

[48] See P. Borsay, 'All the Town's a Stage: Urban Ritual and Ceremony, 1660–1800', in Clark (ed.), *Transformation of English Provincial Towns*, 228–58. The vitality of corporate custom also comes through from a study of the survival of 'mock corporations' which permitted the populace to ape their social betters under official licence—see M. Mullett, 'Popular Culture and Popular Politics: Some Regional Case Studies' in C. Jones (ed.), *Britain in the First Age of Party, 1680–1750* (London, 1987), 129–50.

to receive some personal gratification for his commitment of time and energy to corporate duties, and the assembly principally endeavoured to repay him with status and a sense of self-fulfilment as a local governor. This is not to deny that there were perquisites of a more remunerative nature to be gained in corporate office, but local government could not have functioned purely on the basis of personal self-interest, and assemblymen had to acknowledge the responsibilities of their station in local society. When all of its members were part of the Yarmouth 'community'—residing, working and socializing within the borough—the raising of this civic consciousness was not difficult. However, it was necessary to reinforce this sense of communal identity when the demands of office were so great.

Right from the beginning of their civic career all councillors were left in little doubt that they had joined an exclusive enclave within their own locality, and that they were now charged with duties vital to the future of local society. All newcomers to the assembly had to swear an oath to the current bailiffs to 'be obedient and ready to come to them, to all assemblies and counsels when I shall be summonsed or warned', while also promising to keep assembly debates secret. These obligations reflected the requirement of the charter for only 'good and discrete men' to be elected to the assembly, for the public airing of debate was not deemed to be in the interests of stable local government.[49] Although this gave the assembly a very suspect image as a body whose membership was largely left unaccountable for its decisions, it did not mean that it was arbitrary in its attitude towards town affairs. The elaborate rituals of the election quest and the hefty fines imposed for failure to match up to the required standards of behaviour within the assembly hall were indicative of the seriousness with which the corporation approached its business. However, just as Parliament itself was extremely reluctant for its debates to be reported until the late eighteenth century, so the Yarmouth assembly took a dim view of any who betrayed its agenda. Other corporations displayed a similar vigilance, for the Liverpool assembly actually levied a £40 fine to deter such disclosures, and in 1690 the Nottingham town clerk was debarred from attending town business after divulging sensitive matters 'contrary to his oath and trust'. Even the mid-eighteenth-century Exeter corporation, which was sometimes prepared to call public meetings to discuss matters of general concern, insisted on the secrecy of

---

[49] Y/C18/1. In the tense atmosphere of August 1648, the assembly actually fined two councillors for arguing in the street, believing it to be the immediate catalyst for disorder in the port—Y/C19/7, f. 127.

council meetings on the argument that councillors could speak their minds without fear of reprisal. Significantly, any who dared to publish its debates was regarded as 'a disturber of the public peace'.[50]

Moreover, the severity which marked the assembly's handling of the few recorded cases of internal corruption belied the masonic image of covert illegality associated with this closeted world. For 'the perfidious misdemeanour' of trying to embezzle 40 shillings in 1667, common councillor Edmund Hunton was dismissed from his post, tried at the town's quarter-sessions and threatened with even further punishment.[51] Conscious of its vulnerability to external criticism, the assembly could not allow one councillor to impair its good name. The Lincoln assembly provided a striking demonstration of such concern soon after the Restoration by launching an inquiry into corporate corruption even after the Privy Council had dismissed the original allegations against one of its members. While overt criminality could never be tolerated, it was widely accepted that the councillors could benefit from their position of local authority. Most assemblies could reward its industrious councillors from a well of local patronage, and at Yarmouth the corporation could certainly wield great influence concerning such matters as appointments to salaried local offices, or the granting of licences for building extensions. However, there is no evidence to suggest that the distribution of favours caused dissension within or outside of the assembly. Moreover, the growing number of pensions issued in the late seventeenth century to aged councillors and their families indicated that the corporation had to inspire allegiance by more paternalistic means. By respecting and easing the personal circumstances of its hard-working councillors, the assembly evidently hoped to make corporate service a key element of its personnel's lives. Unfortunately for its public image, the methods employed towards that objective only reinforced the clannish image of its counsels.[52]

The energy which the assembly channelled into this raising of corporate spirit, and the success with which it met in this aim, might be interpreted as an attempt to distance itself from the rest of the locality. However, it is important to recognize that the corporation was not reluctant to play a very public role in local life. Even if the vast majority of

[50] Picton (ed.), *City of Liverpool*, 246; *Nottingham Borough Records*, 364–5; R. Newton, *Eighteenth-Century Exeter* (Exeter, 1984), 34–5.

[51] Y/S1, pp. 204, 210; Y/C19/8, f. 81.

[52] *HMC 14th Report VIII*, 104. The assembly's more obvious concern for the welfare of its members originated in the late 1690s, when it faced increasing difficulties in encouraging members to serve. By 1720 every year would see a new beneficiary of its generosity, ranging from needy ex-bailiffs to the corporation's own cook—Y/C19/9, 10, *passim*.

townsmen had little or no direct say in corporate affairs, the corporation still deemed it necessary to demonstrate its leadership to the Yarmouth populace. Every Sunday the councillors would file into their pews in St Nicholas's to take up their position of precedence in full view of their fellow townsfolk. As one former councillor observed in 1619, the position of the aldermen's gallery was deliberately calculated to ensure that 'those to whom the rule of the people is committed, may the better behold the demeanour of the whole congregation there assembled'.[53] The pervasiveness of civic influence in local life was also acknowledged by the importance of corporate events in the Yarmouth social calendar, with the Black Friday audit and the St John's Day elections featuring among the greatest occasions of popular festivity. Also on a regular basis, the assembly appointed 'scarlet days' to commemorate religious holidays or political anniversaries. These celebrations were marked by a church service and much public feasting, sponsored by the munificence of the assembly and dignified by its begowned progress through the town's main thoroughfares.[54] Such occasions reaffirmed the local social hierarchy, but they also made the councillors more aware of the responsibilities in office. Recent work on the aldermen of Leeds has suggested that a willingness to act on behalf of the community was an important motivating factor for those accepting corporate office. However, the evidence from Yarmouth indicates that this impulse was more a product of office-holding rather than a reason to enter it. Only after the experience of precedence at church, after sensing the respectful gaze of the crowds lining the route of a corporate procession, and having observed the seriousness of assembly procedure, would a true impression of a councillor's responsibilities be formed.[55] Charter privileges might set the corporation apart from the locality which it led, but its position was never so exalted that the views and needs of its neighbours could be totally ignored.

[53] H. Manship, *History of Great Yarmouth*, ed. C. J. Palmer (Great Yarmouth, 1854), 34–6. The importance of the church seat to a local notable's honour was reflected in the strict organization of pew-seating at St Nicholas's Church. In August 1649 ex-MP Thomas Johnson was permitted to retain his alderman's pew-seat following his resignation from assembly office—Y/C19/7, f. 151.

[54] The assembly fined councillors who failed to wear their gowns in church in order to remind them of their duty to uphold civic distinctions in public—Y/C18/3, p. 235. The decision of the Leeds corporation to increase its civic pageantry after 1660 revealed that even a corporation of seventeenth-century origin could appreciate the value of public display to the maintenance of its local authority—Kirby in *Northern History*, 22 (1986), 141.

[55] Ibid. 136. She observed that the aldermen's actions revealed 'an awareness . . . that men of wealth and privilege had a duty towards their less fortunate neighbours'. As often as this obligation might be expounded from the pulpit to the front pews, no corporation could leave its business to be completed merely at the discretion of its membership.

Although keen to provide reminders of its dominance of local society, the corporation revealed that the independence which it truly sought was not from the interference of its fellow townsmen, but rather from the intrusion of outsiders. This concern was clearly demonstrated by the Water Feast, the most spectacular of its annual festivities which saw the bailiffs take command of a fleet of vessels to proclaim the town's jurisdiction of the Rivers Yare, Bure, and Waveney.[56] Rowland Davies, a visiting Yarmouth lecturer, was in attendance in August 1689 to provide an outsider's view of this powerful expression of local autonomy.[57] The leading craft was 'full of young men in white, with caps made like those of our grenadiers', and supporting this aggressive vanguard were the vessels of the two bailiffs, both flying the royal colours and each with a drummer keeping a constant beat at their bows. The next two wherries flew the town's arms as a mark that they contained the foremen of the town's 'inquest of liberties', whose task it was to make 'an inquiry into all the abuses and all the privileges of the town', which was the ostensible purpose of the trip. However, as on all civic occasions, not far behind them were vessels carrying the victuallers and the 'mob', intent on a profitable and enjoyable day out.[58] The fleet separated on Breydon Water to proceed concurrently up the Yare and the Waveney, and when the limit of jurisdiction had been reached, a proclamation would be read out to elicit reports of any 'nuisance or injury' from vessels on that stretch of river.[59] An open-air meal was then served and both fleets would retrace their steps to rendezvous on Breydon Water, where 'there was a stir in firing guns, huzza and drinking healths'. All vessels then returned to Yarmouth for more celebrations, only for the whole process to be repeated the next day by the entire fleet on a journey up the Bure. Such was its perceived importance to the corporation's local popularity that even in times of

[56] Yarmouth's only territorial boundary lay with the manor of Caister two miles to the north of the town, and was marked by the 'Caister Rails'. This was proclaimed during an annual perambulation of the town's liberties, which was also led by the bailiffs. For the bitter disputes between the corporation and the Lords of Caister until 1545, see D. Turner, *A Sketch of the History of Caister Castle* (London, 1842).

[57] See W. R. Caulfield (ed.), 'The Journal of the Very Reverend Rowland Davies', in *Camden Society*, 68 (1857), 35–6.

[58] Davies recorded that the size of the fleet in 1689 was only twenty vessels, but he was informed that normally it was double that complement. The unruliness of the mob on this occasion was of constant concern for the assembly, and in July 1644 it even considered suspending the event for fear of the disorder it might cause—Y/C19/7, f. 41.

[59] The bridges which marked Yarmouth's jurisdictional limits were blockaded by ships during the reading of the proclamation in order to emphasize the town's control of those waterways.

severe financial crisis the Water Feast was maintained. It remained a symbol of the spirit of self-sufficiency which was evident throughout the seaside town, a local character which the corporation did not invent, but merely sought to embody.[60]

These observations were borne out by the town's two earliest historians, Thomas Damet and Henry Manship the Younger, a brace of native councillors who at great length expounded their own sense of civic spirit.[61] Both identified the corporation as the guiding force of the community since the demise of the Guild, but their main concern was to record the defence of the town's privileges against the encroachments of outsiders. The challenge of the Cinque Ports, Lowestoft, and a host of other traditional rivals will be considered later on, but it is significant that these contests were portrayed as the struggle of the merchant community as a whole, on whose success most of the town depended for their livelihoods. Manship, in particular, was eager to highlight the corporation's responsibility for the protection of the local economy, and he ended his account of Yarmouth's past battles hoping that such recollections would serve as an example for 'the posterity to come, especially such as be chosen to the body of the assembly'.[62] Peter Clark, in his survey of urban historians, brackets Manship with Exeter's John Hooker and Ipswich's Nathaniel Bacon as fellow upholders of a 'civic community', but the boundaries of this inner society must be clearly delineated and their permeability assessed.[63] The corporation's proud recantations of Yarmouth's history certainly dwelt on legal successes against its adversaries, but they also paid full tribute to the contribution of local mariners to the port's past achievements. Even the town arms reflected this generosity of spirit, for the three lions rampant with herring tails was conferred by Edward III in recognition of the townsmen's major contribution to the victory of the

---

[60] The expense of the Water Feast, however, was carefully monitored by the assembly. As early as 1619, Manship could comment on its 'superlative' cost, and it proved a drain on corporate resources until the mid-nineteenth century—Palmer, *Perlustration of Great Yarmouth*, i. 290–7; Manship, *History of Great Yarmouth*, 114–15. Some saving was made in 1706 when the assembly decreed that only one river would be visited each year, a change resulting from its recent switch to a mayoralty—Y/C19/10, f. 95v.

[61] T. Damet, *A Booke of the Foundacion and Antiquitye of the Towne of Greate Yermouthe*, ed. C. J. Palmer (Great Yarmouth, 1847); Manship, *History of Great Yarmouth*. Also see T. Nash, *Nashes Lenten Stuffe, with the Praise of the Red Herring* (1599), which gave the town welcome publicity after the author had received a loan from a local resident during his stay at Yarmouth.   [62] Manship, *History of Great Yarmouth*, preface.

[63] Clark, 'Visions of the Urban Community', in D. Fraser and A. Sutcliffe (eds.), *The Pursuit of Urban History* (London, 1983), 105–24. Clark's accreditation of Damet's history to Henry Manship the Elder is thrown into doubt by Rutledge's articles on Damet in *Norfolk Archaeology*, 33 (1963), 119–30, and ibid. 34 (1968), 332–4.

English fleet at Sluys in 1340. This event took its place amongst other significant local episodes recorded on 'the ancient chronological table', a list which had hung in the parish church for centuries and was subsequently moved to the Guildhall. It was still a source of corporate concern and pride in 1712, revealing the assembly's belief that the history of the town should be known and respected.[64] Antiquity might bolster the position of the corporation within the borough, but it also put it under pressure to maintain the town's historic course, binding it even more firmly to the general interest of the locality.

The emphasis which the Yarmouth corporation placed on custom and its stubborn defence of historic rights fulfils yet more of the criteria associated with the traditional oligarchy, but these features must not be seen as artificial supports of the assembly's own making. There were many influences working to unite the social élite of the town together, and the assembly's constitution merely articulated a set of values which had been largely determined by the town's historic development. Economic dependence on the haven affected the hopes of rich and poor alike, and no ordinance was needed to remind the assembly of its duty to maintain its natural advantages. Likewise, the relatively isolated position of the port on the tip of the rump of East Anglia had decisively shaped the attitude of the town's leaders towards outsiders. Jealous of its advantageous geographic position with respect to inland, coastal, and overseas trade, the assembly was wary of encroachments and always eager to strengthen the privileges which were designed to protect its control of the port. Yarmouth society cannot be portrayed as a cosy communal consensus, but economic interdependence must be acknowledged as an unifying bond.[65]

The essential unity of interest concerning the local economy facilitated the corporation's accumulation of power as the spokesman for the locality, and its success in that task left its supremacy unchallenged within Yarmouth itself. The single-parish structure of the town was an especial aid to its authority, for the vast majority of larger boroughs were divided by a number of parochial boundaries. Of course, a parish of such unwieldy

---

[64] For a copy of the table, see T. Hearne (ed.), *Joannis Lelandi . . . De Rebus Britannicus Collectanea* (Oxford, 1715), 285–8. Its descriptions of charter privileges, and of the battles fought to defend them, were noted by antiquary James Brome—*Travels over England, Scotland and Wales* (London, 1700), 133–5. For the transcription ordered by the assembly, see—Y/C19/10, f. 236v.

[65] A timely reminder of the overriding importance of commerce to the early modern town has recently been served by Robert Tittler, and in its determination to protect its trade, Yarmouth was no different than any of its urban rivals—*Architecture and Power*, 155.

proportions presented problems for Yarmouth's administrators, but the assembly's precedence at St Nicholas's faithfully reflected the comprehensiveness of its control. Not even the subdivisions of the wards threatened to undermine its control, for the eight wards actually cut across the South Quay and the market place, which constituted the only recognizable occupational or economic zones in the town. As was the experience of the councillors of Newcastle and Leeds, Yarmouth assemblymen could not fail to notice the deprivations of their impoverished neighbours, and thus the risk of social atomization was reduced.[66] In this busy and densely populated environment, the corporation provided a pole of order and stability which allowed local society to function, and the value of that role was not underestimated by the townsmen who embarked on a civic career. For certain, corporate service was often a thankless task and could threaten the safety of the councillor's person or the size of his purse.[67] However, the sense of duty which the assembly instilled in its members as the heirs of a tradition of responsible self-government did much to appease such personal considerations, thus providing the principal momentum for the continued effectiveness of corporate rule.

Yarmouth's co-opted élite can thus be shown to be a somewhat unsatisfactory candidate to fit the accepted model of corporate oligarchy. It did exert firm control over the town and few dared challenge its position when it had such considerable resources of manpower and influence at its command.[68] However, with that dominance came a commitment to the locality's interests of equally daunting proportions. Such responsibility defined its relationship with its fellow townsmen and required the

[66] The eight-ward system had only been introduced in 1620, in response to the growth of the local population. For an analysis of the distribution of wealth through the wards (named 1st North, 2nd North, 1st North Middle, etc.), see Appendix 2. Yarmouth's lack of identifiable or distinct 'zones' was in some contrast to county capitals such as Exeter and Norwich—see J. Kirby in *Northern History*, 22 (1986), 132; J. Ellis, 'A Dynamic Society: Social Relations in Newcastle-upon-Tyne', in Clark (ed.), *Transformation of English Provincial Towns*, 198–9; Evans, *Seventeenth-Century Norwich*, 14–18; W. T. MacCaffrey, *Exeter 1540–1640* (Cambridge, Mass., 1958), 250–1.

[67] In 1665 Thomas Ouldman, common councillor and overseer of the poor, was attacked with a knife and stave by an ex-assemblyman while going about his duties—Y/S1/3, p. 185. The prominent position accorded to the constables in church came in recognition of their hazardous and onerous tasks, as well as enabling them to react more readily to 'any sudden accident'—Manship, *History of Great Yarmouth*, 36.

[68] In August 1657, local residents were reported to have blamed the 'loftiness of the bench' for the corporation's financial problems, believing that excessive sums were being spent on legal disputes—A. W. and J. L. Ecclestone, *The Rise of Great Yarmouth* (Norwich, 1959), 153–62. In 1723 corporate rebel John Andrews attributed the assembly's local supremacy to 'private men not being willing to spend their own money in suit with the corporation'—Y/MS/4593/T138E.

corporation to act as borough spokesman with a wide range of external authorities. Maintaining its control under such pressures was not an easy task and the assembly had to work hard to ensure the discipline and loyalty of its councillors. The difficulties facing the individual corporator will be examined in the prosopographic section, but as a prelude to that study it is necessary to analyse the corporation's regulation of two of its most important, and problematic, spheres of responsibility. The freeman body, as the reservoir of corporate personnel, inevitably played an important role in civic affairs and remained the most immediate concern of the assembly when debating local matters. Most significantly, an analysis of the fundamental ties which existed between the freemen and the assembly will broaden our conception of oligarchic rule, and highlight still further the complex interaction of the town's politics, society, and economy. An even more delicate connection, however, existed between the assembly and the greater authorities of county and capital. The corporation's vulnerability to interference from outsiders, and its frequent dependence on external sources of aid, forced Yarmouth's leaders to establish contacts on a regional and national basis to maintain control over the town's future. These sections will permit a more well-rounded perspective of the corporation to be formed, paying tribute to its adaptability to the varying demands of locality, region, and centre.

ii. THE FREEMEN

The role of the freedom in the early modern English town has not been a neglected study, but historians of the post-Restoration period have principally focused on its political significance as a qualification for the parliamentary vote. Primary interest in the electoral influence of the freeman has also ensured that research has focused on corporations such as London and Norwich, whose constitutions permitted the freeman body to make an annual choice of local officials, or even to influence the make-up of part of the assembly itself.[69] Such work has an undoubted importance in highlighting the direct participation of large freeman

---

[69] London and Norwich remain the two most intensively researched corporations, an attraction based on their contemporary importance as well as on the relative 'openness' of their corporate constitutions—see Evans, *Seventeenth-Century Norwich*, 8–13, 26–62; G. S. De Krey, *A Fractured Society: The Politics of London in the First Age of Party, 1688–1715* (Oxford, 1985); I. Doolittle, 'The Government of the City of London, 1694–1767', Oxford D.Phil. 1979. However, O'Day has pointed out that the number of active freeman democracies in seventeenth-century English towns was extremely small—O'Day *et al. The Traditional Community under Stress*, 135–6.

electorates in the government of local society, but insufficient attention has been given to the freedom's role as an economic regulator and as a stepping-stone to a civic career. The freedom was a fundamental distinction of local society, and thus it should be seen in its communal context, where it can be shown to be a vital basis of the local social order.

Lack of interest in the economic role of the freedom must be attributed to its image as a medieval relic of a regulated economy, which by the late seventeenth century was already under attack from the ultimately triumphant forces of free trade. Indeed, the unpopularity of freemen privileges was well represented by a critic of the Newcastle assembly in 1699, who described it as 'the epitome of all corporations' and observed that 'the ancient citizens of Rome . . . never boasted more of their freedom than this arbitrary town'. By the late eighteenth century the unscrupulous practices of borough electioneers in purchasing masses of paper freemen to swamp the electorate had irreparably damaged the standing of the freedom. However, there has been little concern to explain why many towns fought to maintain its economic distinction, some of whom battled on until the advent of municipal reform.[70] It will be argued here that the importance of the contribution made by the freemen to the government of the locality lay behind such stubbornness, and that the battle to safeguard freemen trading privileges went beyond political considerations. Without the economic incentives offered to freemen, the task of finding candidates for corporate office would have been impossible, and many corporations came to view the issue of freeman rights as a struggle for its continued survival. The Yarmouth assembly may have given its own freemen very little opportunity to influence corporate policy directly, but it showed itself to be extremely sensitive over freeman rights.[71]

In accordance with the custom of most English towns, Yarmouth confined entry to freeman status to three principal methods of qualification:

[70] History of Parliament, 1690–1715 section, unpublished constituency article, Newcastle-upon-Tyne; S. and B. Webb, *English Local Government*, 402, 529–58. There is plenty of evidence from Leicester, York, Nottingham, Boston, Oxford, Southampton, and Lincoln to show that corporations did not meekly surrender their freeman privileges in the eighteenth century—Greaves, *The Corporation of Leicester, 1689–1836*, 48–60; Dawson, 'Finance and the Unreformed Borough', 255–63: Keith-Lucas, *Unreformed Local Government System*, 26–7; A. T. Patterson, *A History of Southampton* (Southampton, 1966), i. 23–5; F. Hill, *Georgian Lincoln* (Cambridge, 1966), 245–6.

[71] Should an insufficient number of common councillors attend the St John's Day assembly, freemen would make up the quorum of thirty-six required for the selection of the quest. During the plague year of 1665, the names of as many as ten freemen went into the draw for the quest—Y/C19/8, f. 61v. The freemen were also permitted to attend the Black Friday audit, subject to the limitations of space in the Guildhall.

the acceptance of the sons of freemen at the age of 20, the serving of a seven-year apprenticeship under a freeman, or the purchase of a freedom by direct application to the assembly.[72] The assembly kept a close scrutiny over all petitions for the freedom, while also reserving the power to confer it upon deserving townsmen or helpful outsiders.[73] In 1660 the principal motivation for seeking freeman status remained economic. With the freedom came an immunity from paying a wide range of local port dues, and, most importantly, an exclusive right to act as an independent trader within the town. This trading monopoly was most strictly imposed during the late autumn herring season, when all visitors to the port had to sell their catches to freeman 'hosts', a custom which caused great discontent amongst non-free 'strangers'.[74] These were considerable advantages for the local trader, but their attraction only served to emphasize the commitment that the freemen had to make to the service of the locality. Although they would not fill any important corporate offices until they had been admitted to the assembly, their admission to freeman ranks meant that they had to be prepared to take on the onus of local government at some stage in their career. This reality was bought home by the assembly's strict enforcement of the residence requirement for freemen, which aimed to bind the individual's future to that of his locality.[75] Moreover, even if the freeman never entered assembly ranks, there were other unsalaried posts to be fulfilled, most notably that of constable, which needed personnel who were committed to the town's future.[76] The freeman was thus expected to play a key role in maintaining local order, and his obligation to uphold the privileges of the town was clearly signified by the freeman's oath and his 'burgess letter'. It was with this sense of mutual self-preservation that the assembly and the freemen viewed each other, an interdependence which generally acted as a firm bond of unity.

---

[72] The age level for the sons of freemen was set at 20 in March 1644—Y/C19/7, f. 36.

[73] Honorary freedoms were usually bestowed upon the high steward and his family, prospective MPs for the town, or notable naval personnel.

[74] For the best description of the workings of the heyning system, from the perspective of its critics as well as its supporters, see the depositions of witnesses called at the trial of John Andrews in 1728—PRO, E134, 1 Geo. II Easter No. 16, and 2 Geo. II Michaelmas No. 26.

[75] The freemen could not leave Yarmouth for more than a year and a day—Y/C18/3, p. 34.

[76] The unpopularity of the constable's duties was attested by the fines levied for failure to serve, and each incumbent was expected to serve a three-year stint in office. In 1685, schoolmaster Matthew Springall complained that the distractions of the job had almost led to 'an utter overthrow of my school'—Palmer, *Perlustration of Great Yarmouth*, ii. 409.

Although Yarmouth's freeman body numbered only some 600 in 1660, its social make-up inevitably meant that local leaders could not dismiss its views out of hand. The expense involved in the training of apprentices or in the purchase of freedoms dictated that such applicants usually came from respectable backgrounds, and those free by birthright could be expected to come from the town's more established families. Even in the 1720s, when freemen numbers had risen to some 800, a leading merchant commented that 'a great many' of the freemen 'are of the most substantial inhabitants . . . and are generally persons of pretty good circumstances'.[77] Such observations echoed the ideals of Exeter historian John Hooker, who regarded the freeman as 'the chiefest and principal member of the commonwealth of the city', particularly as 'out of his loins do proceed all such as be officers'. The propriety of the freemen was evidently a very important boost to the overall dignity of the Yarmouth corporation, and the assembly dutifully revealed a concern for the general welfare of the poorer burgesses. Every year the aldermen were required to tour their wards to take the names of poor freemen, or their widows and families, so that money could be distributed to needy cases. This 'freemoney' was derived from the town's dues on part of the fishing catch, and proved to be a substantial boon to the corporation's image from the 1690s onwards when it was requested to justify the imposition of local dues. In the early eighteenth century the Exeter corporation introduced similar charitable initiatives to make the freedom more attractive to local traders, and even ensured that local freemen gained contracts for work ordered by the assembly.[78]

Unlike several notoriously venal boroughs, the Yarmouth corporation did not view its freemen merely as a source of income, for it could not afford to be so short-sighted when regulating for its future personnel. By 1660 freedoms purchased directly from the assembly had reached a level of £15, but in the ensuing decade this price more than trebled in some notable cases.[79] However, even these rich newcomers could not expect to

[77] The freeman estimate and the commentary on personal wealth came from Richard Ferrier, a leading corporate figure who had often had cause to use freeman lists in the course of his election campaigns—PRO, E134, 1 Geo.II, Easter No. 16.

[78] The corporation tightened the administration of freemoney after 1711 when the heyning system came under attack, and within a decade as much as £119 was being distributed to poor freemen and their families each year—Y/C19/10, ff. 188v, 622v, 641.

[79] The rise in the price of purchased freedoms can be partly attributed to the port's prosperity, which increased the attractiveness of freeman privileges in the eyes of outsiders. However, the assembly seems to have set its prices in accordance with its own assessment of the wealth of each applicant.

escape from making a contribution to corporate life which went well beyond their entrance fee. In 1645 pewterer Richard Betts was allowed to redeem his freedom for only £10 'in as much as there is good hope of him to be a serviceable man to the town'. The assembly's faith in him was rewarded when he later became an alderman and bailiff, and two of his sons followed him into assembly office.[80] The criterion of utility continued to be the principal merit which the assembly sought in its freemen, for its future could be imperilled if its offices devolved into disinterested or resentful hands. Awareness of the tie between freeman and corporator helps to condition our understanding of the inner workings of oligarchy still further, for it reveals that the assembly often sat on the knife-edge between control and dependence when dealing with a large and important section of local society.

Most importantly, the freemen body must not be seen as a static group, for its size could fluctuate, and the applicants for such privileged status underwent significant change. Analysis of its make-up during the Augustan period suggests that the freeman body was primarily responsive to the fluctuations of the town's trade, rather than regulated by the sinister hand of assembly policy for self-interested ends. Appendix 3 charts the changes in admission rates across the period, and shows that the popularity of the freedom dramatically increased after the Restoration, a pattern consistent with the boom enjoyed by Yarmouth traders until the late 1670s.[81] A combination of over-expansion and the impact of the wars fought by William and Anne had a dramatically adverse effect on the local economy after 1680, and admission rates only began to recover after the establishment of a European peace in 1713. The changes in the rates of apprentice freemen were the most sensitive guide to the economic health of the port, for the expense of such training ensured that it was a major decision for any family to invest in the likelihood of their offspring becoming successful Yarmouth merchants.[82] The purchase of freedoms was similarly affected, for redemptions were generally taken out by new settlers in the town who were attracted by the prospect of good business. Economic prosperity even overcame the reluctance of the sons of freemen to make themselves liable for assembly service, though political consid-

[80] Y/C19/7, f. 63.

[81] Appendix 3 has been compiled from the freeman rolls edited by B. De Chair in *NNAS* 9 (1910). Their reliability can only really be accepted from the 1620s onwards.

[82] For a good illustration of the importance and cost of apprenticeship, see R. G. Wilson, 'Merchants and Land: The Ibbetsons of Leeds and Denton', in *Northern History*, 24 (1988), 77–8. He shows that even the 'respectable' sum of £300 was 'unlikely' to obtain a good apprenticeship for an aspiring merchant in Restoration Leeds.

erations may have boosted the total for the 1680s, as was certainly the case in the 1720s.[83] What is clear from the patterns revealed in Appendix 3 is that the make-up of the freeman body was still largely determined by economic factors well into the eighteenth century, an observation which reflects the primary motivation moving applicants to seek entry into its ranks.

This long-term overview of the progress of the Yarmouth freedom must be kept in mind when trying to evaluate the impact of the most dramatic development in the town's electoral history: the enfranchise-ment of the freeman body on the ruling of the Convention Parliament in 1660. Such a decisive alteration of the town's political structure might be interpreted as the cue for a wholesale change in the balance of power within its upper hierarchy, but the franchise issue must be seen as only one aspect of the relationship between the assembly and the freemen. Derek Hirst, the foremost authority on the early seventeenth-century electorate, viewed the assembly's apparent reticence to surrender its elec-toral monopoly as a complex phenomenon. He found evidence to suggest that the Yarmouth freemen might have participated in the choice of Yar-mouth's MPs as early as 1625, but notes that, unlike the burgesses of other boroughs, they showed little interest in challenging for the vote.[84] However, rather than viewing such apathy as a consequence of the pau-city of freemen, as Hirst suggests, credit should instead be given to the efficiency with which Yarmouth's representatives acted on behalf of the generality of the local populace. Recent studies of the Elizabethan cor-poration have underlined the benefits which the assembly gained for the town, and the role of the MPs in maintaining such advantages remained an important issue at election time. A major recommendation for the Yar-mouth candidate remained his likely effectiveness as the spokesman for the town's interests in Westminster, a criterion supported by councillor and freeman alike, though appearing more of a burden to any local gentle-man or noble. The assumption that freemen were necessarily in constant conflict with the assembly over such matters misrepresents the fundamen-tal basis of their relationship. By concentrating on moments of confront-ation such as the electoral poll, the worst conclusions will be drawn of the assembly's treatment of its freemen. A broader perspective brings home

---

[83] The first evidence of electoral corruption affecting the rate of freedom applications came at the 1722 general election—see Ch. 7. However, similar artifices had probably been employed by royal agents as early as 1687, though no parliamentary election actually took place to reward their endeavours.

[84] Hirst, *The Representative of the People?*, 53–4.

the transient nature of much political strife when compared to the ongoing stability of their mutual interests.[85]

These observations are borne out by the course of the parliamentary election of 1654, when the first consolidated attempt was made to force the assembly to enfranchise the freemen. On the eve of election day one common councillor went as far as 'to open the doors of the assembly' in order to allow non-councillors to enter, an audacious gesture deemed to be 'to the great disturbance of the house'. The corporation's sensitivity over the franchise issue had already been signalled by a recent decision to ban any notice of the poll, for it was thought that local electioneering 'may tend to the destruction of the privilege of the house'.[86] However, this drama was not the result of a wave of democratic self-assertion on behalf of the populace, as has been suggested for contemporaneous events at Newcastle, King's Lynn, or Bedford.[87] The corporator who dared to fling open the doors of the assembly was a member of a Presbyterian group which was attempting to undermine the growing influence of its Independent rivals. His desperate methods only reflected the strength of his political enemies within the corporation, not the momentum of a freeman campaign for the vote. The swiftness with which the assembly closed ranks after this interruption, with even Presbyterian leaders disowning the tactics of one of their own, indicated that the whole episode had served to reaffirm corporate fears for the consequences of open factionalism.[88]

Such reservations over the actual politicization of the freeman body before 1660 obviously condition the significance of its enfranchisement by the Convention Parliament. Following the pattern of the election six years before, the poll of 1660 was decisively influenced by an acrimonious struggle for power between factions within the assembly. Presbyterians

---

[85] For important studies of the corporation's pursuit of the town's economic interests, see D. M. Dean, 'Parliament, Privy Council, and Local Politics in Elizabethan England: The Yarmouth–Lowestoft Fishing Dispute', in *Albion*, 22 (1990), 39–64; G. Elton, 'Piscatorial Politics in the Early Parliaments of Elizabeth I', in N. McKendrick and R. B. Outhwaite (eds.), *Business Life and Public Policy* (Cambridge, 1986), 1–20.

[86] Y/C19/7, f. 246. Also, see Kishlansky, *Parliamentary Selection*, 116–18, where Yarmouth's 1654 election is discussed in the wider context of the growing number of double election returns from the mid-century onwards.

[87] See Howell, *Newcastle-upon-Tyne*, 52–62; G. Metters, 'The Rulers and Merchants of King's Lynn', 21–2; C. G. Parsloe, 'The Corporation of Bedford, 1647–64', in *TRHS*, 4th ser. 29 (1947), 151–65.

[88] The motion condemning the electoral tactics employed by Nathaniel Ashby was passed by an overwhelming 34 vs. 3 majority—Y/C19/7, f. 246. There was no attempt made by the Presbyterians to contest the Commons' decision at the elections of August 1656 and January 1659, both of which were very strictly supervised by the assembly.

and Independents still fought for control, but the imminent restoration of the monarchy further complicated their points of difference. Once again the Presbyterians sought to outmanoeuvre their rivals by an appeal to a wider local electorate, and a double return duly resulted. The Convention predictably sided with the candidates favoured by the Presbyterian faction, for the town's notorious reputation for radical opinions—enforced by the assembly's choice of a regicide—did not endear it to a government trying to end the anarchy of the previous two years.[89] The extension of the Yarmouth electorate can thus be seen as a conservative measure, aimed at undermining the political power of a faction which had seized control of the assembly during a time of unrest. The limited import of the freemen's enfranchisement, moreover, was brought home by their subsequent treatment at the hands of the assembly, which showed little deviation from traditional practice. Rather than choosing to contest the freemen's electoral right, the assembly was content to ensure the strict regulation of the freedom, with particular attention paid to its entrance requirements.[90] Only when another isolated political faction had been raised to power in 1684 would the freemen be denied the parliamentary vote again, but this exclusion was as brief as the supremacy of the Tory regime which had occasioned it. The assembly had no hesitation in reinvesting the freemen with their voting rights in 1689, for the poll did not pose an automatic threat to their general control of the locality. Having maintained the economic status of the freedom up to that point, the ties between the assembly and the freemen were still strong enough to bind them in a pact of mutual benefit.

Chapters 6 and 7, which analyse the bitter struggles fought by the corporation in defence of freemen privileges after 1689, will show how desperately the assembly depended on its freemen for the maintenance of the corporate *status quo*. Whereas Independents and Exclusionists might come and go, and Whigs and Tories change their policies, the assembly was unswerving in its protection of the freemen's economic privileges. In this regard the enfranchisement had changed little, though it might be seen to have rewarded hard-working local officials with a greater influence in the running of the locality. The real threat that the freeman voter

---

[89] The Commons' ruling was given on 18 May 1660—*CJ*, viii. 35. For the controversy surrounding the election of regicide Miles Corbet, see Henning, *House of Commons, 1660–1690*, i. 324.

[90] See, Y/C19/8, ff. 37, 164. G. Metters argued that corporate control over freeman admissions largely negated the effects of the enfranchisement of the freemen of King's Lynn after 1661—'The Rulers and Merchants of King's Lynn', 21–2.

would pose to assembly control would only become evident at the very end of our period, when the intervention of an ambitious and wealthy patron would throw the traditional dominance of the corporation into question. However, even then the corporation proved intransigent on the issue of the freedom, despite the immense pressures working to break its hold over the town's economy and society. The assembly continued to penalize 'strangers' for failing to pay their surcharges as non-freemen, banned the covert sale of freedoms for political votes, and insisted that freemen were local residents ready to fulfil corporate service. In this manner, the freedom can be seen as one of the key barriers employed by the corporation against outsiders, rather than as an ossified medieval relic designed to subject its neighbours. The freedom increasingly invited external interference on account of its political value, but the assembly still fought for its civic distinction. Other trading centres whose privileged trading status mirrored that of Yarmouth faced similar jealousy and censure from outsiders, and their corporations revealed that they too could not compromise over such hard-won advantages. Even when attempting to understand the corporation's relationship with its own locality, attention must therefore be paid to its interaction with the world outside its walls. The next section is thus no adjunct to the examination of oligarchy, but an integral part of its study.

iii. THE OUTSIDERS

The corporation's general policy towards outsiders, in accordance with its basic principles of government, aimed to advance the town's interests while preserving its control of the locality. Of course, when dealing with external authorities, many with influence far greater than that of the assembly, this was a difficult objective to achieve. Resourcefulness thus became a basic requirement for the assembly's approach to the unpredictable outside world. Given Yarmouth's tempestuous history, with many a battle fought against local and national rivals to establish and preserve its privileged status, intransigence might be taken as the watchword of its attitude towards external forces. However, even past successes did not recommend that the town's leaders should automatically adopt a defensive position when dealing with strangers. The corporation recognized that the maintenance of its legal and natural advantages relied heavily on the preservation of a dialogue between itself and outsiders, and thus it attempted to formalize the channels of influence which led to the authorities most regularly involved in Yarmouth's affairs. Reflecting the nature of much early modern government, this system of connections was highly personalized, but for all the precariousness inherent in any network of contacts, it did allow the corporation to participate in the formulation of policies affecting its affairs.[91] The narrative sections will show how fluid and interactive the tie of local and centre could be, especially when further complicated by the influence of regional, or even overseas, interests. However, a basic overview of corporate 'foreign' policy is required to give those sections some coherence, and to illustrate why the assembly's most important self-appointed role remained that of Yarmouth's spokesman in national circles.

With its well-developed structure of officials and committees, the corporation was prepared for most eventualities, but these annually elected posts were essentially local in sphere and transient in their personnel. Significantly, the only long-term appointments made by the corporation were to offices assigned with the task of gaining outside influence or of representing its interests in public. They all accorded the incumbents much honour within the locality, for their contribution to the town's future was generally acknowledged. The status of the high steward was greatest of all, a life-time appointment which had been bestowed on a succession of influential national figures since the reign of Henry VIII.[92] From the town's perspective, the process of seeking powerful friends was always a risky business, because its would-be patron could easily regard his office as an invitation to meddle in its affairs for his own ends. The town's relationship with its high stewards certainly showed many a strained moment as it wavered between the competing demands of dependence and autonomy, but its leaders knew that friends in high places were essential for the defence of its interests in Westminster or Whitehall. Another vital figure was the recorder, 'one discrete man learned in the

[91] Recent historiography is beginning to adopt a less structured view of the links between centre and locality. Kishlansky, *Parliamentary Selection*, 37–48, saw the relationship of patron and locality as one which 'cut both ways'. L. Glassey stressed the danger of exaggerating the dichotomy of local and central perspectives—'Local Government' in C. Jones (ed.), *Britain in the First Age of Party, 1680–1750* (London, 1987), 151–72. D. H. Sacks emphasized the flexibility of the locality when establishing contacts with external authorities—'The Corporate Town and the English State: Bristol's Little Businesses, 1625–41', in *Past and Present*, 110 (1986), 69–105.

[92] When the 4th Earl of Dorset was chosen as high steward in November 1629, the corporation specifically alluded to his offices of Privy Councillor and Admiralty commissioner. At the same time it stressed his responsibility 'to patronise the town in all honest, good, and indifferent causes'—Y/C19/6, f. 141v.

law of England' who acted as the town's chief legal adviser.[93] The corporation was willing to entrust this important office to notable outsiders,
for technical skill was at a premium when so many of the corporation's
disputes revolved around the defence of its charter in the courts. To back
up such expertise, a salaried town attorney was occasionally employed to
preserve local privileges, and this office was usually bestowed upon a
non-resident.[94] The most important life-time appointment which the assembly made from its own ranks was that of the town clerk, whose main
responsibility also lay in legal matters. On the basis of the work completed by a succession of incumbents after 1660, the town clerk's role
would expand and its status increase until it rivalled that of the mayor
and the JPs.[95] The buffeting which the corporate charters took at the
hands of the later Stuarts, and the increasing economic pressure against
local tolls gave these attorneys ample opportunity to prove their worth to
the town. In return, a grateful assembly was never slow to reward their
efforts.

With this impressive array of legal firepower, the assembly could hope
to undermine the strength of any opposition in court, but it was not so
complacent as to believe that the course of law could never be corrupted
by influential figures in the distant corridors of power in London. The
contact with the high steward was a crucial source of strength in these
matters, but at particular moments of crisis the assembly also sent gifts
to helpful governmental officials who could help its cause. However,
the most effective Yarmouth agents in the capital remained its two parliamentary representatives, whether townsmen or strangers. Although elections between 1660 and 1722 were often heavily influenced by regional
patrons or their nominees, the borough maintained a very strong sense of
self-determination over the choice of MPs, usually attempting to ensure
that at least one of the two was a townsman.[96] Even after the vote had

---

[93] The wording is that of the charter of 1608 which introduced the office of recorder to
replace that of the steward. The latter post had predated the reforms of 1491, and had
fulfilled a role very much akin to that of the recorder—Palmer, *History of Great Yarmouth*,
336, 341–50.

[94] The attorney's salary was set at £20 p.a. In 1667, the assembly decided to dispense
temporarily with this extra legal adviser after nine months of inactivity on his part, thereby
allowing the role of the town clerk to expand—Y/C19/8, ff. 12v, 92v.

[95] The attraction and importance of this office was already well established by 1661, for
the assembly estimated that 'the considerable profit' of its various sources of income was
some £120 p.a. at that time—Y/C19/7, f. 383.

[96] The corporation had passed resolutions on the residence requirements of MPs in 1584
and 1620—see P. W. Hasler (ed.), *The History of Parliament: The House of Commons, 1558–
1603* (London, 1981), i. 211–12; Y/C18/3, p. 232.

been extended to the freeman body in 1660, the defence of local interests remained a very strong platform from which a townsman could launch his campaign, and the assembly certainly did not alter its perception of the role of Members after the Restoration. Prior assembly practice had sought to inculcate their loyalty by the payment of expenses in the capital and by rewards for exceptional service in the town's name.[97] However, in return, the MPs were expected to pay constant attention to the issues prescribed by the assembly to be of particular interest, with trading matters remaining the most consistent priority. As recently as 1658 the assembly had issued 'instructions' to Members before the start of the session to ensure that Yarmouth's views and grievances were heard in the national arena.[98] Yet, as much as the assembly valued a spokesman at Westminster, the role of its MPs was not confined to the parliamentary sphere. They were expected to act as the town's lobbyists and informants throughout the capital, appearing at the Privy Council, the Admiralty, the Customs House or any other authority which might influence the town's affairs. In 1689 lecturer Dean Davies had frequent chance meetings with the Yarmouth MPs in various parts of London as they went about their corporate business, although he could generally hope to find them at the Green Dragon Inn in Bishopsgate, the unofficial headquarters of Yarmouth men in the capital.[99] This essential tie of corporate service could be severely tested when political divisions or personal ambition intervened, but the obligation of representing the town could not be ignored by townsman or stranger, particularly if he should wish to seek re-election at some future date.

Recent research into late seventeenth- and early eighteenth-century politics is beginning to recognize the importance of 'constituency' matters to the parliamentary member. In particular, the *History of Parliament*'s volumes for the Restoration period have provided a wealth of evidence to suggest that the corporations expected their MPs to act in their direct interest. For instance, when electoral agents at Preston reported in 1685 on the outlook of local leaders they observed that 'their pulse beats after

[97] See Y/C18/3, p. 268. When fulfilling the dual responsibilities of both recorder and MP in the 1640s, regicide Miles Corbet was twice rewarded with gifts of £50 by a grateful assembly—Y/C19/7, ff. 102, 174.

[98] Y/C19/7, f. 302. The History of Parliament noted the election of instruction committees by the Yarmouth assembly in the Elizabethan period—Hasler (ed.), *The House of Commons, 1558–1603*, i. 211.

[99] See *Camden Society*, 68 (1857), *passim*. The Green Dragon was the terminus for the Yarmouth stage, a service which could convey passengers to the capital with only one overnight stop *en route*.

such a person as may be qualified to do services for their corporation'. Assemblies such as Exeter, Gloucester, and King's Lynn continued to rely on local townsmen to advance their cause at Westminster, and the Liverpool assembly actually used the Lancashire-born Member for Herefordshire, John Birch, commending him for having 'done more for our town than our two Parliament men ten times fold'. Even major politicians such as Lord Danby recognized the necessity to court the provinces through the promise of favour, informing the York assembly in 1673 that his recent appointment as Lord Treasurer meant that he was now in 'a station more capable of doing you service'. Most significantly, although the increasing importance of Parliament as a clearing-house for local business after 1689 has yet to be systematically explored, early research has indicated that the 'traditional' service expected of the corporate Member continued to be exacted during the 'rage of party' of the reigns of William and Anne.[100]

Yarmouth, in common with other important centres such as Chester, Liverpool, and Hull, sought to keep a tight rein on its Members' activities in the capital after 1689.[101] However, the increasing value placed upon a parliamentary seat by patrons and borough-mongers put great pressure on the corporation as it endeavoured to maintain the discipline of the town's representatives. From being at one time an oppressive burden on the local notable, the seat at Westminster became a bargaining counter and a position of status eagerly sought for personal and political ends.[102] Such a development proved a serious challenge to the assembly's independence of action, encouraging the electoral manipulation of the freeman body, while also threatening to diminish the effectiveness of its voice in the capital. The struggle which the assembly mounted against the intervention of the Pastons and the Townshends showed that it was not prepared to compromise over its local control by becoming simply a figure in an electioneer's calculations. Even though its councillors were clearly affected by the great divisions of the day, the assembly demonstrated that the service of the locality remained a major consideration shaping its political outlook. The town's increasing susceptibility to regional

[100] Henning, *House of Commons, 1660–1690*, i. 198, 241, 288, 327, 489; S. Handley, 'Local Legislative Initiatives for Economic and Social Development in Lancashire, 1689–1731', in *Parliamentary History*, 9 (1990), 231–49.

[101] History of Parliament, 1690–1715 section, unpublished constituency articles.

[102] The assembly did recognize the onerousness of the MP's tasks. In September 1645, MP Edward Owner was permitted to decline the office of bailiff in consideration of the demands of his parliamentary service—Y/C19/7, f. 74.

and central interference after 1660 only heightened the cautiousness of the assembly's approach towards outsiders who could undermine the structure of its local supremacy.[103]

However, Yarmouth was not incurably inhospitable to outsiders. Henry Manship, the civic historian, certainly betrayed an open approach to visitors. He delighted in citing the approving observations of his contemporaries William Camden and John Speed on the architecture of the town, but took especial pleasure in mentioning their gratitude for the courtesy shown to them. This led him to recommend that all should follow their example: 'come hither, therefore, gentle reader . . . for the eye will make a deeper impression in thy mind than the best orator with his pen is able to persuade thee to believe'.[104] Such warmth could not, however, be extended to the outsider who wished to make more of his visit than a study of the curiosities of the herring fishery, and Manship faithfully reflected the limits of the assembly's tolerance. For Manship, writing principally for a corporate audience, the town's character had been chiefly defined by the battles it had fought against the Lords of Caister and of Lothingland, the town of Lowestoft, and above all the Barons of the Cinque Ports. He portrayed Yarmouth as a true city state, assailed on each side by ambitious opponents yet defiant within its massive stone defences. As he observed on the challenge of the Cinque Ports to Yarmouth's maritime jurisdiction, 'they were the mightiest, so had longest continuance', a rivalry marked by 'the often jars, contentions and bloodsheds, both by land and sea, that for many hundred years continued between them'. The main flashpoint in this long-running feud had been the question of precedence between the Yarmouth bailiffs and the representatives of the Cinque Ports during the forty days of the annual Yarmouth fish fair, especially the latter's right to preside over the town's borough court for the duration of that season. Over the simple matter of cushion-space, violent confrontations could ensue where death-threats

---

[103] For the town's bitter reaction to the interference of military commanders during the 1640s, see C. Holmes, *The Eastern Association in the English Civil War* (Cambridge, 1974), 188–9. For the conservative reactions of other towns, see A. M. Johnson, 'Politics in Chester during the Civil Wars and Interregnum, 1640–62', in P. Clark and P. Slack (eds.), *Crisis and Order in English Towns, 1550–1700* (London, 1972), 204–37; Howell, 'Neutralism, Conservatism, and Political Alignment in the English Revolution: The Case of the Towns, 1642–49', in J. Morrill (ed.), *Reactions to the English Civil War* (Oxford, 1982), 67–87.

[104] Manship, *History of Great Yarmouth*, 5–6, 62–5. Manship used Camden's *Britannia* (1586) and Speed's *Theatre* (1611) to illustrate Yarmouth's attraction to visitors, backing up their impressions with the approving remarks of Lord Burghley and the Earl of Leicester on their tour of 1578.

were not unknown.[105] Coming at the concluding section of Manship's work, such recollections of past contention were meant to serve as a lasting reminder of the efforts which had been expended in establishing the town's local control. Individually, the councillors could be extremely cordial to visitors, but acting collectively in the town's name, they had a responsibility to proceed more circumspectly.

From this multiple perspective of councillor, freeman, and outsider, the full range of the corporation's influence and responsibilities comes to light. Oligarchic in form it might be, but through its day-to-day administration of the town it came into contact with a wide section of local society as well as a host of rival authorities. It might be fiercely defensive over its privileges in the manner of the archetypal corporation, but this stubbornness only reflected the importance of those rights to the overall structure of its local control. Its omnipotence in local affairs meant that any encroachment could be interpreted as an assault on its supremacy, and its past success against such interference did little to reduce the corporation's sensitivity over its rights. Most of these attacks came from outside of the town, leading the assembly to conduct its affairs on a wide public stage. However, as organized as its external defences were, the corporation recognized that the most effective way to preserve the local *status quo* was to appease the Yarmouth populace itself, particularly the freeman body on which it so heavily depended. Even the lowest members of society benefited from the corporation's fundamental commitment to the locality as it manifested its concern for local order with a series of charitable projects.[106] As local leaders, the councillors had an obvious interest in ensuring the town's general prosperity, but in the unruly and cramped conditions of the port of Yarmouth, there was an especial motivation to underline its supremacy by acts of charity, or to assert its control through the local courts.[107] Even after centuries of predominance, the

---

[105] For the clearest evidence of the bitterness between the two maritime powers, see the reports of the deputies of the Cinque Ports who ventured into Yarmouth each autumn. The last to do so came in 1662—Hastings Gallery: Section A, Yarmouth Herring Fair, A/H Books [a], esp. nos. 15–18. Manship vividly describes the clash of 1302, when in a battle with the fleets of the Cinque Ports Yarmouth lost 37 ships, 171 sailors, and £45,000 worth of goods. However, the Cinque Ports were to suffer a 'grievous requital' soon afterwards— Manship, *History of Great Yarmouth*, 167–89.

[106] Most notably, the erection of a workhouse at a cost of £850 by August 1667—Y/ C19/8, f. 87.

[107] Yarmouth may have ranked seventh amongst provincial towns by its return of 4,705 hearths in the assessment of 1662, but poverty was evidently a serious problem for local

corporation still had to work very hard to maintain its authority within the town for new challenges would continually rise to test its powers of governance.

Yarmouth's experiences were certainly not atypical when compared to those of other corporations, though it might have suffered from problems peculiar to its size and location. The assembly's concern over the discipline and loyalty of its councillors at the time of the 1703 charter mirrored that of the Bristol assembly eight years later. Its growing worries over the devaluation and abuse of freeman privileges after 1689 had been shared by an anxious Lincoln corporation only three years before. Yarmouth's historic rivalry with Lowestoft over the former's monopoly of the autumn herring fishery produced tensions very much akin to those present in Southampton's battle with Portsmouth over the issue of local admiralty jurisdiction.[108] All these examples reveal how corporations viewed their rights and their personnel as key elements of their continued rule, for if either was threatened then the general functioning of local government was seen to be imperilled. The struggles fought to maintain corporate privileges have received most attention from analysts in the past, but they have to be recognized as integral parts of each corporation's campaign to encourage the diligent service of its councillors. The next chapter will undertake a prosopographical analysis of the Yarmouth corporation to highlight the importance of the role played by each councillor in the assembly's task of government. An insight into the corporate merchant oligarchy will also further refine our understanding of the communal pressures working on them in office—an often conflicting set of loyalties which had a direct bearing on the corporation's general outlook. It is appropriate that this section should end with the perspective of a single councillor, who, though a contemporary of the condemnatory Hobbes, only asked for the provincial assemblies to be judged on their own terms:

governors. Although a complete assessment for only two of its eight wards survives from the hearth tax returns of 1664, 20 per cent of the households in that area were deemed too poor for liability to pay. However, even this bleak picture compares favourably with the returns for Leicester (27.5% in 1670), Newcastle-under-Lyme (37% in 1666) and Ipswich (37.9% in 1674). See W. G. Hoskins, *Local History in England* (London, 1959), 177; R. Seaman and M. Frankel, 'The Norfolk Hearth Tax Assessment of 1664', in *Norfolk Genealogy*, 15 (1983); A. McInnes, *The English Town, 1660–1760* (London, 1980), 23–7; M. Reed, 'Economic Structure and Change in Seventeenth-Century Ipswich', in Clark (ed.), *Country Towns in Pre-Industrial England* (Leicester, 1981), 118–19, 131–3.

[108] See R. C. Latham (ed.), 'Bristol Charters, 1509–1899', in *Bristol Record Society*, 12 (1947), 57–60; Hill, *Tudor and Stuart Lincoln* (Cambridge, 1956), 204–5; S. and B. Webb, *The Manor and the Borough*, 371–2.

If the benefit of the corporations were truly weighed and balanced, it would produce better opinions of them, for where hath true religion without faction been better supported of, where [like] civil government observed, or what orderly man could live in such populous places in safety without the help thereof? All which I leave to the judgement of all who without prejudice will rationally consider the same.[109]

[109] Styles, *Corporation of Warwick*, 11.

2
Oligarchy and Community:
The Corporate Personnel

THE reputation of the early modern councillor, just as much as that of the institution he served, has been ill-served by the age of municipal reform. Cooptatively elected, in the 1830s the corporators were denounced as unaccountable to the public they were meant to serve, nepotistic in their recruitment and unscrupulous in their use of patronage to achieve personal ends. A conflict of interest, portrayed as a clash between hereditary oligarchy and democratic rule, was identified as the inevitable outcome of a system of local government which excluded the direct participation of the wider public.[1] However, these lingering impressions have not prevented some historians from analysing the personnel of the corporations as a means to achieve a more thorough understanding of urban society, and excellent work has been produced on the early modern rulers of London, Norwich, Gloucester, and Hull. Significantly, while substantiating many of the criticisms levelled at the corporators, recent prosopographic studies have highlighted the particular pressures working on them as part of the urban 'community' over which they presided. Seeking to understand the position of an urban élite within its own locality rather than to condemn it, they have questioned accepted notions surrounding the supposed homogeneity of the corporations. The applicability of such concepts as 'merchant oligarchy' has certainly been thrown into doubt by their more open approach to urban government, and continuing calls for research into the upper strata of town life reflects the success of their methodologies.[2] Analysis of the intricate networks of kin and business

[1] See B. Keith-Lucas, *The Unreformed Local Government System* (London, 1988), 15–18; P. Clark, 'Civic Leaders of Gloucester, 1500–1800', in Clark (ed.), *The Transformation of English Provincial Towns* (London, 1984), 311; R. W. Greaves, *The Corporation of Leicester, 1689–1836* (Leicester, 1970, 2nd edn.), 2–6.

[2] For the most notable encouragements towards research into urban oligarchy, see W. G. Hoskins's foreword to P. Clark and P. Slack (eds.), *Crisis and Order in English Towns, 1500–1700* (London, 1972), p. vii; and L. Glassey, 'Local Government', in C. Jones (ed.), *Britain in the First Age of Party, 1680–1750* (London, 1987), 151–72. The best prosopographic studies remain J. T. Evans, 'The Decline of Oligarchy in Seventeenth-Century Norwich', in *Journal of British Studies*, 14 (1974), 46–76; Clark, 'The Civic Leaders of Gloucester

contacts which existed within the corporations has revealed how the civic hall could play a very important focal role in local society, concentrating a town's key interest groups within a forum charged with its general advance. An oligarchic form of government did not necessarily preclude responsible rule on the behalf of those outside its charmed confines, and the corporation's dining club image is now being replaced by a more dynamic and realistic alternative.

Increased awareness of the practical strengths and weaknesses of urban government has been the most beneficial aspect of recent work on corporate prosopography. Rather than viewing the corporation in isolation from its urban locality, analysis of the careers of individual corporators has shown how the town hall had to compete for the attention of councillors with work-places, social venues, and homes. As a result, scholars have tried to isolate the particular centripetal effect of corporate office-holding, while balancing it against the more diffuse influences of a councillor's daily life. The urban 'community' has been shown to be a very complex social structure, and research into local government and politics should reflect the diversity of that world, criss-crossed as it was by divisions of wealth, trade, or religion.[3] Particular interests, and even certain families, could dominate a town as well as its corporation, but the traditional concept of oligarchic government does not convey the breadth of influences which affected societies such as Yarmouth. The previous chapter has shown the lengths to which the Yarmouth corporation was prepared to go in order to maintain assembly discipline, and such difficulties highlight the distractions which could affect any councillor's attendance to duty. Any study which purports to represent the corporate outlook has to take into account the centrifugal effect of its own councillors' interests, especially if the corporation's responsiveness to local needs is to be assessed accurately. Even if the assembly could not recruit every single influential member of a local society, personal connections forged outside of the corporate circle would ensure that all important views would be heard by the assembly, although communicated via less formal channels

1580–1800' in Clark (ed.), *Transformation of English Provincial Towns*, 311–45; J. Kirby, 'Restoration Leeds and the Aldermen of the Corporation', in *Northern History*, 22 (1986), 123–74; G. Forster on Hull in *VCH Yorkshire: East Riding* (London, 1969), i. 120–30. For London's rulers, see G. S. De Krey, *A Fractured Society: The Politics of London in the First Age of Party* (Oxford, 1985); and P. Earle, *The Making of the English Middle Classes* (London, 1989), 240–68.

[3] For a discussion of communal models, see J. MacFarlane, *Reconstructing Historical Communities* (Cambridge, 1977); C. Phythian-Adams, *Rethinking English Local History* (Leicester, 1987).

than the civic debating-chamber itself. The delicate relationship between the corporation and the local community is most clearly observed at this personal level, and must be considered as a fundamental influence on the development of corporate government.

However, even though the conventional model of corporate oligarchy fails to take in account the wider experiences of the early modern councillor, it is still important for us to consider the membership of a corporation as a distinct group. Lawrence Stone has rightly pointed out the dangers of constructing communities which meant little to contemporaries, but the attempt to analyse the corporators as a coherent entity has been upheld by the work of Clark, Kirby, and Evans.[4] They have all noted the synonymity of wealth and civic office, but the cohesion of the corporate group should be understood as a consequence of its shared experience of civic office, rather than determined by the more basic dictate of personal fortune. As much as the demands of everyday life might deflect the corporator from his civic duties, the very onerousness of those responsibilities inevitably established the corporation as an important commitment. The burden of office would also determine that his fellow councillors would come from a similar social background, for financial security was a prerequisite for a councillor to be able to devote sufficient time to the execution of his duties. Moreover, for the sake of the corporation's prestige and influence, it was important that the councillors should include as many local notables as possible. Their wealth and vested interest in the town's future would also serve to make them more committed councillors, which was a further reason for favouring those lucrative trades and rich families that most consistently produced the right sort of candidate for civic office. On these pragmatic foundations, the corporation could build a whole edifice of civic obligation, enforced by ordinance and celebrated in custom. Aided by the constant intercourse of official business and social ceremony, the corporations thus encouraged their councillors to view themselves as the 'natural' leadership of urban society. The resultant image of the assemblies might be oligarchic in impression, but its essential priorities were based on governmental continuity and efficiency, rather than aimed at the preservation of the existing local hierarchy.

A comprehensive review of the careers of the 389 councillors who held office in the Yarmouth assembly between 1660 and 1720 will fully illustrate the tensions between the public and private lives of its corporate

---

[4] L. Stone, 'Prosopography', in *Daedalus*, 100 (1971), 46–99; see also P. Burke's chapter on 'The Studies of Élites' in his *Venice and Amsterdam* (London, 1974), 9–15.

membership.[5] The familial, social, and business connections between corporators have remained the principal interest of previous prosopographic
works, but the actual significance of such links must be carefully assessed
against a multitude of other influences. Most importantly, prior to a
study of the effect of kin and work on the Yarmouth councillors, it is
necessary to establish the pattern of corporate recruitment across the
period, for even an oligarchic government could undergo significant development while preserving an outward veneer of stability. The corporation's general electoral policy fluctuated under the strains of economic
and political change, and as a priority these decisive influences must
be mapped out. Only once these parameters have been established will
the impact of personal connection be examined in two further sections,
the first concentrating on the role of the family, the other addressing the
influence of wealth and occupation. These networks of contacts have
been previously denounced as having an insidious effect on corporate
government, but on closer inspection the significance of corporate dynasties and merchant cabals appears less clear-cut. These impressions are
supported by subsequent sections which consider other influences which
might determine a councillor's outlook, such as his religion and his ambitions beyond the confines of Yarmouth. This approach aims to place
the Yarmouth corporators in as wide a context as possible in the hope
that their own perception of civic life might become apparent. In 1703 the
corporation chose to cut its membership by a quarter rather than compromise over the calibre of its councillors. If contemporaries attached so
great an importance to the choice of its personnel, then historians should
continue to commend their in-depth study as a means of assessing the
strengths and limitations of urban self-rule.

i. RECRUITMENT AND THE CIVIC CAREER

Patterns of corporate recruitment have remained the principal study for
analysts wishing to discover the dynamic behind the workings of urban
government. In accordance with the worst impressions of oligarchy, most
studies have found evidence of the rampant influence of nepotism and
economic self-interest in the cooptative process of election practised by

---

[5] This figure covers all councillors who served in the assembly between 29 May 1660 and
29 September 1720. The Restoration day has been used as a starting-point to encompass a
group of Nonconformist councillors who played a significant role in the town's subsequent
political development.

most English corporations.[6] While this type of analysis is undoubtedly an essential focus for the study of any corporation's development, such surveys often fail to place its development in a wider, extra-assembly, context. The compelling attraction of wealth and family as foci of allegiance has meant that the importance of greater forces for change, especially of a political or economic nature, have suffered as a consequence of their more impersonal significance. Moreover, some studies have concentrated too exclusively on the higher echelons of the corporations without sufficient consideration of their more junior brethren, who were often drawn from more diverse backgrounds.[7] Such reservations indeed suggest that our impression of urban rule is too static to encompass its propensity for change and too narrow to recognize its susceptibility to outside pressures. Important influences have thus been overlooked, and our understanding of corporate priorities remains as blinkered as the outlook imputed to the councillors themselves. For instance, a rise in the number of assemblymen's sons entering the assembly has to be measured against the more general pattern of freedom-taking in order to judge whether the pool of freeborn townsmen was itself increasing.[8] As an initial priority, the interval between an individual's attainment of a freedom and his election to the corporation has to be established in order to gauge the relative difficulty encountered by different groups of freemen on their path to the assembly. In order to clarify Yarmouth's corporate selection policy, Table 2.1 analyses the average time taken for a freeman to enter the assembly, delineating methods of freeman entry and any identifiable links with a corporate member.

Table 2.1 immediately demonstrates the advantage of having a father or master who had undertaken office in the corporation, for both categories show a significant preponderance over freemen who did not enjoy such personal connections. Most interestingly, this oligarchic trend can be seen to have sharpened among freemen after 1660, a development which can be more precisely dated to the decades following the Glorious Revolution. Between 1660 and 1690 one in four of the newcomers to the

---

[6] Evans gives the best summary of the traditional image of the oligarchic corporation—*JBS* 14 (1974), 46. The Webbs found that three-quarters of English boroughs were elected by cooptation—S. and B. Webb, *English Local Government: The Manor and the Borough* (London, 1924, 2nd edn.), 381–3.

[7] The forbidding numbers involved in surveying all the councillors within a given council should not dissuade researchers from attempting a complete survey. Evans's and Kirby's work could have been greatly extended by a study of the common councillors of Norwich and Leeds—see *JBS* 14 (1974), 46–76, and *Northern History*, 22 (1986), 123–74.

[8] For a comparison in Yarmouth's case, see Appendix 3.

Table 2.1   *Average Time Taken For Freemen to Enter the Assembly**

Freeman Entry Method	Free pre-1660 (years)	No.	Free post-1660 (years)	No.
Birth (father = councillor)	9.8	30	9.6	61
Birth (no assembly link)	15.9	10	12.4	32
Apprentice (master = councillor)	11.7	45	8.3	60
Apprentice (no assembly link)	18.4	34	16.4	18
Purchase	6.5	33	6.3	40
Gift	5.0	1	5.3	6
Unknown		11		8
Average/Total	11.9	164	9.8	225

* Calculations are based on B. De Chair's transcription of the freeman rolls in *NNAS* 9 (1910). The division at 1660 is made to facilitate comparison with the freeman table in Appendix 3.

assembly was merely replicating the civic advancement of his father; over the ensuing three decades that proportion increased to one in three. This change was even further accentuated by a slight rise in the fraternal connections of newly elected councillors, which increment took the proportion of new assemblymen with corporate kin ties over 40 per cent.[9] However, these figures do not suggest that personal contact was the sole, or even the most important, criterion for civic advancement. Although the table indicates that a personal association with a current or former councillor was an extremely useful launch-pad for a civic career, it was not essential. Moreover, increasing favouritism for candidates with such contacts cannot be blamed simply on the notorious, and largely immeasurable, influence of ever-spiralling nepotism. The assembly would always seek to be sure of the suitability of its choices for office, and the approving testimony of a master or close relative would obviously aid its assessment of a candidate's acceptability. However, such a noticeable change in the

[9] Between 1660 and 1690, 56 assemblymen's sons and 4 brothers of councillors entered the corporation; over the ensuing 30 years the respective totals were 31 and 3.

overall pattern of recruitment demands a fuller and more precise explanation, especially when it could have major consequences for the overall development of the corporation.

Behind the figures in Table 2.1 lies a massive discrepancy in recruitment rates, a development which must be acknowledged as a fundamental cause of this apparent contraction of opportunity in favour of corporate families and businesses. In the period 1660–90, 221 freemen entered the assembly for the first time; thereafter only 83 new elections were made until 1720.[10] There were thus fewer chances for would-be councillors to gain entry to the assembly, thereby increasing competition for places. The established local élite was successful in capturing a greater share of those vacancies, but this development must be recognized principally as a response to the borough regulators' policy of enforcing their selections on the corporation, which had alarmed the assembly and offended local perceptions of social status. Over a third of the 389-man sample suffered political ejection from the corporation in the 1660–1720 period, a significant proportion of the corporation's leadership covering a section of the urban community far exceeding its Nonconformist groups.[11] Particularly in 1662–3 and 1688, when the scale of the purges forced the assembly to rely on less acceptable candidates for replacements, there can be no doubting the instability which national politics had brought to local society. Yarmouth was one of the nation's hardest-hit towns due to its reputation for Dissent, but there has been little effort to measure the immediate legacy of Stuart policies, especially the wealth of mistrust which was created towards central government.[12] Even though a small élite might appear the principal beneficiary of such change, from this wider perspective oligarchic trends can be seen to be the product of influences greater than personal or collective ambition alone.

In order to give further illustration of the impact of borough regulation on the Yarmouth corporation, Table 2.2 examines the relative experience of aldermen and common councillors at twenty-year intervals.

---

[10] The fall in the number of new entrants was partly a consequence of the assembly's decision of 1703 to cut its membership by a quarter. However, even when this change has been taken into account, the scale of the upheavals of 1660–89 is all too obvious.

[11] Some 39 per cent of the sample (151 men) suffered political ejection during our period, some of them on more than one occasion. From a wide range of sources, including Nonconformist registers, sessions books, episcopal visitations, and wills, only 85 (21.9%) of the sample have left a documented link with local Dissent.

[12] However, see J. Hurwich, who has reasserted the significance of Nonconformity for urban politics during the Augustan period—'A Fanatick Town: The Political Influence of Dissenters in Coventry, 1660–1720', in *Midland History*, 4 (1977), 15–47.

TABLE 2.2   *Office Tenure of Assemblymen (in Years)**

Office	1660	1680	1700	1720
Alderman (as an alderman)	7.5	11.1	12.5	16.4
Alderman (as an alderman and common councillor)	15.1	16.2	17.7	27.4
Common Councillor	6.5	9.3	8.4	10.4

* The twenty-year intervals are chosen in the interest of clarity. A simple overview of the tenure of the 389 councillors would have allowed the brief careers of political appointees to obscure the general trend of corporate experience across the period.

The opportunities for promotion within the assembly were, of course, limited by the mortality rate of the existing aldermanic bench, but as Table 2.2 shows, the political intervention of the later Stuarts played a significant role. The rise in average assembly experience between 1660 and 1680 can be ascribed to the relative calm in corporate affairs following the purges of 1660–3, which permitted the assembly more time to settle than after the purge of 1649. This improvement would have continued but for the political upheavals of 1684–8, the effect of which is most noticeable in the actual drop in the level of office tenure in the lower house by 1700.[13] However, the general stability of the ensuing twenty years, which saw much political tension but only a few minor purges, produced a much more settled corporation in which promotion to the aldermanic bench was becoming increasingly difficult. This development might have promoted a 'corporate will' among the members of the upper house, so characteristic of classic oligarchic forms, but the benefits of a more experienced personnel were felt throughout the assembly. Indeed, it was the early eighteenth-century assembly which master-minded the regeneration of the town and its economy. Reference to the experiences of those directly involved in the day-to-day running of local government can help to resolve the dichotomy whereby the foundations for the country's future political stability are perceived to have taken place in the same era as England's 'rage of party'. County JPs might continue to fall

[13] In July–August 1649, 6 aldermen and 16 common councillors were removed, although 6 of them were subsequently reinstated on central orders—Y/C19/7, ff. 147v, 148v–149v. Thirty-one (8 per cent of the total sample) of the councillors who sat in the packed assemblies of 1684–8 never served at any other time.

foul of the political tide, but the corporate charters, though shaken by the regulations of the 1680s, largely proved immune to the political machinations of the court.[14] The quality of assembly personnel certainly benefited from this more assured tenure of office, even though it continued to be affected by party division. As Peter Clark has suggested, corporate oligarchy may well have been facilitated by the general revulsion towards the borough policies of the later Stuarts, but the further advantages of a more experienced magistracy have been overlooked.[15]

Although these oligarchic trends had a significant impact on the assembly's development, the contribution of assemblymen from wider backgrounds must also be acknowledged. Table 2.1 reveals that nearly a quarter of freeborn or apprenticed councillors who were appointed after 1660 did not directly owe their promotion to their fathers or masters, and their importance should not be obscured.

The most striking pattern revealed in the table is the rapidity with which freedom purchasers could enter the assembly, a phenomenon which demonstrates the corporation's willingness to accept newcomers.[16] However, while highlighting the potential flexibility of corporate recruitment, the freedom purchasers also serve to underline the fundamental corporate priority of enlisting councillors who would provide the town with durable service. Promotion was undoubtedly less of a problem for those who could afford to pay the purchase fines, but that did not mean that these individuals could expect an equally easy time in office, for greater wealth usually meant greater responsibility for any councillor. As a result, the purchase of a freedom was often the agency of a newcomer's speedy integration into local society, whether desired or not. In order to emphasize the openness of the town's corporate élite, Andrew Michel cited the example of Peter Caulier, a London merchant who rose to the status of Yarmouth bailiff within two years of purchasing his freedom in 1667. Yet, even a man of Caulier's metropolitan background did not spurn the commitments of corporate life, for he was to provide invaluable service

---

[14] See Glassey, *Politics and the Appointment of the Justices of the Peace, 1675–1720* (Oxford, 1979). G. Forster noted the corporations' concern for their charters after 1689, but concluded that the crown posed no real threat to them—'Government in Provincial England under the Later Stuarts', in *TRHS* 33 (1983), 47.

[15] Clark (ed.), *Transformation of English Provincial Towns*, 324–5.

[16] Evans and Hoskins viewed the freedom purchase as a sign of its holder's non-native origin—*JBS* 14 (1974), 54. At Yarmouth this also seems to apply, though further questions could be asked of the interval between a settler's arrival in the locality and his freedom purchase. Frustratingly, the freemen rolls leave no record of a purchaser's arrival at Yarmouth, and only rarely give his place of origin.

right up until his death in 1708. Moreover, two of his daughters married Yarmouth assemblymen and the third was paired with the son of the local curate, thereby displaying his willingness to be assimilated into the mainstream of town life.[17] Over 40 years after Caulier's arrival, City merchants such as Thomas Steadman were still following his path from the capital and enjoying rapid corporate promotion at Yarmouth. However, his experience was becoming increasingly rare, for in the early eighteenth century the overall rate of freedom purchases dropped significantly. This development was partly the result of economic trends, but there were also important political influences at work as the corporation struggled to control freedom purchases in order to combat a predatory borough-monger.[18] Newcomers still had to show a long-term commitment to the locality in the manner of Steadman, who married the daughter of a councillor in the year of his freedom purchase. Wealth and wisdom were prerequisites for a successful civic career, but they had to be accompanied by some guarantee of personal attachment to the corporate community.

While the freedom purchasers offer a dramatic alternative to the traditional picture of corporate nepotism, the election of freemen without obvious kin or business contacts highlights the consistency with which the corporation searched for able and experienced councillors. Meteoric rises to the top of the corporate ladder did occur, such as the election as bailiff in 1694 of 24-year-old Richard Ferrier, but the assembly did not generally recruit freemen below the age of 30. The average age of the freedom purchasers, 32.4 years, was some ten years higher than those free by birth (20.8 years) or apprenticeship (23.0 years), a factor which conditions the apparent dynamism of their position within Table 2.1.[19] A new councillor would thus have to establish himself within the town, or demonstrate his local status by the purchase of an expensive freedom. The corporation could obviously expect committed and informed service over a long period from candidates boasting these credentials. Even the careers of freemen who only served a short time in the assembly, having taken a lifetime to rise sufficiently highly in Yarmouth society to gain the

[17] See A. Michel, 'Port and Town of Great Yarmouth . . . 1550–1714', Cambridge Ph.D. 1978, p. 41. Caulier certainly used his freedom privileges to secure business—H. Roseveare (ed.), *Markets and Merchants of the Late Seventeenth Century* (Oxford, 1987), 295.

[18] Although the number of freedom purchasers was falling, redemption remained the most assured route for civic promotion. In the period 1700–19 redemptions constituted only 2.7 per cent of the total admissions to freeman ranks, but 14.9 per cent of vacant corporate seats went to freedom purchasers—see Appendix 3.

[19] These averages are mainly based on data recorded in D. Turner, *Sepulchral Reminiscences* (Great Yarmouth, 1848). The thirty-two freedom purchasers whose births have been ascertained took up their freedoms between the ages of 20 and 43.

corporation's notice, revealed that a commitment to the town's interests was a principal recommendation for civic office. For instance, local cooper Robert Parish had to wait until he was 59 before the assembly selected him in 1692. However, he did accept office and served as a common councillor until his death four years later. Moreover, his dying wish was to be buried next to a fellow common councillor at St Nicholas's Church, and his bequests provided his apprentice with the financial security necessary for him to lead a successful career in business and civic life. The experience of such men serves to highlight the potential diversity of corporate opinion, as well as the sense of responsibility which municipal office imposed on its incumbent. Not all would allot the corporate burden as central a place in daily life as Parish did, but the assembly certainly worked hard to inculcate that allegiance in patriarch and newcomer alike.[20]

The soundness of the assembly's recruitment policy, proven by its general success in attracting committed and able officers, was further demonstrated by the loyalty of its common councillors. Most significantly, they appear not to have breathlessly sought civic promotion as a reward for their application to corporate duty. Even though political stability and contraction of assembly numbers made it more difficult to become an alderman after 1689, the common council continued to satisfy many local notables as a source of status. As Table 2.2 indicates, elevation to the aldermanic bench would generally take a common councillor up to ten years to achieve by the end of our period, and was, of course, never guaranteed. Yet there were many examples of outstanding service in the lower house to suggest that political ambition was not the sole determinant of corporate commitment, and that a sense of civic duty helped to eclipse any personal feelings of injustice which might have been engendered by being continually overlooked for higher office. Benjamin Goose, a descendant of a once-influential Yarmouth family, spent 41 years as a common councillor after election in 1662, showing a remarkable ability to survive every political upheaval of the period. In contrast, the founder of a major corporate dynasty, Samuel Colby, was prepared to endure 44 years below the aldermanic bench from 1707 until his death at the age of 76. Their experience clearly suggests that not all corporators desperately sought to establish familial control over many generations. Yarmouth could certainly boast such dynasties, but their influence was confined to only a small minority of councillors.[21] The aldermen themselves would

---

[20] See NAC wills 1696, fo. 385.
[21] For a discussion of dynastic influence, see A. Everitt, 'Dynasty and Community since the Seventeenth Century', in id. (ed.), *Landscape and Community* (London, 1985), 309–30.

have been the first to admit that corporate affairs could only benefit from the presence of able officials in the lower house, even if they might stand as more effective obstacles to any extension of aldermanic power.[22]

This overview of corporate recruitment patterns has portrayed the Yarmouth assembly as a far more diversified body than might have been assumed on the basis of its cooptative selection process. Oligarchy might have been advancing in tandem with increased nepotism, but explanations can be brought forward for such trends which credit the assembly with less self-interested motives. The rising political value of the freedom which prompted an increasing number of freeborn locals to take up their hereditary entitlement in the early eighteenth century must also be acknowledged as an important factor. Likewise, the economic difficulties of the town during the wars of William and Anne sharply curtailed the number of settlers willing to enter Yarmouth society via the purchase of a freedom, thereby causing a significant drain on the pool of suitable candidates for office. However, though the corporation was prepared in 1703 to take as drastic a step as cutting its membership by a quarter, it could never compromise over the essential abilities expected of any new-comer to its ranks. Commitment to duty and to the locality ranked highest on its list of priorities, and such considerations ensured that the corporation came to rely on the town's more established families and trades. Yet even with regard to these preferences, the assembly can be shown to be discerning in its choices and sensitive to the particular needs of the locality. The following sections will show that a freeman could not expect his family name or his position in the local merchant hierarchy to provide automatic promotion, a reality of civic life which only enhanced the attraction of corporate status. By probing the tug of allegiance between work, home, and municipality, the corporation can be seen to have emerged as a focus of loyalty in its own right. It might have often bowed to the influence of connection when choosing its councillors, but, in its turn, it also created new networks of contacts which worked to remind local notables of the town's general interests.

ii. THE CORPORATE FAMILY

The stranglehold of a handful of families on corporate government in 1835 earned Yarmouth a reputation for clannishness and corruption which

---

[22] Note, in particular, the lower house's successful stance against its aldermanic superiors between 1719 and 1721—see below, Ch. 7.

did not win it friends amongst the proponents of municipal reform.[23] However, an initial survey of the surnames of the 389 councillors of the post-Restoration period suggests that the influence of individual families was more ephemeral. A few families do stand out, but even they could suffer temporary or permanent eclipse. For example, the Englands— probably the most dominant force in Yarmouth society with four alder- men and a recorder among its number—experienced almost total ruin in the 1720s after one expensive election campaign too many. Three great names of Yarmouth's early seventeenth-century history—the Cuttings, the Medowes, and the Johnsons—fell from their accustomed position in corporate leadership at an even earlier date for similar reasons of political and financial mismanagement.[24] Their places were quickly taken by am- bitious families such as the Ferriers and the Fullers, but the supremacy of these successors was never assured as they struggled to control both local and external rivals. The family unit, weathered not only by such competition but also by the uncertainties of mortality and fortune, was not an unassailable platform from which to establish long-term author- ity.[25] It was not immune to division either, a fact accepted by vigilant politicians eager for opportunities for advancement. This section will outline the vicissitudes of Yarmouth's civic dynasties across the period, and will analyse several families in detail to highlight local responses to an age of change and uncertainty. Familial influence played a complex role in corporate affairs, but its intricacies can illuminate the social and politi- cal structures of town life.

Such initial caution concerning the impact of the household should not invalidate the significance of kinship as a crucial determinant of local status and power. Marriage remained the most important broker of wealth and connection in early modern England, and the networks of intra- assembly alliance remained a fundamental basis of the corporation's gen- eral cohesiveness. Unfortunately, the shortcomings of the Yarmouth parish records do not allow an exact impression of assembly intermarriage to be achieved, but, on the basis of a wide range of genealogical sources, at least

---

[23] See H. Barret, *The Great Yarmouth Corporation* (London, 1834), where the control of four great local families is bitterly denounced. For a discussion of the veracity of his account, see J. D. Murphy, 'The Town and Trade of Great Yarmouth 1740–1850', UEA Ph.D. 1979, pp. 239–49.

[24] Of the 240 different surnames amongst the 389-man sample, only fifteen appear four times or more. The surname of Ward was shared by eight councillors, five of whom became aldermen.

[25] Note Earle's recent reminder of the pressures working on familial stability—*The Making of the English Middle Classes*, 302–33.

56.3 per cent of the sample can be shown to have enjoyed a close familial relationship with at least one other councillor.[26] This pattern reflects the endogamy of other corporations, for 51 per cent of the Gloucester assembly of the late seventeenth century are known to have had a corporate kinsman, while 61.5 per cent of the aldermanic bench of Leeds in 1662 were related by blood or marriage. Such familial bonds undoubtedly made these assemblies more unified in outlook than the rulers of London and Norwich, whose more 'open' constitutions produced a wider field of recruitment. However, these impressive statistics require further analysis to establish the particular significance of kinship ties, in order that their impact on assembly life might be more closely delineated.[27]

An initial survey of assembly marriage does reveal an upwardly mobile momentum, with common councillors enjoying the benefits of a marital tie to an aldermanic household, while the latter often married into the East Anglian gentry. However, this general impression fails to convey how slow and difficult such processes could be, and it ignores the very real tie to Yarmouth shown by even the most successful of its would-be urban gentlemen. Although the most well-documented family networks naturally centre on the greatest of the aldermanic dynasties, whose concern to propagate the lustre of their name is suggested by pedigrees and sepulchral monuments, their atypicality must be recognized.[28] Alan Everitt has warned against assumptions which over-stress the ambitiousness of civic élites to attain gentle status, and such caution should also be heeded

[26] For the Yarmouth parish registers, complete for the seventeenth century though badly bomb-damaged for the 1650s, see Y/PD 28/3–5. Ninety-five first marriages were found there (24.4 per cent of the sample) and thirty-two second marriages. This network of familial alliance would have probably been extended still further with better source materials, although the completeness of any record has been irreparably undermined by the existence of a rival Nonconformist congregation, whose members were often forced to conduct baptisms, marriages, and funerals in secret—see 'Yarmouth Letters' in *East Anglian*, NS 5 (1893–4), 357–8; Raynham Hall, boxfile of lord-lieutenancy proceedings, 1662–9; A. Suckling, *The History and Antiquities of the County of Suffolk* (London, 1846), i. 376–7. The minister of the local Dutch church even baptized infants in the home—O. P. Grell, J. I. Israel, and N. Tyacke (eds.), *From Persecution to Toleration* (Oxford, 1991), 105–6.

[27] Clark (ed.), *English Provincial Towns*, 325; Kirby in *Northern History*, 22 (1986), 135. J. T. Evans concluded that 'very few' of Norwich's aldermen were interrelated in 1665— *JBS* 14 (1974), 48–52. For the lively debate on the development of oligarchy within London's aldermanic bench, see P. Borsay (ed.), *The Eighteenth-Century Town: A Reader in English Urban History, 1688–1820* (London, 1990), 13–14.

[28] See 'The 1664 Visitation of Norfolk', in *NRS* 4–5 (1934); 'East Anglian Pedigrees', in *NRS* 13 (1940); and W. Rye, *Norfolk Families* (Norwich, 1913) 2 vols. For an insight into the problems encountered by the earliest demographers when using parish registers, see D. V. Glass, *Numbering the People* (Farnborough, 1973), esp. chs. 1 and 2.

when studying the lower reaches of the corporate pyramid.[29] Contemporary opinion certainly saw marriage as a vital stepping-stone to achieving local status, but that is not to say that a match with a member of an aldermanic household was breathlessly sought by every common councillor, or that such a move was a guarantee of social and political acceptance. Despite the attractions of country houses and race meetings, the most important marriage market remained the immediate locality, for Yarmouth's leaders never lost an awareness of their need to maintain social pre-eminence above the local community which they dominated through civic office.[30]

These observations can be illustrated by reference to the highly influential England dynasty, whose marital contacts with local, East Anglian, and even overseas, households are revealed in Appendix Four.[31] The sons of Sir George England, in keeping with the prominence of their father in the immediate post-Restoration period, managed to find good matches outside the town. However, while one daughter also succeeded in this manner, two of her sisters looked no further than the assembly itself, establishing alliances with other civic families. A general survey of the connections displayed in Appendices 4 and 5 indicates that a daughter's marriage was viewed as a very promising means of alliance to other civic households, a development no doubt aided by the social milieu centring on the annual round of corporate festivities.[32]

Of particular interest is the figure of thrice-married Sarah England, whose first marriage in 1659 united the mercantile wealth of her family to the politically influential Burtons. This was to prove a tragically short-lived union when her husband died only six months later, leaving his father to lament how he 'gave a great sum in land and money, of which I lose the most part with him'. This business-like approach to marriage was very much in keeping with contemporary practice, and Sarah's attractiveness as a rich young widow saw her swift betrothal to a Norwich barrister, John Fowle. The match endorses Defoe's observation that Yarmouth ladies not only rivalled their gentry contemporaries for 'beauty, breeding or behaviour', but that they 'generally go beyond them

---

[29] Everitt (ed.), *Perspectives in English Urban History*, 11.

[30] For critiques of L. and J. Stone, *An Open Elite? England, 1540–1880* (London, 1984) in relation to urban social mobility in the provinces, see R. Wilson, 'Merchants and Land: The Ibbetsons of Leeds, 1650–1850', in *Northern History*, 24 (1988), 99–100, and Kirby in ibid., 22 (1986), 163–5.   [31] Rye, *Norfolk Families*, i. 181–2; *NRS* 13 (1940), 67–8.

[32] For the best account of socializing between councillors, see the diary of Dean Davies for 1689–90, in *Camden Society*, 68 (1857), *passim*.

in fortunes'. Sarah did bear her second husband children, but it is significant that even her daughter married into Yarmouth society. Sarah herself did the same in 1668 after the rapid demise of her second spouse, this time taking her vows with alderman Edmund Thaxter. Three marriages in nine years was a quite exceptional experience for a woman not out of her twenties, but her example illustrates the delicate interplay of human mortality with family status and ambition. Thaxter's will certainly paid tribute to the contacts he had strengthened with his 'loving' brothers-in-law, two of whom served terms as bailiffs, while a third acted as the town's recorder and MP. Even non-assemblymen remarked upon the cohesion which such marriages brought to the corporate hierarchy, underlining their importance as a mechanism of local control.[33]

Thaxter left no dynasty to carry on his name despite achieving great prominence in Yarmouth during his lifetime, but an examination of another branch of the England family tree will emphasize the stabilizing effect of a prudent marriage for any household. The Ferrier family first settled at Yarmouth in the mid-sixteenth century, having already gained renown as Norwich merchants. However, until the entry of Robert Ferrier into the assembly in 1630 they had made little impact on local society.[34] The same could be said for the Englands as well, but during the ensuing troubled decades they made far greater strides within the corporation, leaving the Ferriers trailing in their wake. Proof of their respective local advancement came at the Restoration, for while George England survived the purges of 1662–3, the younger Robert Ferrier found himself out in the political cold, despite their both having played a prominent role under the Interregnum regimes. Yet, the latter's marriage to England's daughter linked him with the most influential figure in Yarmouth trade and politics. This obviously facilitated the Ferriers' return to corporate office after the Glorious Revolution, for they proceeded to establish a local dominance in tandem with the Englands which few locals dared to challenge. This alliance proved a stubborn obstacle to ambitious outsiders too, serving to demonstrate how the clannishness of such cliques was often founded in their opposition to external, rather than internal, threats to the local *status quo*. By the 1730s the Ferriers had achieved so great an

---

[33] *CSPD* 1659–60, p. 69; D. Defoe, *A Tour Through the Whole Island of Great Britain* eds. G. Cole and D. Browning (London, 1962), i. 65–71; NRO, NAC wills 1690, f. 94. For another outsider's impression of the town's 'fine women', see Thomas Baskerville's account of 1681—*HMC Portland*, ii. 267–8.

[34] Rye, *Norfolk Families*, i. 202–10; NRO, MC44/119; 'The Journal of Major Richard Ferrier MP', in *Camden Miscellany*, 9 (1895), 3–14.

authority in the town that opponents dubbed the head of the family 'Richard II', a title which displayed an obvious hostility towards their monopoly of influence. However, it is important to trace the source of that power as it was built up uncertainly over a period of decades, for it highlights the steadying role of marriage contacts which could cushion the damage of economic difficulty and political interference.[35]

Less spectacular examples of advancement through marriage can be seen in Appendix 5, which shows the assembly network centred on the Wakeman family. This household had provided bailiffs at Yarmouth since 1568, and thus it was no surprise that two of the sons of Robert Wakeman followed their father into the assembly. In addition, no less than four of his sons-in-law served in the corporation, taking full advantage of their contacts with one of the town's leading families.[36] Unfortunately, the Wakemans' reputation as one of the main pillars of local Nonconformity ensured that Richard Huntington was the only one of those six to enjoy a sustained tenure of office after 1660, although he played a prominent role in corporate affairs. The other five experienced only a brief spell of assembly service as the intervention of national politics largely negated the local influence which they had come to expect from an attachment to the Wakeman name. However, Huntington's high-profile career proved the durable strength of this familial network even while most of its members remained out of office. Most significantly, Huntington consolidated his position by his daughter's marriage to Samuel Fuller, the son of another ousted alderman. This match proved the spring-board for the Fullers' rise to the top of the corporate ladder, a development which ultimately helped to define the structure of political control in Yarmouth in the first half of the eighteenth century. Moreover, the aggrandizement of this solitary branch also facilitated the resurrection of the Wakeman name in assembly circles after 1689. The eventual rehabilitation of the Wakemans after the demise of borough regulation indicated that successive generations of that family had not forfeited the essential assembly requirements of wealth and local status. Just as importantly, however, they had never completely severed their personal contacts with

[35] Changes in familial fortune could be rapid. In March 1676, Richard Ferrier was expelled from the assembly after two years of absenteeism had borne witness to his disaffection. He was back in office in 1688 and seven years later 300 horse paid him the tribute of riding to greet his son's return to Yarmouth on his wedding day—Y/C19/8, ff. 209, 216v, 236v; *Camden Miscellany*, 9 (1895), 7.

[36] Evans is a little overhasty in minimizing the importance of the relationship between in-laws, even if a great many of these contacts were made. Yarmouth's evidence suggests that it proved a very significant personal link—*JBS* 14 (1974), 57–8.

the assembly, which were maintained through an intricate marriage net-work. The Restoration is an especially fine vantage-point from which to view the influence of family connection because of the uncertainty caused by central interference.[37]

All the dynasties mentioned so far established their local pre-eminence on the basis of wealth derived from commerce, a pattern which serves as another reminder of the overwhelming importance of water-borne trade to the local economy. However, at the centre of Appendix 5 stands the figure of Thomas Godfrey, a local attorney whose career reveals how non-mercantile freemen could climb the corporate ladder and take advantage of marital links to established trading families. Godfrey's elevated position within Yarmouth society was founded on his appointment as town clerk in 1681, having already been presented his freedom by an assembly grateful for his 'good service' on its behalf.[38] He was fortunate to come to the post at a time when its duties were rapidly expanding, thereby heightening the esteem in which his fellow councillors held him. Function, rather than family, was thus his initial recommendation for promotion, and his work during the 1680s placed him at the very centre of deliberations concerning the town's economic and political future. However, he undoubtedly consolidated his local influence by the subsequent marriages of his daughters into the Wakeman and Fuller families. As elsewhere, the cachet of marriage into professional families was evidently increasing in the minds of Yarmouth's merchants.[39] Further acknowledgement of Godfrey's reputation came after his death, for in 1710 the corporation chose his apprentice Francis Turner as town clerk. Turner himself had married Godfrey's daughter several years before, and his career stands as a measure of the opportunities open to an ambitious freeman. However, the likely value of his contribution to civic life was an essential consideration for his rapid promotion, and his dynastic contacts should not be credited as the sole cause of his advancement.

Thomas Godfrey's career was not unique, for several other attorneys

---

[37] The career of Giles Wakeman suffices to mark the political and social importance of his family. Expelled from the assembly at the Restoration, this Independent became the port's largest native coastal trader. His standing made him an obvious choice as a trustee of the meeting-house in 1677 and he was to become only one of four purged councillors to return to corporate office in 1688.

[38] In 1670 Godfrey's freedom was cited as a reward for 'writing upon a commission at Yarmouth and at Norwich several days'. Moreover, he promised to donate a piece of plate to the corporate treasury—see *NNAS* 9 (1910), 104.

[39] For the rise of the professions, see G. Holmes, *Augustan England* (London, 1982); W. R. Prest (ed.), *The Professions in Early Modern England* (London, 1987).

enjoyed the social benefits of their profession and gained civic promotion. The synonymity of business interests and familial ties certainly endowed Yarmouth's lawyers with the kind of 'group consciousness' which has been identified among the attorneys of early modern Ipswich.[40] However, as valued as they were by the assembly for their expertise in legal disputes, their position within the local hierarchy was also consolidated by their influence over the private affairs of their civic colleagues. Through their responsibility for administering a councillor's estate in preparation for his demise, the attorneys established for themselves a very trusted and privileged position within the corporate community. In recognition of this, historians are showing increasing interest in probate records as a means to reconstruct the early modern household. Peter Earle has recently shown how wills can identify social networks by providing the names of executors and the destination of bequests.[41] Such qualitative work is replacing previous efforts to determine precise levels of wealth from often ambiguous data, but even when trying to trace indicators of communal association, testamentary evidence can still be undermined by the existence of previous settlements. In spite of these reservations, it is evident that many important insights will be gained by a survey of the 235 assemblymen's wills which survive. Richard Wilson has emphasized the critical decision-making process attending the partition of an affluent townsman's estate, and thus we may assume that these wills provide a realistic guide to personal connections. Table 2.3 thus examines appointments to the key posts of executor and supervisor.[42]

The heavy reliance on members of the nuclear family as executors is hardly surprising given the testator's wish to provide for his immediate household as his main priority. However, the choice of in-laws and friends as executors represents the influence of the assemblyman's social world, for the testator would not entrust strangers with the care of his estate after his death. The selection of supervisors to aid the administration of the testator's estate was a similarly significant decision, and a survey of such appointments reveals the unmistakable influence of assembly connection. Two-thirds of the eighty-one supervisors had some experience

---

[40] M. Reed, 'Economic Structure and Change in Seventeenth-Century Ipswich', in Clark (ed.), *Country Towns in Pre-Industrial England* (Leicester, 1981), 111. Interestingly, the Yarmouth custom officials, whose work seems to have precluded their active participation in corporate affairs, were less cohesive as a social group even though they evidently enjoyed much local status.

[41] Earle, *The Rise of the English Middle Class*, 315–18; see also P. Riden (ed.), *Probate Records and the Local Community* (Gloucester, 1985).

[42] R. Wilson in *Northern History*, 24 (1988), 75–100.

TABLE 2.3   *Executors and Supervisors Chosen by Assemblymen**

Relation	Executor			Supervisor		
	Sole	Joint	(Total)	Sole	Joint	(Total)
Wife	70	44	—	—	—	
Son	15	33	(51)	—	2	
Daughter	3	33	(44)	—	—	
Friend	4	20	(24)	18	1	
Brother	10	13	(14)	4	5	(8)
Son-in-law	2	9		3	4	(6)
Brother-in-law	2	6	(9)	3	5	
Kinsman/Cousin	—	7	(8)	2	2	
Nephew	2	3	(5)	1	—	
Sister	—	4		—	—	
Other	8	12	(14)	3	2	
Not Specified	7	19		6	7	(14)
Total	123			40		

* The table follows the format of Peter Earle's study of 181 'middle-class' wills from London—*Making of The Middle Classes*, 315–18. The 235 Yarmouth wills can be found in the probate records of the Norwich Archdeaconry court (175 wills), the Norwich Consistory court (19), and the Prerogative Court of Canterbury (41)—NRO: NAC and NCC wills; PRO, Prob 11. The figures in brackets in the table give the total number of relatives chosen in each category when joint appointments were made (for the obvious reason that more than one son, e.g., could be appointed as co-executor/co-supervisor).

of corporate service, including three-quarters of the friends appointed and half of those whose relationship is not specified.[43] Such an overwhelming corporate presence highlights the sense of fraternity and mutual trust which evidently existed between assembly members. An analysis of those gathered at the signing of the will—another indicator of a close personal relationship with the testator—confirms this impression, with over half of the wills showing at least one witness who had served in the assembly. Predominant among them were corporate attorneys who played a key role in bridging the divide between a councillor's private and public life. Most notably, John Woodroffe, a prominent civic figure and

[43] The executors and supervisors whose relationship to the testator is not specified could also certainly be classed amongst his 'friends', but in the absence of conclusive proof of this, they have been represented separately. Just over 30 per cent (71) of our sample of wills-makers appointed supervisors, particularly to assist widows acting as sole executrix. Earle's London sample showed 'nearly three-quarters' of executrices assisted by the appointment of supervisors, while Yarmouth's evidence reveals a rate of 57.9 per cent.

the town's greatest creditor, actually witnessed the wills of twenty of the eighty-four assemblymen to die between 1660 and 1685, the year of his own demise. Of course, the witnesses cover a far greater sphere of experience than corporate service alone, but the evidence of the wills suggests that membership of the assembly led to a much wider involvement in the lives of one's fellow councillors.[44]

The assembly can thus be shown to have had a decisive influence on the local marriage market, hardening the ties which already existed between local leaders. Appendices 4 and 5 display the two most important familial networks in Yarmouth during our period, and they show that while some councillors did aspire to a gentry match, no councillor could ignore an opportunity to strengthen social links with other civic households. Of course, these dynasties also boasted more modest local figures, some of whom declined, or even refused, to take up corporate office.[45] While marriage remained a key agency of fortune, it was bound to be influenced by far wider considerations than civic promotion alone. However, as long as a good match could provide the financial and personal catalyst to launch a civic career, then marriage would continue to have a very important bearing on the make-up of the assembly's personnel. A match was unlikely to catapult a complete nobody into the local hierarchy, but it could confirm his status within the town and thereby bring him to the notice of the assembly. The ambitious individual therefore had to establish himself within local society first of all if he was to stand a chance of successfully wooing a bride from a notable corporate household, and this preliminary stage in his career path recommends the study of wider economic forces affecting assembly recruitment.[46] In Yarmouth's case, social status had to be gained via one's performance at the dockside or in the market-place, which remained the town's overriding centres of trade and wealth. By assessing the extent of the dominance of the town's 'merchant oligarchy', and its relationship with the assembly's development after 1660, a fuller understanding of the force of familial connection will be achieved.

---

[44] One hundred and twenty-seven of the wills were witnessed by at least one current assemblyman—54.1 per cent of the wills discovered. A further 6 per cent of them record the signature of a former councillor. In fifty-eight of the wills, the only councillor present was a lawyer by trade. Of the total of 761 witnesses (3.2 per will), 21.7 per cent were councillors and 14.7 per cent women.

[45] Note, in particular, Richard Brightin, an absentee who was actually disenfranchised in 1692; and Thomas Ellys, who refused to join the packed assembly of 1688.

[46] For a well-drawn account of the interaction of aspiration and achievement in urban society, see Evans, *Seventeenth-Century Norwich* (Oxford, 1979), 23–5.

iii. THE CORPORATION, TRADE, AND WEALTH

The role of the merchant in the government of English provincial towns has been one of the primary concerns of urban prosopographers. However, while the merchant 'interest' is perceived to have acquired a significant collective force from the time of the nation's commercial revolution in the late seventeenth century, its impact at a local scale has been viewed in less coherent terms.[47] The fiercely competitive spirit with which traders fought for overseas and domestic markets does not square well with the harmonious image of the local merchant oligarchy, and analysts have sought to question the homogeneity of these commercial élites. For example, a terrific struggle for civic influence amongst the traders of Newcastle at the end of the sixteenth century actually led to the establishment of a complex corporate constitution designed to protect the Merchant Adventurers against their freemen rivals. Bristol experienced a similar battle for control of overseas trade between the Society of Merchant Adventurers and local shop-keepers and manufacturers. Inland, Coventry could not suppress internal conflict either, for during the 1620s and 1630s local textile producers clashed with the retailers and finishers of cloth, who wished to import materials from Gloucester.[48] Yarmouth was fortunate to have a less complex economy which tended to promote unity within its mercantile community, but after 1660 commercial developments would force the corporation to lessen its natural reliance on maritime traders. Merchant opinion remained an unmistakable force while the local economy depended so fundamentally on its dockside, but the emergence of rival sources of wealth and influence must be acknowledged, particularly as the corporation itself felt their impact.[49]

The mutual familiarity established between assemblymen through their mercantile activities must be recognized as having an overwhelming influence on the make-up of the corporation's personnel. When working in such a concentrated trading area as the Yarmouth quays, it is unthinkable that leading merchants could have failed to gain a thorough knowledge of

[47] C. Wilson, *England's Apprenticeship* (London, 1984, 2nd edn.), 160–84; R. Davis, *The Commercial Revolution* (Historical Association Pamphlet 64, London, 1967).

[48] R. Howell, *Newcastle-upon-Tyne and the Puritan Revolution* (Oxford, 1975), 52–62; R. C. Richardson (ed.), *Town and Countryside in the English Revolution* (Manchester, 1992), 74, 105–7. For an account of the decline of the Society of Merchant Venturers at Bristol in the eighteenth century, see P. McGrath, *The Merchant Venturers of Bristol* (Bristol, 1975), 31–6, 94–5.

[49] Richard Cust concluded that economic issues were a force for unity at Yarmouth during its political upheavals of the 1620s and 1630s—'Anti-Puritanism and Urban Politics: Charles I and Great Yarmouth', in *HJ* 35 (1992), 7–8.

TABLE 2.4   *Occupational Structure of the Assembly and the Town**

Occupational Group	Assembly 1660–1720 Number	%	Town 1683–5 %
Distributive Trades	285	73.3	16.6
Food and Drink	25	6.4	13.3
Maritime Industries	21	5.4	9.6
Professions	17	4.4	4.6
Clothing	13	3.3	5.1
Transport	11	2.8	27.1
Metalwork	5	1.3	3.2
Leather Trades	4	1.0	7.8
Building Trades	2	0.5	7.8
Agriculture	—	—	1.3
Miscellaneous	—	—	3.7
Unknown	6	1.5	—
Total	389		

* The table has been classified along the lines of J. F. Pound's survey of Tudor Norwich—see 'The Social and Trade Structure of Norwich 1525–75' in *Past and Present*, 34 (1966), 49–69. The occupations of Yarmouth's councillors have been derived principally from their wills and administrations, though inventories, parish registers, and sessions records have also been used. A. Michel's table is based on parish burial records, a source whose limitations he acknowledged readily—'Port and Town of Great Yarmouth . . . 1550–1714', Camb Univ. Ph.D. 1978, pp. 27–8.

their fellow local traders.[50] Moreover, even the intense competitiveness of commerce could never obscure the underlying consensus of interest which all traders shared in securing the future of the port, and prominence within that mercantile arena would inevitably promote any individual to the forefront of local society. The occupational background of the corporate membership clearly suggests that the predominance of merchants within the assembly must have acted as one of its most unifying features. Table 2.4 compares the corporation's occupational structure with an analysis of the general distribution of trades at Yarmouth.

The dominance of the distributive trades in local government, particularly in proportion to their numerical strength in Yarmouth, faithfully

[50] An indication of the visual familiarity between local traders may be derived from the workings of the town's heyning custom. Any freeman could be challenged by another as he made his way from the quayside to the town's auction chamber in order to ascertain the price of the fish which he had just bought. As a consequence, the larger traders, especially those holding civic office, must have been very well known—see PRO, E134, 1 Geo. I, Easter No. 16; 2 Geo. I, Mich. No. 26.

reflects the fundamental importance of their commerce to the town's economy. Those styling themselves 'merchants' actually account for some 60 per cent of the overall total, with an even higher proportion of their number occupying the highest posts of bailiff or mayor, a pattern which seventeenth-century analysts have discovered for the corporations of York and King's Lynn.[51] However, bald statistics fail to take into account long-term changes in the assembly's occupational distribution, and the difficulty of defining the title of 'merchant' has to be addressed. In 1660 two-thirds of the Yarmouth assembly classed themselves as merchants; by 1720 their number had fallen some way below half the membership. Accompanying this decline was a growing diversity of occupations within the corporation, most notably the entry of professional and luxury trades such as surgeons, haberdashers, and even a carver. Moreover, the election of shipbuilders in the 1690s indicated that the corporation also followed shifting trends in the port's maritime economy, as had the Norwich assembly earlier in the period.[52] Despite this fall in merchant numbers, however, there is no doubt that their influence was still powerful, a reality of Yarmouth life indicated by the desire to be ranked as a 'merchant' in fellow assemblymen's eyes. Economic historians have grappled with the problem of defining what a 'merchant' actually signified in its early modern context and have concluded that it served as much as a mark of social status as it did as a description of economic function.[53] A 'merchant' could be expected to engage in overseas or coastal trade as his main economic activity, but Yarmouth's mercantile community shows many examples of self-styled merchants who did not conform to that model.

---

[51] Over three-quarters of the aldermen styled themselves as 'merchants', while the proportion of merchants occupying the offices of bailiff or mayor in our period was predictably similar. This is very much in line with Metters's findings for King's Lynn in an earlier period. Mercantile dominance of the aldermanic bench at York 1603–84 was less pronounced, but—at 61 per cent—still impressive. See G. Metters, 'Rulers and Merchants of King's Lynn', UEA Ph.D. 1982, pp. 58–9; *JBS* 14 (1974), 67.

[52] The 1660 assembly contained 48 merchants, of whom 19 were aldermen, and 29 common councillors. Sixty years later, there were just 24 in the remodelled corporation, with 12 in each house. For the increase in Yarmouth ship-building from the 1670s onwards, see R. Davis, *The Rise of the English Shipping Industry* (Newton Abbot, 1972), 56–7, 92–3; Michel, 'Port and Town of Great Yarmouth . . . 1550–1714', Camb. Univ. Ph.D. 1978, table 6.2. J. T. Evans found that an increasing number of worsted weavers became Norwich aldermen in the course of the seventeenth century, at the expense of local merchants and grocers—*JBS* 14 (1974), 73.

[53] See R. Grassby, 'The Personal Wealth of the Business Community in Seventeenth-Century England', in *Economic History Review*, 2nd ser. 23 (1970), 220–34. At King's Lynn, Metters links the decline in the use of the title 'merchant' in the 1620s–1630s to the demise of the guild, and concludes that it 'signified little . . . other than actual membership of the urban upper classes'—'The Rulers and Merchants of King's Lynn', pp. 76, 377.

Some still skippered their own craft to sea, thereby deserving the lesser title of 'mariner' or 'shipmaster'. The largest of the town's overseas traders engaged in a wide diversity of other economic activities, investing particularly heavily in the local brewing and inn-holding trades. Local grocers, bakers, and brewers added to this confusion by participating in the local herring trade, and some of their wills reveal substantial owner-ship of shipping shares. This ambiguity does not invalidate the attempt to chart a locality's occupational distribution, but it does indicate the im-portance of economic dependence as a communal bond. Yarmouth could not survive without its maritime and inland water communications, and the significance of trade for the town's prosperity would always keep its main participants at the helm of the community.[54]

These economic circumstances, therefore, limited the potential impact of the broadening scope of corporate recruitment. Moreover, further com-pensation for the shortfall in merchant assemblymen was provided by the rise in the wealth and economic control of a small élite of greater traders. This group consisted of both assemblymen and non-Yarmouth residents, who derived the maximum benefit from the coal and corn boom which the port experienced in the early eighteenth century.[55] Michel has identified the timing of this change as the turn of the century, and contemporaneous developments at Newcastle and Hull suggest that this was a more general phenomenon during an era of massive growth in British overseas and coastal trade.[56] It is tempting to see the emergence of this mercantile élite as a contributory factor towards the corporation's oligarchic growth, but the assembly actually showed great concern at the possible aggrandizement of overambitious councillors. It was even pre-pared to fight a twenty-year legal battle with rebel alderman John An-drews rather than give way to his demand for the abolition of 'heyning', the duty which it levied on the herring catch. This confrontation high-lighted very definite worries within the corporation over the monopolistic activities of some of its members, and while its local supremacy depended

---

[54] Ambiguities in occupational status can be revealed from a simple comparison between a testator's own record and that of the parish clerk in the parish register—see Y/PD28/4. Yarmouth wills and inventories also reveal that at least twenty-four non-merchant council-lors owned shipping shares, and many more appear in the port books—PRO, E190.

[55] See Murphy, 'Town and Trade of Great Yarmouth', pp. 34–49; and A. H. John, 'English Agricultural Improvement and Grain Exports, 1660–1765', in D. C. Coleman and A. H. John (eds.), *Trade, Government, and Economy in Pre-Industrial England* (London, 1976), 45–67.

[56] See Michel, 'Port and Town of Great Yarmouth . . . 1550–1714', pp. 229–31; J. Ellis, 'A Dynamic Society: Social Relations in Newcastle-upon-Tyne', in Clark (ed.), *Transforma-tion of English Provincial Towns*, 204; *VCH: East Riding* (London, 1969), i. 142–3.

TABLE 2.5   *Corporate Influence on Local Mercantile Activity**

| Year/Trade | % Share of Cargoes | | | | |
	Assemblymen (Current)	Assemblymen (Former)	Élite Traders (15 Largest)	Women	Other
Overseas 1661/2	32.5	6.8	20.4	1.3	39.0
Coastal	5.8	5.1	50.1	—	39.1
Overseas 1677/8	22.9	11.0	27.1	3.9	35.1
Coastal	5.5	8.6	52.8	0.9	32.1
Overseas 1698/9	13.9	15.4	25.5	1.7	43.5
Coastal	6.4	8.0	50.0	—	38.7
Overseas 1714/15	17.0	2.8	23.1	1.3	55.9
Coastal	4.0	2.2	61.9	0.2	31.7

* The sample was largely determined by the completeness of the surviving record. In line with the most exhaustive treatment of port book evidence—G. Metters, 'The Merchants and Rulers of King's Lynn', UEA Ph.D. 1982—each cargo listed against a merchant's name was taken as the basic unit for comparison. Her analysis of the problems posed by these sources (pp. 80–90), particularly the influence of smuggling and the recording of merchant cartels, must be heeded alongside R. Hinton's earlier warnings—'The Port Books of Boston, 1601–40', in *Lincoln Record Society*, 50 (1956). The port books used here are PRO, E190 493/8, 493/5, 496/21, 496/22, 513/6, 513/8, 514/6, 529/13, 529/17, 530/7. The column tabulating the share of trade enjoyed by the port's fifteen largest non-assembly traders differentiates between those most prominent in overseas trade and the biggest coastal traders.

so heavily on the recruitment of mercantile influence, it could not afford to allow any particular group of merchants to dominate its policy decisions.[57] In order to illustrate these pressures on the assembly, Table 2.5 analyses the degree of control enjoyed by its members over Yarmouth's trade. Using the evidence the Yarmouth port books, it takes a four-year sample in order to chart the relative strength of corporate influence in comparison to other significant groups using the port.

Although the nature of this sample does not allow firm conclusions to be reached concerning the general development of the town's trade,

[57] For the Andrews affair, see below, Ch. 7.

Table 2.5 does suggest that the assemblymen's share of port activity fell in the 1660–1720 period. As the figures for former assemblymen indicate, this was partly the result of political interference before 1689, but the trend across the whole period was one of decline in direct corporate control.[58] This was principally due to the involvement of outsiders in town trade, especially during the port's boom periods in the 1670s and after the War of the Spanish Succession. Prominent among these non-resident traders were Norwich freemen who used Yarmouth to export textiles or to import a whole host of commodities demanded by the lucrative market of the nation's second largest city. In addition, Norwich's great demand for coal from the North-East is represented by the minimal level of assembly participation in coastal traffic and by the increasing investment of élite non-Yarmouth traders in that market.[59] Of course, as the principal beneficiary of the resultant rise in the yield of local tolls, the assembly had cause to welcome this boost to the local economy. It even sought to win the favour of the largest coal magnates, such as London merchant Robert Atwood, in order to gain leverage in debates on national economic policy.[60] However, the table also reveals that the corporation maintained its policy of recruiting Yarmouth's leading merchants, even though political unsuitability would often frustrate this aim. For the four years studied here, the corporation contained at least two members who ranked among the port's ten greatest overseas traders, who thereby preserved a direct link between the town's governmental and economic élite. The historic symbiosis of mercantile and corporate development centring on the Yarmouth assembly had become a less certain relationship between 1660 and 1720, but there were still merchants of sufficient stature to represent the civic institution's indissoluble tie to its port. There could be no mistaking the determination with which the corporation approached issues affecting local trade, a sense of purpose founded in its informed and active personnel.[61]

[58] The number of assemblymen directly engaged in the port's trade certainly fell—1661/2: 56; 1677/8: 46; 1698/9: 28; 1714/15: 26.

[59] Michel notes that Yarmouth ships seized an increasing proportion of the Newcastle-London collier trade, and that their share of that market rose from 8.1 per cent in 1682 to 36.5 per cent in 1714—'Port and Town of Great Yarmouth . . . 1550–1714', table 6.5.

[60] For the controversy which surrounded Yarmouth's coal duties in the 1690s and 1700s, see below, Chs. 6 and 7. Atwood was appointed as agent for the corporation's public investments in June 1715—Y/C19/9, ff. 587, 614.

[61] The assembly's sensitivity over its economic reputation was exemplified by its dismissal of alderman Thomas Horth in August 1643, after he was deemed to have brought disgrace on the town in Parliament over his administration of the salt patent—*CJ*, ii. 31–2, 44, 70; Y/C19/7, f. 18.

The status of the merchant-assemblyman remained unassailed in our period, for his economic utility was recognized throughout the town, from the corporation to the casual labour force which depended on a busy harbour for its livelihood. The riches to be gained in trade were the personal reward for entrepreneurial flair, but success in business would probably be accompanied by election to a burdensome local office as the corporation sought to buttress its local authority by selecting capable and influential individuals. The correlation between wealth and the holding of local office is a well-established theme for the early modern period, and Yarmouth appears to have conformed to this pattern.[62] However, the manifold problems of measuring personal riches makes it difficult to establish even broad patterns of their distribution. In Yarmouth's case, the paucity of surviving taxation records does not help, although a glut of sources from the start of our period permits some preliminary observations to be made concerning the financial status of assemblymen at the Restoration. It should be emphasized how fleeting an impression of personal wealth Table 2.6 must represent, for the corporation books are sprinkled with pensions granted to impecunious assemblymen who had fallen on hard times after a sudden change in fortune. Moreover, assemblymen's wills frequently allude to the transient nature of their worldly estates when establishing elaborate safeguards to protect their heirs from the worst effects of weather, war, or piracy.[63] Wills can also provide indicators of individual wealth, though their partiality as sources are well understood. Inventories exhibit similar problems as a record of personal estate, though both sources betray much information concerning the equally interesting questions of how fortunes were accumulated and spent.[64] In the light of such methodological reservations, Table 2.6 examines the distribution of wealth among assemblymen and their fellow townsfolk at the beginning of our period.

Both sources used here suffer from their incomplete coverage of Yarmouth society, though for the present purpose of studying the town's governors they do provide a vivid picture of the concentration of wealth

---

[62] See A. MacInnes, *The English Town, 1660–1760* (London, 1980), 31–4; Evans, *Seventeenth-Century Norwich*, 29–32.

[63] By March 1683 the assembly had set up a fund to redeem local mariners captured at sea, having previously made occasional provision for the payment of ransoms in wartime— Y/C19/8, f. 268v, Y/C19/9, f. 44.

[64] Only twenty-four of the inventories of our corporate sample survive, an insufficient figure for statistical comparison. For general discussion on the utility of probate records, see Riden (ed.), *Probate Records and the Local Community*; and J. Johnson, 'Worcestershire Probate Inventories 1699–1716', in *Midland History*, 4 (1978), 191–211.

TABLE 2.6   *Wealth Distribution at Yarmouth, 1660–61**

(1) Poll Tax, November 1660

	Assemblymen			
Assessment	Current (ex 72)	Out in 1660 (ex 26)	New 1660–3 (ex 48)	Whole Town
£20	1	—	—	1
£6	1	—	—	1
£3–6	6	—	—	9
40–59s.	8	2	1	13
30–39s.	7	2	1	11
20–29s.	10	4	7	33
10–19s.	15	6	5	60
2–9s.	7	2	13	214
TOTALS	55	16	27	342

(2) Free Voluntary Gift, November 1661

	Assemblymen			
Gift	Current (ex 72)	Out in 1660 (ex 26)	New 1661–3 (ex 48)	Whole Town
£30	1	—	—	1
£10	2	—	—	2
£6	3	1	—	4
£5	10	1	—	14
£3	8	—	2	13
40–50s.	14	5	3	28
20–30s.	16	8	14	53
Below 20s.	5	4	8	117
TOTALS	59	19	27	234

* PRO, E179, 154/633, 634, 637, 638, 647 and 253/8 (Poll Tax); E179, 253/40 (Free Gift). The Poll Tax (12 Charles II c. 9) was levied at the rate of 1s. per £ for those valued over £2 p.a., with a minimum of 12d. for each single man and 6d. for any other person over the age of 16. The Gift (13 Charles II c. 4) had no set rating system, though a £200 limit was enforced for non-peers—*Statutes of the Realm*, v. 207–25, 307.

in assembly ranks.[65] Although only two-thirds of the poll tax return survives intact and the free voluntary gift was merely discretionary in nature, both records display the 'Eiffel tower' pyramid of financial power which has been shown to have existed in other towns at that time.[66] At the apex of both returns stands the figure of Sir Thomas Medowe, a merchant and major brewer reputed to have had an annual income of £2,000 in 1660 when elected to the abortive Order of the Royal Oak. Immediately below him came George England, who was thought to be worth some £30,000, and was responsible for handling more overseas cargoes in the port than any other merchant in 1661/2.[67] Fifty-two of their assembly colleagues in the period 1660–3 occupied the seventy places below them in order of poll tax assessment. This correlation between wealth and assembly service is even more marked by the contributions to the voluntary free gift, with assemblymen providing sixty-one of the largest seventy-two donations. The pressure to contribute to the gift in the uncertain political climate of 1661 almost certainly influenced such beneficence, but a comparison of individual returns to both levies unmistakably pinpoints the assembly's desire to enlist the service of the town's wealthiest inhabitants. The poll tax's highest non-assemblyman contributor, Leonard Osborne, may not have joined corporate ranks, but his fortune paved the way for his son's entry into the assembly only five years later. The next three non-corporate figures all displayed a sense of obligation towards the town in their respective positions as the current town clerk, a former lieutenant in the town militia, and the widow of an alderman who had been a notable local benefactor. Although no other Yarmouth tax record survives for the latter part of our period to test the development of this pattern of assembly recruitment, there can be little doubt as to its continuation. Only wealth could bring the individual the security, the time, and the social status necessary for the efficient execution of a councillor's duties. Furthermore, throughout the period the assembly was forced to call upon its members for loans to weather cash-flow crises. Therefore, in the interest of corporate government, candidates had to be found who could match up to these exacting requirements.

[65] The Poll Tax returns survive for only seven of the eight wards, and some of them are either damaged or incomplete. The returns for the Gift are complete, but the size of the sums collected (2s. being the smallest contribution) suggests that no real attempt was made to encourage the lowest orders to pay.

[66] See MacInnes, *The English Town, 1660–1720*, 23–8; Evans, *Seventeenth-Century Norwich*, 14–16.

[67] Medowe's knighthood made him liable for a £20 rating. See C. J. Palmer, *Perlustration of Great Yarmouth* (Great Yarmouth, 1872–5), i. 153–9; *CSPD* 1667, p. 186; 1668–9, p. 75.

The relatively narrow horizons of the assembly's recruiting-ground is brought into perspective by the wide base of the poll tax 'pyramid'. In particular, the sub-10s. contribution of assemblymen elected to replace purged members in 1662–3 highlights the assembly's problems in finding a sufficient number of suitable councillors when the scope of its choice was curtailed by forces beyond its control. Other corporations expressed similar fears for the debasement of their personnel through the machinations of outsiders, for the Hereford assembly was so alarmed by the interference of the Foley family after 1670 that it complained its councillors were now 'not of the best and most approved citizens, but persons of mean parts and estates'.[68] Such upheavals apart, the Yarmouth assembly could generally rely on the local mercantile élite as a source of suitable candidates, confident in the knowledge that their business experience would render them familiar with the corporation's concerns, as well as actively committed to the town's general future. Mercantile ties were clearly a more significant influence in the determination of corporate policy than bonds of kinship, although it is often difficult to distinguish their impact given the familial character of trading ventures in the period.[69] However, the diminishing size of Yarmouth's merchant hierarchy may well have forced the corporation to recruit new members from a wider range of occupations. The concentration of the port's trade in an ever-decreasing number of local hands reduced the pool of obvious candidates, and this shortfall was compensated to some extent by the enlistment of local lawyers and surgeons, whose status was increasingly acknowledged. Such a development did not have a decisive impact on corporate policy because the mercantile orientation of the local economy perpetuated the influence of the traders. Yet it was clear that a merchant career was not the only route to advancement in local government, particularly when the local economy was slowly diversifying and providing alternative avenues towards fortune and social acceptability.

Having outlined the way in which political and economic developments could affect the corporation's relationship with a councillor's work and home, this survey now turns to take into account centrifugal forces

---

[68] Henning, *House of Commons, 1660–90*, i. 264. The twelve replacements elected at Yarmouth in 1663 were not only poorer than their assembly colleagues, but, judging by the date of their freedoms, also well below the average age of new common councillors in the period.

[69] Grassby noted that 'the kinship group was the basis of all business dealings' in our period—'Social Mobility and Business Enterprise in Seventeenth-Century England', in D. Pennington and K. Thomas (eds.), *Puritans and Revolutionaries* (Oxford, 1978), esp. pp. 364–9.

which threatened to distract the councillor on a more permanent basis. In the context of early modern urban England, the pull of religion and the lure of the countryside must be considered of particular interest and importance. Religious division dealt a shattering blow to the corporation's hopes for a broad urban consensus from the mid-seventeenth century onwards, while aspirations towards gentility provided a challenge to the assembly's authority as the ultimate source of local status. The corporation could not allow these external forces to undermine its position within local society, and its attempts to control their impact will again highlight the ability of its leadership to accommodate significant change.

iv. THE CORPORATION AND THE RELIGIOUS DIVIDE

For all the similarity in the background of its personnel, and in spite of attempts to impress upon its members the importance of local office, the assembly was not immune to forces of internal division. Of prime importance for the corporation's seventeenth-century development was the influence of Nonconformity in assembly circles, for this innovation threatened to create a rival, and independent, network of allegiance within the town.[70] Some of the best work produced on 'communal' perspectives in early modern England has concentrated on the problems faced by localities which tried to come to terms with the shattering blow of religious pluralism after the Reformation.[71] The significance of the Church as a vital pillar of unity and order was all too evident, with the congregation organized to mirror the social hierarchy on which local government was founded. The complete breakdown of the Anglican supremacy in the aftermath of the Civil Wars was seen to justify the worst nightmares of the nation's rulers as Ranters, Fifth Monarchists, and Quakers emerged to fuel their religious anxieties. The Quakers' challenge to formal magistracy and the Ranters' moral latitude seemed to promise social chaos, forcing even one of the more sympathetic of the nation's rulers—the

[70] Yarmouth's Nonconformist records have been well mined by local and national historians. See, in particular: J. Browne, *The History of Congregationalism in Norfolk and Suffolk* (London, 1877); C. E. Whiting, *Studies in English Puritanism, 1660–88* (London, 1931), 380–91; M. Watts, *The Dissenters* (Oxford, 1978), *passim*.

[71] See M. Spufford, *Contrasting Communities* (Cambridge, 1974); J. Barry, 'The Parish in Civic Life: Bristol and its Churches, 1640–1750', and J. Triffit, 'Believing and Belonging: Church Behaviour in Plymouth and Dartmouth, 1710–1730', in S. Wright (ed.), *Parish, Church, and People* (London, 1988), 152–78, 179–202; D. Hey, *The Fiery Blades of Hallamshire: Sheffield and its Neighbours, 1660–1740* (Leicester, 1991), 249–99.

Protector himself—to impose limits on that freedom once more.[72] Within their own confined sphere of responsibility, Yarmouth's leaders faced equally difficult decisions when reacting to the innovations of the times. A brief study of their response will aid an understanding of the corporate outlook after 1660, especially by providing an insight into the competing allegiances which acted on the minds of all councillors.

Yarmouth had long been viewed by national authorities as a potential source of religious Dissent, principally because of its close maritime relationship with the Low Countries. In the early 1630s clerical and temporal authorities had moved swiftly to suppress a separatist meeting and to remove the town's suspect puritan minister, John Brinsley.[73] However, despite these measures, Yarmouth quickly established itself as the centre of Independency in East Anglia after the Congregationalist divine William Bridge had been appointed by the assembly in 1642 as a town preacher. The corporation initially welcomed his arrival as a major boost to the learning and preaching ability of the town's ministry. This approval rapidly changed to disquiet when Bridge began to organize a Congregationalist meeting independent of its control. In January 1644 the assembly twice voiced its anger at the 'taking of members into any societies as particular churches'. By April 1645 a more conciliatory tone accompanied its wish to re-establish the 'peace and uniformity' of the borough, but such hopes were soon frustrated when 'great divisions and distractions' were blamed on the activities of Bridge's congregation. Only after 1649 with the impetus of revolutionary events at a national level was Bridge's group accorded official local recognition and permitted to conduct services at St Nicholas's Church.[74] However, tension between Brinsley's Presbyterian congregation and Bridge's Independents did not subside even though the two ministers were close friends, thereby creating a fissure in local society which the corporation had always feared as a consequence of Bridge's actions. Even the emergence of a Quaker meeting

---

[72] For a stimulating discussion of the impact of religious pluralism, see B. Worden, 'Toleration and the Cromwellian Protectorate', in *Studies in Church History*, 21 (1984), 199–234.

[73] R. Cust, in *HJ* 35 (1992), 1–26. The separatists, sixty-one of whom were reported to the authorities, came from humble backgrounds—C. Jewson, 'Norfolk Baptists up to 1700', in *Baptist Quarterly*, 18 (1959–60), 308–15, 363–9; *CSPD* 1628–9, p. 429; 1629–31, p. 308.

[74] See B. Cozens-Hardy (ed.), 'Old Meeting, Norwich, and Great Yarmouth Independent Church', in *NRS* 22 (1951); Y/C19/6, ff. 502, 571v; Y/C19/7, ff. 32v, 66, 158v. £900 was spent on partitioning St Nicholas's in order to house both congregations, a costly enterprise which was also undertaken by religious authorities at Hull—see F. Worship, 'On the Crowther Monument, Yarmouth Church', in *NNAS* 2 (1849), 35–42; *VCH: East Riding*, i. 107–9.

in early 1655 failed to bring reconciliation between the two groups. Both censured the Quakers for disrupting local services, but while Brinsley emphatically called for 'the setting-up of the worship and service of God's work in a public, uniform and authoritative way', Bridge accompanied his criticism with a more tolerant plea for 'the law of peace and moderation' in Church affairs.[75] The bitter divisions which had resulted from the national indulgence of conscience would not be a pleasant reminder for the magistrates returning to office after 1660. Yet at the same time Bridge's outstanding abilities as a preaching minister had inculcated respect in the minds of many town leaders for a difference of religious opinion. It was such complex, interacting attitudes which played on the minds of the local magistrates after the Restoration as they considered the implementation of statute law against their neighbours.[76]

The problem of Nonconformity, particularly for those detailed to suppress it, is only really appreciated by an awareness of its impact within the local community. Studies of Bristol, Plymouth, and Coventry have shown the practical difficulties facing magistrates who tried to isolate support for Dissent, and Yarmouth's example suggests the impossibility of that task.[77] The purges of 1662–3 might have ended the corporate involvement of the most suspect of local leaders, but the pervasive influence of Nonconformity in local society would be much more difficult to remove. The presence of some of Yarmouth's leading merchants within Bridge's congregation was a fundamental boon to the survival of Dissent. As the poll tax returns in Table 2.6 show, the resignation of these Independents *en masse* in 1660 robbed the assembly of the services of some of the town's most substantial citizens. Their influence in local society, even when excluded from the corporation, was sufficient to cause grave concern among Anglican supporters, for they represented a significant section of the port's mercantile leadership. Other town authorities experienced the same difficulties as Yarmouth's hard-pressed Anglican magistrates. At Abingdon, one

[75] Evidence of Quaker activity dates from 1651, but George Fox's visit to the town in 1655 was the spark for subsequent controversy—NRO, SF43; *The Journal of George Fox*, ed. J. L. Nicholls (Cambridge, 1952), 215. For local religious reaction to the Quakers, see J. Brinsley's *Two Treatises* (1655) and W. Bridge's introduction to Brinsley's *Gospel Marrow* (1659).

[76] For Bridge's life, see R. L. Greaves and R. Zaller (eds.), *Biographical Dictionary of British Radicals* (Brighton, 1972), i. 99–100. G. Rupp notes his prominence at the Westminster Assembly in 1644–6, and attributes the Independents' disproportionate influence in national circles at that time to Bridge, Nye, and Simpson—*Religion in England, 1688–1791* (Oxford, 1986), 121–2.

[77] S. Wright (ed.), *Parish, Church, and People*, 152–202; J. Hurwich in *Midland History*, 4 (1977), 15–47.

electoral observer complained that 'many of the Dissenters are so rich that many beholden to them, though not of their judgement, dare give no votes', while at Berwick it was reported that 'trade is in the hands of a few rigid Dissenters', ensuring that 'no one with any zeal for his Majesty or the Church can ever hope for . . . any considerable place, traffic, or friendship in the town'.[78]

Moreover, broadening this base of Dissenter support at Yarmouth was the presence of 'hearers', or partial conformists, at Independent meetings who swelled their numbers without becoming full communicant members of Bridge's church.[79] They represented the greatest obstacle to a complete Anglican triumph after 1662 by providing the Dissenters with the numerical support necessary to influence local opinion into accepting their continued existence. Another important group within the Nonconformist circle were the wives of several prominent assemblymen, who evaded the requirements of Charles II's penal tests against the corporators. Perhaps the most significant political role of a Yarmouth woman in the Restoration period was that played by Rose Huntington, wife of one of the leading Nonconformist sympathizers within the assembly. Informers regarded her as a formidable opponent of local Anglicanism, and even her tomb testified to the fact that 'religion was her aim'.[80] The political narratives will explore the delicate interplay of such complex social connections as they affected the Nonconformity issue, but the undermining influence of religious division must be recognized. It complicated every personal, social, and economic relationship within the community, often forcing its leaders into extreme and self-destructive policies.

V. REGION AND REALM

Introspection and clannishness have been too often assumed to be inevitable consequences of oligarchic patterns of assembly intermarriage and recruitment.[81] However, while such painstaking statistical analysis can

---

[78] Henning, *House of Commons, 1660–90*, i. 130, 345.

[79] A. O. Whiteman uses Yarmouth to show the difficulty of accurately assessing the numerical strength of Dissent when partial conformists and hearers have to be taken into account—*The Compton Census* (Oxford, 1986), p. xxxix.

[80] *CSPD* 1666–7, p. 568; 1670, pp. 512–13: Swinden, *History of Great Yarmouth*, 862–3. See Appendices 4 and 5 for the key female members of the Yarmouth Independent Church.

[81] Note J. T. Evans's assumption that oligarchic corporations, unlike the freeman democracy which he found at Norwich, would experience 'greater agreement on religious and political matters, and consequently less conflict within the corporation'. Yarmouth's factious history cautions against such generalization—*Seventeenth-Century Norwich*, 319–25.

illuminate the internal workings of the corporations, attention must also be paid to the position of corporate members within the wider horizons of region and realm. Yarmouth's geographic situation, marooned as it was on the eastern tip of East Anglia, would seem to provide a particularly good example of the general isolation thought to be experienced by corporations outside the ranks of the nation's provincial capitals. However, as a major port with important international trading links, Yarmouth retained a very cosmopolitan outlook, particularly on account of its historic relationship with the Dutch.[82] It also served a large economic hinterland throughout East Anglia which demanded a constant intercourse of people and provisions. Most significantly, its uneasy partnership with the city of Norwich some fifteen miles upstream ensured that the town was directly linked to regional and national developments. London itself was a well-frequented port-of-call for Yarmouth's coastal traders and a mere overnight journey away by land.[83] The corporation would certainly not welcome all the influences which these contacts might bring, but their impact on its members as they went about their businesses ineluctably brought them to consider the town's role outside its fine medieval walls. The more prominent role of the gentry in seventeenth- and eighteenth-century towns has been cited as a major theme of English urban development, but more work should be undertaken to understand the attitudes of the townsmen as they came into increasing contact with the rural environment and the national arena.[84]

Mention has already been made of the civic élite's propensity to marry into gentry families without jeopardizing their place within urban society. This caution over the apparent irresistibility of the country estate to the wealthy merchant has been recently echoed by Richard Wilson's study of the Ibbetsons of Leeds, where gentility is shown to have been a long-term and difficult achievement.[85] The number of important Yarmouth families who completely forfeited their interests in the port was extremely small, as was the number of assemblymen who requested dismissal in order to

[82] See K. H. D. Haley, *The British and the Dutch* (London, 1988), 53–5, 73–4; C. B. Jewson (ed.), 'Registers of Passengers from Great Yarmouth to Holland and New England, 1637–9' in *NRS* 25 (1954); Palmer, *Perlustration of Great Yarmouth*, ii. 219–20.

[83] See P. Corfield, 'A Provincial Capital in the Late Seventeenth Century', in P. Clark and P. Slack (eds.), *Crisis and Order in English Towns, 1500–1700* (London, 1972), 263–310. Dean Davies provides a very good description of the journey along the Yarmouth-London road in *Camden Society*, 68 (1857), 29–30, 40.

[84] For the most comprehensive overview of the gentry's social impact on the towns, see P. Borsay, *The English Urban Renaissance* (Oxford, 1989). For a debate on his conclusions, see *Past and Present*, 126 (1990), 189–202.

[85] Wilson in *Northern History*, 24 (1988), 99–100.

reside elsewhere.[86] Even those families who suffered the chastening experience of removal from office for political reasons generally remained in the town, and those that did leave settled in close proximity to their old power-base. The Coopers are a good case in point with their move to Burgh Castle and Ormesby St Margaret, villages within a four-mile radius of Yarmouth. Four of their family had suffered expulsion for their Nonconformist sympathies after 1660, yet their new residences permitted them to carry on their mercantile activities in Yarmouth at a convenient distance. At Ormesby they were joined by the Castels, two of whom had been dismissed in 1689 as non-jurors. Their willingness to maintain links with Yarmouth was signalled by their sons' entry into freeman ranks, and their prominence in the town was attested by the corporation's grant of a pension to the family over twenty years after their departure from the assembly.[87]

This desire to stay in contact with the urban world can be further illustrated by the general pattern of assemblymen's land-owning. Wills again suffer as evidence here due to their incomplete coverage of real estate, though the scale of the survey permits a realistic impression. Forty-three per cent of the 235 corporate wills reveal ownership of property outside of town, and this finding suggests that Yarmouth assemblymen were less attracted to a country estate than their counterparts in the county capital of Norwich. Moreover, it is important to note that one-third of the estates of the Yarmouth councillors were concentrated within a ten-mile radius of the town. Over two-thirds were situated within twenty-five miles of Yarmouth, and only a handful of councillors mentioned properties outside of Norfolk and Suffolk in their wills. Such individual holdings gave the assembly an extended influence over its immediate rural hinterland, and this position could only have improved after 1700 when trade began to recover and land prices continued in their decline. Yet these properties were clearly meant as country retreats rather than as bases for dynastic aggrandizement. The motivation behind most landed investment was undoubtedly the priority of providing portions for

[86] Only five councillors requested their dismissal in order to settle elsewhere, and the destination of four of them is not recorded. However, the assembly made a significant point in regard to the other petitioner by ruling that his move to the Norfolk village of Ingham in 1689 would leave him more than ten miles away from Yarmouth, and thus incapable of performing his civic duties—Y/C19/9, f. 168.

[87] For the Coopers, see PRO, Prob 11, reel 378, f. 113; NRO, NCC wills 1725, f. 351. For the Castels, see F. Blomefield and C. Parkin, *An Essay towards a Topographical History of the County of Norfolk* (London, 1805–10), xi. 253–4; Prob 11, reel 372, f. 2; NCC wills 1718, f. 44.

offspring, for real estate promised a far greater security than the hazards of ship ownership and trade.[88]

These impressions can be confirmed by a review of the countryside's attitude towards the town, for rural society displayed a similar reluctance towards full integration. Dwarfed as Yarmouth was in social attraction by the regional capital of Norwich, at the start of our period it had little to tempt the gentry by way of diversion. Gentle visitors seem to have gone there with the premeditated desire to examine the curiosities of the herring fishery, judging by their rather surprised reaction at anything else of interest in the town.[89] Yarmouth society enjoyed a somewhat bluff and hearty image in contrast to the more genteel social arenas at Norwich and King's Lynn, and this image was even endorsed by the Customs House in 1667 when describing the port as 'a place of great trade and consumption of drink'. Seven years later Sir John Hobart confessed that he was 'endangering my temperance' by making a personal electioneering visit to Yarmouth, and this view was echoed by Sir Robert Paston when describing the 'prodigious' entertainment he received there in 1675.[90] Such impressions did not promise to overcome the town's comparative social isolation in the immediate future. In 1684 a large section of the Norfolk gentry withdrew from the town's celebrations for its new charter when it was announced that the county's lord-lieutenant would be unable to attend. As the town's minister explained, 'the news of my lord's return stopped the gentry from coming in, for though they honour my lord, they owe very little respect for the town'.[91] A handful of gentlemen did trade out of Yarmouth on a small-scale basis, and some sent their children to be educated there, but the overwhelming gentry interest in the town remained the riches to be won through a prudent marriage into mercantile society. So evident was this attraction that a local ballad, *The Yarmouth Tragedy*, celebrated it in verse:

---

[88] Only ten of the 235 wills specifically or indirectly allude to properties outside of Norfolk or Suffolk. Peter Clark suggests that in the 1680–1700 period a quarter of the Gloucester assemblymen (including half the aldermen) held property outside the town in the 'inshire' area. However, over two-thirds of the wills of Norwich magistrates in 1620–90 record extra-mural properties—Clark (ed.), *Transformation of English Provincial Towns*, 319, 326; Evans in *JBS* 14 (1974), 58.

[89] Gentle visitors included Thomas Baskerville in 1681 and Sir John Perceval in 1702— *HMC Portland*, ii. 267–8; A. Wenger, *The English Travels of Sir John Perceval and William Bird II* (Missouri, 1989), 70–1. The smell of curing herrings was probably enough to dissuade Celia Fiennes from travelling there on her 'great journey' of 1698—C. Morris (ed.), *The Journeys of Celia Fiennes* (London, 1947), 146.

[90] *CTB* 1660–7, p. 730; Raynham Hall, boxfile of 1st Visct. Townshend, misc. corresp. 1650s–1687; NRO, Bradfer Lawrence Ic, Visct. Yarmouth to wife, 1 Oct. 1675.

[91] Add. mss. 36988, f. 231.

Nancy was a merchant's only daughter,
Heir to fifteen hundred a year,
A young man courted her for his jewel,
Son of a gentleman who lived near.

Even this avaricious reason for entering Yarmouth society did not see a flood of gentry suitors come into town. When such matches did occur, it more readily symbolized the entrance of Yarmouth men and women into the wider social horizons of the 'country'.[92]

Despite these reservations concerning the parochial character of Yarmouth's assemblymen, certain families did reveal ambitions far beyond the confines of East Norfolk. Their example does not invalidate observations which have been made concerning the essential sphere of assembly interest, but they do underline the dynamism of urban society, which could promote such upward mobility. For instance, two leading corporate families, the Gooch and Ellys households, had each produced a bishop by the mid-eighteenth century while maintaining their place in Yarmouth society. In addition to this success, another of the Gooch family became a baronet and the Ellyses could also boast a vice-chancellor of Cambridge University. Both families had been settled in Suffolk villages at the start of the seventeenth century, but had found that a move to Yarmouth could provide the financial impetus for a return to a more polite social environment.[93] Even families who had based their entire social advance on mercantile success in the port could aspire to wider recognition. Most notably, the Fullers used their local prestige to secure a consulship at Leghorn for one of their number, who then went on to win a seat in Parliament for a constituency outside East Anglia.[94]

However, the majority of Yarmouth's leaders were content to launch their sons on a career in local office, often hamstrung by financial difficulty to attempt a more ambitious calling. The professions became increasingly popular as an attractive and achievable goal for aspiring parents such as common councillor Christopher Cousens, who in 1683 made provision for his younger son Henry 'to go to grammar school and then to be apprenticed to an apothecary, attorney at law, or a surgeon, or as Henry likes best'. This latitude was by no means unusual among the last

---

[92] See Palmer, *Perlustration of Great Yarmouth*, i. 249–52. A copy of *The Yarmouth Tragedy* at the British Museum has been tentatively dated at 1720.

[93] For the Gooch family of Ilketshall, see J. Venn, *Gonville and Caius College* (Cambridge, 1897–1901), iii. 115–26; *NRS* 4 (1934), 85–6. For the Ellys household of Somerleyton and Raveningham, see Venn, *Gonville and Caius College*, iii. 110–14; *NRS* 13 (1940), 667.

[94] Sedgwick, *House of Commons, 1715–54*, ii. 55.

wishes of anxious fathers, and Cousens's emphasis on the attainment of a good education was one of their notable features. This concern was reflected in the steady rise of Yarmouth applicants to Cambridge colleges up until the 1690s. Caius was their principal destination, and this collegiate link was symbolized by the dominance of two Yarmouth-born masters there between 1702 and 1754.[95] Such a path would normally take the assemblyman's son into a clerical career, but there is no doubt that it was seen as a step into a wider social sphere. As one-time corporator John Castel resignedly observed in 1718 on his son's time at Caius, 'because I have given him a considerable education, so . . . I think he will not live anywhere hereabouts'. His son's ordination clearly gave the young man a greater geographic mobility, even though it might not lead to a parallel rise in status. Castel's remark, however, gave a good indication that even the relative isolation of eastern Norfolk was diminishing in response to a broadening of social opportunities.[96]

The widening of contacts with the outside world must act as a counterbalance to signs of growing oligarchy within Yarmouth's assembly élite. This is particularly evident from the way in which assemblymen perceived their own status within and outside of the town. The memorials to personal prestige which survive in the form of sepulchral monuments are often overly sycophantic, but they do provide subtle indices of the requirements for local recognition.[97] Election to national office was always given prominence but was accompanied by reference to the individual's service to his immediate locality. Thus George England, a long-serving Yarmouth MP though never an assemblyman, is described as 'a true friend to that [town], and to the liberty of his country'. Samuel Fuller's heirs were even more precise concerning the gradations of his local and national status: '*qui huius burgi bis ballivus, dein Praetor, et ad memorabilem illum anno 1688 conventum multaque inde Parliamenta missus hinc burgensis*'. The claims made for the virtuosity of certain individuals must be regarded as suspect, but the recording of familial achievement in one of the town's most frequented concourses provides a vital insight into the prerequisites for local prestige.[98]

---

[95] NRO, NCC wills 1682, f. 65. For Yarmouth's links with Cambridge University, see J. Venn, *Alumni Canterbrigienses* (Cambridge, 1922) 4 vols., where short biographies of twenty-seven sons of assemblymen can be found; also see J. Whitehead, *History of Great Yarmouth Grammar School, 1551–1951* (Great Yarmouth, 1951), 43–8.
[96] NRO, NCC wills 1718, f. 44.
[97] Swinden, *History of Great Yarmouth*, 857–85; D. Turner, *Sepulchral Reminiscences* (Great Yarmouth, 1848), *passim*; Blomefield and Parkin, *Essay towards a Topographical History of Norfolk*, xi. 375–99.   [98] Turner, *Sepulchral Reminiscences*, 30, 35–6.

More generally, the use of the titles 'esquire' and 'gentleman' to signify social station indicated a self-conscious need for personal status. Will evidence suggests that Yarmouth assemblymen were more eager to adopt such distinctions from the turn of the century onwards. Of the sample, only five styled themselves esquire before 1710, compared to seventeen who did after that date. Likewise, only six gentlemen can be found before 1710, while thereafter eleven of the sample described themselves in such a manner.[99] The need for these honorific titles had not been apparent at the time of the Herald's visitation of Norfolk in 1664, when the heads of fourteen leading Yarmouth families disclaimed the right to bear arms, all but one of whom were recent assemblymen. Nine families based in the town did take up arms, but many councillors continued to bear a gentle title without any strict heraldic foundation.[100] The assembly encouraged this ambiguity by addressing its justices as esquires and referring to the other councillors as 'Mr'. This practice could only magnify the elevated position of the judicial bench, but it probably had a wider effect, prompting other local notables to adopt high-sounding titles to demonstrate their prominence in local trade or to hint at the distinction of their ancestry, whether armigerous or not.[101] The professionals within the assembly were very quick to adopt them, thereby providing another indication of the important social adjustments which accompanied their growing stature in the assembly. However, merchants also adopted these titles, a development which suggested that even their perception of status could undergo subtle transformations. Their response to social changes affecting the whole country confirmed how susceptible they could be to external influences, however firmly set they might be in their Yarmouth ways.[102]

In this prosopographic study I have ranged widely, hoping thereby to depict influences which could affect an apparently closeted and unchanging

[99] By the terms of the 1660 Poll Tax, esquires or those 'so reputed' were assessed at £10. Although no Yarmouth individual put himself forward for that liability, Sir Thomas Medowe had to pay £20 as a knight of the realm—see *Statutes of the Realm*, v. 375–99.

[100] Of the nine families claiming arms, only two had no direct familial tie to corporate members. Some disclaimers did subsequently take up arms, most notably George England on his elevation to a knighthood in 1671—*NRS* 4 and 5 (1934); Turner, *Sepulchral Reminiscences*, 153.

[101] Evans notes a similar trend within the Norwich corporation after 1660—*Seventeenth-Century Norwich*, 51.

[102] Merchants account for thirteen of the self-styled esquires and eight of the gentlemen. However, three brewers and six other occupations also claimed the superior title. Six attorneys addressed themselves as gentlemen, while three other occupations were represented in that manner. For an account of the changing status of merchants, see R. Grassby, in D. Pennington and K. Thomas (eds.), *Puritans and Revolutionaries*, 360–4.

institution of local government. The ties binding the assemblymen to their urban society were extremely complex, and our understanding of the corporation's recruitment policies should reflect this. However, the collective momentum of the assemblymen's shared experience at work, at leisure, and in the home, gave the corporation a well-defined identity as the leader of local society. There were indications that the assembly might have become even more oligarchic during the sixty years following the Restoration, but the potential effect of this development was tempered by its membership's willingness to adopt new ideas and influences. Nepotism might have abounded, but its impact has to be judged against the particular needs of the corporation, whose priority was to find councillors who could spare the time and effort required by its affairs. A century later, after significant changes in local society had broadened the pool of potential assemblymen, the injustice of such favouritism would become particularly apparent. However, the benefit of hindsight should not lead us to dismiss the corporation's earlier responsiveness to a different set of social circumstances.[103] The Yarmouth corporation was certainly no meritocracy between 1660 and 1720, but its overall make-up was commendably diverse within the limitations set by the hierarchical assumptions of contemporary society. When buffeted by the effects of dynastic failure, business collapse, political interference, religious division, and personal ambition, the corporation simply could not have relied exclusively on a narrow selection of families and trades, as its reform of 1703 proved. Indeed, the remarkable fact was that it succeeded for so long in attracting the 'good and discrete men' which its charter demanded, persevering in its principle of electing able and committed councillors.

By dint of their social position and the responsibilities of their office, local governors played a key role in all walks of town life, and it is clear that any study of Yarmouth's politics cannot ignore assembly activity. The need for such research is particularly apparent to the analyst of the post-Restoration period, when the methods employed by the crown to overcome corporate resistance throughout the provinces obviously bear great significance for our understanding of the country's general political development. Thus the narratives which follow will address several

---

[103] See Barret, *The Corporation of Great Yarmouth*. J. Murphy asserts that the corporation had yet to succumb to the rule of a few families in 1740, although he acknowledges that the preconditions for oligarchy were inherent in the Yarmouth constitution. He identifies a hardening of distinctions within the élite in the early nineteenth century, when the scale of commercial investment promoted the consolidation of familial fortunes through marriage— 'Town And Trade of Great Yarmouth', 22–3, 239–47.

important themes, even though they are principally concerned to study the way in which political events directly impinged on the largely self-governing rule of the Yarmouth assembly, and to measure the feasible control of central government over such an autonomously minded institution. As these first two chapters have argued, the interplay of town, county, and central government has to be studied if an accurate impression of Yarmouth's post-1660 development is to be achieved, and the narratives have been tailored to portray the nuances of these complex relationships. Moreover, the narrative format will enable us to see the corporation as a continuously resourceful and active institution, heavily reliant on its councillors to respond effectively both to sudden emergencies, as well as to more permanent problems. This approach will highlight the dynamism of urban society, and will serve a timely reminder of the importance of provincial politics during a time of great national upheaval.

3
The Challenge of the Restoration: 1660–74

AFTER years of civil unrest, the only certain prediction which could have been made concerning the restoration of the monarchy in 1660 was that it would usher in a period of painful transition. The settlement of the nation, with which the Great Protector had confessed himself to be 'much taken' amid a series of failed experiments, posed an enormous challenge for the governors of the restored realm, for former parliamentarians and royalists alike.[1] A recent authoritative account of this key period has suggested that it was a landmark in determining the character of local government, as a predominantly royalist gentry seized the opportunity provided by their leader's return to push through a succession of punitive measures against the enemies of Church and State.[2] From a long-term perspective, the extent of their victory, judged in terms of their control over town and countryside, can be shown to have been less than conclusive, but attention has been rightly turned towards the localities as a crucial arena for Restoration conflict. The undeniable attraction of the charismatic Charles II has of late consumed much of the interest of the period's leading analysts, but studies have also appeared to give greater credit to the contribution of the localities to the eventual form of the Restoration settlement.[3]

[1] S. C. Lomas (ed.), *The Letters and Speeches of Oliver Cromwell* (London, 1904), iii. 87 (speech of 21 Apr. 1657).

[2] R. Hutton, *The Restoration* (Oxford, 1985). More recently, Anne Hughes has concluded from her study of mid-seventeenth-century Coventry that the Restoration saw a decline in civic independence in the face of gentry and royal pressure—R. C. Richardson (ed.), *Town and Countryside in the English Revolution* (Manchester, 1992), 94–6.

[3] Hutton, *Charles II, King of England, Scotland, and Ireland* (Oxford, 1989); J. Miller, *Charles II* (London, 1991); J. R. Jones, *Charles II: Royal Politician* (London, 1987). For the studies of the Restoration county, see A. Coleby, *Central Government and the Localities: Hampshire, 1649–89* (Cambridge, 1987); S. K. Roberts, *Recovery and Restoration in an English County: Devon Local Administration, 1646–1670* (Exeter, 1985); P. Jenkins, *The Making of a Ruling Class: The Glamorgan Gentry, 1640–1790* (Cambridge, 1983). Monograph studies of the Restoration town are still rare, but see J. T. Evans, *Seventeenth-Century Norwich: Politics, Religion, and Government, 1620–1690* (Oxford, 1979), and J. Barry's excellent article on Restoration Bristol in T. Harris, P. Seaward, and M. Goldie (eds.), *The Politics of Religion in Restoration England* (Oxford, 1990), 163–89.

The most important advance in recent Restoration historiography is a realization that the process of settlement was not only decisively conditioned by divisions at the centre, but was also compromised by the response of the provinces.[4] The exhaustive efforts of Charles II and James II to control the personnel of local government bore witness to the centre's dependence on the localities for the execution of their policies, particularly with regard to contentious issues such as religion. However, as hard as they tried to subdue the provinces, they were unable to achieve their objectives, and their increasingly desperate methods only served to highlight the failures of the early years of the restored regime. The Anglican Church and its supporters were undoubtedly hampered in their campaign to suppress Dissent by the undermining activities of the court, but analysis of religious conflict in the localities can reveal the deep-rooted strengths of Nonconformity, as well as the practical obstacles which lay in the path of officials detailed to execute the penal statutes. More generally, the provincial case study brings attention to the wide range of issues involved in the quest for local settlement, the interaction of which could defeat the government's intentions. The local perspective also illuminates previously understudied themes, such as the importance of economic interests to provincial political development. Taken together, these new insights recommend a closer study of the interplay of local governors and their superiors in Whitehall and Westminster, in order to subject them to a rigorous scrutiny, akin to that which the provinces underwent under the restored Stuarts. Not surprisingly, historians have increasingly called for work to be completed on the localities as a means to understand this vital period of transition.[5]

Of all the targets deserving of royalist attention after 1660, the towns were one of the more obvious. The speed with which urban governors fell over themselves to send loyal addresses and surrender their fee-farms in the early months of Charles II's reign betrayed widespread guilt over their role under the Interregnum regimes, and hinted at their barely concealed fears for the immediate future.[6] Without wishing to draw too clear a dichotomy between town and countryside, the corporations were evidently perceived as bastions of radicalism in 1660, a verdict proven by the subsequent passage of the Corporation Act which menacingly

---

[4] Harris *et al.* (eds.), *Politics of Religion in Restoration England*, esp. pp. 1–28.

[5] Roberts, 'Public or Private? Revenge and Recovery at the Restoration of Charles II', in *BIHR* 59 (1986), 173; P. J. Norrey, 'Restoration Regime in Action: the Relationship between Central and Local Government in Dorset, Somerset, and Wiltshire', in *HJ* 31 (1988), 789.

[6] Recent research suggests that in general the corporations benefited under the Interregnum regimes—Richardson (ed.), *Town and Countryside in the English Revolution*, 89.

observed that 'many evil spirits are still working' in urban government.[7] However, momentous as the impact of that legislation was, historians are only beginning to understand the complex influences which worked to curb the effectiveness of the early Restoration purges. Question marks have been raised over the coherence of national policy towards the corporations, and the enduring strength of provincial independence has been widely recognized.[8] Concentration on one of the government's clearest subversive targets will demonstrate the compromises of the Restoration settlement, all too apparent to ministers and gentry as they quickly came to learn that the administration of the localities demanded subtle powers of management rather than the blatant use of force. In particular, the corporate perspective helps to focus attention on the processes whereby former rivals re-established their respective positions in local society after 1660, adjusting themselves to life under the restored crown. Yarmouth's development from the Restoration to mid-1670s can thus help us to understand how local, regional, and central governors faced up to the unfinished business of settling the mid-Stuart polity.

Yarmouth's corporation faced the future with trepidation in the spring of 1660. After several years of growing internecine conflict between Independents and Presbyterians, its voice was distinctly unharmonious even before the resurgence of royalist influence. The assembly's decision of March 1660 to elect a regicide as one of the town's Members for the Convention Parliament revealed the stubbornness of its radical core, but the short-sightedness of this action became only too clear as the freemen successfully challenged the corporation's franchise monopoly by an appeal to Westminster. Political bankruptcy was at hand, and the decision of twenty-three Independent corporators to resign in July merely anticipated an inevitable ejection from office. Earlier in the year their leader

---

[7] W. Costin and J. S. Watson (eds.), *The Law and Working of the Constitution 1660–1914* (London, 1967), i. 15–17. Also note Clarendon's allusion to the 'factious humour' of the corporations—*The History of the Rebellion and Civil Wars in England* (Oxford, 1888), ii. 470. For a discussion of Dissent as an urban phenomenon, see Harris, *Politics under the Later Stuarts: Party Conflict in a Divided Society, 1660–1715* (London, 1993), 9–12.

[8] See Miller, 'The Crown and the Borough Charters in the Reign of Charles II', in *EHR* 100 (1985), 53–84; P. Seaward, *The Cavalier Parliament and the Reconstruction of the Old Regime, 1661–67* (Cambridge, 1989), 151–7; M. Watts, *The Dissenters* (Oxford, 1978), 244–6, 286–7. In particular, much more work is needed on the impact of the Commonwealth charters on the independence of the corporations. Hutton, for one, has recently modified his views on their effect—*The Restoration*, 158–161, and *The English Republic, 1649–60* (London, 1990), 85–6. R. Howell has provided the most reliable account of Interregnum policy towards the boroughs—'Resistance to Change: The Political Élites of Provincial Towns during the English Revolution', in A. Beier *et al.* (eds.), *The First Modern Society* (Cambridge, 1989), 433–55.

William Burton had expressed a less than confident faith in the future, lamenting that 'he would not trust the state for one penny . . . for here was one state today and another tomorrow'. His suspicions were born in bitter past experience and they were unlikely to be dispelled by the promises made in the Declaration of Breda.[9] His departure in December 1660 confirmed that the assembly's political complexion had altered, but his removal resolved none of the town's urgent problems. The most immediate concern for local merchants was a privateering offensive which operated under the licence afforded by the nation's upheavals. However, much more significantly, the town's permanent legacy from the Inter-regnum period was a community firmly divided by religion. The outlook for local recovery was decidedly gloomy, and just as surely as their economic plight would force the town's leaders to seek national aid, so central government itself would inevitably focus much attention on the problem of Yarmouth's Nonconformity. The struggle for the control of the corporation would obviously be the crucial test for local and national governors in the early years of the Restoration.

The resultant conflict saw an apparent royalist victory severely curtailed by the enduring realities of local political life. Despite the removal of twenty-six Independents in the course of 1660 and the expulsion of thirty-five mostly Presbyterian members by the Corporation Act purges of August 1662 and March 1663, some of the town's leading Interregnum figures remained in office. Four aldermen in particular—John Woodroffe, George England, Richard Huntington, and Edmund Thaxter—were significant and costly oversights on the commissioners' part. All four had signed a loyal address to Richard Cromwell in December 1658, congratulating him on his succession and couching the event in the providentialist language which marked out the Protectorate's closest supporters and associates. However, despite such prominence, they proved immune to exclusion and eventually joined the other 'good and discrete men' listed as councillors in the town charter of 1664. All were to be instrumental in protecting local Dissenters throughout the reign of Charles II, and it must be asked why they remained in office.[10]

[9] *CSPD* 1659–60, pp. 403–4. Burton had already been imprisoned by the Convention as one of the twenty men specifically exempted from the proposed general pardon for activities under the Interregnum regimes—*CJ*, viii. 50, 63.

[10] Y/C19/7, ff. 352–3, 359, 392–7v; Y/C19/8, ff. 9v–11. For a copy of the 1658 petition, taken in 1676, see PRO, SP18/184, f. 85. For a comparison with other corporate purges, see J. Kirby, 'Restoration Leeds and the Aldermen of the Corporation, 1661–1700', in *Northern History*, 22 (1986), 124; P. Styles, 'The Corporation of Bewdley under the Later Stuarts', in *University of Birmingham Journal*, 1 (1947–8), 98–9.

That is the question which local informer Richard Bower posed to under-secretary of state Sir Joseph Williamson for sixteen years, although he knew only too well the essential reason for their continued tenure of corporate office. Quite simply, their local status rendered them indispensable while they were still willing to perform their corporate offices. They were active representatives of the mercantile élite which had dominated the town for centuries, and even central governors were prepared to acknowledge their importance, recognizing that the administration of the provinces was heavily dependent on local initiative and knowledge.[11] Bower might describe them as 'changelings' who had enjoyed office 'in more or less all the governments', but influential men could retain their offices, even if they adopted a politique stance of submitting to the restored crown while still sympathizing with Dissent. Their familiarity and evident support for local interests could override the political dictates of the moment, for not even the dramatic events of 1660 could erode their enduring ties to the urban community. As has been noted in the previous chapter, Anglican supporters at Abingdon and Berwick experienced similar difficulties with merchant princes who offered protection to local Dissenters, and the Corporation Act clearly failed to have a lasting effect on the governors of such towns as London, Chester, Coventry, Bristol, Gloucester, Hull, and Bedford.[12]

The strength of such localist sentiment was most keenly felt by the officials saddled with the responsibility of managing the town. In the period 1660–4 three principal figures emerged, all of whom had little experience of the locality and its problems. Sir William D'Oyly, a former royalist commander who was elected by the Yarmouth freemen as their MP in 1660 and 1661, had the unenviable task of representing the inter-

---

[11] G. C. F. Forster, 'Government in Provincial England under the Later Stuarts', in *TRHS*, 5th ser. 33 (1983), 48. John Woodroffe, although an attorney by trade, was a key figure in the local mercantile community as the corporation's largest creditor for its expenditure on haven maintenance, owed some £1,200 by 1667—Y/C36/6, piece 3.

[12] *CSPD* 1676–7, pp. 155–7; Henning, *House of Commons, 1660–90*, i. 130, 345; Watts, *The Dissenters*, 245–6; D. Lacey, *Dissent and Parliamentary Politics in England, 1661–1689* (New Brunswick, 1969), 306–7; M. Mullett, 'Deprived of our Former Place: The Internal Politics of Bedford, 1660–88' in *Bedfordshire Hist. Rec. Soc.* 59 (1980), 3–4. The Corporation Act has belatedly received the attention of historians wishing to understand the development of the provinces after the Restoration—Norrey in *HJ* 31 (1988), 809–12. As Hutton's list of seventy-eight possible urban case-studies indicated, much more work could still be completed on the impact of that act—*The Restoration*, 338–9. However, for a clear exposition of the mechanics of a purge, see R. Austin, 'The City of Gloucester and the Regulations of Corporations, 1662–3', in *Transactions of Bristol and Gloucestershire Arch. Soc.* 58 (1936), 257–74.

ests and views of a severely divided borough.[13] His immediate superior
in the task of securing the town for the crown was Horatio, Viscount
Townshend, the chief architect of Norfolk's submission to Charles in
1660, a service which led to his appointment as lord-lieutenant of the
shire in August 1661.[14] In turn, he was directly accountable to the Earl of
Clarendon, his patron and lord chancellor, whose interest in the town
was secured in January 1661 by election to the high stewardship. In a
time of extreme uncertainty, it was an astute move on the corporation's
part to establish a link with such a prominent figure, but it would also
mean that it risked closer scrutiny from central government.[15] All three
officials found their responsibilities for the town onerous, and such
difficulties would ensure that the policies of the restored crown were
sporadically enforced. The corporation's traditional suspicion towards
external authorities was only heightened by royal policy in the early
1660s, and such inbred caution would continue to condition its reaction
to the great issues of the day. Indeed, one of the few sources of Yarmouth's
internal unity in this trying period was its leaders' sensitivity to the
encroachment of county or national figures.

It was the lasting influence of local Independents and Presbyterians
which proved the most immediate obstacle for the enforcement of national policy. D'Oyly, heavily reliant on the support of local Dissenters
for his parliamentary seat, was from the very beginning compromised.
Even Lord Townshend was overwhelmed by the strength of local Nonconformity on his first visit to Yarmouth in September 1661, informing
Clarendon that 'I could not have imagined that there had been such a nest
of schismatical rogues within his Majesty's kingdom'. His concern only
grew over the next few years as the town established itself a safe haven for
Nonconformist ministers driven from East Anglian parishes, and such
notoriety earned the corporation savage treatment at the hands of the
Corporation Act commissioners in the course of 1662–3. Yet, even in the
wake of the dismissal of over half the corporation, Townshend was no
less pessimistic of his ability to control the town. He blamed D'Oyly
for the town's current predicament, accusing him of ingratiating himself
with leading Yarmouth Nonconformists to the discouragement of local

[13] Henning, *House of Commons, 1660–90*, ii. 230–3. D'Oyly's fellow Yarmouth Member
in the Convention, Sir John Potts, 1st Bt., played no decisive role in corporate politics after
1660.
[14] J. M. Rosenheim, *The Townshends of Raynham* (Middletown, 1989), 18–25.
[15] Clarendon succeeded Henry Cromwell as high steward, the latter having been elected
to that position in June 1654—Y/C19/7, ff. 245, 370–1.

Anglicans, who had come to view their MP as 'the head of the faction'. Even more seriously, D'Oyly was accused of undermining the reformed corporation's authority by passing government directives to purged assemblymen, thereby circumventing the crown's more assured supporters. D'Oyly was certainly not unsympathetic towards the Dissenters, but, as he was later to protest to Townshend, he was not an active adherent of the Nonconformist cause. His precarious position only highlighted the problems encountered by all politicians who tried to secure influence in a divided town.[16]

Although these fundamental religious difficulties remained, Townshend found some cause for encouragement from his responsibility for the military supervision of the town. On his elevation to the lord-lieutenancy, he undertook a thorough purge of officers of the Yarmouth militia, ousting seven of the nine officers, including the commanding figure of George England. Among the replacements, Townshend confirmed Sir Thomas Medowe as the leader of the 'loyal' group within the town, a position which he would retain for nearly thirty years. Medowe's attachment to the royal cause could not be questioned, for he had refrained from taking assembly office under the Interregnum regimes, and in the Restoration year had been listed as a member of the abortive Order of the Royal Oak. More importantly, he subsequently established himself as an effective leader of a group of Anglican hardliners who stubbornly opposed any compromise with Yarmouth's Dissenters. In common with informer Richard Bower, he displayed a profound hatred of 'recusants and sectaries', and his views indeed suggest that the principal feature of Yarmouth 'loyalism' was support for the Church of England. Their intransigence ensured that Nonconformists could not expect to escape the penal statutes with complete impunity, for these loyalists represented a pole of religious extremism to rival the leaders of the Independent congregation, and proved equally vigilant for opportunities to advance their cause if events turned in their favour.[17]

Medowe set about the task of securing the locality with a gusto, closely scrutinizing the passage of papers and persons through the port, and acting swiftly to rumours of fifth monarchist and other plots.[18] By the

---

[16] Raynham House archive, boxfile, 1st Visct. Townshend, misc. corresp. 1650s–1687; boxfile 74, file of misc. papers.

[17] Raynham House archive, boxfile, 1st Visct. Townshend, misc. corresp. 1650s–1687, Medowe to Ld. Townshend, 21 Nov. 1664.

[18] See R. L. Greaves, *Deliver Us From Evil* (Oxford, 1986), 81, 91, 130–1; *CTB* 1660–7, p. 74; PRO, SP29/18, f. 57; Raynham House archive, boxfile 74, general certificate of the

essential criterion of public order, the town had been most efficiently settled, but the militia were not as effective in suppressing covert Nonconformist meetings. The Independent meeting-house was closed by Medowe in November 1661, but conventicles were arranged in private houses or outside of local magisterial jurisdiction in nearby Norfolk and Suffolk parishes. The Clarendon Code did drive many Presbyterians back into the Anglican fold, or at least into partial conformity, and within a few years Bower could identify a 'moderate episcopal' group who had been 'formerly understood to be rigid Presbyterians'. However, the Independents remained intransigent, and their conventicles soon attracted the attention of the Privy Council itself, which swiftly dispatched orders to Townshend to intervene directly in town affairs. The Independents simply regrouped and waited for a more opportune time to resume their meetings, confident as they were of their influence within the locality.[19] As compliant as the corporation could be made, the contacts and social status of local Nonconformist leaders would continue to block the most indefatigable efforts of regional magnates to remove them. The personal influence of ousted Dissenting councillors could not be ignored by their replacements, since the purged members continued to represent the town's permanent interests. Two key conflicts, both resolved in the course of 1663, underline the difficulties of those officials as local circumstances conspired to undermine national policy.

The election of a new town curate, necessitated by the purge of the local ministry under the authority of the Act of Uniformity, was evidently expected to polarize religious differences within an already divided Yarmouth. However, controversy did not simply revolve around the question of Nonconformity, for the issue of corporate rights had a decisive impact on the configuration of the groups party to the affair. Ever since its clashes with the Dean and Chapter of Norwich in the late 1620s, the corporation had stood firm over its claim to nominate candidates for the curacy, and as early as August 1660 it had made preparations for defending its right against any future challenge.[20] However, the Dean

---

Norfolk and Norwich militia, 1661. Yarmouth's militia consisted of three companies, with a complement of 408 men in 1661.

[19] Y/FC31/1, 18 Nov. 1661; *CSPD* 1667–8, p. 186; PRO, PC2/56, f. 676; PC2/58, f. 130. Local Quakers probably suffered the most thorough persecution—J. Besse, *A Collection of the Sufferings of the People Called Quakers* (London, 1753), 490–3. For evidence of Quaker meetings at Yarmouth throughout Charles's reign, see Y/SF53, pp. 1–99.

[20] R. Cust, 'Anti-Puritanism and Urban Politics: Charles I and Great Yarmouth', in *HJ* 35 (1992), 1–26; Swinden, *History of Great Yarmouth*, 834–56; A. G. Matthews, *Calamy Revised* (Oxford, 1934), 5, 74–5, 489; Y/C19/7, f. 359.

and Chapter proved equally keen to advance the Anglican cause in the town, and so the inevitable skirmishes between the two corporate bodies began. The Yarmouth assembly was unable to prevent the dismissal of its incumbent ministers in 1662, but it stubbornly refused to recognize the Dean and Chapter's replacement, Edmund Duncon. By May 1663, after the Dean had been unable to secure Duncon's acceptance, Clarendon himself was drawn into the dispute, but his contribution was merely to urge the two sides to put an end to their differences in the cause of local unity. The assembly responded to his intervention by putting the matter to a vote in early June, knowing that it would be the first great test of corporate unanimity in the wake of the Corporation Act purges. In a dramatic division, twenty-five assemblymen signalled their opposition to Duncon's appointment by walking out of the Tolhouse, leaving thirty-three of their brethren inside to pass the motion. However, this majority was so dependent on recently appointed councillors that the result rang very hollow, particularly in the minds of local parishioners over whom Duncon now had to preside. For the sake of the town's longer-term settlement, both local loyalists and government officials knew that the corporation's rights would have to be respected if the disaffected councillors were to be reconciled.[21]

The apprehension of Lord Townshend in the summer of 1663 spoke volumes for the potential resonance of the dispute. He observed that the Nonconformists stood to gain a significant political advantage from the disunity which the affair had sown in the remodelled assembly, though he realized that any climb-down on Duncon's part would be interpreted as a sign of weakness in the Anglican camp. He thus urged Clarendon not to appear to be 'willing to waive the right of the Church' in the matter, and implored him to become the direct arbiter of the contest. Clarendon responded by putting forward Dr Lionel Gatford, a solidly conformist minister, who was propounded to the assembly on 23 August after Duncon had agreed to step down. In order to ensure a smooth passage for this proposal, both the Bishop of Norwich and Townshend travelled to Yarmouth to attend the assembly vote, the latter having promised Clarendon to use his 'little interest' in the town to support Gatford's appointment. On the eve of the decisive vote Bishop Reynolds, a cleric of former Presbyterian leanings, preached a sermon 'tending to unity' at St Nicholas's, and

---

[21] Y/C19/7, ff. 380, 386; Y/C19/8, ff. 16, 17v–18v. Of the thirty-three Duncon supporters, all but three had come into office since the Restoration. On the aldermanic bench, Duncon's opponents outnumbered his supporters by 10 to 8. Six of the departing aldermen had previously served under the republican regimes.

the lord-lieutenant strove to assure local Anglican leaders that Duncon's resignation was not a sign of Nonconformist influence over the Lord Chancellor. Their efforts were rewarded the next day when Gatford was accepted by the corporation, though its members only did so, as the bishop wearily noted, 'avowing their own right'. He hoped that Gatford would help to resolve tensions within 'that divided people', though his companion Townshend was more pessimistic, especially while D'Oyly remained as Yarmouth's MP. The episode had shown that local circumstances could impose great pressures on government officials, especially when their attention was distracted by other responsibilities. Moreover, in Yarmouth's case, these officials also had the misfortune of having to weather a concurrent storm raging over the corporate charter.[22]

Local concern for the town charter was a natural response to the aggressiveness of national policy towards the corporations in the early Restoration period. However, it was not until April 1663 that the Yarmouth assembly was alerted to the possibility that a dreaded *quo warranto* might be served against it. D'Oyly was the first to bring the corporation's attention to the attorney-general's brief to investigate the activities of suspect corporations, and the assembly decided to anticipate events by petitioning the crown for a new charter. Nothing was heard until December, but when news of the attorney-general's report came, the assembly was thrown into turmoil. The report recommended that the choice of three of the corporation's most senior officials—the high steward, recorder, and town clerk—should henceforth be subjected to royal approval, a proposal which could only be interpreted as a direct attack on corporate independence.[23] The corporation immediately appointed a committee to argue its case in the capital, urging the town's MPs to aid them. Its main hope, however, rested with Clarendon, whose responsibility it was to brief the crown on the attorney-general's findings. In the most important test of his utility as high steward, Clarendon was not to disappoint, for by representing 'the good character . . . of this corporation's loyalty' to the King, he succeeded in having the offending clauses removed. His recommendation was a little disingenuous given his personal experience of Yarmouth's current state of unrest, but he was happy to support the corporation if it might aid the stability of the turbulent borough. The

[22] Raynham House archive, boxfile, 1st Visct. Townshend, misc. corresp. 1650s–1687; boxfile 74, file of misc. papers; Bodl. Clarendon mss 80, ff. 161–2, 167–8; Y/C19/8, f. 21. For Reynolds's views, see Evans, *Seventeenth-Century Norwich*, 245.

[23] Y/C19/8, ff. 15v, 27. These changes were very much in line with government policy towards other corporations, and had been first proposed in May 1661—see Miller in *EHR* 100 (1985), 64–7.

corporation was, for once, unanimous in voting him thanks for his service, and registered the importance of the new charter in late January 1664 by ordering that it should be read out in public. However, the barrels of fish sent to Clarendon to mark the corporation's gratitude would also remind him that it was only while working on the town's behalf that he could expect its acquiesence or favour.[24]

Other corporations revealed similar vulnerability in the face of royal pressure in the early years of the Restoration, and in towns such as Liverpool and Leeds the charter issue remained a sensitive subject well into the next decade. However, it is important that the boroughs are not portrayed as being at the mercy of the crown and its gentrified allies. Recent research has suggested that both local and central governors trod a wary path in the early 1660s, with Charles and his deputies only acting decisively when informed that disaffected elements within a borough were posing a serious threat to local order. John Miller has recently highlighted the inconsistency of Charles II's borough 'policy', concluding that the King preferred to respond to local initiatives rather than impose his will indiscriminately. Given the ineffectuality of the Corporation Act purges, and the general uncertainties of the 1660s, it seems extremely unlikely that Charles could have been more combative towards the boroughs without provoking widespread disorder. Even though his prerogative powers gave him great leverage over the corporate towns, his room for manœuvre was invariably more restricted in practice. Moreover, during the 1660s towns such as Bristol, Leicester, Norwich, and Wigan sought new charters not only to confirm existing privileges, but also to extend them, thereby indicating that their loyalty to the restored crown had a price. Thus the continuing flow of new charters granted in the 1660s and 1670s did not necessarily suggest a crisis for the proponents of civic independence, for the dependency between ruler and ruled was yet sustained by the fragility of the restored regime.[25]

The clarity with which the Yarmouth corporation viewed its own

---

[24] Y/C19/8, ff. 29v–30v. The corporation, having spent £156 on the renewal, ordered all relevant correspondence to be recorded in the assembly book, a sure sign of its vulnerability over the issue.

[25] Miller in *EHR* 100 (1985), 53–84; Mullett, 'The Politics of Liverpool, 1660–88', in *Transactions of the Hist. Soc. of Lancashire and Cheshire*, 124 (1972), 45–6; Kirby, 'Restoration Leeds and the Aldermen of the Corporation, 1661–1700', in *Northern History*, 22 (1986), 137–8; R. C. Latham (ed.), 'Bristol Borough Charters 1509–1899', in *Bristol Rec. Soc. Publs.* 12 (1947), 39–41; C. Stephenson and F. G. Marcham (eds.), *Sources of English Constitutional History* (London, 1938), 592; Evans, *Seventeenth-Century Norwich*, 240–2; Henning, *House of Commons, 1660–90*, i. 293–4.

interests, and their unifying effect even in time of serious upheaval, were the most notable features of the curacy and charter disputes. However, beyond the political sphere, there were further agencies working to heal internal rifts, and their impact must be recognized as a significant influence on the town's early Restoration development. Economic difficulty, in particular, distracted town leaders as they considered the import of the national events. However, their success in mercantile affairs also did much to appease local opinion at this difficult time. The port's problems on the eve of Charles's return had been signalled in March 1659 by its petition to Parliament to encourage domestic consumption of fish. It continued this campaign after the Restoration with a virulently anti-Dutch tirade to a parliamentary committee investigating the state of the English fishing trade, taking the opportunity to lecture the board of MPs on the nation's debt to its 400–500 strong fleet of sail as a nursery of wealth and mariners.[26] The town's mercantile anxieties were further demonstrated by the election as MP in March 1661 of William Coventry, secretary to the Lord High Admiral, whose advice was eagerly sought by the corporation concerning fishing matters. The subsequent passage of the 1663 Herring Act indicated that Parliament was responsive to Yarmouth's pleas, and by directly affirming Yarmouth's status as the leading port authority in that industry, this statute inspired both hope and pride among the town's merchants. Even the non-mercantile figure of Viscount Townshend could appreciate the importance of satisfying local trading opinion, advising Coventry that 'the town depends so much upon their seamen that they will not, . . . in common prudence, must not, disoblige them in point of interest'. No local official could ignore the views emanating from the town's dockside, and in the appeasement of that body of opinion lay the greatest hope of any would-be patron for the advancement of his interest in the town.[27]

The corporation had always prided itself as the articulator of mercantile concern, and while keen to advance the cause of the fishing trade in

[26] Y/C19/7, ff. 324, 366. Yarmouth had not been negligent of its mercantile grievances during the Interregnum, for by June 1657 it had successfully agitated for the removal of the Navigation Act's ban on the export of fish in foreign ships—see R. Ashton, *Financial and Commercial Policy under the Cromwellian Protectorate* (London, 1934), 20.

[27] Y/C19/8, ff. 8v, 15v; *Statutes of the Realm*, v. 498–9; Raynham House archive, boxfile of lord-lieutenancy proceedings, 1662–9, Townshend to Coventry, Oct. 1664. By March 1661 Coventry had also been appointed a commissioner for trade, and for the plantations, thereby making him in the eyes of the Yarmouth freemen a much more attractive prospect than their Member in the Convention, Sir John Potts, 1st Bt.—Henning, *House of Commons, 1660–90*, ii. 157–63; iii. 267–8.

the parliamentary arena, it also proved stubborn over the defence of its exclusive commercial advantages. Despite the distractions of central government interference, most of the assembly's time in the early Restoration period was consumed by a drawn-out battle against a more traditional and immediate rival, the town of Lowestoft. Yarmouth's jurisdiction over the waters of Kirkley Road to the south of the town was the key point of difference, a centuries-old struggle centring on Yarmouth's right to retail all fish caught within a seven-mile radius of its port.[28] By late 1660 the Privy Council itself had become embroiled in the dispute, but it would still take another eighteen months and the arbitration of the House of Lords before the matter was finally resolved. The Lords recognized the validity of Yarmouth's chartered right, but decreed that a new measurement of the seven-mile limit be taken in order to appease the Lowestoft petitioners. Even though this ruling came with the backing of the Upper House, the Suffolk officials attending the measurement in May 1662 were treated by the Yarmouth mob to 'many insolencies, provoking languages and several disturbances' while the town magistrates stood idly by. When economic benefit was so evidently allied to historic right, the corporation would show itself at its most intransigent, and could even count on the wider support of the populace to bolster its formidable defence against outside interests.[29] However, despite these residual strengths, the corporation would continue to be tested by the succeeding challenges of Charles II's reign. The upheavals of 1660–4 might have left the corporation battered and divided, but the defence of local rights and privileges would yet sustain and unify its membership.

Even though the assembly had survived the chaos of purges and the expense of court cases, it had yet to meet the most serious threat to its local control. This challenge came from Sir Robert Paston, a Norfolk gentleman whose schemes to resurrect his family's fortunes clashed decisively with the assembly's own plans.[30] Paston's sustained campaign to develop his lands at Southtown, a hamlet directly opposite the town across the

---

[28] This right had been originally granted by Richard II's charter of 1386. The last measurement of the seven-mile limit from Yarmouth quay had been taken in 1596. For the disputes over the privilege, see Y/C36/7.

[29] Y/C19/7, f. 338v and ff.; PRO, PC2/55, ff. 51, 108, 199, 212; *LJ*, xi. 265, 510–11, 513–14; *HMC Townshend*, 26.

[30] For an account of the life of Sir William Paston, see R. Ketton-Cremer, *Norfolk Assembly* (London, 1957), 17–40. The Paston estate had been crippled by Sir William's conspicuous extravagance and the burden of a £5,594 sequestration liability (the highest in Norfolk)—*Calendar of the Committee for Compounding*, 96, 115.

River Yare, represented a fundamental threat to the Yarmouth economy and had to be overcome if the corporation were to maintain its traditional supremacy. Moreover, as the controversy developed, the rising stature of the town's opponent, and his identification with the policies of the court, would endanger Yarmouth's political independence. Although on appearance a purely local matter, the struggle was fought out in a wide arena, drawing many other issues into the eye of its storm. Historians have rarely accorded urban development the significance of political, religious, or commercial affairs, but the Southtown 'business' was to be all-embracing in its resonance, serving to highlight the continuing interaction of a town's economy, society, and politics. The Pastons had tried to build at Southtown before, but in the person of Sir Robert they had a rising court favourite who could test Yarmouth's defences with everincreasing central influence. His manifold difficulties reveal an active relationship between urban, county, and national governors, which vividly illustrates the nation's troubled development after the turbulence of the mid-seventeenth century. The experiences of this quintessential Restoration figure will certainly question the feasible extent of the 'triumph' of his fellow gentle governors in the later Stuart period when in conflict with established urban interests.[31]

Paston first came to the corporation's notice in a not uncontroversial manner, but the occasion gave little hint of the stormy relationship which was soon established between them. Indeed, many local leaders were undoubtedly heartened to hear that Sir Robert Paston had risen in the Commons on 25 November 1664 to move for a £2,500,000 supply to fund the now-inevitable military exchanges with the Dutch.[32] They may have been unaware of the ministerial intrigue which lay behind Paston's motion, but the town's recent bellicose attitude towards Dutch trading

---

[31] The most recent overture for Southtown development had been made in 1658 by Paston's father, Sir William. The corporation had turned down his offer, even though an agent of Paston's reported that 'it is most notoriously visible that they have more than a desire to have the land'—Add. mss 27447, f. 300. Legal proceedings had already commenced by the time of Sir William's death in February 1663—Y/C19/7, ff. 386–7.

[32] Only four days before the supply debate Sir Thomas Medowe had informed Townshend that local merchants, apprehensive at the probable outbreak of hostilities, were 'not willing to adventure until they understand more of his Majesty's resolutions as to the Dutch War'—Raynham House archive, boxfile, 1st Visct. Townshend, misc. corresp. 1650s–1687, Medowe to Townshend, 21 Nov. 1664. S. Pinkcus has recently argued that Anglican royalists saw the war as an opportunity to undermine the principal foreign ally of the English Nonconformists, but there is no clear evidence to suggest that loyalists at Yarmouth shared such a view—'Popery, Trade, and Universal Monarchy: the Ideological Context of the Second Anglo-Dutch War', in *EHR* 107 (1992), 1–29.

rivals suggested that his initiative would have found support in the port.[33] However, earlier that very day another bill had been introduced to 'compose and prevent differences between the towns of Great and Little Yarmouth . . . concerning the lading and unlading of herrings and other merchandise', which soon altered the countenance of the town towards Paston, its author. When it became clear that the bill aimed to extend the trading privileges of the port to the west bank of the Yare, a furious battle ensued. Thanks to his loyal service on the supply vote Paston had considerable resources of influence, but even with royal backing he found to his cost that the port was no pushover. While attempting to portray himself as the public-spirited gentleman, only interested in the rights of the inhabitants of Little Yarmouth, he met a thorough and aggressive defence from a corporation determined to control its maritime locality. Fortunately for us, his surviving correspondence has left a fulsome account of this battle, providing an unrivalled account of the manœuvring which could accompany the passage of a local bill in the later Stuart period.[34]

The initial campaign in the Commons revolved around a pamphlet war, the corporation determined to expose Paston's self-interestedness, and to assert its charter rights; the courtier keen to stress the oppression of Yarmouth over its neighbours. His letters to his wife from the House of Commons committee certainly do not betray that innocence, but at the crucial report stage on 4 February 1665, he could rely on such allies as fellow Norfolk MP Sir John Holland to champion the bill as 'consonant to reason, agreeable to law and common right and the liberty of the people'.[35] However, the six-hour debate which followed the report soon dispelled any illusions over his opponents' defence, and when the House divided on the bill, Paston achieved the slimmest of majorities—81 versus 80. In a dramatic gesture, he then withdrew his vote in order to display his supposed indifference. However, this pantomime was only undertaken in the knowledge that the Speaker of the House, Sir Edward Turnor, was 'my friend, who decided the quarrel for me' by his casting vote.[36] The façade of complacent public spirit was thus kept up, but as

---

[33] For Clarendon's wildly misleading account of Paston's role in this affair, see *The Continuation of the Life of Edward, Earl of Clarendon* (Dublin, 1759), ii. 440–5. It is corrected by both R. Ketton-Cremer, *Norfolk Portraits* (London, 1944), 29–32, and Seaward, *The Cavalier Parliament*, 121–3.

[34] For a much fuller account of this parliamentary battle, see P. Gauci, 'The Urban Perspective in Early Modern England', Oxford M.Phil. 1988, pp. 33–40.

[35] Bodl. Carte mss 78, f. 691; BL, 816m. 8, f. 78; 816m. 16, f. 29; Tanner mss 239, f. 42.

[36] *CJ*, vii. 594; *PL*, Paston to wife, 4 Feb. 1665. Even in this predominantly local matter Paston identified his opponents as those 'angry with me for the King's cause'—PL, Paston to wife, 14 Jan. 1665.

the bill went to its engrossment a much-chastened Paston still doubted the outcome, even though royal messengers had sent him promises of direct courtly aid. The engrossment on 9 February actually saw a major switch in his tactics, for a proposal to incorporate Paston's lands within the jurisdiction of the Yarmouth corporation was forced through by 26 votes in the 'hardest driven battle' Sir Robert had seen. He had the unusual (and commanded) appearance of Lord Arran's 'gallants' to thank for that majority, and, unable to compete against such court patronage, Yarmouth's assembly reluctantly consented to negotiate an incorporation as a means to limit the possible inconveniences of the bill. However, the assembly was keen to stress to its representatives that no final settlement was to be concluded without its prior approval, reaffirming its obdurate stance against Paston as the bill went up to the Lords.[37]

The bill passed its first two readings and was committed on 13 February, and once again Paston was able to use his court and familial contacts to effect. The committee's chairman, the Earl of Dorset, was summoned for a personal interview with the King, where he was told bluntly that Parliament would remain in session until Paston's bill was passed. Meanwhile Paston's uncle, the Earl of Lindsey, ensured suitable entertainment for a 'great many' of the committee at his London home.[38] In response to these intrigues, Paston himself noted that the Yarmouth representatives 'grumble like dogs and swear they have yet £3,000 to spend at law', but having satisfied the Lords' committee that he would do nothing to prejudice the royal interest, he became increasingly excited at the prospect of success. He assured himself that 'Acts of Parliament are pretty sure cards' to play against the Yarmouth corporation, and when the bill finally passed the Lords on 23 February, he gleefully recorded that the King had turned down a £4,000 bid for Paston's bill, declaring that he deserved 'ten times as much' for his loyal service on the supply bill.[39]

At this late stage both the Yarmouth assembly and its representatives in the capital were still trying to salvage some advantage for the town, even if Paston might describe them as 'out of their wits' to do so. The corporation had revealed a customary readiness to react swiftly to a developing crisis, and the frequency with which it met during this parliamentary battle (eight times in 12 weeks) highlighted the potential mobilization of civic effort when sufficiently roused. However, even though assembly

[37] *CJ*, viii. 598; Add. mss 27447, f. 336; Y/C19/8, f. 50v. Richard Butler, created Earl of Arran in May 1662, was listed as a court dependant in 1664—Henning, *House of Commons, 1660–90*, i. 756. [38] *LJ*, xi. 656–7; Add. mss 27447, f. 338.
[39] *LJ*, xi. 663; Add. mss 27447, ff. 334, 338.

leaders were generally willing to heed the advice of the committee in London, some persuasion was needed before they accepted that the incorporation scheme was the best means to limit the impact of the bill. The Yarmouth representatives had requested the assembly for 'further power' to treat with Paston while the bill lay before the Lords' committee, but permission had been denied them. However, only three days later they were given the go-ahead to conclude articles of incorporation.[40] By 25 February Paston had cautiously accepted Yarmouth's overtures, even though he realized that this provision would render his bill void in exchange for the promise of full trading rights for his own lands. Subsequent events suggest that agreement between the two parties had been reached by 2 March when Charles came to prorogue Parliament.

On that occasion the King honoured Paston with a public acknowledgement, and within weeks the courtier was buoyed up by reports that Charles wished to reward his loyalty with a title.[41] Soon he was chasing more tangible and immediate gain in the service of the crown at the Customs House. When the Yarmouth representatives, the apparent losers, came back to report to the assembly on 17 March, all they could offer as consolation was the option of incorporating Paston's lands as a means to annul the Act. For an outlay of £180 in defence costs (some 16 per cent of the corporation's average annual income), that might have seemed a scant reward, but they had at least managed to confine the benefits of the statute exclusively to Paston's lands, and allowed themselves a three-year breathing space in which to assess the likely impact of incorporation. As he organized his business interests in the snowy London of March 1665 Paston was already speculating on a return of £2,000 p.a. on his Southtown property, and ordered a draft of the area to be drawn up to advance his plans. However, he had already experienced the dourness of grumbling Yarmouth men, and it was such opposition that brought him to this conclusion: 'I have learnt this—refuse nothing. Therefore if the King gives me honour, I shall be the harder beggar for somewhat to support it.' The aspirant courtier had emerged victorious from his first experience of local politics, but was to be corrected many times in his ensuing years of frustration.[42]

Subsequent relations between town and courtier, until the provisions of the act required their direct co-operation to secure the incorporation of Paston's lands by letters patent, were limited by the nature of their

[40] PL, Paston to wife, 25 Feb. 1665; Y/C19/8, f. 51.
[41] PL, Paston to wife, 2, 25 Mar. 1665; *CSPD* 1667–8, p. 173.
[42] Y/C19/8, f. 52; PL, Paston to wife, 2 Mar. 1665.

respective concerns—Yarmouth preoccupied with local emergencies, while Paston concentrated on consolidating his interest in London. Fortune continued to smile on Paston, for by April 1666 he had gained the lease of the wood farm, which promised an annual income of some £2,000 for the next thirty-one years. Expectation of further royal preferment followed in 1667 when he was elevated to the status of gentleman of the Privy Chamber.[43] Yarmouth, on the other hand, was rocked by a terrible visitation of the plague which carried off some 1,800 of its inhabitants, rendering it a ghost town in the summer of 1665. At Michaelmas the King intervened to deliver a *mandamus* for the choice of bailiffs, such was the perceived weakness of the borough and its magisterial authorities. Given the assembly's recent opposition to royal interference over the charter, it was entirely predictable that some councillors tried to obstruct the *mandamus*. However, despite the town's current weakness, a faction led by John Woodroffe successfully campaigned for the rejection of one of the crown's two nominees.[44] The plague also exacerbated the difficulties faced by local traders on account of the Dutch war, which, in turn, had heightened concern for the state of the town piers protecting the haven-mouth from drifting sand banks. In January 1665 the Yarmouth committee on the Southtown bill had been requested to seek a supply for haven repair, but the Paston affair had forestalled this lobby. From December 1667, once the town had recovered from the ravages of plague, the haven would become the corporation's absolute priority.[45]

By that time, the process of incorporation had been under way for some eight months, the town having sent a deputation to Paston's Oxnead estate to notify him of its willingness to proceed. However, only after the incorporation had passed the royal seal in January 1668 did Sir Robert display the central importance of Southtown to his hopes for familial enrichment. Now that he had secured the trading rights of the ancient borough for his own tenants, he had a marketable proposition with which to lure prospective investors, and by August a thousand 'encouragements' for building a new town at Southtown had been printed and were ready for distribution. Surviving copies reveal the determined preparation of

[43] The wood farm included duties levied on imported glass, stone, earth, lemons, and oranges, as well as timber—*CTB* 1660–7, p. 697. It would not be an easy farm to manage, for in the wake of the Great Fire the crown demanded an extra £3,800 p.a.—*CTB* 1672–5, p. 516.

[44] A. G. E. Jones, 'Great Plague in Yarmouth', in *Notes and Queries*, 202 (1957), 108–12; Y/C19/8, ff. 54–100; *CSPD* 1664–5, p. 527; Raynham House archive, boxfile, 1st Visct. Townshend, misc. corresp. 1650s–1687, Yarmouth bailiffs to Townshend, 30 Aug. 1665.

[45] Y/C19/8, ff. 50v, 90v; *CJ*, ix. 32.

Paston, and, of a more general significance, demonstrate the dissemination of contemporary ideas in urban development.[46]

Not surprisingly, the proposals betrayed a sharp eye for exposing the topographical and mercantile shortcomings of Great Yarmouth. Paston's 'New Yarmouth' was to have all the benefits of regularity which his undeveloped site could afford, and such advantages were most effectively displayed in juxtaposition to the cramped rows of the old town, straitjacketed by its fortress walls. Paston could patriotically declare that a shortfall in Yarmouth shipping, caused by the east bank's incapacity for expansion, needlessly allowed the Dutch to benefit, and he pointed to his uniform grid pattern as the surest path towards commercial growth. A spacious quayfront, regulated wide streets, and the prescribed grandeur of New Yarmouth dwellings all contrasted markedly with Great Yarmouth's maze of narrow rows. The old town had been praised in the past for its fine brick and stone buildings, especially the houses of its wealthy merchants on the South Quay, but Paston had directly hit a local mercantile nerve by highlighting obvious difficulties of overdevelopment.[47]

The expertise behind these proposals was supplied by Stephen Primatt, the author of *The City and Country Purchaser and Builder* of 1668.[48] However, Paston's own experience of the parliamentary debates on London's rebuilding after the Great Fire would have given him some insight into urban development, and his lease of the wood farm no doubt encouraged his interest in such matters. Moreover, he had only recently recorded his own house-hunting activities in the most fashionable West End district of Lincoln's Inn Fields, and thus would have been familiar with the

---

[46] Y/C19/8, f. 80v; Add. mss 27447, f. 313. For copies of the proposals, see Swinden, *History of Great Yarmouth*, 309–35; Bodl. Wood mss. 276A, f. 292; BL, 816m. 8, f. 80. The dearth of work on urban development was recently noted by C. Chalklin in his article 'Estate Development in Bristol, Birmingham, and Liverpool, 1660–1720', in Chalklin and J. Wordie (eds.), *Town and Countryside* (London, 1989), 102–15.

[47] For a discussion of Yarmouth's topographical development, see R. E. Dickson, 'The Town Plans of East Anglia', in *Geography*, 19 (1934), 37–50; A. Michel, 'Port and Town of Great Yarmouth . . . 1550–1714', Cambridge Ph.D. 1978, pp. 270–7; B. O'Neil, 'Some Seventeenth-Century Houses in Great Yarmouth', in *Archaeologia*, 95 (1953), 141–80. The narrowness of the rows had led to the invention of a trolley cart (in the early sixteenth century), and to the passage of an ordinance in 1618 forbidding the doors of row-houses to swing outwards—Y/C18/3, f. 227.

[48] Paston may well have been put in contact with Primatt by his creditors William Morris and Sir Robert Clayton, both of whom invested heavily in the rebuilding of the capital—see F. T. Melton, 'Sir Robert Clayton's Building Projects in London, 1666–72', in *Guildhall Studies in London History*, 3 (1977), 37–42; D. C. Coleman, 'London Scriveners and the Estate Market in the Later Seventeenth Century', in *Economic History Review*, 2nd ser. 4 (1951–2), 221–30.

idea of the regulated residential unit which William Newton had helped to popularize there since the 1630s. Paston provided for both a market and a chapel in his new town, thereby saving its inhabitants from having to cross the Yare bridge into Great Yarmouth for such facilities, and thus ensuring the independence of the community on the west side of the haven. His offer of long-term building leases was another recent London innovation, and his promise of cheap and readily available building materials (most emphatically brick) revealed a similar understanding of current construction practice. His plan showed how quickly London styles and ideas could penetrate the provinces in the post-Fire period, and its sophistication underlined the seriousness of the threat which Paston posed to established interests in Yarmouth. The success of fellow MP Sir John Lowther in developing Whitehaven from the 1660s while employing a similar grid-block plan, suggests that New Yarmouth cannot be dismissed as a mere pipe-dream.[49]

However, despite such thorough preparations Paston failed to gain any immediate building conveyances. There can be little doubt that he secured sufficient publicity for his scheme, for in October 1669 the King's chief engineer, Sir Bernard de Gomme, noted on his survey of the Yarmouth area the precise site which Paston's draft map had earmarked for development. Unfortunately, the circulation of the proposals cannot be measured with any certainty, but with contracting agents in London, Norwich, and Yarmouth itself, they were probably most densely dispersed within East Anglia and the South-East.[50] Equally frustratingly, although there is no firm evidence that any serious approaches were made to Paston, there are certainly indications that the project was successful in attracting the interest of investors. For instance, in August 1669 Paston's Parisian correspondent Thomas Henshawe rejoiced 'to hear your affairs at Yarmouth are so prosperous', and Paston's estate records reveal that in March 1671 Southtown was his only property to have risen in value since 1664. Moreover, its new rental was noted as being 'without anchorage and other duties confirmed by a late Act of Parliament and not settled in a certain rent, but will be very considerable'. In the absence of conclusive

---

[49] Add. mss 27447, f. 336; J. Summerson, *Georgian London* (London, 1970), 27–43; Chalklin, 'The Making of Some New Towns, *c.*1600–1720' in Chalklin and M. Havinden (eds.), *Rural Change and Urban Growth, 1500–1800* (London, 1974), 231–2, 239–42; J. V. Beckett, *Coal and Tobacco* (Cambridge, 1981).

[50] PRO, WO 78/1401. A surviving copy is addressed to a don at Lincoln College, Oxford, a destination which can be attributed to Stephen Primatt's familial association with that institution—Bodl. Wood mss 276A, f. 292; J. Foster, *Alumni Oxonienses* (Oxford, 1891), 1213.

proof of any signed conveyance, or house built, this does suggest some element of success in promoting the scheme, even if it fell short of firm investment.[51]

The difficulty of ascertaining whether anyone did make a firm financial commitment to Paston has led most researchers to dismiss the whole project as whimsical and impracticable, but this would be to ignore the more certain evidence of approaches made in later years, as well as to underestimate the forces working against speculative building at this time. The crucial consideration playing on the minds of all potential investors must have been the likely response of Yarmouth's mercantile élite, and the town's eighteenth-century historian Henry Swinden thought that the threat of a charter withdrawal through their influence was the principal cause of Paston's failure. By January 1669 one of Paston's tenants had successfully petitioned for the freedom of Yarmouth for the payment of a £10 fine, but there was no mass influx of new settlers in his wake.[52] The town's merchants did not see that there was sufficient cause to embark on a hazardous enterprise, and, especially up to April 1670, their attention remained fixed upon the passage of the haven repair bill through Parliament, on which the economic fate of both sides of the haven was seen to hang. It took three attempts and over two years to get the bill past the Commons' committee stage, but in its final form it provided £12,000 for the immediate restoration of the havenmouth piers from the proceeds of a 12*d.* duty on all imports, except fish.

The corporation's principal adversary on this occasion was the city of Norwich, which was prepared to go into print to prevent the levy of additional tolls on the large supplies of coal, corn, and other goods which its merchants shipped through the outport. To champion its cause the Norwich assembly also employed Lord Townshend, who later claimed the credit for smoothing the bill's passage through the Upper House. Deprived of a high steward to fight its corner following the exile of Lord Clarendon, Yarmouth showed some willingness to compromise, but in the end all the county capital had to show for its efforts was the promise of an annual £50 grant from the haven duty to aid the navigability of the Yare between the two towns. There is no evidence to suggest that the Yarmouth assembly endeavoured to enlist Paston's support for this contest, and it is unlikely that at that stage in his career he would have felt sufficiently confident to challenge Townshend's authority. However, for

---

[51] Add. mss 36988, f. 99; PRO, C111/120, part 1, piece 19.
[52] Swinden, *History of Great Yarmouth*, 335; Y/C19/8, f. 109v.

Townshend himself it was a perfect opportunity to act as the arbiter of the county, able as he was to portray himself as a purveyor of central influence. By their very nature, issues such as river navigation and harbour maintenance often concerned a variety of interest groups, and offered prospective patrons ideal opportunities for extending their influence. At the Thetford by-election of 1669 Sir Joseph Williamson had promoted a candidate on a platform of reviving the Norfolk borough as a port, and a bill to that effect was passed in the 1670 session. Moreover, even when such a campaign failed, as was the experience of Tregony MP Charles Trevanion later in the reign when supporting a bill to improve the navigation of the River Fal, such efforts worked to secure a Member's interest in the constituency. As Yarmouth had found to its cost, the irregular meeting of Parliament did not help local interests to plan their appeals to Westminster, and not until after the Revolution would such a fundamental impediment to the passage of legislation be removed. However, while haven blockage posed such an urgent threat to the livelihoods of the local populace, town leaders were prepared to dig deep in their pockets to seek favour at the centre.[53]

The corporation's haven campaign again testified to the inner resilience of the Yarmouth mercantile community when motivated by economic necessity. However, such efforts had evidently distracted attention from Paston's scheme, and the haven issue could only have cast further speculation over Southtown's commercial viability. A recent inquiry into corporate finances had also highlighted the pressure which haven maintenance exerted on the assembly, revealing a £9,000 debt and an annual deficit of some £1,000. Clearly, local merchants were reluctant to gamble on a major building project which would require a massive injection of capital with no sure sign of success, and by late 1671 Paston had signalled his own disillusionment with the scheme by offering to sell Southtown to the King. Ironically, this despairing proposal resulted from the huge expenses he had incurred in receiving the King and Queen at his Oxnead home in September of that year. The shortfall between his expected lifestyle and his actual income was the leitmotif of Paston's financial difficulties, but the depression caused by his first failure at speculative investment did not last long as events turned to favour him. The assuredness of Yarmouth's short-term economic stability due to the Haven Act ensured the competitiveness of the Southtown scheme into the 1670s,

[53] BL, 816m. 8, f. 77; *HMC Townshend*, 28; Swinden, *History of Great Yarmouth*, 896–910; Y/C36/6; Tanner mss 311; Henning, *House of Commons, 1660–1690*, i. 180, 333.

and continuing royal favour, as witnessed by the court's visit to Oxnead, only made him more determined to succeed.[54]

However, stacked against him, there was not only the proven organization of Yarmouth's representatives, but also the increasingly significant problem of Nonconformity within the town. Government informer Richard Bower attributed the renewed rise of local Dissent to the installation of Edmund Thaxter and Richard Huntington as town bailiffs in 1666. As if to underline Paston's direct concern in the issue, he reported that the clemency afforded to conventicles stemmed from the fear of local inhabitants that leading merchants would destroy their trade should anyone dare to oppose Dissenting activity.[55] Bower felt particular unease at the return of Independent minister William Bridge to Yarmouth in 1667, for a collection openly undertaken to support him was led by contributions from bailiff George England and Thaxter. The financial muscle of these negligent magistrates impressed Bower greatly, and in December 1668 he thought that he stood to lose his business just for informing London that 'Presbyterian grandee' John Woodroffe had unsuccessfully attempted to pass an assembly motion to deregulate religious 'scarlet' days.[56] A month later, such agitation led to the banishment of Bridge from Yarmouth as the Norwich Assize chose to enforce the Five Mile Act. Lord-Lieutenant Townshend played an uncharacteristically forthright role in Bridge's ejection, but only after Lord Arlington had informed him that the King himself had been 'infinitely scandalized' by the activities of the Yarmouth Nonconformists. Further trouble came the lord-lieutenant's way when Sir Thomas Medowe resigned in 1670 as major in the town militia in protest at the promotion of Nonconformist sympathizer Richard Huntington to a captaincy. Undoubtedly wearied by Yarmouth's divisions, Townshend not only ignored Medowe's stand but also a Privy Council order to investigate reports of magisterial support for conventicles held in the town and its vicinity. Indeed, his reaction suggested that the best opportunity to suppress the Yarmouth Dissenters had already been missed, and that even new initiatives such as the Conventicle Act of 1670 would only have a short-term impact. The assembly did take legal counsel about the Act, but, as Anthony Fletcher's survey of its enforcement in

---

[54] Y/C36/6, piece 3; *CSPD* 1671, p. 516. Within a year Paston's heir, William, had married Charlotte, a natural daughter of the King (by Elizabeth, Viscountess Shannon), and Paston's wife could enthuse that Charles was willing to grant the family anything it could 'reasonably ask'—Y/NRS 4008 13F7, Rebecca Paston to R. Clayton, 16 July 1672.

[55] See, in particular, *CSPD* 1667–8, pp. 67–8, 85, 88, 97, 145, 161, 186, 232–3, 250, 300, 446.   [56] *CSPD* 1667–8, p. 186; 1668–9, pp. 99–100.

several English counties concluded, the statute appears to have had little more than temporary effect.[57]

Religious divisions within the town may not have surfaced during the royal visit to Yarmouth in October 1671, but their absence merely reflected its leaders' priority of presenting a united face to impress important visitors. The assembly invested some £1,000 which it could ill afford on entertaining the court, enlisting the services of its recorder to deliver a remarkably sycophantic speech in honour of the King. However, amid the deferential plaudits was the telling observation that Charles's presence renewed 'the long continued series of the charters of privileges, enlargements, and other mercies' granted to the town by his royal ancestors. Furthermore, the present of three golden herrings on a gold chain, and the serving of the freshly caught local produce for the royal meal, were calculated reminders of the town's economic importance within the realm. Although the eloquence of the recorder's speech to the town's 'most dread and most gracious sovereign' made the town appear in a subservient mood, the account of the royal visit by Norfolk wit Matthew Stevenson bespoke its communal resilience, which had been recently proved by the passage of the Haven Act:

> When the town sparkled with such courtiers
> Yarmouth was sure nobly supplied with piers.[58]

Informant Bower was less happy with the occasion, grumbling that the factions were 'striving to outvie one the other' to gain royal recognition, although he did note that they were 'unanimous as to the King's reception'. However, the knighthoods given to James Johnson, the King's host, and to George England, only further cemented local Nonconformist influence, and any authority aspiring to secure control of Yarmouth would have to tackle the issue of religion head-on.[59] Thus, by the time Paston had embarked on a second wave of building proposals in late 1672, Yarmouth was still in a state of flux, its government strengthened by improved economic fortunes, yet rocked by religious division.

Paston's new printed proposals were principally inspired by a royal

---

[57] *CSPD* 1668–9, p. 159; Raynham House archive, boxfile of lord-lieutenancy proceedings 1662–9, Arlington to Lord Townshend, 20 Oct. 1668; Y/C27/2, Michaelmas 1670/71; A. Fletcher, 'The Enforcement of the Conventicle Acts 1664–79' in *Studies in Church History*, 21 (1984), 235–46. An episcopal survey of 1669 cited the Yarmouth Independents as 400-strong—C. Turner, *Original Records of Early Nonconformity* (London, 1911), ii. 896–7. Also, see *CSPD* 1670, pp. 512–13; PRO, PC2/62, pp. 247, 352.

[58] M. Stevenson, *Norfolk Drollery* (1673).

[59] Y/C19/8, ff. 159–167v; Tanner mss 311, f. 96; *CSPD* 1671, pp. 491, 517.

declaration of June 1672, which offered special immunities to Dutchmen willing to settle in England. At a stroke this offer promised to overcome a serious difficulty which the Yarmouth assembly had recently thrown in Paston's path. In October 1672 an inhabitant of Southtown, Thomas Bendish, was forced to submit to a town assistance that he had committed an offence by landing coals from the vessel of a 'stranger' at a quay on the west side of the haven without seeking the permission of the town bailiffs. A £6 fine was levied despite Bendish's protest of ignorance of local laws as the town signalled its determination to remain the controlling commercial authority in the area, whatever the changed circumstances of the incorporation. Paston's bill of 1664 had only ever aspired to secure the claimed right of Little Yarmouth inhabitants to land goods in their *own* ships on the western bank, and Great Yarmouth was quick to forestall any major commercial exchange at Southtown via the influx of ships owned by foreign merchants.[60]

The opportunity for naturalizing settlers, however, might circumvent this obstacle if they brought their ships and wealth with them to Southtown, and the Dutch text inserted into Paston's second printed proposal was obviously designed to attract foreign investment.[61] Like the 1668 edition, it stressed the advantages of the regular new town over Great Yarmouth's overdeveloped site, but the additional emphasis on naturalized citizens— even to the provision of a 'Dutch church' nearby—forced Yarmouth's leaders to reconsider their position. That Paston could expect stiff opposition from them there was little doubt, for the English envoy at the Hague had observed as early as 1661 that Yarmouth would bitterly oppose any attempt to make foreigners freemen of the town, even with the authority of a parliamentary act behind it, for such a challenge would be seen as 'a breach of their privileges'. Familiarity of trading relations had certainly cemented firm links between the Dutch and Yarmouth merchants, as was most evident from the assimilation of Dutch architectural styles by local builders. However, an influx of settlers of the magnitude proposed by Paston's plans could only be viewed as an economic threat to existing interest groups. In particular, a royal assurance in the declaration of 1672 that Dutch ships owned by settlers would be treated as English-

---

[60] Y/C19/8, f. 179v. The 1668 charter of incorporation had acknowledged that the hamlet of Little Yarmouth was now under 'the rule, government, jurisdiction, scrutiny, taxation, correction, punishment, precept, and arrest' of the Yarmouth assembly—Palmer, *History of Great Yarmouth*, 37–8. Other corporations were finding greater difficulty in controlling unregulated suburbs—see T. Reddaway, *Rebuilding London after the Great Fire* (London, 1940), 42–8; J. M. Lee, 'Stamford and the Cecils, 1700–1885', Oxford B. Litt. 1957, p. 10.   [61] For copies, see *CSPD* 1673, pp. 150–1; BL, 816m. 8, f. 79.

built could be perceived as a harbinger of direct commercial growth at Southtown.[62]

Paston sent a copy of these proposals to under-secretary of state Sir Joseph Williamson in April 1673, reminding him of a prior royal promise to aid Paston's 'interest at Yarmouth', and in the following September he received word from fellow MP and entrepreneur Thomas King that surveyor general of the customs William Dickenson had approved the scheme. Moreover, King enthusiastically promised him that 'I hope in five or six years to build your lordship as good a street as is upon Yarmouth quay', estimating that it would profit the Paston family to the tune of £40,000–50,000. Yet he was equally sure, as one who had married into one of Yarmouth's leading merchant families, that the town would oppose the plan. He advised Paston not even to consult Yarmouth's leaders, disingenuously reasoning that 'they cannot apprehend the depth of it'. However, he did emphasize that his building-plans would only be realized 'if your lordship hath the houses', and again, on that vital criterion, there is little evidence of certain success. Paston ventured into construction himself by building a quay right opposite the town's customs house, but for all his lobbying of powerful authorities in London, it remained the extent of proven development. A major reason for this failure must lie with a factor over which Paston had little control—the Dutch war itself.[63]

Bower noted at the outbreak of hostilities that initial Dutch military reverses met with a mixed reception in the port: 'we are so Dutchified here that a Dutchman cannot be more dejected than our people are generally for the sad condition we understand the Hollander to be in'. The practical effect of the war on a mobilized and fortified Yarmouth was to preclude any thoughts of extensive urban development when there was little assurance of protection for their shipping. The state papers reveal evidence of Dutchmen attempting to naturalize, but they found the royal proclamation to be no security against many obstacles on arrival, and both crown and courtier were disappointed in their hopes for pecuniary advantage.[64] Paston did achieve his much-desired elevation to the peerage by his

[62] A Dutch chapel had been established at Yarmouth in 1600, but closed in 1680, after which it became one of the town's notable social centres—O. P. Grell, J. I. Israel, and N. Tyacke (eds.), *From Persecution to Toleration* (Oxford, 1991), 105–6; *HMC Portland*, ii. 268. Also, see Clarendon mss 104, ff. 160–1; W. Kuyper, *Dutch Classicist Architecture, 1625–1700* (Delft, 1980), 115–25; K. Haley, *The British and the Dutch* (London, 1988), 53–5, 73–5.

[63] *CSPD* 1673, pp. 150–1; PL, Thomas King to Paston, 6 Sept. 1673; Paston to wife, 14 Apr. 1676.

[64] *CSPD* 1672, p. 272. A warrant of January 1673 specified that all Dutch passengers arriving on the East coast were to be arrested save those wishing to settle. However, this order only came after Dutchmen at Falmouth had complained that their goods had been

creation as Baron Paston and Viscount Yarmouth in August 1673, but, as he so often observed, such an objective would have to be accompanied by financial gain. With probable debts of some £10,000 by this time, his annual £13 stipend as peer of the realm highlighted the hollowness of Paston's elevated social position. However, such promotion gave him hope of future economic reward, opening new channels of influence to the desperate nobleman. Viscount Yarmouth had discovered that a gentleman could rise rapidly in the service of his monarch, but he still could not challenge the town of Yarmouth from a position of true authority.[65]

Somewhat surprisingly, the promotion which suggested his next campaign for Southtown development came from Yarmouth itself, for in December 1674, following the death of the exiled Clarendon, the assembly elected its namesake peer as its new high steward. It might seem strange for the town to elect a recent rival, but the requirements of that office made Paston an obvious candidate. The high steward had to act in the town's name in the highest political circles, and in its previous battles with Sir Robert, the town had found him a promising link to the court, the Customs House, and Parliament itself. Most remarkably for a borough which had been riven with division for some time, the assembly's vote to elect him was unanimous, but this may have simply reflected an absence of viable alternative candidates. Lord Townshend had acted on the town's behalf on a few occasions during Clarendon's exile, but his political star was already on the wane, and he simply could not boast sufficient clout to perform the services expected by the corporation. In contrast, Paston was the leading pretender for control of the shire, and town leaders sensibly agreed to elect a patron who was likely to be welcomed in the corridors of power in the capital. In reply to the offer Paston demonstrated understanding of his new role, observing that the assembly's consensus over his election would remain a 'stricter tie' on him to act always in Yarmouth's interest.[66]

seized when they tried to naturalize there in July 1672—*CSPD* 1672, pp. 358–9; 1672–3, p. 417.

[65] *CTB* 1672–5, p. 381. Paston's elevation was viewed by Charles Hatton as the work of Lord Danby, whom he described as Paston's 'great friend'—'The Correspondence of the Family of Hatton', in *Camden Society*, NS 22 (1878), 115. For his debts, which might have been as high as £20,000 at this time, see Y/NRS 4017 13F7, and Y/MC107/4. However, in the summer of 1674 he was still willing to advance £6,000 to ensure that he did not lose Southtown through the marriage of his daughter to an alien (for the lands were held in her name)—Guildhall Lib. mss 6428, ii. 158–9. I will continue to refer to Viscount Yarmouth as 'Paston' to avoid confusion between town and peer.

[66] Y/C19/8, f. 216v; Add. mss 28261, f. 29; J. M. Rosenheim, *Townshends of Raynham*, 36–41. Although Townshend had acted on the town's behalf during Clarendon's exile, most

Political commentators saw many divisive issues awaiting the new incumbent. Bower, in particular, expressed grave concern at the renewed confidence of local Dissenters since the introduction of Charles's Declaration of Indulgence, in the wake of which eight Yarmouth Nonconformists had taken out preaching licences. The withdrawal of the Indulgence in March 1673 had allowed the loyalists to recover some ground, and in the following September they actually ousted eleven councillors from the assembly for failing to take the oaths required by the Test Act.[67] However, the Declaration had a lasting impact, for it gave substance to the rumours spread by local Nonconformists of their support at court, a claim which, as at Coventry, had undermined the Anglican position ever since the Declaration of Breda. Bower still hoped that Paston's election would prove a major victory against the officials whom he perceived to be the pillars of local Nonconformity, Lord Lieutenant Townshend and Sir William D'Oyly. Significantly, Paston's own informant noted the hesitancy of 'one or two fanatics' in the assembly who wished to postpone the vote until they had 'taken advice' in the matter, and the new high steward could have had few illusions as to the dangers of becoming embroiled in urban politics. His subsequent actions show that the election encouraged his dreams of material advantage, but such an addition to his authority and honour brought responsibilities and problems which he could not ignore.[68]

The travails of Lord Townshend since the Restoration would have given Paston sufficient warning of the potential dilemmas ahead. The lord-lieutenant's experience was clearly shared to some degree by Charles II's other provincial deputies, all of whom were saddled with responsibility for the execution of often controversial, and sometimes contradictory, royal policies. Having raised such fundamental issues as religion and

notably in December 1670 to obtain a royal pardon for the town's minting of brass farthings, no source mentions his possible candidacy for the high stewardship—*CSPD* 1670, p. 562.

[67] *CSPD* 1673–5, p. 475; PL, R. Flynt to Paston, 6 Jan. 1675. In response to the Declaration, five Independents, two Baptists, and one Presbyterian had taken out licences to preach at Yarmouth, while an Independent and a Baptist meeting-house were also licensed—Turner, *Original Records of Early Nonconformity*, ii. 887, 896–7, 901. Significantly, after the purge of September 1673 one of the ousted aldermen gained immediate reselection to the upper house—Y/C19/8, ff. 192v–195. When Sir John Hobart went electioneering in Yarmouth in March 1675, he found the Nonconformists still mindful of recent persecution—Raynham House archive, boxfile, 1st Visct. Townshend, misc. corresp. 1650s–1687, Hobart to Townshend, 19 Mar. 1675.

[68] PL, R. Flynt to Paston, 6 Jan. 1675; J. J. Hurwich, 'A Fanatick Town: The Political Influence of Dissenters in Coventry, 1660–1720', in *Midland History*, 4 (1977), 21.

municipal independence, the disputes of the early 1660s were unlikely to have been resolved without decisive and sustained central intervention. The government quickly revealed it lacked the will or the courage to mount such a campaign, thereby allowing divisions and uncertainties to continue to plague both central and local government. Indeed, the most lasting consequence of Charles II's intervention at Yarmouth was a lingering suspicion of royal motives, and after a series of changes in court policy both loyalists and Nonconformists regarded Whitehall with little confidence. Paston had been lucky to avoid any direct involvement in those early Restoration disputes, but as a rival economic interest to the Yarmouth mercantile élite had come to understand the obstinacy of the corporation when thrown onto the defensive. Now, as high steward, he would learn that the interplay of centre and locality, as maintained by his mediation, was a partnership of extreme sensitivity. His experience of the cares of local office between 1676 and 1681 highlights the more acute difficulties of the Restoration period, which, on a national scale, came to their climax with the Exclusion crisis.

4
The Challenge Met: 1675–81

HISTORIANS of English political development have credited the late 1670s as a period of key significance, regarding it as a decisive era for the emergence of party. Contemporaries certainly saw those years as a turning-point in Charles II's reign, as fears for the court's swing towards France and Rome reached a hysterical pitch. The campaign to exclude the Catholic James, Duke of York from the succession caused the most intense political activity of the reign, as both the court and its opponents mobilized every supporter for a parliamentary confrontation. Although the King emerged victorious from the show-down at the Oxford Parliament in March 1681, the crisis had an undeniable long-term impact, passing the unflattering soubriquets of Whig and Tory into the nation's political vocabulary. From a historiographic perspective, the subsequent popularization of such labels only further magnified the significance of the Exclusion controversy, for this development suggested that the organization of English politics had undergone important change during that time. However, most recent work has expressed reservations concerning the coherence of the political groupings between 1679 and 1681, and has questioned whether the contesting rivals were the direct forerunners of the Whig and Tory parties which assumed a more permanent existence after the Glorious Revolution. In particular, scholars have disputed the primacy of the Exclusion issue as the sole objective of the court's opponents, casting even further doubt over the degree of party discipline during that period.[1]

The evidence from Yarmouth, although frustratingly sparse at times, endorses such a challenge to accepted views, for during these critical

---

[1] Path-breaking work on the Exclusion crisis came with J. R. Jones, *The First Whigs: the Politics of the Exclusion Crisis, 1678–83* (Oxford, 1961). However, for a stern critique of his findings, see J. Scott, *Algernon Sidney and the Restoration Crisis, 1677–83* (Cambridge, 1991). For an assessment of their relative merits, see T. Harris, *Politics under the Later Stuarts: Party Conflict in a Divided Society* (London, 1993), ch. 4. Also note the work of M. Knights, who argues that the first Exclusionist election was far from being tied to that single issue alone, with cross-currents of religious factionalism, the court-country divide, and local issues all playing their part—'Politics and Opinion during the Exclusion Crisis 1678–81', Oxford D.Phil. 1989, to be published as *Politics and Opinion in Crisis, 1678–81* (Cambridge).

years its political complexion was principally determined by problems which had bedevilled local society for some time, most evidently the issue of Dissent, and not by the immediate controversy surrounding Exclusion. That is not to say that the town's leaders were immune to the impact of national debates, but that their reaction to the most dramatic crisis since 1660 was unavoidably influenced by divisions which had continued to spark contention since the Restoration. The configuration of local parties reflected that simple fact of political life; the leaders of the respective factions seeing little reason to change their positions at the onset of the Exclusion campaign. However, the same could not be said for potentially the dominant figure in Yarmouth politics, Robert Paston, lionized by both contemporaries and historians as a staunch servant of the King. The manner in which he strove to serve both his own interest and that of the court between 1675 and 1681 deserves close attention in order that the complexities of local politics might be recognized. His difficulties were evidently of a very singular nature, but they demonstrate the workings of the political process in detail, providing insights into the general responsibilities of the provincial governor at this difficult time. Furthermore, an in-depth assessment of his relationship with Yarmouth's leaders will help to place electoral politics in its proper context, highlighting the particular pressures which a run of parliamentary contests exerted on both patron and borough.

In all probability, it was only at his official inauguration at the Michaelmas assembly of 1675 that Paston fully acknowledged the significance of his election to the high stewardship. The patent of office had already been presented to Paston in person by a Yarmouth delegation the preceding April, and on that occasion Paston had promised to make an address to the crown on the town's behalf, having 'methodized' some propositions with Sir George England and Sir William D'Oyly. No address appears to have been made, but during that summer England was certainly negotiating with Paston concerning a possible settlement on the west side of the haven, and early September saw the assembly move its ships to Paston's bank in order to ease congestion in the port during the fishing season. In that time Paston had the misfortune to fall foul of a robber's gun, but he recovered quickly, and the episode only increased expectancy for his return to Norfolk. Bower excitedly forecast that Paston would be met by crowds at Yarmouth 'greater than has been at any time to wait upon any person of honour whatsoever'. The corporation itself, evidently viewing hospitality as an essential support of its dignity, was even prepared to accommodate a guest who had already caused more than a decade of unease for his hosts. However, although the presentation of the communal 'face' could often override inner dissension, descriptions of the visit revealed that tensions could underlie such expressions of joyful unanimity.[2]

If Paston had any trepidation about the warmth of his reception as he travelled towards Yarmouth on 28 September, it must have been dispelled some two miles out from the town walls at Caister, when he was met by the whole of the corporation and some 300 other riders.[3] As one, they saluted the high steward with a toast and acted as a magnificent and orderly escort into the town. Yarmouth itself was packed with crowds lining the processional route around the town and, as Paston's coach passed, guns on the eastern battlements and on the ships moored at the quayside thundered out their welcome. Paston was to be housed at bailiff Thaxter's house, which stood at the centre of the main quayfront, and as he alighted from his coach to spontaneous cheers from the crowd he could not have failed to be impressed by the hundreds of ships bedecked in full regalia, and the similar ceremonial grandeur of the South Quay. At his temporary home he received town notables who had been unable to meet him at Caister, and was entertained to a 'very great supper' that night. The next day he was taken to the Tolhouse to be inaugurated into civic life by receiving the freedom of the town, the instrument of which was presented in a silver box. He then heard prayers conducted in his honour at a church service where he sat between the two retiring bailiffs, and later attended the swearing of recently elected officers at the Guildhall. As the new bailiffs took up their position on either side of him, in an assembly resplendent in aldermanic scarlet, Paston could have been forgiven for thinking that he had finally established some true authority within the town, and that such respect might be turned to financial gain. However, beyond the pomp there was hard bargaining to be done, and as Paston informed his wife that very evening, having escaped the suffocating hospitality of his hosts for a hastily scribbled note, he had not missed the chance to promote his designs among Yarmouth's leading merchants.[4]

Paston's principal revelation was that one of the England family had

---

[2] PL, Paston to Yarmouth bailiffs, 29 Apr. 1675; Paston to wife, 29 Sept. 1675; Y/C19/ 8, f. 227v; *CSPD* 1675–6, p. 319.

[3] F. Heal, in her *Hospitality in Early Modern England* (Oxford, 1990), 311–12, 314–15, provides a fine account of this visit, but she does not note the significance of the meeting at Caister. The boundary between the Paston estate at Caister Castle and the town limits had proved a bone of contention for centuries, and in 1659 the impecunious Sir William Paston had been forced to sell his lands there to two Yarmouth traders for the settlement of a £6,500 debt—see D. Turner, *A Sketch of the History of Caister Castle* (London, 1842); National Register of Archives reports, Middlesex 19.

[4] PL, Paston to wife, 29 Sept., 1 Oct. 1675; J. Fisher to Lady Yarmouth, 29 Sept., 1 Oct. 1675; J. Gough to Lady Yarmouth, 1 Oct. 1675; R. Flynt to Lady Yarmouth, 8 Oct. 1675.

begged the high steward to be patient, assuring him that 'the growth of
the town in shipping and trade will necessarily throw them upon me'.
However, although Paston agreed that it was not yet time for concluding
an agreement with the corporation, he found its leaders 'nibbling' in
negotiations. What Paston really wanted was for 'Mr Fits [Fitch]', the
architect of the Fleet Ditch, to come down from London to boost the
commercial attractiveness of the scheme, and he repeated the request to
his wife after he had just left Yarmouth, noting that 'it is impossible but
I must now reap advantage'.[5] One of his entourage endorsed this view,
observing that an eighty-ship increase in Yarmouth's merchant marine in
the past year would at the very least force the corporation to lease Paston's
lands. Even more encouragingly, another aide revealed that several aldermen had made private overtures to fix terms for Paston's property, with
Sir George England singled out as Paston's 'great honourer'.[6]

The secrecy with which such approaches were made suggested that
suspicions over Paston's plans still lingered among town merchants. Reports from Paston's entourage certainly suggest prior unease within the
viscount's party concerning local opinion on the new high steward. Paston's
attendants were all struck by the unanimity of joyful expressions towards
their master, and one emphatically stated that he 'could not discern the
least shadow of a cloud in the eye of any one person'. For his own part,
Paston must have been as happy to hear that, in spite of the extremely
cordial entertainment, none of his retinue had been the worse the wear
for drink. The presentation of his own interest was as much on trial as the
attitude of the Yarmouth corporation towards him, and right to the end
of the visit he was keen to play the part of the beneficent patron. Paston's
request to pay for the gunners and bell-ringers, the corporation's polite
refusal of this largesse, and his successful renewed offer to tip his hosts'
servants and donate £10 to the town's poor, formed a pantomime of
social graces to aid the attainment of such mutual respect. It was repeated
at both Norwich and Thetford on Paston's triumphal progress through
Norfolk, but at Yarmouth the singing of 'loath to depart' by the corporators as they took leave of him must have seemed that much sweeter in
consideration of past frustrations and hopes of future reward.[7]

---

[5] PL, Paston to wife, 29 Sept., 1 Oct. 1675. For Fitch's Work, see H. Colvin, *Biographical Dictionary of British Architects, 1660–1840* (London, 1978), 308–9.

[6] PL, J. Fisher to Lady Yarmouth, 1 Oct. 1675; R. Flynt to same, 8 Oct. 1675. For
analysis of the town's economic boom of the 1670s, which can be mainly attributed to the
gradual recovery of the herring fishery since the Restoration, see A. Michel, 'Port and Town
of Great Yarmouth . . . 1550–1714', Cambridge Ph.D. 1978, pp. 23–4, table 3.1.

[7] PL, R. Flynt to Lady Yarmouth, 8 Oct. 1675; J. Gough to the same, 1 Oct. 1675.

Paston received further good news in November when the corporation promised to keep in communication with him while they waited for their mutual interests to become 'mature'. In the meantime, he endeavoured to monitor developments in the town by ordering his contacts to keep him informed of Yarmouth opinion on parliamentary affairs. By way of response, the Yarmouth assembly ordered the driving down of mooring piles on the west bank of the haven, thereby indicating a further rapprochement between town and high steward.[8] However, the subsequent elevation of Paston to the lord-lieutenancy of Norfolk on the dismissal of Lord Townshend in February 1676 was not greeted with unanimous enthusiasm by the Yarmouth corporation, despite the likely additional influence which the town might gain from the growing distinction of its high steward. Bower rejoiced to see the downfall of the man he saw as the Nonconformist champion of the county, but Paston's new status threatened to upset the delicate relationship between town and patron. Even though the corporation sent a deputation to congratulate Paston, its members realized only too well that he now had a much more wide-ranging authority, which necessarily plunged him deeper into the governance of the town.[9] Yarmouth's volatility in the very month of Paston's appointment was only too clear, for the Compton census estimated the strength of the town's Dissenting community to be 1,090 members, a sizeable minority of the local population when compared to the 6,466 conformists reported in the parish. If he was to consolidate on his recent peace-making with the corporation, he would have to remain sensitive to the position of this powerful lobby of Dissenters. Bower was already reasserting the militia as a critical support for local Nonconformity; a troubled omen for the new lord-lieutenant. Nevertheless, in the spring of 1676 Paston was quick to use his rising influence to forge a new pathway towards development at Southtown.[10]

---

[8] PL, Yarmouth bailiffs to Paston, 22 Nov. 1675; J. Gough to the same, 29 Nov. 1675; Y/C19/8, f. 233v.

[9] Townshend's fall had been threatening ever since Danby's accession to power, and Paston was an obvious, pro-Anglican, alternative—see J. M. Rosenheim, 'Party Organisation at the Local Level: The Norfolk Sheriff's Subscription of 1676', in *Historical Journal*, 39 (1986), 713–22; Jones, 'The First Whig Party in Norfolk', in *Durham University Journal*, 46 (1953–4), 13–21. However, the previous autumn Paston had temporarily moved into opposition to the ministry in order to prove his worth to the court—R. Davis, 'The Presbyterian Opposition and the Emergence of Party', in C. Jones (ed.), *Party and Management in Parliament, 1660–1784* (Leicester, 1984), 15–16.

[10] *CSPD* 1675–6, pp. 567–8. See A. O. Whiteman (ed.), *The Compton Census* (Oxford, 1986), pp. xxxix, 191, 194. The census also noted five papists at Yarmouth. Most significantly, Anne Whiteman cites Bower's views on the instability on religious allegiance as a

In mid-April Paston played the genial host to a group of eleven Yarmouth councillors at Oxnead, who had come to congratulate him on his recent promotion. In order to ensure both their favour and respect, he allowed them liberty to wander through his highly adorned estate, and after a fine dinner 'set a bottle at each man's trencher'. This hospitality was only to be expected from the King's deputy in the shire, and it did have the intended effect of leaving them 'in stark love and kindness'.[11] Paston had not been slow to forward his plans for Southtown on this occasion, particularly as he was ready to embark on a new scheme on the advice of John Dawson, Yarmouth's customs collector. Dawson proposed that Paston take advantage of a recent rift between the Yarmouth customs house and the corporation, which had arisen over a rent increase imposed by the town on the collectors' headquarters. Customs officials were now renting a private house inconveniently sited for the main town quay and Dawson suggested that Paston should erect a new customs house on the west side of the haven, which, he argued, would act as a catalyst for making Southtown 'built all over'. The attraction of the plan was obvious to Paston, for it could again be marketed as in the King's interest, thereby maintaining his own veneer of public-spiritedness. Just as importantly, it could also be effected through channels of influence with which Paston was most intimately connected. His management of the wood farm had evidently left him thoroughly conversant with the daily workings of the London Customs House, but it was his long-term acquaintance with the current lord treasurer, the Earl of Danby, which promised an effective route towards his goal. A distant kinsman of Danby's, he had befriended the then Sir Thomas Osborne as a young man, and ever since Paston's rise to the lord-lieutenancy, Danby had expressed his full support for him in his new position of authority, most recently on 12 April in person at Holkham. Dawson reckoned that the lord treasurer could 'do it in a word', and offered to build the customs house for Paston as a testament to his confidence in the project.[12]

critical consideration in evaluating the accuracy of the census. Bower usually cited the size of the conventicle to be 2,000-strong, but even the census's lower estimate suggested that 14.4% of local parishioners over 16 were Nonconformist. The Congregational register for the 1670s is too incomplete for any worthwhile calculation to be made upon it. The episcopal visitation of the following year recorded only fifty-two non-church attenders (including two women), 4 Baptists, 3 Quakers, and 2 papists—NRO, VIS 7/3.

[11] PL, Paston to wife, 14 Apr. 1676. For an account and an engraving of Oxnead Hall, see R. Ketton-Cremer, *Norfolk Assembly* (London, 1957), 212–22.

[12] PL, Paston to wife, 12, 14 Apr. 1676. Danby was certainly familiar with Paston's constant scheming—A. Browning (ed.), *Thomas Osborne, Earl of Danby and Duke of Leeds, 1632–1712* (Glasgow, 1944–51), ii. 13.

Paston was quick to adopt Dawson's plan, for he had become increasingly disillusioned with the Yarmouth merchants, whom he thought would 'battle and battle and never do anything'. Encouraged by Dawson's assurance that he already had names of investors ready to start building if the new customs house was erected, Paston wrote to Danby to enlist his direct support for the scheme.[13] However, the lord-lieutenant could not ignore signs of growing political unrest in Yarmouth, which would soon impinge on his financial dealings. Even as he strove to organize the customs house business, his newly established responsibility for the county militia dragged him into the cauldron of local religious conflict which had been threatening to boil over for a decade. The ensuing scandal was not only to destroy Paston's financial hopes, but also to expose the contradictions of his position as Anglican champion, lord-lieutenant, rising courtier, and local entrepreneur. The generally factious nature of Norfolk, which had been recently highlighted by bitter controversy surrounding a county by-election, ensured that his role as the King's deputy was particularly onerous. However, the manner in which he attempted to tackle such widespread problems as Dissent can illuminate the intractability of that issue for all the nation's governors. Several scholars have already gained wider insights by analysing his difficulties, and even a proponent of the 'triumph' of the Restoration gentry felt compelled to qualify his perception of Paston's supremacy in Norfolk, admitting that his control was 'at the mercy of the entanglements of urban politics'.[14]

In May Paston had been forced to confront the problem of Yarmouth Dissent when making his first appointment of militia officers, for loyalist leader Sir Thomas Medowe refused to serve alongside Nonconformist sympathizer Richard Huntington. Most surprisingly, Paston decided to isolate Medowe by promoting allies of Huntington such as Thaxter and the Englands 'to disappoint the other party'. By this puzzling policy of keeping the peace through support for the law-breakers, he thought that the matter would be resolved. He grumbled that Yarmouth's inhabitants were 'the stubbornest, most ill-natured men in the world', but was sure that 'all will be over' once his militia policy had been enforced.[15] He was

---

[13] PL, Paston to wife, 30 Apr. 1676; BL, Egerton mss 3329, f. 111. Significantly, in his letter Paston vacillated between commerce (at Southtown), Nonconformity, and the militia.

[14] A. Fletcher, *Reform in the Provinces* (New Haven, 1986), 340.

[15] PL, Paston to wife, 19, 26 May 1676. Paston's militia regulation may have been designed to gain local support for his Southtown plans, but it is important to note that he applied the same accommodating policy towards his deputy-lieutenants. In contrast to the situation at Yarmouth, Nonconformist deputy-lieutenants withdrew of their own accord, thereby avoiding the contention of a purge—Rosenheim, 'An Examination of Oligarchy', 220–2.

to be proved disastrously wrong when that same faction took offence at a scandalous libel penned on 12 June by the informer Bower, who accused them of lenience towards Dissenting activity. Bower's importance in this affair lay not so much in the revelations themselves, for he had often attacked the Huntington–England–Thaxter group. However, this time he communicated his findings to Paston as well as to Secretary Williamson. Bower had never tried to influence the previous lord-lieutenant, since he believed Lord Townshend to be unsympathetic to the Anglican cause, but he held much better hopes of Paston. By expressing his alarm at militant 2,000-strong conventicles, by stressing the divisiveness of Huntington's refusal to kneel at services in St Nicholas's, and by pinpointing the militia as the basis of Nonconformist power at Yarmouth, Bower had delivered Paston a problem of intimidating magnitude and complexity. Moreover, instead of a peaceful locality where Paston might finally capitalize on his schemes, he found one riddled with division, rendering the establishment of his political or financial interest impossible.[16]

The storm of controversy over Bower's letter broke with great speed within Yarmouth. Only two weeks later Bower noted with alarm that copies of his narrative were circulating the town, as were rumours that Paston 'will take me to task'. However, Paston was already intimating that he would prefer the informer's repentance to 'a dangerous scandal'.[17] Such a hope began to recede rapidly when Thaxter, Huntington, and the Englands wrote to Paston to demand satisfaction against the upstart scandalmonger. From that moment the lord-lieutenant found that balancing the public interest and statute law against local circumstances and private gain was an exceedingly difficult art to master. He had lamented to his wife in May 1676 that 'it's impossible to please all' and his observation was to be proved correct with frustrating and wearying repetition. Reports of local interest in the customs house scheme, when combined with hopeful signs of its acceptance in Whitehall, were heartening tonics for Paston. However, when seeking advice on the problematical Bower issue from one of his favoured attorneys, William Thursby, Paston's doubts were only multiplied.[18]

In his methodical, legalistic manner, Thursby delivered a cautionary

[16] *CSPD* 1676–7, pp. 155–7. M. Kishlansky has rightly stressed the importance of the militia as 'another social connexion', and the Bower affair again suggests that its basic inefficiency should not lead its socio-political significance to be overlooked – *Parliamentary Selection* (Cambridge, 1986), 151–5.
[17] *CSPD* 1676–7, pp. 179–80; PL, Paston to wife, 17 June 1676.
[18] PL, Paston to wife, 19 May 1676.

verdict on the likely effectiveness of the informer's defence. First of all, he delineated Bower's three most damaging allegations, identifying them as slurs against the town magistrates for leniency towards conventicles, against the town militia officers for their records of Cromwellian service, and against Sir William D'Oyly for influencing Paston to neglect 'the Church party'. Encouragingly for Paston, he thought that any Privy Council hearing would deliver a 'smart check' to Bower for his scandalous words against local officials. However, he then queried whether Bower might not be able to justify himself with regard to the local conventicles and the presence of commonwealthsmen in the militia hierarchy. Thursby noted that it was 'impossible to be otherwise' that in every local magistracy there were always incumbents who had served under the usurped regimes, and that even in the most vigilant towns Nonconformists continued to thrive. His observations highlighted the contingent success of penal legislation in the Restoration period, and it is particularly significant that he was ready to express such views to a royal deputy in confidence. Thursby, in fact, noted that the king and Privy Council had 'unhappily' taken note of the growing dispute, but the only reassurance he offered Paston was that Bower was 'too mean a fellow' to damage his reputation as lord-lieutenant. It was obvious that Bower had hit a raw nerve of Restoration society, and Thursby had not underestimated the potency of such charges in difficult times.[19]

A week after receiving this letter Paston could only comment that 'all is so uncertain in this world'. Desperate to avoid a damaging public scandal, he urged the Yarmouth magistracy to close down Bower's coffee-house for unlicensed sales of alcohol. The order was carried out, vindicating Bower's own conviction that economic intimidation was the most reliable force in Yarmouth society.[20] Within a few weeks Paston learnt that Giles Dunster, a surveyor of customs, had agreed to support his customs house plan and would represent it in the capital after his circuit of port inspections. Paston now had six weeks in which to organize an effective lobby at the Customs House to press his scheme, and, as a first step, ordered Yarmouth's magistrates to bind Bower over for his insolent narratives. They needed little encouragement here, causing the

---

[19] PL, Thursby to Paston, 20 July 1676. These comments certainly help to explain the half-heartedness of Paston's predecessor, Viscount Townshend, whose problems had been even more demanding in the immediate Restoration period.

[20] As Sir Thomas Medowe had remarked on his loyalist initiatives in November 1664, 'factions and trade unite to lay rubbs in the way'—Raynham House archive, boxfile, 1st Visct. Townshend, misc. corresp. 1650s–1687.

informer to hurry to London in the hope that his correspondent Sir Joseph Williamson would ensure a fair trial at the forthcoming Yarmouth quarter-sessions. Williamson himself needed all his diplomatic skills to avoid the matter being broached at the Privy Council, for the Yarmouth magistrates, as supported by Paston, were eager for a hearing there. The town's quarter-sessions subsequently bound over Bower for a second time, leaving the Huntington group to gloat that 'it is ill dallying with sharp-edged tools'. With the full backing of urban, county, and national authorities behind them, they were now confident that the Bower affair had decisively swung in their favour.[21]

Paston shared their delight at Bower's humiliation, but his financial enterprise was not going to plan. Although commissioners began to inspect and appoint lawful quays at Yarmouth and Southtown in October, the goal of the new customs house, on which his greater hopes pivoted, was lost. No precise explanation for the failure of the scheme can be given, but official misgivings over the cost of a great extension of customs activity at Yarmouth, aired by William Montagu, chief baron of the Exchequer, probably proved the greatest stumbling-block.[22] The viscount immediately reverted to his previous project of simply leasing his west bank to the town, and, encouraged by Huntington's recent election to the position of senior bailiff, he made a direct approach to the corporation. In order to accelerate proceedings, Paston sent a gift of a Michaelmas doe to Huntington, who in turn requested a set of proposals and supporting reasons for presentation to the next assembly meeting. However, the bailiff did warn him that some of his 'friends' had aired grave doubts concerning the town's ability to pay the touted annual rental of £1,000. Moreover, the general discord caused by the Bower affair was cited as a major obstacle to any long-term agreement. One of Paston's agents cautioned his master in similar terms after interviewing Huntington on 18 October, reporting that 'when Bower's business is over, some proposals may be made to your lord which will be supported by Huntington'. The informer continued to campaign for himself in the name of the Anglican Church, perpetuating a dispute which the lord-lieutenant would have preferred to see quietly resolved. Most worryingly for Paston, the Yarmouth magistrates continued to press Paston to provide some public

[21] PL, G. Dunster to Lord Danby, 10 Aug. 1676; Yarmouth magistrates to Paston, 25 Sept. 1676. For a much more detailed analysis of this episode, see P. Gauci, 'The Urban Perspective in Early Modern England', Oxford M.Phil. 1988, pp. 75–9.

[22] Montagu had first aired such doubts to Paston on 14 Aug.—see PL, Montagu to Paston. For the Exchequer commission's report, see PRO, E178/6367.

forum, preferably the Privy Council, at which to vindicate their own reputation, always emphasizing that they were working on the 'just principle' of maintaining local government and order.[23]

Bower, for his own part, concentrated on trying to win a sympathetic hearing from Williamson over the closure of his coffee-selling business. Having described his coffee-house as the place where 'the divisions he makes are the common topic', the Yarmouth magistrates were understandably reticent to grant Bower a licence, reflecting a widely prevalent governing attitude towards these still-novel centres for news and debate.[24] Yet, even in the corner in which he perceived himself to be, Bower continued to assess the strength of his enemies with clarity, supplying Williamson with an account of the marital ties binding the leading Yarmouth townsfolk together. In particular, he lamented how his affair had been monopolized by the familial network of Thaxter, Huntington, and the Englands, and observed how 'they want no will to take my life'.[25] As winter set in at Yarmouth, the issues of religious division, magisterial leniency, and urban development were all unresolved. However, given their indissoluble linkages, Paston was not able to master them individually, and was forced to use his authority to settle them all. Procrastination, while there were such pressures from all sides to advance their respective causes, was likely to achieve only further discontent; conversely, the sensitivity of local circumstances argued against decisive external interference. The New Year therefore promised more unrest, and Paston found to his cost that such divisions could severely limit his local influence and his entrepreneurial interest.

In February 1677 Yarmouth delivered a pointed reminder to its high steward that his local authority was conditioned by his utility to the town, whatever his standing at court. In that month Paston made an official approach to the Yarmouth corporation for a lease of his Southtown lands, and caused a rare adjournment in assembly proceedings. The offer of a ninety-nine-year lease, presumably at an annual rental of around £1,000 which Paston had sought the previous October, was thus given the town's 'full deliberation'. However, the bailiffs informed Paston a week later that the 'expected improvement is beyond the purses and credit' of the town,

---

[23] PL, J. Doughty to Paston, 2, 9, and 18 Oct. 1676, Yarmouth magistrates to Paston, 25 Sept. 1676; *CSPD* 1676–7, p. 382.

[24] PL, Yarmouth magistrates to Paston, 6 Oct. 1676. For a discussion of government policy towards the coffee-houses, see B. Lillywhite, *London Coffee-Houses* (London, 1963), 17–22.

[25] *CSPD* 1676–7, p. 366. For the familial links within the England–Huntington–Thaxter group, see Appendices 4 and 5.

and, as if to emphasize their financial worries, they implored his aid to obtain a supply for the maintenance of the now-repaired havenmouth piers. They cleverly pointed out that Paston himself could only gain by an act of Parliament which would maintain the commercial viability of his own side of the haven, but the snub to him was obvious.[26] To reject his proposals and yet ask for his influence speaks volumes for the apparent confidence of the town, but the bold diplomacy of the assembly towards its high steward was vindicated, for he did accede to the request. However, the corporators also approached the out-of-favour Lord Townshend to bolster their campaign, evidently unsure of Paston's reliability, and aware that the former lord-lieutenant was eager to gain support against his rival.[27]

Such caution was well advised, for the swift passage of the second Haven Act through Parliament masked the direct hostility of the Norwich corporation, which had also enlisted the support of Lord Townshend over this issue. However, the Norwich assembly achieved little through their lobbying, and again had to settle for an annual grant of £50 to maintain the navigability of the Yare. A jubilant Yarmouth corporation voted in April to thank Paston for steering the bill through the House of Lords, but such amicability was obviously strained by the disappointment he had received in February. His valuable service for the corporation on this occasion demonstrated that even the disgruntled peer acknowledged a sense of responsibility for his position in authority. The competition offered by his rival Townshend was undoubtedly a key consideration here, and the town was equally keen to praise Townshend's contribution, noting that the bill's 'speedy dispatch' came 'through the assistance we had from friends in the management thereof, which must be in a great measure imputed to your lordship's influence and mediation in our behalf'. Paston knew that he had to maintain local support by his good offices in the capital, just as surely as the assembly leaders recognized that their loyalty had a price. It was a dangerous game for any borough to secure favours by playing off local magnates against each other, especially as it could easily jeopardize longer term interests. In Yarmouth's case,

---

[26] PL, B. England and R. Huntington to Paston, 26 Feb. 1677. For a contemporaneous example of corporate intransigence towards noble patrons, note the policy of the Leicester assembly towards Lords Huntingdon and Rutland—C. Stephenson and F. Marcham (eds.), *Sources for English Constitutional History* (London, 1938), 596; Henning, *House of Commons, 1660–90*, i. 296–8.

[27] Only two years before, a report suggested that Townshend still had backers at Yarmouth, most notably Sir James Johnson, a leading Nonconformist sympathizer—Raynham House archive, boxfile, Visct. Townshend's misc. corresp. 1650s–1687.

prudence prevailed on both sides, and an open rupture between town and patron was avoided for the time being.[28]

Relations between town and patron had certainly cooled. The Bower controversy continued to simmer as the informant unsuccessfully tried to arrange a Privy Council hearing though the agency of Williamson, and by the summer of 1677 tension between Yarmouth and its high steward had increased thanks to a new source of contention. From July the Yarmouth corporation proceeded to auction off the only undeveloped site within the old town, a narrow belt of land some two-thirds of a mile in length, known locally as the Deneside. The hard-pressed corporation ultimately raised £2,260 from this sale, all the purchasers coming from Yarmouth itself.[29] Paston could only have seen the Deneside development as a major blow to his hopes for investment at Southtown, for it absorbed residual demand among Yarmouth merchants for building space. He quickly signalled his displeasure by refusing the assembly permission to place mooring piles at his west bank for the fishing season, and although both sides agreed to go to arbitration to resolve their differences, nothing was resolved before the New Year. By that time an additional urgency had been instilled into the dispute through the death of Yarmouth MP Sir William D'Oyly, in the wake of which the town became 'full of noise' at the prospect of an imminent by-election. Most significantly, it would give Bower an opportunity to recall some of his favourite political themes as Richard Huntington competed against Sir Thomas Medowe for the vacant seat. After an interval of sixteen years without a parliamentary election, local factions would obviously see the poll as an opportunity to test their strength, permitting them to focus the attention of the Yarmouth freeman body on the issues which had for so long divided the town.[30]

Unfortunately, narratives of this, and the succeeding elections of 1679–81, are relatively sparse, and are overwhelmingly loyalist in character. However, even as vituperative a commentator as Bower can provide valuable information concerning the political motivation of the Yarmouth

[28] *CJ*, ix. 399–421; *LJ*, xiii. 109–20; *HMC Townshend*, 29; Swinden, *History of Great Yarmouth*, 910–12; PL, Yarmouth bailiffs to Paston, 20 Apr. 1677. Note the limited success of Stamford when attempting to shake off Cecil domination in the 1670s—C. Holmes, *Seventeenth-Century Lincolnshire* (Lincoln, 1980), 36. Even modestly sized towns such as Clitheroe could maintain some electoral independence by exploiting the rivalry of local magnates—M. A. Mullett, 'Men of Known Loyalty: The Politics of the Lancashire Borough of Clitheroe 1660–89', in *Northern History*, 21 (1985), 108–36.
[29] Y/C19/8, ff. 255, 256, 258, 264. For the deeds of the sale, see Y/C18/7, ff. 76–108. Thirteen plots were sold by September 1677, the smallest £54 in value, the largest £122.
[30] Y/C19/8, f. 264v; *CSPD 1677–8*, p. 496

electorate prior to the Exclusion crisis. He certainly acknowledged the resourcefulness of his rivals, for he condemned several of their under-hand electioneering tactics, which included threats against the trades of poor freemen, and an attempt to create fifty new freemen at the assembly immediately prior to the election. More significantly, he concluded that the election essentially revolved around the question of 'a Church or no Church', thereby displaying the fundamental importance of the Dissent-ing issue in the minds of local voters. The loyalist cause, however, re-ceived little help from Paston, who was concentrating on a simultaneous by-election at Norwich, for which his son, Sir William, was to stand successfully. Yet it is doubtful whether he could have played a decisive role at Yarmouth, for as early as December it was reported that 'the townsmen will not hear of any stranger'. Interestingly, such wariness towards outsiders mirrored the response of other corporations during by-elections to the Cavalier Parliament. In 1673 the York assembly had rejected the candidacy of the son of Lord Treasurer Latimer (later Danby), observing that it ''twas thought fit to choose one of our own body'. Latimer sarcastically replied that it was 'the first time that any man's interest was thought equal to the lord treasurer's in promoting of trade in England', but he did not prevail. Two years later he was less forthright when assisting the campaign of his son-in-law at King's Lynn, and his entreaty found greater success, the corporation having thanked him for 'nobly leaving them their freedom in electing . . . without which they cannot be said to send representatives to Parliament'. If a magnate of the stature of Danby had to tread carefully when trying to manage a large borough, then Paston, who had recently shown great insensitivity to local opinion, could only have proved an electoral liability for the Yarmouth loyalists.[31]

Betraying a weariness with the hard-headedness of the town's cor-poration, Paston actually confessed that he did not care much for either Yarmouth candidate. On the same day as he imparted such views to his wife, the assembly were preparing to send its fourth deputation to nego-tiate the haven matter with him, but little progress was expected whilst the town's political future was in the balance. As election day drew nearer Paston reluctantly chose to back Medowe, but only because Sir Thomas was likely to bring some fifty voters for his son's election at Norwich. News of Medowe's victory by fifteen votes reached Oxnead on 13 Feb-ruary, permitting Bower to exult that 'the old tribe are now so disheart-

---

[31] *CSPD* 1677–8, pp. 496, 531, 555–6, 559; Henning, *House of Commons, 1660–90*, i. 328, 489–90.

ened'. However, far from heralding an era of dominance for Yarmouth's loyalist Anglicans, the election only served to stir up local divisions. Worryingly for Paston, the defeated factions sought to compensate for their electoral reverse by resuming proceedings against Bower for his narrative of June 1676.[32]

As informant, Bower had maintained a continuity between the divisiveness of his current neighbours and that of the Cromwellian period, but in March 1678 it was the turn of the magistrates to perpetuate that vein of contention by insisting on satisfaction for their slighted reputations. Bower reacted in his accustomed manner by sending Williamson a full narrative of Nonconformist activity in Yarmouth since the early 1660s, and expressed his long-held fear for the outcome of a local trial, currently set for the ensuing Thetford assizes. However, in an unexpectedly decisive move, Paston used his local authority to contain the growing controversy. Despite the severe misgivings of Thaxter and Huntington, he persuaded them to cancel the trial at Thetford by promising to stand personally for their reputations, hoping that moderation would yet save a scandal. He also directed Williamson to control Bower's outbursts, but these initiatives did not secure Paston's interest in the town. Unlike the Yarmouth magistrates, Paston did not face the 'insolences' of Bower as he left for his abortive trip to Thetford, and with similar irresolution remaining over the haven issue, the high steward had far from defused a potentially explosive situation.[33]

Proof of the polarization of local society by mid-July 1678 was provided by Sir Thomas Medowe, who drew up a list of 'the loyal' and 'the faction' for the benefit of Secretary Williamson. Significantly, Medowe was concerned not only to record the allegiance of seventy assemblymen, but also that of ninety-four other townsmen, all of whom were freemen. This list was a logical progression from Bower's narratives and testimonials in the loyalist cause over the course of the previous thirteen years, but it gave the clearest evidence of the strength of local division on the eve of the discovery of the Popish plot. His survey revealed a healthy majority of loyalists within the assembly, but, disturbingly for his own allies, a preponderance of factious opponents outside.[34] Most significantly, the factious non-assemblymen betrayed a strong Nonconformist character,

[32] PL, Paston to wife, 14 Jan. 1678; J. Hildeyard to Lady Paston, 13 Feb. 1678; *CSPD* 1678, pp. 1–2, 9–10; Y/C19/8, ff. 264, 265, 270. For the Norwich by-election and the ensuing inconclusive battle over the control of aldermanic bench, see J. T. Evans, *Seventeenth-Century Norwich* (Oxford, 1979), 252–67. [33] *CSPD* 1678, pp. 20–2, 45.
[34] PRO, SP29/408, f. 121. Medowe recorded a loyalist majority of 49 to 21 within the assembly itself, thereby supporting Bower's recent argument that a Nonconformist tactic to

for no less than twenty-four of them were former councillors who had been ousted during previous purges. Long-term divisions thus continued to influence the formation of local groupings, and the very identity of the list's compiler suggested an increased tempo of conflict within the town. Given the generally volatile state of Norfolk, government officials like Williamson evidently wished to quell local factionalism. However, even though showing moderation over the Bower issue, Paston was still determined to vindicate his exclusive right to lay down mooring piles on the west side of the haven. In August 1678 he wrote a frank letter to the corporation to announce that, regretfully, he was to begin legal proceedings against the town.[35]

At this point Paston once again revealed his readiness to compromise loyalist principles for reasons of self-interest, for his decision to force the haven issue largely negated one of the greatest Anglican advances in Yarmouth since the Restoration. At an assembly on 23 August Sir Thomas Medowe had managed to overcome the opposition of the current senior bailiff, John Woodroffe, to pass an order enforcing the taking of the Anglican sacrament as a qualification for the freedom of the town. It was an audacious move to introduce a local Test Act, but its successful implementation would have at a stroke cut the political and economic power of Yarmouth's Dissenters. However, within a week the corporation felt obliged to utilize the negotiating experience of Nonconformist sympathizers Sir James Johnson, George England, and Huntington in an attempt to persuade Paston to settle their differences via arbitration. Pragmatism had thus prevailed over ideology, but not even the factious leaders could bring about an accord with Paston. Subsequent meetings only hardened the points of difference between town and patron, and the latter eventually decided to take the law into his own hands.[36]

On 29 September three of Paston's menservants set about the removal of the town's mooring posts on the west bank, only to be apprehended by a party of townsmen under the direction of bailiff Woodroffe. He took

confine the parliamentary franchise to the assembly would not have prevented a loyalist victory—*CSPD* 1677–8, p. 625. Medowe's survey suggested that the faction held sway outside the assembly by 68 to 26.

[35] PL, Paston to Yarmouth bailiffs, 11 Aug. 1678. For the county's political tensions, see J. M. Rosenheim, 'An Examination of Oligarchy', 213–51; V. L. Slater, 'Continuity and Change in English Provincial Politics: Robert Paston in Norfolk, 1675–83', in *Albion*, 25 (1993), 193–216.

[36] Y/C19/8, ff. 281, 283; *CSPD* 1678, p. 347. Paston was particularly antagonized by the corporation's claim that the incorporation of 1668 permitted the ships of both Yarmouth and Southtown to moor at either bank.

them back over the Yare bridge, formally charged them with criminal damage, and threw them into jail. An emergency assistance was then called, which approved the bailiff's actions and methodically prepared for Paston's retaliation, politely informing him of their actions, and notifying the recorder to organize the town's defence once more. Bower attributed these gathering storm-clouds to the erection of twenty houses on the Deneside in the past month, which offered a physical rebuke to Paston's own plans for development at Southtown. The assembly temporarily forgot its religious divisions, ordering piles to be set down on the west bank, and answering the delivery of a writ from Paston in late October with the election of a sizeable committee to 'manage the business . . . until the same be tried'. Having drawn its ranks, the town was ready to give its high steward proof of its obdurate powers of defence, and in the succeeding months its commitment to the Southtown issue was sufficiently strong to condition the impact of national political upheaval on the locality.[37]

Taken together, Bower's letters and the assembly's general handling of its representatives in London clearly demonstrate that the town was never slow to gather information concerning national events, and though it was the Paston affair which dominated local interest at this time, the Popish plot and ensuing Exclusion crisis did make a firm impression in Yarmouth. In late 1678 a local merchant was chastised for spreading rumours that Dutch arms were being shipped via Yarmouth to Ireland for the use of papist insurrectionists, and Bower also reported that thirty Dutchmen were interrogated on arrival at the port under suspicion of being Jesuits.[38] Such incidents suggest that the town was seized by an anti-Catholic hysteria leading up to the parliamentary elections of February 1679, and Bower indeed observed that Sir Thomas Medowe was seen to be in danger of losing support as 'a friend to the Duke of York's interest'. However, the attacks made by his rival candidates indicate that the poll was not solely dominated by the succession issue, and that the Yarmouth electorate was not motivated by purely ideological arguments. Most significantly, Medowe's opponents were the familiar group of Nonconformist sympathizers—Huntington, Thaxter, George England (son of the knight), and Sir James Johnson—who derived continuing

---

[37] Y/C19/8, ff. 285–8; *CSPD* 1678, p. 421. Paston evidently wished to make a deliberately emphatic point by removing the mooring posts on one of the major days in the civic calendar. His current standing in the capital impressed Henry Savile, who described him as 'no small' figure in the House of Lords—*HMC Bath*, 162.

[38] *CSPD* 1678, pp. 500, 509, 557–8. Significantly, the notebook of a Yarmouth customs officer, William Jackson, dated 1715, is full of transcriptions from political propaganda of the 1678–81 period—see CUL, Oo. 6. 115, ff. 71–84.

support from the 'partial conformists'. Their principal target remained Medowe, for they realized that Sir William Coventry's outstanding value as a parliamentarian and government official would make him a fairly automatic selection, should he wish to stand. Moreover, Bower noted that Medowe's enemies were seeking to undermine his candidacy by spreading rumours that the loyal candidate had been responsible for supplying information which had incriminated three local merchants for contravening temporary trading restrictions. These allegations were seen as a 'great prejudice' to Medowe's chances, and Bower urged Williamson to clear him of any responsibility for the prosecution of these men, recognizing that commercial interests had an important part to play in so tight a contest. A truculent Paston exerted little influence on the election, contemptuously referring to Medowe's opponents as 'not worth naming'. However, he did think it would be 'soundly tugged by both parties, [they] being confident of their own strength'.[39]

The lack of any poll figures for the first election of 1679 is particularly disappointing, for it would have been interesting to discover if any changes had occurred in local political groupings since Medowe's list of the preceding July. Despite their absence, Medowe's assessment of the strength of the 'faction' outside of the assembly was seemingly endorsed by the election on 20 February 1679, since Huntington successfully ousted Medowe to be returned alongside Sir William Coventry. The result can certainly be seen as a victory for local Dissenters and their allies, but the immediate relevance of economic issues argues against the application of too pure an ideological divide to this specific contest. Coventry's election was even made against his will, and the corporation was willing to spend £45 to secure his services, displaying a unity which was sadly lacking over the choice of the other Yarmouth Member.[40] Furthermore, local divisions could boast a continuity which spanned the whole Restoration period, not just the immediate emergency which Oates and Shaftesbury were seen to have created. Parliamentary elections were key events in establishing the course and 'pace' of local politics, but there were numerous other opportunities in the civic calendar for skirmishes to occur. For example, within a few weeks of the election the choice of a new curate had focused reli-

---

[39] *CSPD* 1679–80, pp. 65–6; Add. mss 28621, f. 35.

[40] Y/C27/2, fiscal year 1678/9. Coventry's possible retirement, as well as irregularities in his election of February 1679, are reported in Bodl. Carte mss 103, ff. 221–2. His unwillingness to sit in the Commons was noted after the election, as was the House's unwillingness to part with this able member—see H. C. Foxcroft (ed.), *The Life and Letters of Sir George Savile, Marquess of Halifax* (London, 1898), i. 141.

gious tensions once more. In some contrast to the parliamentary election, the loyalists in the assembly fought a successful campaign in support of Luke Milbourne, and he subsequently repaid them by uncompromising leadership in the cause of the established Church. The town might thus be decisively influenced by parliamentary elections and national issues, but local politics also possessed an independent timetable and agenda.[41]

Paston himself was too dismissive of the Yarmouth candidates, and too busy organizing the loyalist effort in the county election, to exert any influence on the borough. Although taking note of the choice of Coventry and Huntington, he showed far more interest in his forthcoming hearing for the haven issue at the Bury assizes. He was already anxious at the cost of the protracted dispute, and he rued that if he carried the trial he would be 'quits with Yarmouth favours', displaying a frustration born in the hopes raised and dashed since his election to the high stewardship. He initially scorned to use any influence with the assize judge, but by late March, when further burdened by an inquiry into his electioneering prior to the recent Norfolk poll, he thought it prudent to send gifts of fish to the Lord Chief Baron in order to prepare some ground for the Bury hearing. Yarmouth itself sent six representatives to argue its case, and, by including Nonconformist sympathizers such as Woodroffe alongside loyalists like Thomas Gooch, reiterated its united stance over issues which threatened the town's interest so directly. However, the Bury hearing produced no conclusive result.[42]

Such irresolution was in some contrast to the outlook of the Yarmouth electorate, for at the parliamentary contest of August 1679 the Nonconformists made even further gains at the expense of the loyalists. Richard Huntington managed to keep his seat, and his ally George England secured the spot vacated by the retiring Sir William Coventry. Medowe was again the loser in the loyalist cause, and there is no evidence to suggest that he received any significant aid from High Steward Paston. Indeed, the presence of two local men in Parliament accurately represented the town's aggressive stance against external interference at this time, and Paston must be held largely responsible for the eclipse of the Anglican cause at Yarmouth. He might have been elevated to an earldom six weeks before for his loyalist services in Norfolk, but no added dignity was likely to intimidate the assembly into submission over the haven

---

[41] Y/C19/8, f. 294. Milbourne secured the approval of at least thirty-seven assemblymen.

[42] PL, Paston to wife, 24, 26 Feb., and 29 Mar. 1679; Y/C19/8, ff. 292v, 301–2v.

issue. The corporation was even prepared to consider a lease of his lands as a sign of their willingness to reach a compromise, but obviously at an insufficient rental, for another meeting at Norwich in late September broke up with no agreement in sight.[43]

This stalemate was eventually to see in another New Year with little leeway given by either side. Although the assembly strengthened its negotiating committee in the spring of 1680, it was only through the personal mediation of its recorder, Sir Robert Baldock, that articles of agreement were eventually drawn up. By that time Paston had started proceedings against Yarmouth in the Court of Common Pleas, and it was his readiness to withdraw his action of trespass in that court which forged the path towards a settlement. For its part, the corporation agreed to remove the mooring piles which had sparked so much controversy, though it sought to minimize the loss of quay space by adding new posts to the southern stretches of its own riverbank, beyond the town walls. These delicate negotiations were in the balance right up to August 1680, but the willingness of the town to spend some £160 on defence costs in the previous year highlighted its determination to neutralize the Paston threat. From Paston's perspective, the defence of his rights in Southtown had left him with few illusions over the extent of local opposition to his plans. The battle had also obstructed any effective campaigning for the loyalist cause in Yarmouth while Paston remained in conflict with the town, a dereliction in political duty which stands in great contrast to his successful campaigning at the Norwich elections of the Exclusion period.[44]

However, it seems doubtful whether Yarmouth's dominant mercantile élite could yet be dragooned into organized parties, or even temporarily politicized into pro- and anti-Exclusionist groups. A loyalist group of Anglican hardliners had clearly taken advantage of the Exclusion crisis to advance their cause, viewing the frequent parliamentary elections as an opportunity to expose magisterial lenience towards local Dissenters. Despite the advantage which the loyalists held in the assembly, the strength of the Nonconformists and their local allies within the freeman body proved too great for them, and in January 1681 no serious opposition was

[43] Y/C19/8, f. 302v. M. Knights notes that at this time election propaganda urged voters not to choose anyone tainted by association with the court—'Politics and Opinion during the Exclusion Crisis', pp. 172–3.

[44] Y/C19/8, ff. 310v, 312, 316v, 319; Y/C19/9, f. 4; Add. mss 27447, f.485; Evans, *Seventeenth-Century Norwich*, 267–77. Papers from the Chancery hearing in 1678–9 survive at the PRO—C10/195/5. The actual agreement between the two parties, by which the town agreed to pay £122 towards Paston's costs, can be found in the Arundel Castle archive, Norfolk House document, packet 27.

raised against the return of Sir James Johnson and George England to the Oxford Parliament. Fortunately, Johnson's victory speech to the Yarmouth freemen survives, and its text reflects the interplay of local and central issues which had such a decisive influence on the fate of the borough's seats. For certain, Johnson saw cause to bring his audience's attention to the great political issues of the day, expressing his desire to uphold 'the true Protestant religion', to secure the King's safety, and to preserve the 'tranquillity and peace' of the kingdom. However, the predominant theme of his oration was his promise to act 'for this poor town, for its prosperity, for the well being of it, and if it were possible, for every individual in it'. In particular, he praised the utility of his fellow Member George England, whom he lauded as 'so worthy a personage, whose knowledge, whose ability, and whose experience in employments of this nature may hereafter be of great use and advantage to me'. The manner in which previous MPs had been managed by the town suggested that they had little option but to represent Yarmouth's interests to the best of their abilities. Awareness of such responsibilities cautions the automatic application of party labels to local politicians, and the speech's generalized tone warns against categorizing men and events too conveniently.[45]

Paston would certainly have agreed with this wary approach, having served for five years as one of the town's senior representatives. Indeed, it took a significant change of heart on the part of his political masters in the capital to stiffen his resolve. Only in the aftermath of the court's victory at the Oxford Parliament would he dare to influence the town's political course, and even then he was heavily dependent on the bullishness of local contacts to play such an effective role. Although the corporation had remained broadly loyalist in outlook during the Exclusion crisis, Anglican hardliners within its membership had been unable to gain control of assembly policy, and it was soon apparent that they regarded the dissolution of the Oxford Parliament as a long-awaited opportunity to go on the offensive. Their views were clearly expressed in May 1681 when the assembly ordered an address to the crown to thank the King for his recent proclamation, rejoicing to see 'the preservation of the Protestant religion as now established by law', and the downfall of 'all popish and schismatical rogues'. However, they had rarely displayed such confidence

---

[45] Swinden, *History of Great Yarmouth*, 949–50. The cessation of Bower's reports after March 1679, evidently caused by Williamson's removal from the secretaryship in December 1678, is a sad loss, especially as it leaves the resolution of his struggle with the Yarmouth magistrates in doubt (if any occurred). The assembly were quick to block Bower's admission to freemen ranks in August 1684—Y/C19/9, f. 70.

over the previous five years, and loyalist leaders must have prayed that the crown and its deputies would be more consistent in support of their cause. Even as rabid a loyalist as curate Luke Milbourne could recognize the strength of his opponents, for he would later accuse Dissenters of having employed 'fair and plausible pretences, and sometimes justifiable subtleties, to make the votes of the populace concur with their own desires'. Yet, if the crown was at last prepared to confront its enemies, then there was hope for the loyalists that genuine political change was at hand. Having presented the Yarmouth address to the King, Paston himself acknowledged that his relationship with the town had reached an important watershed, observing, with a personal significance, that it was the first service which he had performed for the town at court.[46]

The controversies of 1676–81 had shown that the interplay of town, county, and national interest was a complex meeting of influence. A courtier's private gain, the issue of magisterial negligence, or the desperate electioneering of competing factions were all powerful considerations when evaluating the town's stability at any one moment. However, credit must also be given to the corporation as a pole of order amid so much strife. The pace of local politics was often determined by central events, and national issues had a significant impact on the Yarmouth consciousness, but such influences were far from passively received. Having experienced twenty years of contention at first hand, town leaders needed little guidance in forming opinions upon the great issues of Church and State, nor did they need lecturing on the importance of healing and settling.[47] Yarmouth's development demonstrates that the Exclusion crisis cannot be treated as the simple orchestration of Shaftesbury's London powerbrokers, and the town's subsequent response to the 'Tory reaction' also warns against oversimplifying the ease of the royal triumph. Central government could obviously impinge more effectively than any one of its deputies on the provincial arena, but such encroachment was still conditioned by local circumstances. Paston might enjoy the favour of Yarmouth for the first time since Michaelmas 1675, but it was while acting in its service that he did so, as the town strove to determine its course through the upheavals of another turbulent Stuart decade.

---

[46] Y/C19/9, ff. 12, 20; L. Milbourne, *The Origin of Rebellion* [1683].

[47] Significantly, in the fiscal year 1678/9 the corporation was prepared to pay for troops 'when the election was', an expenditure which could have been applied to either of the parliamentary contests of February or August 1679. However, the assembly made no such payments for the 1681 election, which marked the climax to the Exclusion campaign—Y/C27/2.

5

Regulation and Revolution: 1681–88

DURING the 1680s the crown subjected local government to the most sustained intervention of the Stuart period, culminating in James II's premeditated campaign to pack Parliament with supporters amenable to his control. The boroughs took the brunt of the royal attack, and historians have recognized the mass surrender of charters and the successive purges of the corporate benches as key elements of the court's struggle to subdue opposition. However, recent work on the 'Tory reaction' of the last years of Charles's reign has raised questions concerning the aims of government policy towards the corporations, and has credited local leaders with a greater role in determining the political complexion of their communities.[1] Most importantly, recent studies of provincial politics have highlighted widespread opposition to the regulation of the boroughs. Hitherto, such resistance has been overlooked as scholars assumed that the flood of charter surrenders bespoke the meekness of the provinces to the royal will. Although the court's opponents failed to save the charters, the provincial response to central intervention merits closer attention to illuminate the issues which divided fellow townsmen in the crucial run-up to the Revolution.[2]

Yarmouth's experience was no different from the vast majority of English boroughs during this time of upheaval. Although its leaders were of the generation which had suffered the central intrusion of the early

[1] R. Pickavance, 'The English Boroughs and the King's Government: A Study of the Tory Reaction, 1681–5', Oxford D.Phil. 1976, esp. pp. 228–41; J. Miller, 'The Crown and the Borough Charters in the Reign of Charles II', in *EHR* 100 (1985), 53–84. For local studies, see C. Lee, 'Fanatic Magistrates: Religious and Political Conflict in Three Kent Boroughs, 1680–84', in *HJ* 35 (1992), 43–61; M. A. Mullett, 'Conflict, Politics, and Elections in Lancaster, 1660–88', in *Northern History*, 19 (1983), 61–86; J. Kirby, 'Restoration Leeds and the Aldermen of the Corporation, 1661–1700' in ibid. 22 (1986), 150–1.

[2] The need for research on the boroughs during the 1680s is still evident some twenty years after J. R. Jones identified them as an essential area of study for understanding the upheavals of that time—*The Revolution of 1688 in England* (London, 1972), 142–3. However, see the constituency articles in Henning, *House of Commons, 1660–90*, i. *passim*. Even those few, fortunate boroughs which did keep their charters throughout the 1680s, such as Southampton, could not ignore the implications of crown policy for their future development—see A. T. Patterson, *History of Southampton* (Southampton, 1966), i. 13.

Restoration period, even they were unprepared for the thoroughness of the purges of that decade. The expulsion of large numbers of assembly-men clearly failed to have its intended effect, and royal regulators found that their draconian methods only caused further unrest. Some local loyalists actually welcomed the royal onslaught, but repeated crown inter-vention inevitably provoked a hostile response from Yarmouth leaders of all political opinions. Indeed, the development of political groupings after 1681 cannot be interpreted simply as a conflict between 'Whigs' and 'Tories', for controversial issues such as the surrender of the charter altered allegiances at critical points. Most significantly, even in as highly a politicized society as Yarmouth's, where rival factions were keen to anticipate central events, it was not until February 1684 that the terms of 'Whig' or 'Tory' came to be used by a local figure. Yarmouth politi-cians continued to apply the labels of 'the loyal', 'the faction', or even the 'commonwealthsmen', thereby echoing the importance of longer-term divisions. Since the Restoration local differences had principally revolved around religion, but royal policies, particularly those of James II, even managed to confuse the townsmen's loyalties over that contentious issue. The committed core of the respective Anglican and Nonconformist par-ties certainly made hay as they took turns to bask temporarily in the sunshine of royal favour, but it would be wrong to polarize the whole of the local élite. Even though central intervention encouraged fluid political loyalties, the extremities to which the crown was prepared to go to secure support worked to unify the townsmen against it. In particular, local con-cern for traditional rights of self-government helped to rally opposition against the perceived threat of an increasingly absolutist regime.

In the immediate aftermath of the Oxford Parliament the town's lead-ers clearly had more on their minds than politics. When a visitor to Yarmouth in May 1681 discussed current affairs with some of the port's leading Nonconformist sympathizers, including the Englands and Hun-tington, economic, not political, problems dominated debate. 'The town, as some persons of quality told me, is now over-built or too numerous in shipping, so that they are now at a loss for want of trade', the traveller observed, identifying the pivotal importance of the haven to local devel-opment.[3] Of course, an end to Yarmouth's commercial boom of the 1670s further complicated Paston's role as local patron, and he was well aware that for the sake of his local interest he had to avoid controversy over

---

[3] *HMC Portland*, ii. 267–8. It is significant that these Nonconformist sympathizers were seen socializing together in public.

the thorny issue of Southtown. However, as Sir Thomas Medowe and other loyalist corporators took up Bower's mantle as the scourge of local Nonconformity under the protection of a now-intrusive central government, Paston could act as the corporation's link to the court, acceptable at least to the predominant political faction within the town. Although in appearance an alliance of irresistible strength, the lord-lieutenant and his Yarmouth allies could not afford to underestimate the resilience of their opponents. Ensuing battles, especially over the charter issue, where influence could only be gained by careful, stage-by-stage advances, serve to re-emphasize the fallacy of tracing too deterministic a triumph for the 'Tory reaction'.[4]

Even though the assembly's thankful address to the King in May 1681 had betrayed a loyalist elation at the defeat of the Whig cause at Oxford, a succession of incidents proved that local divisions lived on. In June Sir Thomas Medowe and other loyalists reported to Paston that successive assemblies had broken up unproductively due to 'the same persons continuing still in their same ill-temper'. Moreover, on the same day, the bailiffs informed the new secretary of state, Sir Leoline Jenkins, that Sir James Johnson had uttered disrespectful words towards the King, the Dissenting leader having wittily opined that 'the King of France could whore well and govern well; our King could whore well but not govern'. More worryingly, their report also revealed that Johnson and his allies had forced two witnesses against him to flee the town in fear of reprisal.[5]

The loyalists were not slow to respond to these challenges, renewing at the town's quarter-sessions in August their previously desultory campaign of harassing local Dissenters.[6] By that time Paston had already resolved on the more decisive step of effecting a 'total alteration' of the Yarmouth militia. Past experience had taught him that the control of the militia could bolster the confidence of any group within Yarmouth, and he finally decided to make a remodelling in line with his avowed political principles, spurred on by such influential figures as the Bishop of

---

[4] As a sign of the centre's reliance on the local knowledge of its supporters, it is interesting to note the unfamiliarity of secretary of state Sir Leoline Jenkins with the borough constitution, for on two occasions he addressed his letters to the 'mayor' of Yarmouth rather than the bailiffs (even after receiving letters from them!)—*CSPD* 1680–1, pp. 305–6, 312, 338, 525.

[5] Add. mss 27448, f. 22. Johnson was later fined £500 at the Norfolk summer assize of 1682—*CSPD* 1680–1, pp. 338, 349; 1682, p. 352.

[6] Y/S1/4, pp. 35–6. Between 1664 and 1681, few Nonconformists had been prosecuted at the town's quarter-sessions, but in August 1681, fifty-six were indicted, including most of the leading civilian members.

Norwich.[7] In contrast to his stance in May 1676, Paston was now prepared to work with Medowe and his allies, eagerly grasping the opportunity to divide and at least gain favour (if not rule) for himself at Yarmouth. An inquiry into the town's militia had been ordered in May 1680 to enforce the Corporation Act, but had apparently achieved little advantage for the loyalists. However, in the wake of the inquest of January 1682, which sought to discover 'the names of such persons as may be intrusted with the command of the militia', the beginnings of serious political change were perceived in the town. By the time of the July muster, Thaxter, Huntington, and Thomas England had disappeared from the militia command, and this loyalist coup was soon followed by further success at the St John's Day elections, where Sir Thomas Medowe was returned as one of the new bailiffs. The loyal knight could now optimistically boast that the town charter would soon 'be laid at his Majesty's feet to attend his determination for the future government of this town'.[8]

Loyalist hopes continued to soar, particularly after the Duke of York himself was treated with 'all the demonstrations of joy' on landing at Yarmouth in March 1682. However, Medowe had underestimated both the latent strength of his rivals, and, more significantly, the attachment of the corporation to its charter. Thus, though the Bishop of Norwich might relish Medowe's assurances that one of the county's 'nurseries of faction' would soon mend its ways, and Paston might already have examples of charter breaches from local loyalists to seek a *quo warranto* against the corporation, the battle was to go on for a further fifteen months.[9] To invite central government to tamper with the document which guaranteed the town's mercantile privileges and political independence was a step which would not be immediately welcomed by any local interest, even in the politicized aftermath of the Exclusion crisis. Other boroughs showed a similar sensitivity towards their charters. A staunch opponent of the surrender of the Chester charter regarded such a move as 'self-homicide', and gained support from the local grand jury, which urged that 'all lawful means should be used to defend the rights and liberties' of the city. At Poole it was reported that a fighting fund had been set up to defend the town charter, while surrenders were openly opposed at Hull,

---

[7] Add. mss 27448, ff. 24, 26. Bishop Sparrow had visited Yarmouth in 1677, but only actively supported a campaign against the Dissenters in the wake of the Exclusion crisis—J. T. Evans, *Seventeenth-Century Norwich* (Oxford, 1979), 245, 253–4.

[8] B. Cozens-Hardy (ed.), 'The Norfolk Lieutenancy Journal, 1676–1701', in *NRS* 30 (1961), 30–1, 34, 37; Y/C19/9, f. 34; *CSPD* 1682, p. 363.

[9] *CSPD* 1682, pp. 118–19; Tanner mss 35, f. 107; Add. mss 27448, f. 147.

Nottingham, Norwich, and, most significantly, London. Some towns conducted more covert campaigns, choosing like the assemblies of Tewkesbury, Stafford, and Southampton to prevaricate in the face of central intervention, complaining of the cost involved, or trying to establish conditions for their surrender, as was the strategy of the Canterbury corporation. As a result, the court and its deputies had to work hard to prise the charters from reluctant borough leaders, and ministers quickly realized that provincial governors would not meekly fall into line when royal policy posed such a fundamental threat to the local *status quo*.[10]

At the outset of the charter campaign Yarmouth's loyalists were determined to flex their political muscle, forcing through directives to oblige all councillors to attend church on Sundays, and to ensure the use of prayers for the royal family at assemblies.[11] However, Medowe found his co-bailiff, Nathaniel Symonds, a powerful source of opposition for the duration of the corporate year 1682–3. More than any other individual, Symonds represented local suspicion towards outside interests, and personified an important political swing within the Yarmouth leadership. Five years before he had offered £500 to build a new Anglican church in Yarmouth, but the secretary to the Bishop of Norwich reported that he had since mixed with some 'very ill-affected persons', and thus 'could not say well of him now'.[12] A potentially amenable town figure had clearly been alienated by recent loyalist initiatives, and Symonds would remain an effective and persuasive focus for local feeling against external interference. By December 1682 Symonds had already shaken the uneasy peace within the town's hierarchy by refusing to submit the town's admiralty seal to senior bailiff Medowe, and by swearing in George England as a town JP despite Medowe's protestations.[13] Displaying a lack of confidence in their local strength, the loyalists sought rectification of the matter at the Privy Council, which ordered Symonds to relinquish the seal, and declared England to have been sworn 'illegally and unduly'.

---

[10] Henning, *House of Commons, 1660–90*, i. 153, 219, 244, 256, 277, 356, 389; R. O'Day *et al.* (eds.), *Traditional Community Under Stress* (Milton Keynes, 1977), 123–5; Evans, *Seventeenth-Century Norwich*, 284–5; J. Levin, *The Charter Controversy in the City of London, 1660–88, and its Consequences* (London, 1969), 17–55. Note that at Wigan even High Churchman Sir Edward Chisenall opposed the surrender of the charter—Henning, i. 294.

[11] Y/C19/9, f. 38v.

[12] Tanner mss 130, f. 140. Significantly, on his death Symonds received great praise in 1720 from Yarmouth's Anglican pastor, who saw him as a magistrate acting 'with great prudence, with great courage, and great integrity'—*Sermon Preached at the Funeral of Nathaniel Symonds* [1721].

[13] The admiralty seal was required for the calling of assemblies, and therefore its holder could decisively affect the pace of local politics.

Such news gladdened the hearts of local loyalists, one of whom had been
so alarmed by Symonds's opposition that he lamented that 'Sir Thomas
and all honest men had as good be in Algeere as be here'. However, he
also reported that Symonds had called an assembly to assure the councillors 'that he would stand firm by them to maintain their privileges',
a rallying call well tailored to that audience. Symonds even pursued a
Bower-style policy of collecting signatures to demonstrate his loyalty to
the crown, but stubbornly defied the Privy Council order. Medowe gloomily informed Paston on 12 February that Symonds was 'yet obstinate',
and expressed doubts whether any assembly called at that time could
successfully defeat the 'irregular aldermen'.[14]

Symonds was not the loyalists' only problem, for their supporters
encountered much opposition outside of the assembly. Indeed, such was
the delicate balance of power between the competing factions in early
1683 that a fire at St Nicholas's Church became a political issue. Allies of
the Dissenters claimed that the lightning which had caused the blaze had
struck the church at the exact time that one of its meetings was broken up
by local magistrates. This charge was taken seriously by Yarmouth loyalists, who even went into print to refute any suggestion that divine judgement might be against them. However, a more worrying development
was an outbreak of violence among the populace, for in January the local
fort had to be strengthened following 'several insolencies' committed by
townsmen in its vicinity. There is no clue as to the identity or aims of the
members of this mob, but their gathering at the haven fort suggests that
they may have wished to make a stand against a symbol of royal authority.
Whatever the motivation of the rioters, the corporation did not take further steps to eliminate disorder, appearing to have had little difficulty in
maintaining control even in this time of heightened political tension.[15]

Although these events indicated widespread political unrest, the main
arena for political manœuvre remained the assembly. On 20 February
Symonds made a spirited defence of his own actions as bailiff, disputing
the wording of the Privy Council order, and declaring that it should only
be recorded in the assembly minutes as a precedent for future incumbents. On a subsequent vote on the matter, the faction carried it 30 to 29,
and Medowe's despair was complete when Symonds kept the seal, thereby
obstructing any loyalist attempt to arrange assemblies at their own con-
venience. Medowe's list of the respective sides on that vote, when com-

---

[14] PRO, PC2/69, pp. 596, 613; Add. mss 27448, ff. 175, 201.
[15] *A True Relation of the Firing of the Great Church at Yarmouth* [1683]; Y/C19/9, f. 42.

pared to the divisions which he had recorded in July 1678, revealed that the charter issue had had a decisive impact on the corporation's personnel. Of the forty-three councillors who appear in both lists, nineteen showed a steady commitment to Medowe's loyalist stance. However, he had lost the support of eleven councillors on the vote of February 1683, including such important figures as aldermen John Woodroffe, Peter Caulier, and Benjamin England. Twelve councillors remained in opposition, led by Huntington and Thaxter, and only one of their allies had broken ranks to join Medowe's side. Symonds's stand on the charter had thus successfully split his opponents over that crucial division, and he would continue to play upon the town's fear of external intervention. Just as Michael Mullett concluded that 'Whiggism' in Liverpool derived its principal strength from the defence of borough rights, so the 'faction' at Yarmouth reaped advantage from local fears for traditional privileges and liberties.[16]

At this point, the loyalists faced a further setback with the death of the permanently sickly Earl of Yarmouth on 8 March, which robbed them of their most likely intermediary at court. This loss was then compounded by the choice of the Earl of Arundel as Paston's successor as lord-lieutenant, a moderate figure whose election, it was hoped, would dissolve some of the political tension which riddled the county.[17] However, loyalists could at least take some heart from the subsequent appointment of William Paston, the second earl, as Yarmouth's high steward, which ensured a continuity of interest between Oxnead and the town. Reports circulated that the Dissenters and their allies had endeavoured to promote the Earl of Arundel, but the success of the younger Paston was apparently uncontested. The cause for such unanimity is easy to see, for even though his election could be claimed as a political victory for the loyalists, the importance of the office demanded that the corporation make an apolitical assessment of any candidate. The second earl had impeccable credentials as a patron, having first gained royal favour and lodgings at Whitehall in 1672, and having stood successfully as MP for Norwich on four occasions.

[16] PRO, SP29/408, f. 121; SP29/422, f. 90; M. Mullett, 'Politics of Liverpool, 1660–88', in *Transactions of Hist. Soc. of Lancashire and Cheshire*, 124 (1972), 47.

[17] J. M. Rosenheim, *The Townshends of Raynham* (Middletown, 1989), 58–60. Robert Paston was cited by R. G. Pickavance as 'one of the foremost exponents of the Tory Reaction in the entire kingdom', but his previous inconsistencies in his role as regional deputy before 1681 only serve to highlight the changed circumstances of the post-Exclusion period—'The English Boroughs and the King's Government', pp. 298–304. Contemporaries evidently saw him as a loyalist champion—J. Hildeyard, *A Sermon preached at the Funeral of . . . Robert, Earl and Viscount Paston* [1683].

Moreover, his father had largely steered clear of the great divisions of the county since 1681 by a permanent residence in London, and thus a younger and more accessible interest at court, in Parliament, and in the county was an obvious asset for the town. With the second Haven Act due to expire in less than two years, all corporators acknowledged the necessity of choosing a figure active in central politics, yet sympathetic to local needs. Conversely, the earl himself could have had few illusions concerning his influence over the corporation, for the assembly took the opportunity provided by his election to reassert its right to choose its recorder.[18]

As his father had belatedly come to recognize, William Paston saw that his only hope of securing control of the town was to place his influence at the disposal of one of the competing factions. Such a strategy clashed with the wishes of Secretary of State Jenkins, who in the summer of 1683 had been urging Yarmouth curate Luke Milbourne to concentrate on 'the great essentials of Christian duties' rather than stir up further contention in the town. However, Milbourne continued to vent his spleen against the Dissenters, accusing them of seeking a republic, rather than an indulgence. Furthermore, following the Rye House Plot he dedicated the publication of his latest diatribe to the second earl, declaring 'that which bears so great a name in its front must be by all concluded loyal'. Local events were thus spinning out of the control of the centre, and once the new high steward had taken up the loyalist cause, hopes for a peaceful accommodation within the borough all but disappeared.[19]

Attempts made by central government to quash all sedition in the wake of the Rye House plot did little to eradicate local divisions. Paston himself intervened to prevent the execution of an order for searching the houses of twenty leading townsmen for arms caches in August 1683, rightly surmising that it would provoke disorder, and probably earn sympathy for his opponents.[20] However, he was already acting as go-between for Sir Thomas Medowe and Sir Leoline Jenkins as they cautiously plotted the

---

[18] Y/C19/9, f. 47; Henning, *House of Commons, 1660–90*, iii. 213. The Earl of Arundel was an unlikely figurehead for the Dissenting party, particularly after he had endorsed Paston's militia commissions—Add. mss 27448, f. 237. The corporation had ample cause for fearing interference from Paston, for he displayed a singular insensitivity towards assembly feeling at Norwich, where controversy over his nomination of a deputy recorder would rage from July 1683 to April 1684—Evans, *Seventeenth-Century Norwich*, 300–5.

[19] *CSPD* 1683 (Jan.–June), pp. 287–8; L. Milbourne, *The Origin of Rebellion, or The Ends of Separation* (Jan. 1683); *Samaritism Revived* (Sept. 1683).

[20] *NRS* 30 (1961), 46. Thaxter, Huntington, and four other councillors were on that list, as well as seven ex-councillors. In addition, two locals were arraigned for echoing their approval of the Rye House plot—*CSPD* 1683 (July–Sept.), p. 213.

surrender of the town charter. Medowe still feared the strength of his local adversaries, advising Paston that a preliminary *mandamus* would be required to ensure the compliance of the bailiffs as a necessary step before a *quo warranto* could be executed against the corporation. Significantly, the secretary of state was against such a move on grounds of constitutional propriety, observing that although precedents for such a procedure existed, 'the usage now all over England is otherwise'. Medowe himself had experienced the controversy caused by the *mandamus* served against the Yarmouth assembly during the emergency of the 1665 plague, and probably agreed with Jenkins's forecast that opponents would commence legal proceedings to counter another such writ. Fortunately for the court's allies, the bailiff elections of St John's Day 1683 helped to resolve the issue, for loyalists George Ward and Thomas Godfrey were chosen. However, Godfrey's offices of town attorney and clerk were taken over by his rival, John Woodroffe, whose massive corporate experience rendered him an indispensable member of the corporation.[21]

The loyalist alderman Thomas Gooch imparted this news to Paston on 12 September, but even though confident of the surrender of the charter, he still thought that a *quo warranto* had to be issued to satisfy 'some of the moderate sort of people (as they call themselves) whom we must a little gratify'. This was a most significant observation concerning the politicization of the Yarmouth élite, for it demonstrated that even at this critical juncture there was still an important interest unwilling to be committed to the rival camps. This moderate group was evidently well informed of recent events, and their independence of mind suggests that local 'parties' were more fluid in composition than the simple polarity of Anglican and Nonconformist. Accounts of the political orientation of other boroughs reveal a similar picture, for a tripartite division between Whigs, Tories, and moderates was reported to have existed at Norwich, while at Northampton the members of the middling group between rival factions were described as 'following men'.[22] At Yarmouth, it was clear

---

[21] *CSPD* 1683 (July–Sept.), pp. 104–5, 150; Y/C19/9, f. 50. Woodroffe, who had led local opposition to the *mandamus* of 1665, would obviously have made immense political capital out of the threat of a new writ.

[22] Henning, *House of Commons, 1660–90*, i. 331, 341. On the basis of his study of Restoration Bristol, Jonathan Barry warns that party conflict was not simply a matter of Whig Dissenters against Tory Anglicans—T. Harris *et al.*, *The Politics of Religion in Restoration England* (Oxford, 1990), 163–89. Moreover, the bitter polarity between 'the loyal party' and 'the factious' at York in late 1682 was attributed by a contemporary to economic coercion, for 'several there have confessed that they dare not act according to their judgments (viz. for the government) for fear of being undone in their trade'—*Memoirs of Sir John Reresby*, ed. A. Browning (London, 1991, 2nd edn.), 579–81.

that the charter issue had created such waverers. Corporate attachment to the charter merely reflected its fundamental value to local society, and all politicians had to respect such sentiment. Gooch paid further tribute to the force of local opinion by hinting that it might be more acceptable if the surrender was postponed until the town had received all its dues from the herring catch, even though bailiff Godfrey had recently travelled to London in an attempt to speed up the process. Gooch also begged secrecy over the *quo warranto*, evidently anticipating local opposition. The struggle might appear to have tipped decisively in the loyalists' favour, but their correspondence reveals a caution forged in their understanding of corporate affairs.[23]

Symonds, for one, battled on until the last week of his bailiwick, obstructing the prosecution of Nonconformists at the town quarter-sessions, much to Medowe's displeasure. Despite his efforts, once the bridles of local government were in loyalist hands, and Paston had emerged as a reliable intermediary to ensure a smooth surrender of the charter, then Symonds and his allies were fighting a rearguard action. However, before the surrender of the charter local loyalists still thought it necessary to deliver a telling blow to their opponents *outside* of the assembly. On 21 February 1684 loyal councillors introduced a motion requiring all freemen in the town to give proof of their baptism, having already compiled a list of 110 offenders who they wished to disenfranchise. Although only two assemblymen opposed the proposal at first, when the names of the accused were read out 'and proved to be all of the Whiggish side, it received more debate'.[24] However, 'not above ten' assemblymen voted against the ordinance, thereby allowing it to pass comfortably. Within three weeks orders had been given for a writ of *quo warranto* to be sent down to Yarmouth, and the loyalists soon busied themselves with the compilation of a list of assemblymen to be removed. Even at this late stage, events could take unexpected turns, for on 21 March the assembly formally agreed to surrender its charter, thereby obviating the need for a *quo warranto*. Indeed, ten of the town's leading loyalists admitted to Paston that they had only sought the writ due to 'our fears that some of our members were seduced by the adverse party'. However, they now begged their high steward to ensure an economical surrender procedure, stressing the extreme poverty of the corporate treasury, and pointing to the incipient termination of the Haven Act as a sign of local desperation.

---

[23] Add. mss 27448, f. 262.
[24] Y/C19/9, ff. 59v–60v; Add. mss 27448, f. 279.

The discipline of the loyalist charter campaign had ensured that the haven issue did not distract local supporters from factional objectives, but the ascendant group would soon have to assuage mercantile concern over that matter.[25]

The passage of the surrender took four more months of negotiation, and the problems which dogged the loyalist managers only re-emphasized the charter's importance as the keystone of the corporation. In April Sir Leoline Jenkins had to dispel persistent rumours that the King intended to use the surrender as an opportunity to seize town lands. Further difficulties were caused by an intrusive petition from the town of Lowestoft, which sought to define the extent of Yarmouth's admiralty jurisdiction, proposing the substitution of seven English miles for the current contentious distance of seven 'leagues'. Reviving memories of the struggles of 1659–62, such interference was understandably regarded as a potential subversion of local privileges. Moreover, as late as mid-July the town contacted the attorney-general in order to confirm the inclusion of the recent Deneside development within the liberties of the new charter.[26] However, the official presentation of the new charter to the town on 31 July extinguished any lingering doubts, permitting Luke Milbourne to gloat that 'only the discontented party hung their heads' on its arrival. The protracted campaign now over, local loyalists openly heralded William Paston as their champion, and, as a token of their gratitude, in the charter itself there was a provision for safeguarding 'the rights of the Earl of Yarmouth in respect of Southtown'.[27]

The new charter highlighted the priority accorded by both local and central government to the suppression of any source of opposition.[28] Its key clauses centred on the reduction of the assembly from seventy-two members to fifty-four, all of whose tenure was subject to the King's pleasure, and the institution of a mayor as chief officer in the place of the two bailiffs. In the wake of the Medowe-Symonds dispute, the elimination of discord within the town hierarchy was a vital precondition for the smooth running of local government, and, with royal control over appointments to the remodelled assembly, a submissiveness to central

---

[25] *CSPD* 1683–4, p. 325; Y/C19/9, f. 62; Add. mss 27448, f. 281.

[26] *CSPD* 1683–4, pp. 363–4; 1684–5, pp. 13–14, 32; *CTB* 1681–5, p. 1,223. The loyalists' determination to secure the charter surrender led them to accept Lowestoft's proposal, a significant change in corporate policy from the intransigence of 1659–62.

[27] Add. mss 36988, ff. 231, 291; Y/C19/9, f. 65v. Miller observes that the crown's charter policy was generally cautious until the autumn of 1684, and that it rejected moves to hasten the charter surrenders at both Yarmouth and Chester—*EHR* 100 (1985), 77–80.

[28] Palmer, *History of Great Yarmouth*, 38–41.

authority was promised with effect. However, even though twelve alder-men and eighteen common councillors were immediately removed, six of their chosen replacements refused to take up office, thereby suggesting opposition to the new charter. Their stance did little to derail the loyalist campaign, for the charter also undermined the faction's support outside of the assembly by limiting the parliamentary franchise to the corpora-tion.[29] Accompanying these changes came specific reassurances that Yar-mouth's corporate privileges were not to be harmed in any way, and, as if to reaffirm such promises, the position of understeward was created to aid the town's legal counsel. Unlike the loyalists of towns such as Bed-ford, Hull, and Ripon, Yarmouth's leaders did not attempt to gain local support by obtaining additional liberties from the crown, but they were evidently aware of the need to bolster the authority of the new civic order. For example, a swordbearer was provided for the first mayor George Ward, thereby dignifying the transition to a single corporate figurehead.[30] Not surprisingly, the remodelled assembly quickly ordered a grateful address to the crown, and were subsequently informed that Charles had been 'highly pleased' with Yarmouth, particularly as it had been the first borough to respond to the grant of a new charter in that manner. However, the town was soon making approaches to Oxnead on less politicized matters, eager for the earl's aid to ease local anxiety over the decay of the haven. For all the excitement of the surrender, the town's new political leaders had yet to address a more permanent source of local concern, and such challenges would force them to work hard to maintain their position, whatever security royal support might bring them.[31]

Whether motivated by hopes of private gain or not, the second earl's involvement in the charter surrender had certainly cemented his interest within the remodelled corporation. As early as December 1683 William Paston had discovered that financial gain could be reaped from his cor-

[29] The six replacements for the purged members who actually refused to serve were then fined £25 each—Y/C19/9, ff. 69, 71v. The limitation of the parliamentary franchise was a significant feature of government charter policy at this time, although, once again, Miller notes major inconsistencies over this issue, and views such changes as the work of local initiative—*EHR* 100 (1985), 81–3.

[30] Mullett, 'Deprived of our Former Place: the Internal Politics of Bedford, 1660–88', in *Bedfordshire Hist. Rec. Soc.* 59 (1980), 22; *VCH: Yorkshire, East Riding* (London, 1969), i. 120. At Ripon the decision to seek a new charter was taken explicitly with the aim 'not only to allay all jealousies, but to procure some advantages to the town about their fairs and such things'—Henning, *House of Commons, 1660–90*, i. 485.

[31] Y/C19/9, ff. 67, 70, 74v. The town's first understeward was the crypto-Catholic Henry Bedingfield, an appointment which suggests that the court itself was drawing direct advantage from the surrender of the charter.

porate office, when the town purchased £150 of his estate's timber for haven repair. At a time when the family estate might have been encumbered with debts to the tune of £22,000, Paston was undoubtedly keen for any source of revenue. Furthermore, in April 1684 he was approached by scrivener Stephen Primatt, the author of his father's Southtown proposals, who avariciously observed that 'it now consists with your lordship's interest to make your own terms, and have an advantage to make them more considerable to you'.[32] However, Paston realized that it was only while working in partnership with the town's mercantile élite that any permanent gain might be won, and he rested content with the insertion into the new charter of the clause protecting his Southtown rights. Before the year was out, the assembly had gone as far as to propose rates for mooring posts on Paston's land, a notable gesture of support for Paston given his father's experience. However, the offer was also calculated to ensure the high steward's participation in the town's campaign to renew the Haven Act, since it was accompanied by a request for advice on 'the ruinous condition of Yarmouth haven'. Even if he might have ideas of ulterior gain in his relationship with Yarmouth, the corporation was not paying Paston favour without hopes of advancing its interest at court and in Parliament.[33]

Paston initially advised the assembly to look to its own precedents for raising money from crown and locality, but reaffirmed his willingness to serve the town by acting in February 1685 as the presenter of an address from the corporation to James II, offering him congratulations on his accession to the throne. The address stressed the corporation's joy at the enthronement of James as 'the true and undoubted heir', thereby demonstrating the efficiency of the regulation of the previous year. The new charter also ensured that the assembly would return loyalist Members to James's first Parliament, and on 24 March it made a decisive break with recent practice by electing two outsiders, Sir William Cook and John Friend. Both lacked the local or mercantile credentials which successful candidates since 1660 and earlier had boasted, and the former even revealed that his election was 'against my inclinations'. Such a significant change in representation clearly ran the risk of antagonizing local

---

[32] Y/C19/9, f. 58; Y/NRS/4013/13F7, piece 2; Add. mss 27448, f. 283.

[33] Y/C19/9, ff. 75, 76, 78v. In contrast to the golden dreams of his father in 1676–7, the mooring rates put forward by the town were to be 1*s.* per week for vessels over 100 tons, and 6*d.* per week for those under 100 tons. In August 1687, six mooring posts were set down on the Southtown bank with the earl only asking a 'small acknowledgement' for them, and he accepted a £20 p.a. offer from the assembly the following March—Y/C19/9, f. 112; Add. mss 27448, f. 333.

divisions, and it has been suggested that the 'freemen at large' staged their own election to put forward Huntington and George England as the town's true representatives.[34] For certain, discontent within Yarmouth continued to surface throughout the year. In June several locals were imprisoned for treasonable words in connection with Monmouth's rebellion, and in the following month the militia conducted a round-up of twenty local Nonconformists. Most menacingly, in December the local garrison anxiously reported gatherings of large crowds of townsmen, although no violent confrontation ensued. In response to these tensions, the magistrates maintained a vigilant watch over Nonconformist activity, keeping the town's quarter-sessions busy with a continuing stream of mass prosecutions.[35] The assembly was particularly keen to preserve its loyal demeanour, ordering the prolonged pealing of St Nicholas's bells at each stage of the royal victory against Monmouth's rebels to demonstrate its commitment to the Stuart line. Helping to fuel that allegiance was the achievement of a third Haven Act, which provided a supply for haven repair for the next fourteen years. This was a notable success in James's only Parliament, and the corporators were not slow to acknowledge the promoters of the statute, passing on sincere thanks to Paston and the Duke of Norfolk. Both the assemblymen and their patrons must have hoped that the unifying concern of the haven would continue to dampen memories of past factionalism.[36]

In general terms, the ensuing two years appear to have cemented the interest of both crown and courtier in the town. Having left the anxieties of borough regulation and the Monmouth rebellion behind, loyalist leaders used Paston's growing influence to build on the achievement of the third Haven Act. In March 1686 Paston was instrumental in securing the services of the King's finest engineer, Sir Henry Sheers, for an extensive survey of Yarmouth's havenmouth. His expertise was not secured without cost, but the corporation was quick to thank its high steward for assuring the mercantile community that everything possible was being done to secure the town's commercial future.[37] The advantages of an

---

[34] Y/C19/9, ff. 78v, 82, 83; Palmer, *History of Great Yarmouth*, 214–15. Sir William Cook hoped for 'a short but happy Parliament'—Tanner mss 31, f. 17. Friend had actually married the niece of the factious Richard Huntington—Henning, *House of Commons, 1660–90*, i. 326.

[35] Y/C36/6, pieces 31–3; *NRS* 30 (1961), 71, 75; Add. mss 41085, f. 99; Y/S1/4, pp. 71, 91. The prosecutions for non-attendance reached their last peak in September 1685, by which time fines of up to £20 had been levied for one month's absence from church.

[36] Y/C19/9, ff. 89v, 90v. For the Act, see *Statutes of the Realm*, vi. 17–19.

[37] Y/C19/9, ff. 96v, 114, 131. Sheers was expected to play the same saviour's role as

association with Paston only became more evident, for in February 1687 the earl was appointed lord treasurer of the royal household. His father had never risen to such a high office under Charles II, in spite of his great service to the crown over the 1664 supply bill. The corporation was quick to identify itself with the second earl's rising star, ordering that not only the anniversaries of the Stuart Restoration and James's succession were to be celebrated as scarlet days, but also those of the King's coronation and birthday. Paston's position at court was now seemingly secure for the foreseeable future, and the town eagerly sought to maintain his favour by admitting his sons Robert and Thomas as freemen of the borough. However, neither town nor patron had reckoned on the upheaval which was subsequently caused by the recklessness of their royal master.[38]

Analysts of the rule of James II have stressed how fundamentally royal policy had isolated the crown by late 1688, particularly through the methods employed to enforce his controversial religious policies. The ruthless regulation of local government in pursuit of a compliant Parliament and populace has been credited as a significant cause of James's ultimate defeat, especially as it exposed the King's inability to secure any substantial basis of support for his particular brand of toleration. Indeed, a recent work observed that even though these purges might have been less spectacular than the Magdalene College affair, 'they probably alienated more people'.[39] By paying due attention to the pressures working on local magistrates, some of whom had not only experienced the onslaught of central government in 1681–4, but also that of 1661–4, the strain which royal policy imposed on the English state becomes all too evident. Yarmouth was a potentially amenable borough in 1686, its leaders handpicked and the locality boasting a Dissenting community whose leaders James was endeavouring to woo on a national scale. However, in a turnabout of remarkable rapidity, both Anglicans and Nonconformists were progressively distanced from any support for the legitimate monarch. Religion was once again at the root of local upheaval, but it was the massive offensive against local government which most directly precipitated the alienation of the Yarmouth élite from the crown.

Dutch engineer Joyce Johnson, who from 1567 had built Yarmouth's seventh (and last) haven—see Swinden, *History of Great Yarmouth*, 419–54. He was paid 100 guineas plus expenses for his visit, and his report, which includes details of a purpose-built dredging engine, survives at Arundel Castle, MD 1012.

[38] *CSPD* 1686–7, p. 364; Y/C19/9, ff. 112v, 123.

[39] See Jones, *The Revolution of 1688 in England*, 128–75; W. Speck, *Reluctant Revolutionaries* (Oxford, 1988), 160–1. See also P. Murrell, 'Bury St Edmunds and the Campaign to Pack Parliament, 1687–88', in *BIHR* 54 (1981), 188–206.

Factionalism within the town still appeared to be receding at the beginning of 1687. The regulated assembly dutifully celebrated its scarlet days in honour of the King, and its Anglican leaders could take heart at the lowly condition of local Dissent after several years of persecution at the quarter-sessions. However, within a few months James's publicized support for toleration would completely alter this picture. Only a week after the Declaration of Indulgence had been issued in April 1687 'a great auditory' of Congregationalists had been held in the town, and local Nonconformist leaders rushed to send a thankful address to its royal author. As Yarmouth's MP Sir William Cook gloomily reported to Archbishop Sancroft, 'our Dissenters have greedily swallowed the bait, and everywhere expressed their joy with bells and bonfires'.[40] In their first experience of official toleration since 1672–3, such enthusiasm for James's policy was understandable, and in June the Yarmouth Congregationalists receive further encouragement when news reached them that their address had been 'well accepted' at court. In contrast, the assembly was more dilatory in its response, waiting until September to inform James that it was 'entirely satisfied' of his concern for the liberties of his subjects. Subservient as the corporation had been since 1684, the U-turn in government policy was clearly a little difficult for it to stomach. However, the address showed that its members were sufficiently trustful of royal motives to accept the implementation of James's Indulgence.[41]

Unfortunately for local Anglicans, the chorus of approval emanating from Yarmouth made the town appear ready to support the crown's policies, and they would now have to face James's campaign to produce a subservient Parliament. Even before the corporation had presented its thankful address, the Earl of Sunderland had written to the mayor to recommend Sir John Friend as one of the town's MPs at the 'approaching election', stressing his virtues as 'a person of approved loyalty and known affections to the peace and welfare of the government'.[42] Moreover, by this time expectation of an imminent poll was doubtless widespread within the town, judging by the fifty-three freedoms ratified by the assembly in early August. There is no evidence of organized electioneering at

---

[40] Y/FC31/1, 10 Apr., 20 May 1687; Tanner mss 29, f. 10. However, contemporaries such as Sir John Reresby noted significant differences between the reaction of Dissenting groups in Yorkshire to the First Indulgence—J. Kirby, in *Northern History*, 22 (1986), 154. Unfortunately, the Baptists and Quakers of Yarmouth have not left any evidence of having publicly recognized the Indulgence, although the former, having re-established their church in 1686, may have already gained great encouragement from the crown's religious policy—Dr Williams Lib. 38. 109.   [41] Y/FC31/1, 10 June 1687; Y/C19/9, f. 121.
   [42] *CSPD* 1687–9, p. 271.

this stage, but the sudden leap in the number of freemen petitions cannot be solely attributed to the inspiration of Sheers's employment at the havenmouth. Most significantly, eight of the new freemen created in 1687 had Nonconformist links, thereby illustrating the renewed confidence of their co-religionists since the time of the freeman purge of 1684. The government certainly kept its pressure on the corporation to advance the Dissenting cause, for the royal response to the September address expressed hope that the town would soon choose MPs 'as should concur . . . in taking off the penal laws and tests'. Initial signs of support from one of the realm's major towns had only encouraged the crown to accelerate its reforms, heedlessly disregarding the likely response of local governors to significant changes in policy. As the New Year approached, caution was cast aside, and along with it, James's chances of peaceful reform.[43]

January 1688 saw the first major purge of the Yarmouth corporation for four years, a move evidently designed to silence assemblymen who could not accept toleration without a troubled conscience. Sir James Johnson was employed as agent to oversee the removal of six aldermen and eleven common councillors, but his presence could do little to sweeten the pill of central intervention.[44] Most significantly, the identity of the purged councillors revealed that the crown had already alienated the loyalists who had engineered the charter surrender of 1684, for among the six ousted aldermen were the venerable Sir Thomas Medowe; the town's first mayor, George Ward; and Paston's contact, Thomas Gooch. Moreover, seven of the dismissed common councillors had been listed as loyalists by Medowe at an earlier date. In their place, an open-handed welcome was extended to Medowe's declared enemies, with the most distinguished figures of the Congregationalist community gaining admission to the assembly, several of whom had suffered ejection from it in the early years of the Restoration.[45] Interestingly, there was no apparent attempt to

---

[43] Y/C19/9, ff. 117v–19, 124; *NNAS* 9 (1910), 120–3; Y/FC31/1.

[44] Y/C19/9, ff. 127v–28v. Johnson's role here, acting as a royal agent despite a past conviction for slandering the crown, highlights the changeability of the times. His previous disgrace had not been forgotten by Bishop Lloyd of Norwich, nor had his ties to the Dissenters—Tanner mss 137, f. 135. For a discussion of the difficulties of such so-called 'Whig collaborators', see M. Goldie, 'James II and the Dissenters' Revenge: The Commission of Enquiry of 1688', in *BIHR* 66 (1993), 53–88.

[45] PRO, SP29/408, f. 121; SP29/422, f. 90. Bishop Lloyd identified the new aldermen as 'six Independents', who had replaced 'six honest men'—Tanner mss 29, f. 133. There is no evidence to suggest that these new replacements were necessarily of lower-class origin, or that such a complaint was levelled against them, as was made against new councillors at Bedford and Norwich—Mullett, in *Bedfordshire Hist. Rec. Soc.* 59 (1980), 34; Evans, *Seventeenth-Century Norwich*, 314.

court the councillors who had been purged in 1684, the royal supporters evidently unwilling, and probably unable, to rebuild bridges with that faction. However, as a result none of the replacements had experience of corporate office, and the purge was carried through with little local support. Assemblyman John Urwen informed Paston of the drama which surrounded the execution of the royal order, and even noted that Johnson had made a shame-faced denial of personal responsibility for the remodelling. Urwen himself was physically assaulted by ousted loyalist alderman Abraham Castle and other 'discontented persons'. Most significantly, he identified the permanent attachment of the town to its charter as a key cause of contention, observing that 'many discharged are men that . . . have great anger against myself and others for serving his late Majesty according to those methods he was pleased to require'. The struggle over the charter has to be considered alongside James's Catholicism as a determinant of local allegiance, for the methods of crown policy were instrumental in undermining local confidence in James's ultimate objectives.[46]

Within weeks crown agents were already speculating that another round of corporate dismissals would be needed. Urwen's account of the violence attending the purge must have been rapidly communicated by Paston to his superiors in London, for in late February the Privy Council issued a warrant for the removal of a further seventeen councillors.[47] Prudence, however, at last prevailed, for the order was not executed immediately, probably for fear of provoking more widespread disorder in the town. Yet the decision to wait upon events left the town's government in a state of permanent suspense, and in mid-March town clerk Thomas Godfrey noted the circulation of rumours concerning 'a new regulation'. Moreover, Urwen informed Paston that speculation about the parliamentary election was rife. When royal informants reported the town's political situation in April, they confirmed the need for a further regulation of the corporation if the borough was to return MPs amenable to the crown's policies. That month also saw the passage of the second Declaration of Indulgence, as James chose to ignore the warning signs which were clearly emanating from the extensively canvassed provinces.[48]

---

[46] PL, J. Urwen to Earl of Yarmouth, 17 Jan. 1688. For instance, at Bristol, where thirty-four officials had been removed in early 1688, the corporation still refused to send thanks for the Second Declaration of Indulgence, such was the disaffection of the city's political élite—R. C. Latham (ed.), 'Bristol Charters 1509–1899', in *Bristol Rec. Soc. Publs.* 12 (1947), 55–6.

[47] PRO, PC2/72, pp. 616. Bishop Lloyd expected a 'strong working purge' at Yarmouth in late February—Tanner mss 137, f. 135v.

[48] Add. mss 27448, f. 333; PL, J. Urwen to Earl of Yarmouth, 19 Mar. 1688; C. Duckett,

The spring and summer of 1688 was a period of unrelieved anguish for Yarmouth's governors. In March Sheers's proposed plan for haven repair was finally presented to the corporation, but the ambitiousness of the £10,000 scheme must have daunted local spirits as the seriousness of the haven's condition was laid bare. Furthermore, as if to compound the town's mercantile worries, the government then ordered an inquiry into the corporation's administration of Haven Act revenues, following allegations that misappropriation of funds was to blame for the haven's current decay.[49] The growing influence of the Nonconformists continued to cause tension within the town, particularly after the Congregationalists publicly celebrated the inauguration of their pastor James Hannot at a ceremony attended by Dissenting ministers from all over East Anglia. The news of the birth of a royal heir, when it reached Yarmouth on 15 June, could only have fuelled fears that this hastily erected new order was to be of a more permanent existence. The confidence of the government, which finally undertook the long-expected remodelling of the assembly in late August, was obvious. However, this bold action sounded the death-knell for the hopes of James's supporters within Yarmouth.[50]

Sir James Johnson again executed the order for the purge, targeting the seventeen assemblymen earmarked for expulsion in February. However, news of the government's intentions had clearly leaked, for all but one of the seventeen was absent when the royal order was served to the assembly.[51] More worryingly for the crown agent, their replacements were also opposed to the regulation. No fewer than nine members of the Independent congregation had been nominated to serve in the assembly, but three of them refused to take up office, reasoning that 'they humbly conceived themselves not qualified for the same'. Within two weeks, these three men and four others, coming significantly from loyalist and Nonconformist

---

Penal Laws (London, 1882), 314. The ministry, as represented by Lord Dartmouth, wanted Yarmouth to choose Samuel Pepys as one of its MPs. He may have had impeccable Admiralty connections, but his known support for the repeal of the penal laws made him a controversial candidate, as was to be shown by his performance at Harwich in 1689— Henning, *House of Commons, 1660–90*, iii. 226–8.

[49] Y/C19/9, ff. 131, 143v.

[50] *CSPD* 1687–9, pp. 219–20; Y/FC31/1, 12 June 1688; Y/C19/9, f. 141. G. Rupp cites Hannot's inauguration as a sign of the Dissenters' public rebuke to the existing penal laws, but he overstates his case by suggesting that they were risking imprisonment for acting so openly in June 1688, for, as in 1672–3, the royal Indulgences had undermined magisterial authority in religious affairs—*Religion in England, 1688–1791* (Oxford, 1986), 121. However, in June 1688 the government had to issue a warrant to reassure new councillors at Yarmouth that they could retain their offices without taking the oaths required by the Test and Corporation Acts—*CSPD* 1687–9, pp. 219–20.   [51] Y/C19/9, f. 145.

groups, were removed, bringing the total number of officials ousted in the year to forty-one. As elsewhere, the court was rapidly finding that such exertions of force had failed to rally support for its policies, and had only caused further suspicion and mistrust of its aims. In a tightly knit corporation such as Yarmouth's, where an attack on the assembly had been the surest means to unite local leaders in the Restoration period, the methods of policy largely defeated their own ends, creating wary opposition long before the crown had any chance to clarify its objectives.[52]

The court had obviously gone too far, having alienated a corporation which only three years before had enthusiastically welcomed the new reign. In September government agents advised their masters that Johnson and one of Paston's sons should stand for the forthcoming parliamentary election, as candidates with local connections to recommend them, but the town was not to be won over so easily now.[53] The borough's reaction to James's volte-face restoration of charters in mid-October 1688 revealed that its leaders were in little mood to compromise, for they greeted the initiative with suspicion, even though it aimed to combat an enduring and damaging criticism of government policy. On the return of the members of the 1684 assembly, the corporation's first decision was to seek the counsel of its recorder and Whiggish attorneys Sir John Holt and Henry Pollexfen, anxious to determine the full implications of the restoration of the charter. The proclamation clearly failed to achieve any last-ditch support for James in the wake of William of Orange's declaration of late September, and on the day the Dutch landed at Torbay the Yarmouth assembly was busy with the election of Medowe's old rivals John Gayford and Benjamin England as new bailiffs. Moreover, George England was brought back as the town's 'counsel at law' to aid the inquiry into the current legality of the town charter, and a committee was appointed to write an account of the upheavals of 1687–8 for the minute book, emphasizing 'the restoration of this burgh to its ancient charters and franchises'.[54]

---

[52] Y/C19/9, ff. 146–7v; PRO, PC2/72, p. 728. The Yarmouth charter might have survived the upheavals of 1688, but the thoroughness of the purges mirrored the work of the 'amazingly productive', but ultimately self-defeating, committee for regulating corporations—see R. H. George, 'The Charters Granted to English Parliamentary Corporations in 1688', in *EHR* 55 (1940), 47–56.   [53] Duckett, *Penal Laws*, 315.

[54] Y/C19/9, ff. 155v, 157, 159. From mid-October the corporation was already preparing the town for 'the invasion apprehended from the Dutch'—Y/C19/9, f. 152v. D. Davies notes that the ministry, predicting an invasion on the north or east coasts, had moved a fleet to Harwich, and that Yarmouth was one of the expected invasion-sites—'James II, William of Orange, and the Admirals', in E. Cruickshanks (ed.), *By Force or By Default? The Revolution of 1688–89* (Edinburgh, 1989), 83.

Regulation and Revolution: 1681–88

171

During the uncertain period between William's landing and James's flight, the assembly seemed only concerned to set its house in order. Although it was naturally as eager for news of national developments as any other authority in the country, this introverted attitude was calculated to present an impartial front to the eventual victor of the unresolved national struggle. Such caution was well advised, but at least one group within the town sought to influence events more decisively, for in early December the bailiffs had to strengthen the guard at the pierhead fort in order to secure 'the peace of the town' against 'the late riotous and tumultuous concourse of the rabble'.[55] Unfortunately, there is again no clue as to the identity and objectives of this mob, but such violence prompted the assembly to issue a declaration on 18 December in order to preempt further unrest. It may well have been drafted in ignorance of the King's return to London two days before, but while thanking the Prince of Orange for rescuing the nation from 'popery and slavery', and airing support for the calling of 'a free Parliament', the corporation still qualified its allegiance by declaring that there should yet be 'a due regard to his Majesty our sovereign King and the laws'. The address went on to make significant demands for securing the rights and properties of the subject, and even for 'a due liberty to Protestant Dissenters', but a fundamental caution came through in its valedictory flourish: 'God save the King, Lord prosper the Prince of Orange.' In the light of bitter past experience, this unwillingness to give either protagonist full backing was both characteristic and prudent while the issue of the day was still in doubt.[56]

Although the assembly awaited the outcome of the national struggle with trepidation and carefully judged impartiality, its high steward remained loyal to his royal master. Paston was one of four courtiers sent to Faversham on 13 December to bring James back to London, and his

[55] Y/C19/9, f. 161. The assembly's immediate response was to raise twelve extra constables, a move which suggests that the mob was of modest proportions. Moreover, they only employed them for three days—Y/C27/3, Mich. 88/89. The riot may have been associated with an attempt to assert the freemen's right to choose Richard Huntington and George England as Members for James's abortive Parliament. The election writs had been sent out on 27 November, and on 6 December the assembly disingenuously informed Sir John Friend that it could not reveal the town's choices because the freeman body was so numerous. C. J. Palmer maintains that Huntington and England *were* elected by a vote of the freemen, though there is no clear evidence for this—Y/C19/9, f. 160; Palmer, *History of Great Yarmouth*, 214–15.

[56] James II's full regnal title was preserved in the assembly minutes until at least 7 January 1689, only to be finally replaced in March 1689—Y/C19/9, ff. 161–2. For the complex response of the provinces to the invasion, see E. Cruickshanks, 'The Revolution and the Localities: Examples of Loyalty to James II' in id. (ed.), *By Force or By Default?*, 28–43.

identification with the toppling regime would soon rebound on him.[57] He certainly could not expect the continued support of the Yarmouth corporation after the part he had played in the town's political upheavals of the 1680s. He may have been welcomed by a group of councillors, but the means whereby the loyalist supremacy was secured had thrown the assembly into total confusion. Its constitution had been used as a factional tool, prepared as the loyalists had been to allow central government to tamper with the civic charter. It now stood bankrupted by the demands of a locally stationed garrison, while the town's commercial and political future remained decidedly uncertain. The policy of borough regulation had completely misfired as the leaders of one of the nation's largest provincial towns rejected an assault of unprecedented speed and thoroughness on its traditional powers of self-government. Papism might prove the most immediate focus for the widespread fear of James's objectives, but the sheer impact of his attack on the nation's towns and county commissions should not be underestimated as a cause of unrest. Indeed, the disarray in which local government had been left by the royal campaign of 1687–8 should be acknowledged as a significant factor to explain why the Williamite regime was established with such apparent ease. For certain, the governors of other important towns such as Hull and Bristol were in no position to offer co-ordinated opposition to the invading forces.[58]

The study of the locality can thus demonstrate the ultimate futility of James's attack on the government of the provinces. As has been shown by Pat Murrell's analysis of Bury St Edmunds, the King could not even reduce a borough with a corporation franchise to subservience, despite a sustained campaign on the part of local and regional agents. Moreover, Michael Mullett's work on Lancaster and Bedford has demonstrated the divisiveness of crown policy, which even managed to alienate James's natural Tory supporters.[59] Although the court had at its disposal such feared weapons as the writ of *quo warranto*, it found that it could not hope to rule without the consent of a significant proportion of the local

[57] R. Beddard, *A Kingdom without A King* (Oxford, 1988), 50; *HMC Hastings*, ii. 206, 208.

[58] The Hull corporation failed to meet for two months after the dismissal of the assembly *en masse* in May 1688, and it is not clear whether the assembly which was installed under the charter of September 1688 ever met. At Bristol, the assembly did not meet between November 1688 and August 1689—*VCH Yorkshire: E. Riding*, i. 120; Latham in *Bristol Rec. Soc. Publs.* 12 (1947), 55–6.

[59] Murrell, in *BIHR* 54 (1981), 188–206; Mullett, in *Northern History*, 19 (1983), 61–86, and *Bedfordshire Hist. Rec. Soc.* 59 (1980), esp. 27–35.

élite.[60] The restoration of the charters in October 1688 suggested that James had belatedly come to recognize this, but only after he had failed to secure sufficient support among the various factions he had successively tried to win over. One of his principal agents, the Earl of Bath, was keenly aware of the errors of regulation, observing with regard to the members of the Exeter corporation: 'you may easily imagine it to be a great mortification to them to see the most substantial, rich, loyal citizens turned out of the government for no offence . . . and this in such a hurry that they [the regulators] destroyed their charter for very haste'.[61] Such methods were destined to alienate all but the most radical Anglicans and Dissenters, whose zeal took precedence over any respect for traditional rights and privileges. Tellingly, John Western's contention that James's charter policy could have produced subservient Parliaments if he had only managed to secure the allegiance of either Whigs or Tories, makes little reference to the force of municipal independence as a unifying bond against the crown.[62] The charters themselves paid tribute to the delicate balance of interest between ruler and ruled, defining the respective powers and responsibilities of local and central government. In his rashness to achieve his political aims, James had evidently pushed his prerogative to the limit, thereby presenting the constitutional legislators of 1688–9 with the daunting challenge of restoring confidence in the workability of the late Stuart regime. Even though they ultimately failed to provide a satisfactory settlement for local governors, in one very significant way the Revolution did mark a watershed for the municipal corporations, for their vulnerability to crown intervention was never to be exposed so brutally again.

[60] Note the confidence of the Earl of Ailesbury regarding royal control over the charters—'there is not a corporation in England but have forfeited their privileges, what by extortions, false weights, and measures, etc.'—Mullett in *Bedfordshire Hist. Rec. Soc.* 59 (1980), 19.

[61] Henning, *House of Commons, 1660–90*, i. 200. In contrast to Exeter, Yarmouth did not surrender its charter in 1688, royal agents probably determining that it would have been too dangerous a step.

[62] J. Western, *Monarchy and Revolution* (London, 1972), 69–77.

6
Uncertainty and Unity: 1689–1702

THANKS to the celebrations attending the tricentenary of the Glorious Revolution, of late there has been no shortage of work on the events of 1688, as historians still struggle to define their significance for the nation's subsequent constitutional development.[1] However, although a rush of publications has revealed a healthy level of interest and debate in the subject, there has been little concern to analyse the response of the provinces to the Revolution, or, more specifically, to the challenges of the 1690s. Some of the best work on the politics of the Augustan period has chartered the growth of the state apparatus in response to the demands of the wars fought by William and Anne, but there has been little concern to gauge the reaction of the localities to the expansion of central government.[2] Moreover, even though a great deal of research has been completed on the advent of frequent parliamentary elections and the 'rage of party' after 1689, there have been few studies which have tried to approach politics from the provincial standpoint. The handful of local studies to have appeared have certainly advanced our understanding of a key decade for the nation's political development, and have only led to further calls for research into provincial perspectives.[3]

[1] W. A. Speck, *Reluctant Revolutionaries* (Oxford, 1988); E. Cruickshanks (ed.), *By Force or By Default? The Revolution of 1688–9* (Edinburgh, 1989); O. P. Grell, J. I. Israel, and N. Tyacke (eds.), *From Prosecution to Toleration: the Glorious Revolution and Religion in England* (Oxford, 1991); R. Beddard (ed.), *The Revolutions of 1688* (Oxford, 1991); J. R. Jones (ed.), *Liberty Secured: Britain Before and After 1688* (Stanford, 1992); L. G. Schwoerer (ed.), *The Revolution of 1688–9: Changing Perspectives* (Cambridge, 1992). For a review of the historiography of the Revolution, see J. Morrill, 'The Sensible Revolution', in J. Israel (ed.), *The Anglo-Dutch Moment* (Cambridge, 1991), 73–104.

[2] J. Brewer, *The Sinews of Power: War, Money, and the English State, 1688–1783* (London, 1989).

[3] The most important monograph of 'local' political development remains G. S. De Krey, *Fractured Society: The Politics of London in the First Age of Party* (Oxford, 1985). However, for important studies of provincial political development, see L. K. J. Glassey, 'The Origins of Political Parties in Late Seventeenth-Century Lancashire', in *Transactions of Hist. Soc. of Lancashire and Cheshire*, 136 (1986), 39–58; S. N. Handley, 'Local Legislative Initiatives for Economic and Social Development in Lancashire, 1689–1731', in *Parliamentary History*, 9 (1990), 14–37; C. Brooks, 'Interest, Patronage, and Professionalism: John, First Baron Ashburnham, Hastings, and the Revenue Services', in *Southern History*, 9 (1987), 51–70.

For certain, one of the more surprising lacunae in the historiography of the 1690s remains the fate of the corporations in the aftermath of the regulatory policies of the later Stuarts.[4] It is a measure of this gap in our knowledge of local government that the Webbs remain the most useful guide to the corporations for the Augustan period, even though their main interest lay in the developments of the early nineteenth century. The Glorious Revolution has rightly been accredited as a watershed in the crown's relationship with its local governors, but only a deafening silence has greeted calls to define its specific importance.[5] The previous chapter endeavoured to convey the massive impact that borough regulation had on corporate rulers, and it was this bitter memory of central interference which had a profound effect on the development of the corporations after 1689. The failure of contemporaries to address many of the problems spawned by the upheavals of the 1680s should not lead modern researchers to ignore the significance of these issues for the political settlement of the country under William III. Yarmouth's example, as a port which felt the direct burden of the Nine Years War, and as a corporation that had much rebuilding work to do if it was to mend the divisions of the past forty years, provides an excellent insight into the nation's painful adaptation to the consequences of James's flight.

The Yarmouth corporation had first revealed its equivocal attitude towards the events of 1688 by its declaration issued in December of that year. However, the eventual establishment of William and Mary as co-monarchs two months later did little to ease the concern of its members, such was the scale of the economic and political challenges which lay ahead of them. The port's silting havenmouth continued to prey greatly

---

[4] For a valuable chapter on the development of corporate politics, though only with little reference to the Augustan period, see P. Corfield, *The Impact of English Towns* (Oxford, 1982), 146–67. Only heavily politicized provincial corporations, where the charter was openly used for factional ends, have received much attention—e.g. P. Styles, 'The Corporation of Bewdley under the Later Stuarts', in *Univ. of Birmingham Journal*, 1 (1947–8), 92–134. London, as usual, is more fortunate with its attractiveness to researchers—see I. Doolittle, 'The Government of the City of London, 1694–1767', Oxford D.Phil. 1979; De Krey, *Fractured Society*, esp. ch. 2.

[5] See Glassey, on 'Local Government', in C. Jones (ed.), *Britain in the First Age of Party, 1680–1750* (London, 1987), 157; Glassey, *Politics and the Appointment of the Justices of the Peace* (Oxford, 1979). G. Forster accepts the end to royal interference in the corporations after 1688 with a casualness that would have surprised contemporaries—see his 'Government in Provincial England under the Later Stuarts', in *TRHS* 5th ser. 33 (1983), 46–8. However, some historians have noted the corporations' continuing concern over James's proclamation of October 1688—J. Carter, 'The Revolution and the Constitution', in G. Holmes (ed.), *Britain after the Glorious Revolution, 1689–1714* (London, 1969), 39–58; J. R. Jones, *The Revolution of 1688 in England* (London, 1972), 175.

on mercantile minds, but this familiar problem was now compounded by the outbreak of a widespread European conflict, which could only cause further disruption of trade. Furthermore, the fate of the town charter remained uncertain, and a serious reassessment of local religious observance was inevitable.[6] Taken together, these issues threatened to undermine the local *status quo*, and as the assembly settled down to tackling them, its members knew that these problems had been the cause of serious divisions in the immediate past. However, the sheer scale of the assembly's difficulties helped to overcome these fresh and bitter memories, working to unify its membership in a more durable manner than at any time since 1660. The self-imposed isolation of James II and his supporters by late 1688 undoubtedly promoted internal unanimity, but a self-conscious reaction to the intrusions of central government also aided this process. Yarmouth politics during the 1690s cannot be understood without recognition of this underlying consensus, even though war and religion would severely test the local accord at key moments. Indeed, the achievement of greater political stability was not a linear development whereby old divisions were buried for good in a step-by-step progression towards unity. Rather, it was more often a case of three steps forward and two steps back, as local circumstances continued to play a decisive part in determining the outlook of the provincial leaders. Given the significance of the issues which the Revolutionary settlement had left unresolved, it is not surprising that during the 1690s many boroughs faced near anarchy as local politicians continued to fight the battles of the 1680s. Unlike Yarmouth, corporations such as Thetford, Ludlow, Dunwich, and Orford were unable to curb factionalism after 1689, and divisions within these boroughs would actually lead to the formation of rival local assemblies. However, Yarmouth provides a timely reminder that some preconditions for political stability were being established in the provinces during the 'rage of party'. At a grass-roots level the difficulties of William's reign are shown to great effect, but, just as importantly, such a perspective also demonstrates the influences which worked to resolve contention.[7]

Caution had been the keynote of Yarmouth's Revolutionary address, and such hesitancy in the face of the political unknown was again revealed in January 1689 when the Yarmouth freemen returned two townsmen to

---

[6] The corporation may have restored its former constitution in response to the royal proclamation of October 1688, but evidently doubts remained over the wisdom of this reversion. Note the open-minded attitude of the town's lecturer Joshua Meen in March 1689, whose will directed that a benefaction for poor mariners be distributed by 'the bailiffs or the chief of the said town'—Norwich Archdeaconry court wills 1689, p. 273.

[7] *History of Parliament, 1690–1715 section*, unpublished constituency articles.

the Convention Parliament, George England and Samuel Fuller. Both have been credited with Whiggish tendencies by analysts concentrating on their voting record at Westminster.[8] However, in accordance with the wishes of their leading constituents, their principal task during the immediate post-Revolution period was not the pursuit of party gain. The assembly books for 1689 reveal the most prolific correspondence between corporation and town MPs in the late seventeenth century, the former eager to secure from them both influence and information. In response, Fuller and England showed an exemplary awareness of their responsibilities as local representatives by responding with industrious and loyal service in the corporation's interest. However, even though their Commons' activity encompassed a broad range of issues, their overwhelming priority in that Parliament clearly lay with the passage of a bill to confirm the duties and powers conferred on Yarmouth by the terms of the 1685 Haven Act.[9] That act had only invested the mayor with authority to collect the haven tolls, and thus it was imperative for the port's continued survival that it be adapted in line with the corporation's reversion to a two-bailiff hierarchy. Despite the competing demands of the great constitutional issues dominating the Convention, within the space of three weeks the two MPs managed to steer such a bill through both Houses.[10] This success testified to their undoubted utility as agents of the corporation, and the bankrupt assembly's readiness to spend £88 on securing a confirmation of its rights highlighted the importance of the act for the town's prosperity. However, within the new act itself was a clause catering for any further alteration in the town's governing structure, which provision indicated continuing local unease over the 'revolutions' of the previous five years.[11]

Despite this early success, the town had good cause to fear for its privileged position. Controversy surrounding the corporation bills of 1689–90 clearly caused much concern, and the response of Yarmouth's leaders to such debates suggested that they viewed the Revolution as the restorer of lost rights, rather than as the instigator of radical constitutional reform.

---

[8] See H. Horwitz (ed.), *The Parliamentary Diary of Narcissus Luttrell* (Oxford, 1972), 492–3, and his *Parliament, Politics and Policy in the reign of William III* (Manchester, 1977), 346–7, where both England and Fuller are credited as 'mixed voters'. Concentrating on their voting record in 1696–1702, I. Burton, P. Riley, and E. Rowlands cite them both as Whigs—*BIHR*, special supplement 7 (1968).

[9] Henning, *The House of Commons, 1660–90*, ii. 266–7, 371.

[10] *CJ*, x. 78–103, *LJ*, xiv. 182–90. The assembly had given its order to seek the confirmatory act in early March 1689, thereby making its first important decision since the flight of James three months before—Y/C19/9, f. 162.   [11] *Statutes of the Realm*, vi. 62.

The assembly was probably well informed of Parliament's deliberations, for one of its MPs was appointed to three of the four committees which discussed the repeal of the Corporation Act, or the introduction of a bill to confirm charters which had suffered regulation since 1683.[12] By October 1689 the assembly was showing impatience with the inconclusive wrangling of the Convention, and decided to give it direct notice of its specific grievances.[13] In contrast to the partisan politicking which later scuppered both the corporation bill and the Convention itself in January 1690, the Yarmouth assembly had more positive interests to serve in that debate, for its chief concern was for the inclusion of a clause in any future Corporation Act which would preserve the distinction of the trading privileges accorded to freemen in corporate towns. Seeking to justify such rights, it railed against 'the injustice and inequality' of non-freemen taking away the trade of freemen, 'who serve the corporation at great expenses and charges'. This call revealed a more deep-rooted worry over the continued viability of corporate government, for without the inducement of commercial advantages for freemen the assembly would have found it impossible to staff its offices. Three weeks later the assembly sent thanks to Fuller and England for lobbying on this issue, and urged them to maintain pressure over freeman privileges. The enforcement of assembly service had been a long-term problem at Yarmouth, as in other corporations, but the Stuart assault on the charters in the 1680s had evidently resown doubts in the minds of assembly leaders.[14]

The crisis of January 1690, which saw a Whig attempt to amend a corporation bill so as to oust their Tory rivals from local government, could only be viewed in Yarmouth as a threat to chartered privileges.[15] Such was the bitterness of this controversy that even the two Yarmouth

---

[12] *CJ*, x. 43, 119–20, 277. For the Convention's debates, see Horwitz, *Parliament, Politics and Policy*, 17–49. However, his analysis of the corporation bill debates concentrates on the key question of the repeal of the municipal tests, thereby failing to address the wide range of issues involved—pp. 22–6, 29. L. Schwoerer notes the controversy surrounding the regulations, but only discusses the significance of the charters in relation to parliamentary elections—*The Declaration of Rights* (Baltimore, 1981), 78–81.

[13] The assembly's interest in such parliamentary debates is attested by its purchase of a 'copy of the Corporation Act' before the end of September 1689—Y/C27/3.

[14] A new corporation bill was ordered on 30 October 1689—*CJ*, x. 277; The assembly had issued directives to the MPs on the 22nd of that month, demonstrating that its principal interest lay with the restoration of charter privileges. In March 1689 the Commons' committee of grievances had ordered the introduction of a bill to tackle the problem—Y/C19/9, ff. 177v, 178v; *CJ*, x. 51.

[15] See Horwitz, *Parliament, Politics, and Policy*, 42–3, where he notes that the prime role allotted to William Sacheverell in this party initiative has been 'somewhat misleadingly attributed'.

MPs, after months of productive co-operation, were divided on the key vote of 10 January. However, rather than trace this rare point of difference between Fuller and England to a true ideological divide, it is more appropriate in this instance to analyse their respective careers in the service of the town as the most direct influence working upon them. Samuel Fuller, a veteran of the 1684 charter purge yet still with eleven years of civic service behind him, chose not to support the proposed exclusion of Tory sympathizers from local office. George England, one of Yarmouth's MPs at the bitterly divisive Parliaments of 1679 and 1681, but with no assembly experience at all, backed the motion.[16] Corporate interest can thus be seen to be at work here, for though the assembly had no ultimate sanction on the voting behaviour of the town's MPs, it could wield great influence over its councillors. Significantly, even while outlining the shifting pattern of party politics at Westminster, Henry Horwitz also identifies a group of hard-working MPs, Yarmouth's among them, who remained loyal to the service of their urban constituents. The timely intervention of a royal prorogation, and subsequent dissolution, prevented the split between Fuller and England from widening into a deeper personal antipathy. However, their role as representatives of the borough at such a crucial time would ensure a more permanent accord between the two local leaders. Their unopposed re-election in February 1690 was a sign of local confidence that their differences in Westminster would continue to be submerged by the discipline of enduring corporate obligations.[17]

In the high spirits of 1688–90 it was understandable for the town's representatives to waver in an alliance based on the service of the constituency. However, it was the failure of the Convention to settle such contentious matters as the charter question which worked to preserve their basic agreement. The passage of London's Confirmatory Act in May 1690 assuaged some of the concerns of corporate governors, but in practice the statute failed to provide widespread reassurance.[18] Many corporations

[16] See D. Rubini, *Court and Country* (London, 1967), 265. England was elected to the corporate post of recorder after the death of Sir Robert Baldock in late 1691, a prudent move on the corporation's part if it wished to ensure his service—Y/C19/9, ff. 211v, 213v.

[17] Horwitz, *Parliament, Politics, and Policy*, 323–4.

[18] *Statutes of the Realm*, vi. 171–3. Horwitz notes that even this confirmation of rights was not without its politicking, for the Tories succeeded in blocking a Whig move to declare the charter surrender simply as void—*Parliament, Politics, and Policy*, 64. Yarmouth had been swift to demand the return of its deed of surrender in October 1688—Y/C19/9 ff. 153–4. R. C. Latham notes the uncertainty of Bristol's corporation over the government's failure to return its cancelled deed of surrender, which lasted until 1708—'Bristol Charters 1509–1899', in *Bristol Rec. Soc. Publs.* 12 (1947), 59–60.

went to great expense and effort to obtain new charters after 1689 in order to remove doubts over their existing rights, hoping thereby to end factionalism which had thrived in the uncertainty of rival charter claims.[19] Continuing unease over chartered liberties was signalled by the Commons' orders for corporation bills in May 1690 and October 1691, while a renewed assertion of royal powers over the corporations from the pen of Robert Brady could only increase concern among town leaders. Brady in fact used the Yarmouth corporation as one of his case studies, citing medieval Exchequer records to conclude that the port was '*villa Regis*, the King's town'.[20] The contentiousness of the charter issue at Yarmouth was attested by the assembly's decision to seek legal advice over James II's proclamation of October 1688 nearly six years after its introduction. Yarmouth's predicament is a highly salutary tale of the consequences of an often ambiguous Revolutionary settlement, which, for the corporations at least, brought little comfort despite the demise of direct royal intervention.[21]

Even though the charter issue posed fundamental doubts concerning local government, after 1688 the most potent cause of division awaiting resolution at a national and local level was the religious question. Yarmouth's declaration of December 1688 had firmly aligned it with the campaign to license Nonconformist worship, a view undoubtedly put forward by Fuller and England when they were appointed in May 1689 to the committee on the toleration bill.[22] It was clear that the success of that bill was the absolute precondition for the establishment of an accord between Anglicans and Congregationalists at Yarmouth. The Convention

---

[19] From the evidence of the unpublished constituency articles of the History of Parliament's 1690–1715 section, the following parliamentary boroughs all obtained new charters under William III: Poole (1689); Fowey (1690); Chester (1691); Ludlow (1692); Nottingham (1692); Colchester (1693); Dunwich (1693); Warwick (1693); Liverpool (1695); Malmesbury (1696); Plymouth (1696); Eye (1697); Tewkesbury (1698).

[20] See *CJ*, x. 417, 544. Horwitz, *Parliament, Politics, and Policy*, 85–6, makes little comment on these bills. Also R. Brady, *An Historical Treatise of Cities and Burghs or Boroughs* [1690], 3, 35–6, and the appendix, pp. 1–9. For Brady's writings, see J. G. A. Pocock, 'Robert Brady, 1627–1700: a Cambridge Historian of the Restoration', in *Cambridge Historical Journal*, 10 (1951), 186–204.

[21] There is no reference to the specific issue which caused the corporation to order legal counsel, though it is interesting to note that the assembly actually enlisted the aid of the recorder of Bury St Edmunds as well—Y/C19/9, f. 247v. Little has been produced to alter M. A. Thompson's view that the corporations' reaction to the proclamation of 1688 remains 'very obscure'—*A Constitutional History of England, 1642–1801* (London, 1938), 454.

[22] *CJ*, x. 133. Both MPs had close marital ties to leading Nonconformist families in the town—see Appendices 4 and 5. For the debates on the toleration bill, see D. Lacey, *Dissent and Parliamentary Politics in England, 1661–89* (New Brunswick, 1969), 209–43.

duly fulfilled these essential hopes for local settlement, though the continuing exclusion of Nonconformists from civic office remained a potential source of friction.[23] However, in common with their co-religionists in the South-West, the Yarmouth Dissenters could still boast some of the leading mercantile families amongst their 'hearers', and as early as January 1689 the Congregationalists sought to protect themselves by appointing local notables as trustees of their meeting-house.[24] Moreover, they could take heart from the return to assembly office of many sympathetic councillors who had suffered expulsion at the time of the charter surrender of 1684. Indeed, the only real threat to corporate unanimity in the immediate aftermath of the Revolution was the resignation of eight assemblymen in August 1689 for a failure to take the oaths recognizing William and Mary. Compared to the purges of 1660–3, 1684, or 1688, these removals were a mere hiccup in the assembly's political development, but they did show that even members of the laity were unprepared to accept the all-too-apparent innovation of the succession settlement. On the other hand, many of their colleagues who had actively participated in the advancement of Stuart policies in the 1680s accepted the new regime and remained in office. Their presence may have easily served as a basis for continued factionalism, but it was a testament to the broad consensus of local opinion that they did not seek to perpetuate past differences. The diary of Dean Davies, who officiated as temporary lecturer at Yarmouth during the winter of 1689–90, provides a sharper focus with which to analyse this delicate political situation.[25]

As an Irish cleric fleeing from the Catholic threat of the Jacobite

---

[23] For the best account of the compromises inherent in this act, see J. Spurr, 'The Church of England, Comprehension, and the Toleration Act of 1689', in *EHR* 104 (1989), 927–46. Unfortunately, there is no direct evidence concerning local views on the question of comprehension.

[24] J. Triffit, 'Believing and Belonging: Church Behaviour in Plymouth and Dartmouth, 1710–30', in S. Wright (ed.), *Parish, Church, and People* (London, 1988), 179–202; Y/FC31/1, 31 Jan. 1689. These trustees came forward despite the fact that no official toleration had yet been granted. Seven of the nine Independent trustees or proprietors had served in the packed assemblies of 1688. Although the trustees of the Yarmouth Quakers were less influential, their trust deed reveals none of the fears for a revocation of toleration which have been noted in other towns—Y/SF259; M. Watts, *The Dissenters* (Oxford, 1978), 263–7.

[25] Twenty-three of the thirty-one councillors expelled in 1684 returned to office in October 1688, only for three of them to resign for previous non-attendance. Six of the eight non-jurors can be identified as crown supporters in the 1678–83 period, though a further ten 'loyal' councillors submitted to the new regime and kept their places. Eight of those ten had held office since the 1660s, compared to only two of the non-jurors, therefore suggesting that experience in office was a prime influence in their decision-making—Y/C19/9, f. 171v; PRO, SP29, 408/121, 442/90.

insurrection in his homeland, Davies displayed an antipathy to papism which only bitter personal experience could engender. However, his fears for the Protestant faith led him to adopt a much more accommodating attitude towards the Dissenters, and in his sojourn at Yarmouth he socialized with both Anglican and Congregationalist communities. Significantly, his main concern centred on the poor turnout of communicants at Anglican services at St Nicholas's Church, rather than on the presence of Nonconformists in the parish. Of five estimates of communicant numbers over the space of six months, the average only came to some 120, a very low return for a town of some 11,000 inhabitants. Congregationalists and Quakers also experienced a fall in numbers, and thus it is possible to conclude that the most immediate effect of the Toleration Act at Yarmouth, as elsewhere, was to increase lay indifference towards religion by making it easier to escape attendance at church.[26] A major problem for the Anglican congregation was the continuing militancy of curate Luke Milbourne, whose ardour had not been cooled by the events of 1688–9. He proudly showed Davies his treatise in defence of the Church's established orders as well as his satirical 'lampoon' on the parish, but his hardened views increasingly isolated him from moderate opinion in Yarmouth. Davies sensed the instability which such hard-headedness could create when discussing 'the danger of being a Dissenter' with his landlord Anthony Ellys, a recently appointed alderman who had been excluded from corporate office for over twenty years due to his links with the Congregationalists. Ready to mix with leading Nonconformist townsmen, Davies was obviously sympathetic towards their predicament, but even he was mistrusted by some Dissenters, who accused him of preaching 'universal redemption', and branded him an Arminian.[27]

Such suspicion and anger, with fertile roots of contention stretching

---

[26] *Camden Society*, 68 (1857), 32, 54, 69, 70. Note D. Spaeth's recent conclusion that most laymen only took communion three or four times each year—'Common Prayer? Popular Observance of the Anglican Liturgy in Restoration Wiltshire', in Wright (ed.), *Parish, Church, and People* (London, 1988), 125–51. The record of baptisms at the Congregational church in the 1690s (12.6 p.a.) shows a notable drop from the 1650s (31.8 p.a.), the only previous decade when official licence permitted a full record to be kept—Y/FC31/1. The Quakers finally established their own meeting-house in 1694, but their baptismal records for the Augustan period also show a fall from a peak in the 1680s—SF259, SF42. The Yarmouth Baptists, having only been re-established in 1686, were also in a precarious position—J. Browne, *A History of Congregationalism . . . in Norfolk and Suffolk* (London, 1877), 558.

[27] *Camden Society*, 68 (1857), 44, 68. Significantly, Ellys's fretful conversation came less than four months after the passage of the Toleration Act. Ellys had entered the Congregational church in May 1661, rising to become one of its civilian overseers by October 1677—Y/FC31/1.

back over the previous forty years, were not going to disappear overnight at the instigation of a limited indulgence to Dissent. However, the deaths and departures of many of the leading protagonists in those bitter struggles contributed towards a spirit of reconciliation in the town. Sir Thomas Medowe and Thomas Gooch, the two townsmen most directly responsible for the charter surrender of 1684, both died in 1688–9, as did Richard Bower, the self-appointed scourge of the Nonconformists.[28] Most importantly, by Easter 1692 Luke Milbourne had chosen to leave the town, and his replacement Barry Love prudently decided not to follow his fractious example.[29] Conversely, the Nonconformist cause lost three of its secular champions in 1688–9, through the deaths of Richard Huntington and Edmund Thaxter, and the disappearance from public life of Sir James Johnson. With them departed personal experience of the earliest battles fought by the Congregationalists to achieve official acceptance, and the new generation of licensed Dissenters could not fully empathize with this militant past. The priority of the recently ordained Congregational pastor James Hannot lay simply with the re-establishment of his church after decades of suppression, not with the continuation of ecclesiological dispute. The unity of his flock proved a continuing source of unease, and ill-health would not ease his burden.[30] Religious tensions were clearly receding by the time of the visit of preacher Nathaniel Hindle in January 1692, for the sermon he gave at St Nicholas's dwelt on the evils of 'this licentious age', rather than the struggle between competing churches.[31] The Revolutionary religious settlement, however unsatisfactory to many, had given new priorities to direct the enthusiasms of lay and clerical leaders, and irreligion was now the principal target for attack. Nevertheless, as a prelude to the achievement of a religious and political accord in the town, no other development could be more significant than the eclipse of the Earl of Yarmouth.

As architect of the charter surrender of 1684 and as an official in James

---

[28] The last record of Bower's activities is a significant one, for he helped to compile the inventory of Sir Thomas Medowe's estate in April 1688, thereby suggesting that he maintained his contacts with loyalist leaders throughout the 1680s—PRO, Prob 4/17907.

[29] The choice of Milbourne's replacement, an occasion for much friction in the past between the town and the Dean and Chapter, was peacefully resolved, largely due to Dean Prideaux's concern to see the spiritual needs of 'so populous a place' speedily met—Tanner mss 134, f. 94.

[30] Dissenting commissioners noted Hannot's 'great congregation' in 1690–2, but also that there were 'some Presbyterians in their membership'—A. Gordan (ed.), *Freedom after Ejection* (Manchester, 1917), 74, 177. In addition, a member of the Congregationalists was expelled in March 1690 for opposing paedobaptism and psalm-singing—Y/FC31/1.

[31] NRO, MC 117/1, pp. 27–42.

II's own household, the earl personified the upheavals of recent times. His past actions would have been sufficient to make him a controversial figure in Yarmouth after 1688, but the earl's continuing identification with the exiled King rendered him a dangerous political embarrassment for the town. In March 1690 he failed to appear in the House of Lords to take the oaths of supremacy and allegiance alongside his fellow peers, and only four months later he was imprisoned in the Tower under suspicion of abetting Jacobite conspiracies.[32] The corporation was in a particularly difficult position for its high stewardship was a life appointment, and since the present incumbent was only 37 at the time of the Revolution, the town stood to lose a vital channel of influence on a long-term basis. A timber contract just before his incarceration in the Tower constituted the assembly's last official contact with him for over six years, aware as local leaders were that the earl could do little for them while remaining in the political wilderness. The earl's failure to retain the wood farm after the expiration of his lease in 1688 was a clear sign of his estrangement from court, and the coolness with which he was now greeted by the Yarmouth corporation was symptomatic of an inevitable decline in his regional control. His continuing Jacobite connections, highlighted by another spell in the Tower in May 1692, ensured that the assembly kept him at arm's length, while his impoverished estate conspired to push him still further from the centre of political activity.[33]

The Yarmouth corporation's prospects were not dissimilar to those of the suspect earl. Further financial decline was likely while haven blockage continued to threaten the trade of the port, but the assembly now suffered a diminished ability to resolve the problem through the loss of an important contact in the capital. The town's MPs had managed to save the Haven Act, but the assembly had no obvious heir to replace the Earl of Yarmouth's backstairs influence in the royal household. The current lord-lieutenant of the county, the Duke of Norfolk, was a familiar and well-treated visitor to the town, but the corporation had hitherto neglected to cultivate his favour. Most frustratingly, the duke declined to

[32] *LJ*, xiv. 431. The earl twice excused his appearance at Westminster with dubious claims to an incapacity to travel from Norfolk—*HMC House of Lords, 1689–90*, pp. 114, 279. N. Luttrell, *A Brief Historical Relation of State Affairs from September 1678 to April 1714* (Oxford, 1857), ii. 67–8, 72–3. Roger North noted his arrest as 'done for security in dangerous times'—A. Jessop (ed.), *The Autobiography of Roger North* (London, 1887), 224.

[33] *Camden Society*, 68 (1857), 37; Y/C19/9, f. 185; *CTB* 1689–92, p. 277; *CSPD* 1691–2, p. 284; Luttrell, *Brief Relation*, ii. 452–3, 458. By December 1693 Paston was described by a local observer as one who 'lives obscurely and yet increaseth his debts'—see 'The Letters of Humphrey Prideaux to John Ellis, 1674–1722', in *Camden Society*, NS 15 (1875), 165–6.

play an active role on the shire's behalf, preferring to secure his position at the new court by a more permanent residence in London and the Home Counties. Beyond him, there was no county figure who might be reckoned to be of truly national prominence, and this situation did not seem likely to change for some time.[34] The Yarmouth corporation was evidently desperate to find contacts in London, for in June 1693 it was still using its former MP Sir John Friend to secure the town's remission for its fishery beer from the Excise Office, some three years after his dismissal from that department for Jacobite sympathies.[35] Predictably, local leaders turned to their parliamentary representatives to provide the most effective lobby for the town's interests. Most significantly, in response to England's and Fuller's sterling activity during the Convention Parliament, the assembly introduced an annual £15 reward for each of their MPs, acknowledging their 'good services' for the town. In the recent past Yarmouth Members had received payments from the corporation, but never on a regular basis, irrespective of the success of their efforts.[36] It would be too simplistic to suggest that the corporation's decision to concentrate on the parliamentary arena stemmed from Whiggish principles, for the town had pressing motivations of a practical nature to demand such a move. It was as much the scale of the war effort after 1689 as the radical import of the Revolutionary settlement which prompted the Yarmouth corporation to place an ever-greater reliance on its MPs. Such a dependence could only grow as the frequency of parliamentary sessions became more assured, and the war forced the trading community back onto already stretched resources.

Just as the outbreak of hostilities in 1665 and 1672 had been greeted with trepidation by the mercantile community at Yarmouth, so William's inevitable turn against France saw no effusion of patriotic fervour on the part of the corporation. Haven blockage and a worrying decline in the

---

[34] J. M. Rosenheim, 'An Examination of Oligarchy: the Gentry of Restoration Norfolk, 1660–1720', Princetown Ph.D. 1981, pp. 265–6, 293–5. The duke was not only lord-lieutenant of Norfolk, but of Berkshire and Surrey too. His most recent visits to Yarmouth had been in September 1688 and July 1689, both for military inspections—Y/C19/9, f. 149v; Y/C27/3; Y/C39/3.

[35] See Y/C19/9, ff. 180, 184v, 199v, 216v, 228. The need for such influence was highlighted in June 1693 by the Customs commissioners' attempt to cease payment of the £160 annuity—*Calendar of Treasury Papers*, 1557–1696, p. 303. The assembly broke contact with Friend only three years before his execution for his role in the Fenwick plot—Henning, *The House of Commons, 1660–90*, ii. 369–70.

[36] After the parliamentary session of 1685, the assembly had made its traditional non-monetary gift of fish and wine—Y/C19/9, f. 96. The £15 reward was continued until 1741, when it fell victim to an economy drive—Palmer, *History of Great Yarmouth*, 218.

herring fishery were already well-established causes for concern by 1688, and the war against Louis XIV promised to hit the town's traders even harder. Since 1660 French shipping had ranked only behind coastal colliers and Dutch flyboats among Yarmouth's leading importers, and only two years before the outbreak of war local merchants had begun to favour French wines instead of Portuguese produce.[37] All this business ceased abruptly with the embargo on enemy goods, and the menace of the French privateers further worsened the port's predicament. The war might bring with it some compensatory benefits for the local shipbuilding industry, but such demand could never make up for the loss in markets and shipping caused by the constant threat of enemy attack.[38] In the summer of 1689 the corporation busily organized fortifications and artillery to defend its haven and sheltered coastal waters, its urgency born in the experience of three Dutch wars. However, its familiarity with wartime hardship also warned the assembly that it would need central influence if it was to provide protection for its traders offshore. Dwyryd Jones has recently re-emphasized the massive impact of the war on the national economy, and the local perspective reinforces his arguments, clearly demonstrating the disruption which the Nine Years War brought to the country at large.[39]

As early as July 1690 the corporation was already complaining of a 'stop of trade' which prevented them from paying their haven-workers' arrears. Moreover, it also had to deal with the unwelcome distractions of securing French prisoners, and of ensuring public order while the press-gangs were at work. There was little that the assembly could do to improve its haven in the present emergency, for the war-induced decline in trade meant a corresponding fall in the revenue from haven tolls. By August 1690 the assembly's cash-flow problems were so bad that it had to default on a payment of £200 to the Norwich corporation, which was outstanding by the terms of the Haven Act.[40] These manifold difficulties help to explain the assembly's reliance on the town's MPs. They were

[37] A. Michel, 'The Port and Town of Great Yarmouth . . . 1550–1714', Cambridge Ph.D. 1978, pp. 34, 45–8.

[38] Ibid. 214, table 6.2. From the period 1686–90 to 1691–5, the town's shipbuilders increased their output from 982 tons p.a. to 2,352 p.a., reaching their peak for the whole Augustan period in 1694–6.

[39] Y/C19/9, f. 166; D. W. Jones, *War and Economy* (Oxford, 1988). See also Brewer, *The Sinews of Power: War, Money, and the English State, 1688–1783* (London, 1989).

[40] Y/C19/9, ff. 188, 188v, 197; *CTB* 1689–92, pp. 733–4, 1,009; Y/C27/3. The revenue from the Haven Act duty fell sharply from the £1,900 p.a. level achieved in the late 1680s, and it would not reach it again until 1702—Y/C27/3.

soon pressed into service at the Admiralty Board to lobby for a convoy to accompany the town's herring fleets, and in May 1691 the assembly sought to further its cause by sending ten guineas to Samuel Fuller to pass on to Admiralty Secretary Southern.[41] The MPs were in equal demand for attendance at the Ordnance Office as the town strove to gain control of the royal magazine sited at Yarmouth, and to ensure sufficient supplies of ammunition to ward off any unwelcome intruders in the vicinity of the haven. Fortunately for those largely inadequate defences, the only force to shake the town's fortifications was an earth-tremor in September 1692, while the visit of the King to Yarmouth a month later gave the local gunners their most profitable opportunity for practice.[42]

The reception for William was slightly muted when compared to the corporation's entertainment of Charles II, though given the town's current predicament, the sum of £106 expended was sufficient testament to the loyalty of the assembly. Soon after William's departure, the assembly decided to celebrate both the King's birthday and 5 November as 'scarlet' days to reaffirm local allegiance, while the occasional scare of Jacobite activity in the locality saw swift action from the magistrates in full co-operation with central government.[43] However, despite these signs of unanimity, the assembly did not naïvely take this accord for granted, recognizing the frustrations of the town's merchants in the face of prolonged warfare. Tensions certainly came to a boil in the autumn of 1693, the year in which English shipping probably incurred its heaviest losses.[44] Although no reason was specified for the assembly's decision to revive its standing orders concerning the balloting of councillors in disputed motions, and for propriety in debate, such moves suggest that the broad consensus of the immediate post-Revolutionary period was under severe strain. The spark for such an outburst of anti-war feeling was probably the news of the loss of the Smyrna convoy in late June, a disaster which

[41] Similar inducements were sent to Southern in May 1692 and June 1693—Y/C19/9, ff. 201, 216, 228.

[42] Y/C19/9, f. 166; CUL, Oo. 6. 115, f. 150. One observer dismissively remarked in 1694 that a 'little platform . . . is all the security the town hath at present'—Arundel Castle archive, MD 010, pp. 27–8.

[43] Y/C19/9, f. 223; also *CSPD* 1691–2, p. 1. In May 1692 the Duke of Norfolk ordered out the Yarmouth militia for four days in readiness 'if the enemy attempt to land upon their coast'. The naval victory at La Hogue ended this immediate threat—*NRS* 30 (1961), 128.

[44] Jones, *War and Economy*, 158–9; J. A. Johnston, 'Parliament and the Protection of Trade, 1689–94', in *Mariner's Mirror*, 57 (1971), 399–413. One of the few sources for ship losses in this period suggests that the towns of Yarmouth, Hull, and Aldeburgh lost a total of 133 ships in the 1690–3 period, costing their shipowners £35,000 in tonnage alone—BL, Harleian mss 7018, f. 97.

could have only increased local concern for the remnants of the town's herring trade to the Mediterranean. A crackdown on assembly discipline would not remove the essential source of contention, but it could hope to control the hotter heads within the town leadership so that problems could be discussed without resort to violence.[45] As the war dragged on, it was imperative that local dissatisfaction be channelled along ordered lines, though it ultimately befell central government to provide real succour to the nation's hard-pressed merchants.

The discontent of Yarmouth's leaders was evidently communicated to the appropriate authorities in Whitehall, for plans were directed to the Admiralty in 1694 for the creation of a convoy 'in continual motion' between the North Sea and the Baltic. Furthermore, even the English consul in Denmark took note of the 'considerable trade' driven from Yarmouth and Hull by enemy privateers, and the three-hour engagement heard off Yarmouth in March of that year added further urgency to local calls for naval protection.[46] Significantly, the corporation was not alone in its efforts to impress central authorities over the seriousness of Yarmouth's commercial position, for a petition was presented to Parliament in the name of the town's fishing merchants, who sought relief from a proposed salt duty. Recognizing the mood of the House of Commons, they prudently concentrated on the value of the industry to the nation's mercantile marine to justify special consideration, arguing that the fishing industry was 'the best nursery for breeding able seamen and always had the favour of Parliament'. Despite such reasoning, their entreaty met with only limited success. A salt duty was imposed, but there was some consideration shown to the fishing trade by the award of a bounty on exported catches.[47] The Commons had thus resolved that the national interest had to overrule local concerns in this instance. However, there can be little doubt that the petitioners were communicating genuine grievances. Local hardship clearly underlay the workhouse's difficulties in 1693 and 1695, while the assemblymen would retain into peacetime the memory of how the 1692 land tax assessors took 'the very rack-rents' of

---

[45] Y/C19/9, ff. 230, 233. For a renewed emphasis on the importance of the Mediterranean trade to the rise of English shipping in the late seventeenth century, see Jones, *War and Economy*, 47–9. In December 1694, the town's merchants had to petition the Privy Council before two small vessels were allowed to take herring cargoes into the Mediterranean—*CTB* 1693–6, p. 876.

[46] *CSPD* 1694–5, pp. 243, 301. Yarmouth was successful in its plea for protection during that desperate year—*HMC House of Lords, 1693–5*, p. 465.

[47] *CJ*, xi. 121. *Statutes at Large*, iii. 507–15. Exported red herrings—Yarmouth's specialty—were to have a bounty of 2s. per barrel.

their estates. The town's merchants had occasionally shown enthusiasm for confrontation with its Dutch rivals in the course of the seventeenth century, but William's war was not to their taste in being both prolonged and of an increasingly dubious commercial value.[48]

Despite the upheavals of war, Yarmouth's parliamentary election of October 1695 suggested that mercantile difficulties had far from dissolved local unity. Political disaffection was not regarded as a serious problem by the government's agent at Yarmouth, Anthony Ellys the younger, who earlier in the year had dismissed local 'restless tempers' as 'few and those too mean to be regarded'. Moreover, on 14 October he noted that even though county politicians were anxiously canvassing for votes in the borough, the townsmen themselves were more concerned with the herring catch, observing that 'we here are so full of the affairs of the season for the present as to be diverted from talking zealously about our choice'. Two weeks later the sitting MPs were returned without opposition, and Ellys simply remarked that 'seven years' experience of our late Members' services deserved this gratitude'. Significantly, there appeared more than a little pride in his boast that the election had gone off 'without any so much as the least previous arts either of verbal persuasion, drinking or procuring compellations'. In response to such unanimous support, the new Members knew that they would have to deliver assurances that the town's hardships were not being ignored by national authorities in the capital.[49]

However, measures taken by Parliament during the ensuing session did little to improve local conditions, which were indeed worsened in the short-term by the legislation passed to resolve the nation's coinage crisis. Ellys was particularly keen to lecture Under-Secretary Ellis on the dangers of unrest among the poor, observing that the withdrawal of smaller denominations threatened the lives of 'such of them as have but a just sufficiency for a day or two's expense'. On a more general note, he felt constrained to warn his superior of the dangers of ignoring the plight of the lower orders, and suggested 'gentlemen who are above the world' were 'little conversant in those difficulties that occur in the case in question'.

[48] Y/C19/9, ff. 228, 262v; *CJ*, xii. 607. See Jones, *War and Economy*, 156–68, where he concludes that convoy protection was 'grossly inadequate' during the war. Note that in August 1695 Dutch observers feared that Yarmouth, unlike well-defended Harwich, 'might easily be ruined' by a bombardment from Du Bart's squadron—*HMC Downshire*, i. 539.

[49] Add. mss 28924, ff. 71, 83. Ellys himself expressed hope for the success of the policies earmarked in the King's speech, especially 'the last paragraph', i.e. for Parliament to 'consider such laws as may be proper for the advancement of trade'—Add. mss 28924, f. 99; *CJ*, xi. 339.

There is no evidence of any serious disturbance at Yarmouth, but this was probably due to the alertness of local magistrates such as Anthony Ellys, who, unlike his out-of-touch superiors, was 'feelingly sensible' of the wretched conditions suffered by his impoverished neighbours. Earlier that year the corporation had endeavoured to ease the plight of the poor by enlisting labourers to help remove haven blockage. It was obviously intended as a stop-gap measure designed to ease local hardship, for the haven required much more than manual effort to cure its tidal problems. 'Many labourers' responded to this call, and thus the assembly's positive approach to the difficulties of the masses can be seen to have met with local approval.[50]

Beyond its responsibility for the poor, the assembly faced a major challenge in maintaining the loyalty of its own membership to the Williamite regime. This priority had been demonstrated in February 1695 by its address of condolence to the King on the death of Queen Mary. Yet even this loyal gesture was accompanied by an expression of hope that William's campaigns would be 'the restorer of a just and durable peace to Europe'.[51] However, the emergence of William as sole ruler placed an even greater onus on local governors to stamp out political disaffection. Following the discovery of the Fenwick assassination plot in early 1696, the Yarmouth corporation marked its determination to root out any possible Jacobite sympathizers in its midst by organizing an Association subscription seven weeks in advance of the compulsory enforcement initiated by Parliament. The Yarmouth Association clearly demonstrated the resolve of town leaders to stamp out any lingering signs of discontent in their hard-pressed community, for unlike the requirements of the subsequent Act, the assembly did not limit their attention to office-holders, and sought to obtain the sworn oaths of as many of their inhabitants as possible. The declaration of allegiance was thus displayed under guard at the Tolhouse for six days while constables toured their wards urging their neighbours to signify their loyalty.[52]

As a result of this stringency, over 1,100 inhabitants signed the Association.[53] However, before it could be presented to the crown, objections

---

[50] Add. mss 28924, f. 103; Y/C19/9, f. 255.   [51] Y/C19/9, f. 256.

[52] *CJ*, xi. 472; Y/C19/9, ff. 272–3. This was one of the assembly's few orders to allocate aldermanic duties on the basis of the ward system, thereby further emphasizing the importance which the corporation attached to the efficient execution of the task.

[53] PRO, C213/186—1,117 names appear on the list, all of them male. The assemblymen head the list, though the only officers specified were the six gunners at the town's havenmouth fort. The social range of the sample is attested by the 316 marks found on the rolls, representing 28.3% of the subscribers. Ellys actually insisted that 1,600 townsmen had

were raised that it was 'not exact with that which had its rise from the Hon. House of Commons'. Ellys wrote feverishly to Under-Secretary Ellis to ensure that Yarmouth would not be 'thought ill of undeservedly', and the town's Association was eventually presented in April. The assembly was most concerned that its reputation might be tarnished in the eyes of central authorities, and four months later it demonstrated its allegiance by expelling two aldermen and three common councillors for failing to recognize William as monarch 'by law'. Unlike the non-jurors of 1689, none of these councillors had played a significant role in the reigns of Charles II or James II, and their removal stands as a measure of how deeply the succession question had affected the locality. In addition, three non-juring ex-assemblymen and the town's bookseller were briefly detained by the militia as suspects 'thought to be dangerous to the present government'.[54] Although this handful of cases highlighted the general acceptance of the Revolution at Yarmouth, the presence of such disaffection cautions any total dismissal of potential division in the town during the Nine Years War. Only six months later, one observer could still note with some alarm that the Jacobite former Archbishop of Glasgow was 'much caressed' during a visit to Yarmouth. The port's strategic importance would magnify any trace of sedition, and the vigilance of national and local governors was again revealed in April 1696, when the town's militia was called out 'in case the French should attempt to land'. Although these military fears were not realized, there was no doubt in the minds of the corporate leadership that decisive moves had been taken in the interest of the town's political stability.[55]

The national emergency had thus achieved the objective of a unified corporation, and the cause of internal solidarity was even further advanced by renewed attacks on the town's chartered privileges. From the autumn of 1696 the assembly was to be locked in two fierce struggles: one concerning the defence of its admiralty court against the claimed superiority of the jurisdiction of the High Court of Admiralty; the other over

signed the roll, and that 500 more would have if not at sea in the service of the King—Add. mss 28880, ff. 92–3.

[54] Add. 28880, ff. 92–3; Y/C19/9, ff. 279v–280; *NRS* 30 (1961), pp. 135–41. One of these non-jurors had been arraigned for seditious words before the Yarmouth quarter-sessions in June 1689, charged with boasting that Jacobite conspirators in London 'make nothing of the juice of an Orange, but wring it out and make dirt of it'—Y/S1/4, p. 116. He, and one other non-juror, refused to sign the Association.

[55] *Camden Society*, NS 15 (1875), 181–2; *NRS* 30 (1961), 140. A garrison force of two companies of fusiliers had been stationed at Yarmouth in April 1696 at the height of the invasion scare—Y/C19/9, f. 276.

its right to impose discriminatory tolls and prohibitions on non-freemen who used the port.[56] Their immediate relevance for the political development of the corporation was obvious, for the assembly achieved consensus most easily while preoccupied with matters of fundamental importance for its continued control of the town. Lionel Glassey has rightly warned that the riches of a corporate archive can mislead the researcher concerning the significance of local disputes, but there is little doubting the seriousness of these controversies at Yarmouth.[57] For instance, the defence of the admiralty court was cited by the assembly in September 1696 as 'a matter of great moment both respecting the honour of the town and the care and benefit of its inhabitants'. Such an all-embracing significance might seem inappropriate for a court which had seen little activity over the previous half-century, but it did express the corporation's determination to maintain its privileges, even during the distractions of wartime.[58] Moreover, the threat of central interference reanimated the assembly's search for viable contacts in positions of influence in London. The strength of the corporation's opponents, and the perceived importance of these issues, forced the assembly to work hard, for it had to ensure that its well-documented defence was not subverted by the machinations of favour. These struggles would reinvigorate the assembly even as the war reached its eighth year, provoked as it was, once again, to prove its commitment to its own cause.

A major aid in the analysis of this critical time for the Yarmouth corporation comes in the form of over fifty letters between assembly leaders and the town's MPs in the winter of 1696–97.[59] This correspondence demonstrates the variety of roles expected of the town's representatives while in the capital, and also indicates that their responsibilities to

[56] The admiralty court quarrel had a history of contention stretching back to the 1590s—Y/36/17, piece 10. The port's freeman privileges had also caused friction with visiting merchants in the past, but no concerted challenge had been mounted against them before 1696.

[57] Glassey, in *Transactions of Hist. Soc. of Lancashire and Cheshire*, 136 (1986), 47–8.

[58] See Y/C19/9, ff. 282v–84v. The inactivity of the court, in the absence of any record of business before 1712, is manifested by the negligible sums raised by it in the town's audit books—Y/C27/2 and 3 *passim*. However, the town's defence of the court in the early nineteenth century would make much of the High Court of Admiralty's own demise between 1648 and 1689—Y/C16/6, piece 37, ff. 38–58. For the history of the national court, and its jurisdiction over salvage cases, see E. J. Roscoe, *Admiralty Jurisdiction and the Practice of the High Court of Justice* (London, 1920), esp. pp. 144–6, 180; and id., *Studies in the History of the Admiralty and Prize Courts* (London, 1932), 12–13, 17–18.

[59] Y/C36/15. Their survival only serves to emphasize the degree of co-operation between MPs and constituents which may be obscured elsewhere by a less fortuitous preservation of evidence.

their constituents conditioned their political activity. These exchanges came at a time when the Members were under especial pressure from assembly colleagues to attend to local matters, but they betray the essential requirements of loyalty and diligence generally expected of them. There could be little time for personal political conviction when acting for a corporation whose demand for news was ferocious, and whose quest for influence was equally unbridled. The town's Association had marked an advance in the assembly's search for influential allies, for the Duke of Norfolk had agreed to present the subscribed rolls to the King, but the day-to-day burdens of corporate service in London and Westminster remained firmly on the shoulders of Fuller and England.[60] In response to the continued efficiency of its MPs, the assembly was fair and open to suggestions from its leading agents in the capital. It could not prescribe the manner in which the MPs might vote on every issue, nor would its annual £15 gift buy their general compliance. However, their occasional pronouncement of ideological allegiance came against a background of sustained service at the behest of their constituents, the corporation above all.[61]

Significantly, other towns may have placed even greater strictures on their Members during the upheavals of wartime. The mayor of York felt it necessary to lecture one of its MPs in 1693 on the latter's failure to meet the assembly's expectations, remarking that 'I have received your several letters with the votes of the House, but hope that is not the whole work our Members have to do, for those I can have from our common intelligence upon more easy terms'. Even the well-bred Sir William Robinson found the York assembly exhausting in its demands, for he bemoaned the 'vast trouble in discharging the duty of a Parliament man', and lamented that there were 'so many different interests . . . so much expected to be done for the citizens or their friends during the sessions of Parliament'. The correspondence of the Members of Chester, Bury St Edmunds, and Liverpool suggests that Robinson's was by no means an isolated lament, and that the provincial towns had fully recognized the potential of an annually sitting Parliament. Following the Revolution, boroughs such as Plymouth, Bristol, Northampton, and Appleby sent

[60] Y/C19/9, f. 273. Once again, it was the MPs who were requested to approach the duke to see if he would 'do us the honour' of presenting the Association.

[61] Compare to G. Jackson's summary on Hull's representatives in the eighteenth century—'whatever their political affiliations, the responsibility of Members for Hull was to the Bench, and their duty was representing Hull's interests in Parliament'—*Hull in the Eighteenth Century* (Oxford, 1972), 300–2. The heavier demand for legislation from the port towns can, in part, explain this stricter tie of service evident at Yarmouth and Hull.

instructions to their Members on both political and practical matters, while a much larger number petitioned the Commons for the resolution of economic grievances. The marked increase in local legislation after 1689 indicated that these lobbying tactics were not without success, and thus Parliament can be seen to have played a vital role in ensuring that the body politic remained in tolerable health during the disruptions of wartime.[62]

When subpoenaed to attend the Court of Exchequer by the attorney-general in September 1696 for the first hearing of the admiralty court issue, the corporation could only turn to its MPs to provide assistance for its legal counsel in the capital. Indeed, the assembly's first instinct when dealing with another admiralty matter—the redemption of a prize ship captured by Yarmouth mariners—was to petition Parliament. Fuller and England swiftly redirected the corporation towards the Admiralty Board, where its representatives met with 'so favourable a reception'.[63] Of course, such news did not halt the assembly's considerable preparations for the Exchequer case, especially when a writ arrived soon afterwards to summon them for a contest over the port's tolls on non-free 'strangers'. The writ had been issued in the name of a Norwich trader, Joseph Haddock, whose cargo of deals had been seized as goods 'foreign bought and sold' when he tried to sell them at the Yarmouth quayside.[64] This threat to the trading monopoly of the town's freeman body was viewed with understandable alarm by an assembly which had demonstrated its concern over the issue at the time of the Convention Parliament. Sensing that any sign of weakness would only encourage more opportunistic encroachments from rival interests, the corporation was quite prepared to expend time and effort to defend its privileges on two fronts.[65]

The assembly's uneasiness only grew as the identity of their opponents was revealed, and as the difficulty of defending these rights became clear. Haddock was reported to have the backing of the Norfolk shrievalty

---

[62] History of Parliament, 1690–1715 section, unpublished constituency articles. See also Handley, in *Parliamentary History*, 9 (1990), 14–37.

[63] Y/C36/15, Yarmouth MPs to bailiffs, 29 and 31 Oct. 1696.

[64] Haddock came from a notable family of mariners, most prominent among whom was his brother, Admiral Sir Richard—J. Charnock, *Biographia Navalis* (London, 1794–8), ii. 49; E. M. Thompson (ed.), 'The Correspondence of the Family of Haddock, 1657–1719' in *Camden Miscellany*, 8 (1883), esp. 39–41.

[65] Since the Revolution the Commons had continued to debate corporate commercial rights. For instance, in January 1693 a bill to suppress hawkers gave rise to a debate on freemen monopolies, with its opponents branding the measure as 'for the advantage of some few tradesmen in corporations'—Horwitz (ed.), *Parliamentary Diary of Narcissus Luttrell, 1691–3* (Oxford, 1972), 132–3.

to try the town's privileges, and even a corporate committee admitted that the town would have problems in court because 'the plea is a charter of prescription against common rights'.[66] Such awareness of the prevailing support for freer trade was echoed by Fuller and England, who doubted whether the 'good' of these freeman privileges could be proved, even if the corporate archive would attest to the town's prescriptive right to enforce them. The MPs enlisted the aid of one of the capital's leading advocates, Edward Northey, but even he predicted 'no good success' in the corporation's case.[67] Rather surprisingly, the first note of encouragement came from some 'gentlemen of Lynn' who informed the Yarmouth representatives in mid-December that they had recently had their own freemen rights upheld by 'eminent counsel'. The struggles of King's Lynn over the same issue underlined the contentiousness of corporate privileges at a time when the nation's traders were already burdened with heavier wartime impositions. Despite news of King's Lynn's success, Yarmouth's representatives remained sensitive to this tide of mercantile grievance, and thus advised the assembly to seek the less public solution of an out-of-court settlement.[68]

However, the incident which most directly highlighted the anxiety and hesitancy of Yarmouth's London agents at this time was the Members' first contact with the Earl of Yarmouth since his return to public life. Paston had decided to take the oaths acknowledging William as the legitimate monarch on 23 November, thus enabling him to resume his seat in the House of Lords.[69] Only a month later the town's MPs nervously reported to the assembly that 'on a solemn invitation' from the earl they had recently dined with him. Significantly, they noted that the earl had 'expressed himself ready at all times to serve the corporation to the utmost of his power', thereby demonstrating the impecunious peer's desperate search for influence. Yet, recognizing the earl's suspect reputation,

---

[66] Y/C36/15, Richard Ferrier to MPs, 19 Nov. 1696.

[67] For a discussion of the free trade debates of the 1690s, see J. O. Appleby, *Economic Thought and Ideology in Seventeenth-Century England* (Princeton, 1978), esp. pp. 99–128. Northey, elevated to the attorney-generalship only five years later, was consulted by Yarmouth's agents on at least ten occasions before the end of the year—Y/C36/15, M. Kendall (Yarmouth's understeward) to Yarmouth town clerk, 4 Dec. 1696.

[68] Y/C36/15, M. Kendall/G. England to bailiffs, 17 Dec. 1696; MPs to bailiffs, 24 and 29 Dec. 1696. On 4 December 1696 Kendall had advised the town clerk, Thomas Godfrey, 'that you make an end of it upon any reasonable terms'.

[69] *LJ*, xv. 16. This was a very tardy acceptance of the new regime on the earl's part, and probably explains why Horwitz fails to cite him alongside the three other non-juring peers who eventually recognized William III. This leaves only four peers who remained consistent in their non-juring stance—*Parliament, Politics, and Policy*, 45.

the MPs went on to voice their hopes that 'what we have done, though without your express authority and command, will not be taken amiss'. Aware of the town's pressing need for allies, but rightly assessing that the earl was not a figure to supply them, the MPs displayed a less than confident faith in the one-time master of the borough. Probably unbeknown to them, the assembly had actually voted the day before to permit official overtures to its high steward, but such favour was rooted in desperation rather than in a personal or political attachment. His part in the charter surrender of 1684 would hardly bring back happy reminders of his past influence, especially given the town's present predicament. His return was a little too sudden for him to be pressed into immediate service on the town's behalf, and the assembly sensibly waited for a more opportune time to employ his interest.[70]

Accordingly, when the town made its first appearance at the Exchequer to contest its admiralty rights on 5 January 1697, it looked to its two MPs to lead the attack against the vice-admirals of Norfolk and Suffolk. The presence in their opponents' ranks of Sir Robert Rich, a member of the Admiralty Board, could not have eased Fuller's and England's minds.[71] Suspicions of an Admiralty-based conspiracy grew rapidly amongst the Yarmouth representatives, and these fears were soon communicated back to the assembly. An overture for a compromise solution from Dr Beau on behalf of the Norfolk vice-admiralty was swiftly rejected by the bailiffs, convinced as they were that 'he will do all the mischief he can do as to our admiralty court, it being in his interest to subvert it'. By mid-February the town's relations with the Admiralty Board had deteriorated to such an extent that bailiff Richard Ferrier actually feared that Yarmouth might lose a convoy because of the way 'the commissioners stand affected towards us'.[72] Despite the minor success of forcing a six-month postponement of the Exchequer trial, the town's agents were under severe pressure not to jeopardize long-term interests by alienating the Admiralty Board on account of its legal activity. When Samuel Fuller did overstep the mark by castigating the Board's members for the late arrival of a convoy at Yarmouth, he earned a stinging rebuke from bailiff

---

[70] Y/C36/15, Yarmouth MPs to bailiffs, 29 Dec. 1696; Y/C19/9, f. 288v. The reticence with which the MPs approached their high steward is borne out by their correspondence over the subsequent three months, for no mention of him was made by any Yarmouth official.

[71] Rich's family seat was at Roos Hall, near Beccles in Suffolk, and thus the vice-admiralty of his own shire was an important mark of local prestige—Henning, *House of Commons, 1660–90*, iii. 328–9.

[72] Y/C36/15, bailiffs to MPs, 15 Jan. 1697; Ferrier to Godfrey, 10 Feb. 1697.

Richard Ferrier. 'Great men will be courted and 'twere pity for want of a little smooth language to lose what is of so much importance to our trade', Ferrier observed on 15 February as he hastily strove to minimize the damage which Fuller's outburst had caused.[73] Fuller might have acted as MP for eight years, but such durability did not absolve him of his duty to corporate service. Only when the Admiralty Board confirmed its order for a convoy to be sent to Yarmouth two weeks later could Fuller be even partly forgiven. In spite of this success, the other Yarmouth agents in London still faced great difficulties, and they knew that outspoken protest would not aid them to secure cherished objectives.[74]

The assembly's worries were further increased in February 1697 by the latest development in the Haddock case. In that month the Exchequer ruled that the matter should be heard in East Anglia, despite the pleas of Yarmouth's agents for the trial to remain in London. The town's counsel had argued that the corporation would not receive a fair hearing in either Norfolk or Suffolk, for rival interests in the region stood to gain from any ruling against Yarmouth's freeman privileges. However, their arguments were rejected and the trial was set for the Norfolk Lent assize at Thetford. The reaction of the assembly's town clerk Thomas Godfrey, who could only console his employers with the hope that presiding justice Sir John Holt would not allow any jury to be influenced by local pressure, betrayed the desperation of the beleaguered corporation. Godfrey argued that Holt 'will not leave it in the power of a jury to hurt us if we have right on our side', echoing the belligerent faith which the Yarmouth assembly had always placed in the legal system as a buffer to outside interference. On 9 March the assembly appointed a seven-man team to travel to Thetford to defend their case, knowing that on these councillors rested both the profit and, as importantly before the county gentry, the honour of the corporation.[75]

---

[73] Y/C36/15, R. Ferrier to T. Godfrey, 15 Feb. 1697. Fuller remained critical of the Board's actions, and the town's agents prudently delegated him the task of seeking repayment for local wartime expenditure at the Office of Sick and Wounded. The pressures of negotiating with Norwich merchants over the timing of the convoy, as well as the threat of ice on the Yare, probably caused Fuller's outburst.

[74] Y/C36/15, T. Godfrey to [Admiralty Board], 22 Feb. 1697. Interestingly, Ferrier begged Godfrey to keep his views on Fuller's rashness 'inter nos'. In the light of future rivalry between Ferrier and Fuller, the former can already be seen to be planning to undermine the latter's local standing—Ferrier to Godfrey, 15 Feb. 1697.

[75] Y/C36/15, T. Godfrey to R. Ferrier, 16 Feb. 1697; Y/C19/9, f. 289. This concern over the possible bias of a county assize is very similar to that expressed by Richard Bower in 1676–7, and it gives another direct insight into the 'siege' mentality which accompanied the corporation's defence of its rights. Holt had been used by the assembly as counsel to examine the legal standing of the charter after its restoration in 1688—Y/C19/9, f. 159.

However, in a dramatic turnabout of events, the apprehensive assembly proved triumphant when Joseph Haddock chose not to appear before the assize, and agreed to pay a 20s. fine to the town for contravening local customs. His climbdown followed a meeting with two Yarmouth aldermen, and beyond speculation that bribery or threat of force was used to influence him, his decision is still more than a little surprising in consideration of the powerful interests which supported him.[76] Yarmouth's opponents were later to accuse Town Clerk Godfrey of brow-beating Haddock into dropping the case with such threats as 'the town was rich, and believed their custom was against law, yet it would cost him money to try it with them'. There is an echo of the corporation's menaces towards Sir Robert Paston in 1665 in this allegation, and it is significant that the town did not seek to deny the charge, nor the further claim that Godfrey had actually refunded Haddock's fine. In contrast to his powerful backers, Haddock was only a merchant of modest means, and it is most likely that his will to contest the issue buckled under the pressures to which he was subjected from both sides. Nevertheless, his climbdown left Yarmouth's custom of 'foreign bought and sold' unvindicated in the courts, even if it might permit the town more time with which to attend to its other urgent affairs in London.[77]

The corporation had little time to celebrate its victory in the Haddock affair for the continuing European conflict ensured that there were still many problems to be tackled. When requesting ever-greater efforts from the town's agents to secure a convoy in February, Bailiff Ferrier had lamented that local losses had been 'so considerable, as to daunt the boldest amongst us'. By late March the assembly had already spent some £250 on securing French prisoners and a further £500 on provisions for the garrison recently quartered in the town. Such expenditure pushed the corporation into a serious financial crisis, and an emergency assistance at the end of the month concluded bluntly that 'our public stock is exhausted and . . . money cannot be borrowed'.[78] Whitehall mandarins at

---

[76] Y/C19/9, f. 292. The last mention of the Haddock affair in the correspondence of the Yarmouth agents was Ferrier's pessimistic 'lament' at the town's failure to achieve a London hearing for the affair—Y/C36/15, R. Ferrier to T. Godfrey, 24 Feb. 1697.

[77] The charge against the corporation came at a Commons' committee in early 1705, when the town faced another battle over freeman rights—*CJ*, xiv. 511. For Paston's discomfort, see Add. mss 27447, f. 334. In the port books for 1698/9, Haddock imported nine cargoes through Yarmouth itself, thereby ranking him only twenty-sixth among merchants using that port—PRO, E190, 513/6. The cargo of deals in question was valued at £160.

[78] Y/C36/15, R. Ferrier to T. Godfrey, 5 Feb. 1697. The only record of this assistance comes on the back of a letter addressed to the bailiffs in Y/C36/15, dated 20 March 1697. It indicates that many more semi-formal assemblies of councillors might have taken place than have been recorded in the assembly books.

the Office of Sick and Wounded showed particular insensitivity by dismissing Yarmouth's appeal for repayments with the contemptuous remark that 'it grieves us that so small a sum . . . should obstruct his Majesty's service'. Two days later it behoved Samuel Fuller to explain to the same officials why a lack of local credit had forced the Yarmouth bailiffs to turn away a consignment of French prisoners put ashore at their haven.[79] Such an episode pinpoints the vital role of the MPs as a channel of communication between the corporation and central authorities, particularly when the town wished to represent its difficulties to ill-informed or indifferent national bodies. Equally importantly, the MPs performed a crucial service by supplying the corporation with a constant stream of information concerning national affairs. Their letters during the session of 1696–7 provided a full report of all Commons' business, ranging from Fenwick's attainder to the terms of the supply and electoral regulation bills. However, their greatest vigilance was reserved for mercantile issues. Salt, coal, and malt duties were all discussed in detail, and the Members even acted as advisers for the town of Bridlington when it sought to obtain a Haven Act. More so than any survey of division lists, telling activity, or committee attendance, their correspondence proves that Fuller and England were true representatives of an abiding town interest which had little respect for faction or party.[80]

Despite their industry, the two MPs could do little to ameliorate the effects of the war itself. Even as the conflict entered its final year, the town was still on constant alert for enemy activity off the Norfolk coastline. In June the Norfolk militia was put on standby for 'any emergent occasion', but this alarum was merely a prelude to a full-blown invasion scare in July, when French ships were seen off Yarmouth and were thought to be 'threatening to land'.[81] Peace negotiations had begun at Ryswick in May, but the dangers for shipping remained, keeping the corporation under continued pressure to obtain convoys for the port's merchant marine. However, relations with the Admiralty remained tense, and in the summer of 1697 the forthcoming trial at the Exchequer over Yarmouth's admiralty court promised to prolong, if not intensify, the

[79] Y/C36/15, Commissioners of the Sick and Wounded to bailiffs, n.d.; bailiffs to Fuller, 22 Mar. 1697. The bailiffs blamed local victuallers for refusing to supply the gaolers on credit.

[80] Y/C36/15, *passim*. The Bridlington representatives were wise to seek the co-operation of the Yarmouth MPs, for both the ports of Dover (in January 1692) and Whitby (in April 1702) suffered serious set-backs when they sought to oppose Yarmouth's plea for exemptions from proposed pier tolls—Horwitz (ed.), *Parliamentary Diary of Narcissus Luttrell*, 152; *CJ*, xiii. 836, 858–9.   [81] *CSPD* 1697, p. 74; *NRS* 30 (1961), 145, 150.

town's difficulties. In desperation the assembly decided to mend relations with the Earl of Yarmouth, evidently keen for him to play an effective role as high steward. Unfortunately, the very next day after the assembly had voted to renew its practice of sending gifts to Oxnead, the earl was called before the Lords Justices to answer charges that he had conspired in a Jacobite plot to secure Norfolk for the exiled King. He was cleared of any involvement, but his past prominence at James II's court would remain a stigma on his reputation, and minimize his potential utility to the town.[82]

The Exchequer hearing of the Admiralty affair gave the corporation little cause for comfort, for in its wake its agents confirmed that the town's opponents included the attorney-general, the Admiralty's solicitors, and the vice-admiralty of Norfolk.[83] However, despite this formidable opposition, Yarmouth's counsel put up a robust defence to frustrate the immediate hopes of these rivals. Alderman Anthony Ellys the younger, against whom the attorney-general's writ had been served, successfully moved for an Exchequer commission to take depositions at Yarmouth to provide precedents for the town's seizure of wrecks within its admiralty jurisdiction. The depositions were taken in late October, and added immeasurably to the strength of the town's case. Moreover, having already supplied Ellys with the services of three of the town's foremost attorneys, the assembly soon drafted the town MPs into Ellys's counselling team, such was the perceived threat to the 'honour and just perquisites' of the corporation.[84] All this activity was to reap dividends at the subsequent hearing of the matter in mid-November, when judgment on the matter was postponed for yet another year. The town might not have achieved recognition for its admiralty court at the Exchequer, but a platform of legal defence had now been established from which it could continue to justify its rights against encroaching interests. On the other hand, the

[82] Y/C19/9, f. 299v; *CSPD* 1697, pp. 326–7, 359–60, 384, 389. The principal objective of the supposed plot was the seizure of Dover Castle, but 4,000 men were expected to be raised in Norfolk to spread the uprising.

[83] Y/C19/9, f. 302v. In the summer of 1697 attorney-general Sir Thomas Trevor had begun three other processes to contest the rights of manorial lords to seize wrecks washed up on their coastline, two of them in Norfolk and one in Yorkshire. Yarmouth was thus the only corporation to be tried at law, but these concurrent hearings indicated the determination of central authorities to establish the supreme jurisdiction of the High Court of Admiralty—PRO, E134/9, Will. III/Mich. 35, 45, 47, 58.

[84] PRO, E134/9, Will. III/Mich. 58. Ellys had been bailiff at the time of the seizure of an anchor and cables which was used by the attorney-general as the test case for Yarmouth's admiralty jurisdiction. A copy of the depositions can also be found amongst the corporation's own papers—Y/C36/7, piece 3.

complexity of the issues involved would spawn multiple opportunities for attack and counter-attack on both sides.[85]

While the initial outcome of the Admiralty issue invested the corporation with a degree of optimism in its immediate future, nothing could lift the spirits of its members more readily than the actual cessation of the war. Continuing military activity in the vicinity of Yarmouth throughout the summer of 1697 counselled caution right up until the signing of the Treaty of Ryswick, but in December an assembly address to the King heralded the achievement of 'the happy peace'.[86] However, even as the celebratory fireworks at the quayside died away the town's leaders knew that serious challenges lay ahead of them—most dauntingly, the recovery of the port after eight years of disrupted trade. Ten months after Ryswick local merchants such as Benjamin Ward could still blame 'the decay of trade in that port' for his failure to obtain payment at Yarmouth. Moreover, the difficulty of restoring trading links overseas was highlighted as late as October 1699 by alderman Benjamin England, who urged patience on a client with the plea that 'nothing is done to commerce with the French, matters are not right for it'.[87] The responsibility for the regeneration of the town lay principally with the assembly, whose powers of leadership would be severely tested over the succeeding years. In particular, its problems were compounded by the possible resurfacing of local divisions, for the war had not been a popular one and with its end the absolute necessity for a public consensus was perceived to be a less important priority. Even the political hot-house of London had enjoyed some respite from factionalism during wartime, but the long-awaited peace represented an ideal opportunity for competing groups to advance their respective causes.[88]

The parliamentary election of July 1698 certainly testified to Yarmouth's

---

[85] The honour of the corporation was doubtless insulted by the report of Chief Justice Ward after the Exchequer hearing, for he failed even to recognize its status as a functioning organ of local government. He described the whole affair as the 'combination and confederacy' of Ellys and his friends without a single reference to his position within the corporation, or to the powers enshrined in Yarmouth's charter—Y/C36/7, piece 8.

[86] Y/C19/9, f. 303v.

[87] *CTB* 1697–8, p. 379; Arundel Castle archive, A735, B. England to J. Aylward, 18 Oct. 1699. England was very keen to assure his London correspondent of the continuing viability of Yarmouth as 'a good and safe road'.

[88] De Krey, *Fractured Society*, 31–2. An early sign of the corporation's determination to capitalize on the advent of peacetime came with the presentation of the thankful address to the crown in February 1698. The assembly managed to secure the services of the Earl of Yarmouth as presenter, but alongside him it wisely enlisted the Duke of Norfolk, a confirmed Williamite—Y/C19/9, ff. 303v, 304v.

unsettled condition, for the freeman body made the first break in its post-Revolution choice of MPs, returning Captain John Nicholson alongside George England. Most significantly, in the run-up to the election there were indications that religious divisions were appearing in the town for the first time since 1689.[89] In the very first meeting after the signing of the Treaty of Ryswick, an attempt had been made to force two leading Congregationalists to take up seats in the assembly. They both refused office, and also declined to pay the fines levied for such recalcitrance, in reaction to which the assembly began legal proceedings against them.[90] However, even though this dispute had not been resolved by the time of the election, Nicholson's success did not herald a return to the factionalism of the 1680s. Yarmouth's minister, Barry Love, was clearly of the opinion that the town's post-Revolutionary accord had held, for in the wake of the election he could still take comfort in the 'unity, which is at present so visible and praiseworthy' in his locality. Moreover, the lack of a contest suggests that the acrimony of the 1678–81 elections had not returned to the borough. These were encouraging signs, but the harassment of local Dissenters suggested that religious tensions still threatened to boil over, and Yarmouth's leaders would need to be vigilant if they wished to avert serious division so soon after a European peace had been achieved.[91]

The town may have chosen an outsider as a Member for the first time since 1685, but it had not made a complete break with prior electoral behaviour. Although not a native townsman, Nicholson was very much in the mould of the typical Yarmouth representative, rather than that of a creature of party. His experience as a naval commander and as an East India trader rendered him an instantly attractive candidate to the

[89] Rosenheim, 'An Examination of Oligarchy', 310–15, sees the electoral changes in Norfolk at this time as symptoms of a transitional stage, as one county élite replaced another, and cites Nicholson's success as a Tory victory.

[90] John Smith and William Luson were two of the town's leading merchants when elected to the assembly in October 1697—Y/FC31/1; Y/C19/9, ff. 302v, 303v, 307. Religious tension may have been fuelled by national developments, see G. Bennet 'Conflict in the Church', in G. Holmes (ed.), *Britain after the Glorious Revolution* (London, 1969), 155–75. However, signs of religious factionalism have to be qualified by reference to the refusal of two other townsmen to accept assembly places only a month before, neither of whom had documented links to local Dissent. The corporation may simply have been seeking to raise money, following the practice of other boroughs such as London— I. Doolittle, 'The Government of the City of London, 1694–1767', pp. 10–11, 36–7, 58–61.

[91] B. Love, *The Catechism of the Church Resolved into Short and Easy Questions and Answers* (London, 1699, 2nd edn.), the dedication. The History of Parliament suggests that there might have been a contest, but there is no evidence to support this thesis. By the time of the Yarmouth election, Nicholson had already fought and lost a poll at Dunwich—History of Parliament, 1690–1715 section, unpublished biography and constituency articles.

town's mercantile community, especially at a time when the corporation welcomed every source of aid to improve relations with the Admiralty Board.[92] Indeed, it may have been Fuller's outburst at the Board in February 1697 which first put his position in doubt, and may have ultimately cost him his place in the Commons. The assembly could not suffer Yarmouth's MPs to jeopardize the town's interests, and its leaders may have viewed Nicholson as a possible arbitrator to smooth over past differences.[93] Although Nicholson was not an assemblyman, the corporation had revealed its regard for him seven years earlier by granting him the freedom of the town. Such bequests were never made without the hope of future service, and that responsibility now lay even more heavily on his shoulders as he took his seat in the Commons. The session of 1698–9 demonstrated how expectant his constituents were of his dutiful tenure of office at Westminster.[94]

Alongside George England, Nicholson faced a barrage of requests to present Yarmouth's grievances at Westminster. The town clearly hoped that the end of hostilities would yield greater opportunities to gain legislative favour, but such lobbying also echoed a faith in the efficiency and loyalty of its two serving Members. In the preceding session England had represented the town's fears over the possible demise of the herring fishery, but had achieved little more than the referral of Yarmouth's petition to committee.[95] However, in the 1698 Parliament the renewal of the Haven Act was a matter of even greater urgency, for the statute in force was due to expire in July 1699. Worryingly for the town, unlike its campaigns to obtain the Haven Acts of 1677 and 1685, on this occasion it did not have the aid of a noble patron. Furthermore, soon after the introduction of the bill the corporation took note of the circulation of

---

[92] See Charnock, *Biographia Navalis*, i. 399; Add. mss 22186, ff. 31–59; *CTB* 1693–6, pp. 359–61.

[93] The parliamentary voting records of Fuller and England showed no divergence from the time of the corporation bill division of 1690, thus suggesting that party issues did not promote England ahead of Fuller—*BIHR*, special supplement 7 (1968), which is fortunate in having a cluster of surviving parliamentary lists for the year 1696, thereby answering criticisms levelled at the selective nature of such source material.

[94] *NNAS* 9 (1910), 126–7. The corporate service for which Nicholson was rewarded with a freedom is not specified, but it may have been for his command of a convoy frigate. In the same year Captain John Davison also received a gift of the freedom, and this reward was certainly a token of the town's gratitude for the protection which ships under his command had provided for North Sea traders. Unlike Nicholson, he later entered the assembly in 1700 and received rapid promotion to the aldermanic bench—Charnock, *Biographia Navalis*, ii. 308–9.

[95] *CJ*, xii. 151. The petition had requested that a ban, or duty, be placed upon the export of Irish red herrings.

pamphlets by 'country gentlemen' attacking the haven duty. Given its current weakness, the assembly thought it best to seek arbitration rather than risk the complete loss of vital revenue. Therefore a team of seven Yarmouth councillors met with representatives from Norfolk and Norwich while the bill lay before the Commons committee, and renewed the agreement to contribute an annual £50 from the haven duty towards the navigation of the River Yare. Such preparations worked to the town's advantage, for the bill actually received the backing of its former Member Sir William Cook, who enthused that 'the port of Yarmouth is of such consequence to the counties and city as all encouragement ought to [be] shown to the preserving it'. Such an argument impressed both Houses, and the bill quickly passed to reward the assembly's efforts with an extension of haven tolls for another twenty-one years. The new Haven Act also gave the town liberty to experiment with 'new works' at the havenmouth for the first time. At the end of an extremely testing decade for local traders, the success of the MPs was a heartening tonic for the port, and highlighted the wisdom of having representatives directly familiar with the frustrations of their constituents.[96]

The MPs gave the townsmen further satisfaction by their support for Yarmouth's petition to make Billingsgate a free market for fish, a campaign which received the backing of Lowestoft. The ports went into print to attack monopolists at the market, and, somewhat hypocritically, had the cheek to censure the tolls levied there by the mayor of London. Wilson has remarked on the essentially self-serving ends of many free-trade initiatives in the late seventeenth century, and Yarmouth was no exception in attacking the privileges of others while jealously guarding its own exclusive rights. Although Yarmouth's specific requests were not granted, an Act was passed to ensure that Billingsgate would remain open to all merchants, again indicating the current strength of opinion in favour of free trade, which had caused the town so much discomfort during the Haddock case.[97] In March 1699 another petition was received from the borough to draw attention to the 'considerable sums of money' owed to Yarmouth ship-owners for the use of their vessels in royal fleets during the war. The matter was more appropriate to a hearing at the Admiralty Board, but the townsmen's faith in their MPs was vindicated

[96] Y/C19/9, ff. 317v, 319, 330; *CJ*, xii. 358, 360, 449, 485, 495; Suffolk Record Office (Ipswich), Gurdon mss 2, p. 27; *Statutes of the Realm*, vii. 460–2. In the next session, the assembly invested time and effort to ensure that Yarmouth was exempted from the tolls levied by the Dover Harbour Act—Y/C27/3, Mich. 1699/1700.

[97] *The Case of Great Yarmouth and Lowestoft in Relation to the Bill for Making Billingsgate a Free Market for Fish*; *CJ*, xii. 510–11, 590; *Statutes of the Realm*, vii. 513–14; C. Wilson, *England's Apprenticeship* (London, 1984, 2nd edn.), 270–1.

once again when the House resolved to refer the petition to committee.[98] Significantly, it was only with the assembly's petition seeking relief over its land tax assessment that the MPs met immediate rebuttal in the House, when their plea of past wartime hardship was deemed unworthy of special consideration. However, the corporation could not have been but very grateful towards its parliamentary representatives for their efforts in that session, for they had clearly emulated the loyalty of their predecessors.[99]

The corporation, of course, was not totally reliant on its MPs to provide services. However, its other initiatives at this time suggest that it generally looked to the capital to seek resolution of its difficulties. Finance remained the most worrying problem, threatening to stall any plans for local improvement, but the cessation of hostilities at least permitted the assembly a short interval in which to renew efforts to secure its fiscal future. In March 1699 it took the significant step of investing in public stock for the first time, accepting a proposal to place £1,200 in the Bank of England.[100] The assembly's public investments grew in sophistication and importance over the succeeding two decades, demonstrating greater readiness to look to external remedies for local ills. The corporation continued to study ways in which it might revitalize the town independent of outside aid, but the evident utility of its MPs over the decade had impressed upon all assemblymen the benefit of preserving strong links with the capital. Important internal reforms were undertaken after Ryswick, such as the reorganization of the town's committee structure, but even these changes reflected the town's greater involvement with national authorities. In November 1699 a standing committee was appointed to defend the town's admiralty court, as the town responded to continued harassment from the Admiralty in the High Courts.[101] However, London

[98] *CJ*, xii. 583. Michel notes a rise in ship-ownership at Yarmouth by the end of the century, attributing such growth to the desire of local merchants for a safer means of investment—'Port and Town of Great Yarmouth . . . 1550–1714', p. 232. R. Davis ranks Yarmouth as the third leading provincial port after Bristol and Newcastle in terms of ship-ownership in 1702; by 1730 it had overtaken Newcastle—R. Davis, *The Rise of the English Shipping Industry* (Newton Abbot, 1972, 2nd edn.), 34–6; J. D. Murphy, 'The Town and Trade of Great Yarmouth', UEA Ph.D. 1979, p. 264.

[99] *CJ*, xii. 607. In this petition Yarmouth claimed that there had been a 25% fall in the value of local property between 1692 and 1698. Appendix 2 reveals that the town's tax assessments rose by 26.8% between 1689 and 1694—PRO, E182/686.

[100] Yarmouth's Members kept the town informed of the Bank's affairs. In November 1696, they informed their corporate colleagues of the House's resolution that the Bank was an aid to trade in general—Y/C36/15, MPs to the bailiffs, 10 Nov. 1696.

[101] Y/C19/9, f. 328. The assembly also established a standing committee to oversee its investments in London in October 1701, following a major review of local finances—Y/C19/10, f. 2.

did not simply present a confrontational prospect in local life, for the town's growing self-confidence was signalled the following year by a proposal for the erection of a hospital for retired mariners, an idea no doubt sparked by the national scheme at Greenwich.[102] In a period of difficulty and uncertainty, the corporation was naturally more open to consider any source of aid, but the increasing hold of the capital on the minds of its leaders suggested a significant shift in the town's general perspective.

The greatest attraction of London for the assembly, however, remained the powerful institutions of central government, and the cultivation of personal interests there promised the surest route towards local improvement. Fortunately for the town, the death of the Duke of Norfolk in April 1701 provided the corporation with an opportunity to shake off its worrying dependence on the Earl of Yarmouth. The whole of Norfolk, starved of an effective leader for over a decade, now turned to court his replacement as lord-lieutenant, the young Charles, 2nd Viscount Townshend.[103] The future secretary of state had already been tipped as a potential statesman by local observers, one of whom suggested that he was 'fit for the greatest employments in the state, but that innate modesty forbids such ambitious thought'.[104] Such modesty could yet be overcome by the solicitation and support of the shire, and Yarmouth did not hesitate to flatter him by arranging a great entertainment in his honour in August 1701. For the first time since 1684 the assembly conferred an honorary freedom on a visiting nobleman, thereby establishing a basic contact with this most promising source of favour. By October it had prevailed upon Townshend to present an address to the King expressing outrage at Louis XIV's recognition of the Old Pretender as rightful monarch. Townshend did not hold the office of Yarmouth high steward, but from that moment he was effectively fulfilling that role.[105]

---

[102] Y/C19/10, f. 4. A previous project for a hospital for aged mariners had come to nothing in 1673, even though it had gained national backing as a scheme to encourage enlistment in the Royal Navy—*CSPD* 1673, pp. 625–6.

[103] Rosenheim notes that many county politicians hoped that the new incumbent would bring an end to the sterile and bitter contests of the past—'An Examination of Oligarchy', pp. 313–15.

[104] *HMC Egmont*, ii. 202. Note Dean Prideaux's warm praise of the 19-year-old viscount, four years before he even took up his seat in the Lords—*Camden Society*, NS 15 (1875), 165–6.

[105] Y/C19/9, ff. 359v, 360v, 363; Y/C19/10, f. 2v. The entertainment cost the corporation £63, a figure almost twice the sum spent on the celebrations for his father's visit as lord-lieutenant in August 1663 (when the 1st Viscount had also been accompanied by the Bishop of Norwich)—Y/C27/2.

However, even as the town united to close ties to the Townshends, it became apparent that open divisions had re-emerged in the locality for the first time since 1688. In January 1701 the freemen had returned George England and Samuel Fuller as its MPs for the fourth time in twelve years, after an uncontested election which signalled the latter's swift rehabilitation in the eyes of the local leadership. However, by the end of that year religious matters had once again come to a head. Assembly affairs gave little clue to the origin of these tensions, for in August it awarded the town's curate Barry Love a £20 annuity for his catechizing endeavours, thereby demonstrating its members' support for the local battle against irreligion and spiritual indifference. This resolution was in marked contrast to the aggressive moves which had been made against Dissenting leaders in 1697, but such vindictiveness had evidently reanimated divisions within the populace. In particular, the Atterbury affair, which helped to encourage spiritual militancy on a nationwide basis during 1701, may well have prompted Yarmouth's Dissenters to close ranks in defence of their hard-earned rights, and the parliamentary poll in November was an obvious occasion on which to make their stand.[106] The election had a momentous impact on local leaders, for the town saw its first contested poll for twenty years, and both the incumbent MPs were removed. One of their replacements was the familiar figure of John Nicholson, who may well have taken Samuel Fuller's place in a pre-arranged agreement. There was no mistaking the contention surrounding the other seat, however, for England's successful rival was John Burton, the most prominent figure in Yarmouth's Dissenting community. The swift succession of parliamentary elections had finally provided factious minds with the opportunity to break the local consensus which had been shakily maintained since the end of the war, and it was familiar religious tensions which underlay this return to local conflict. In this regard Yarmouth's experience was certainly not atypical, since recent research has represented the events of 1701 as a watershed in national politics, with religion portrayed as an ideological fuse for an explosion of party rivalry.[107]

---

[106] Y/C19/9, f. 359v. The sermons of Independent minister Hannot at this time reveal no bitterness against the Established Church, and his only allusion to local suffering was of a mercantile nature—CUL, Add. 4356. For the Convocation Crisis, see Bennett, *The Tory Crisis in Church and State*, 44–63.

[107] Holmes, *The Making of A Great Power* (London, 1993), 337–8. Moreover, Lionel Glassey found that Whig and Tory labels were not commonly used in Lancashire until Queen Anne's reign—*Transactions of Hist. Soc. of Lancashire and Cheshire*, 136 (1986), 54–5. John Burton was declared the victor at Yarmouth 'after a scrutiny'—*Post Boy*, 29 Nov.–

In a letter which provides the first evidence of Townshend's intrusion into Yarmouth politics only five months after visiting the town, Samuel Fuller blamed England's defeat on 'the slippery trick the Dissenters acted in our election here'.[108] This charge possibly refers to the belated entrance of John Burton as a candidate against George England, whose own preparations may have been affected by a long-term illness. This impression accords with the prediction made by a Norfolk election manager only a week before the poll, for he observed: 'it will be the old ones, tho' now I hear there is opposition at Yarmouth.'[109] Fuller echoed the disgust of 'those of the Church part' at Burton's tactics, and forecast that it might alienate some of Townshend's supporters at the subsequent county contest. At this stage of his political career, such a consideration was obviously Townshend's main interest in securing contacts at Yarmouth, and thus he must have been gladdened to hear that 'a particular obligation' to his interest would save him many of those votes potentially jeopardized by the actions of Burton's allies. His Whiggish opinions were evidently known to the Yarmouth electorate, but the county election of the following year would show how his value as a patron could override political affiliations, for some of the town's Anglican leaders voted alongside their Dissenting neighbours in the Whig interest, thereby vindicating Fuller's reading of local political sentiment.[110]

The Yarmouth Nonconformists were unable to maintain their ascendancy for long, and within eight months Burton had lost his place to Benjamin England at the election called on the accession of Queen Anne. Another contest took place, but the return of Nicholson and England did not herald a backlash against the recent assertiveness of local Nonconformity. Benjamin England was clearly no bigot, for his family had acted as the chief lay supporters of religious toleration at Yarmouth, and his corporate career suggested that his undoubted Anglicanism bore none of the vindictiveness displayed by its local champions in the 1680s. He thus

2 Dec. 1701. He was the son of William Burton, the despised governor of the town in the last years of the Interregnum, and had been approached to become elder of the Congregationalists in May 1694—Y/FC31/1.

[108] NRO, Sotheby Purchase S154D, Samuel Fuller to Visct. Townshend, 12 Dec. 1701. As a Member Fuller could easily assume the role of Townshend's chief correspondent on Yarmouth affairs. However, he did not play host to the viscount when the latter visited Yarmouth—Y/C19/9, f. 359v.

[109] *HMC Portland*, iv. 27. Corporate officials expressed doubts concerning England's life-expectancy as early as February 1697, and he was to die in July 1702—Y/C36/15, 10, 24 Feb. 1697.

[110] *NRS* 8 (1935), 39–70. Only the poll book for the fourth-placed candidate Sir Edward Ward survives, but the names of 148 Yarmouth residents appear on it.

characterized the less militant 'Toryism' of his assembly colleagues, who since 1689 had identified their principal enemy as irreligion and vice.[111] Significantly, the bailiffs themselves regarded the contest as an 'unhappy dispute' when communicating the result to Townshend, and warned him that the Yarmouth electors would not come to the county election 'in so united a manner' as they had hoped. Moreover, even though the assembly had demonstrated its attachment to the Church of England by its congratulatory address to the new Queen in April 1702, it had refrained from castigating Dissenting groups. Love's catechizing campaign had certainly preceded the factionalism described by Fuller, and though the minister's efforts would be insufficient to suppress all memories of past contention, the respite from the polls could only aid the cause of religious settlement.[112] The elections of 1701–2 marked a painful transitional stage in Yarmouth's religious development, but even at the start of Anne's reign there were signs that the most damaging aspects of intra-communal strife would not be suffered to return in perpetuity.

The renewal of European conflict in the last months of William's reign helped to curb local division. However, even though the assembly's address of October 1701 had expressed firm support for the Hanoverian succession, the methods required for its defence against Jacobite usurpation would not be to the liking of the town's merchants. On a visit to Yarmouth only three months before, Sir John Perceval observed that the vulnerability of Yarmouth's herring exports to the Mediterranean 'make[s] the townsmen dread a war'.[113] Indeed, the new reign began in very much the same manner as its predecessor, with local concerns over the succession, a European war, and the possible return of religious conflict. Yet Yarmouth's leaders had witnessed important changes during the intervening fourteen years, and had given notice of their determination to

[111] W. Speck, *Tory and Whig: The Struggle in the Constituencies, 1701–15* (London, 1970), 128. Benjamin England had entered the assembly in 1668, and had been identified as an ally by loyalists in 1678. However, he was one of the most notable converts to the 'factious' by 1683, indicating that his support for the crown wavered in the face of borough regulation—PRO, SP29, 408/121, 442/90.

[112] Raynham Hall archive, box 65, William Browne and Henry Borret to Visct. Townshend, n.d.; Y/C19/10, f. 8. No first edition of Love's catechism has been traced, but the second edition reveals that his positive drive against irreligion was well under way before 1699.

[113] The address did not, in fact, make any reference to a possible call to arms, but the town had already taken an estimate of repairs at the fort in August 1701, and an inspection of the town walls was ordered in December. Both produced scathing reports—NRO, MS 11408/29/A2; Y/C19/10, ff. 3v, 7; M. Wenger (ed.), *The English Travels of Sir John Perceval and William Bird II* (Missouri, 1989), 71. Perceval's correspondent, Peter Le Neve, had noted the 'decay' of Yarmouth's trade only four weeks before Perceval's visit—*HMC Egmont*, ii. 199.

regenerate the town and its trade. The courting of Viscount Townshend was but one part of its overall plan for local improvement, since there were already moves under way for public rebuilding schemes, and even for the reform of the corporate structure itself.[114] Renewed warfare could only threaten the progress made by the corporation since Ryswick, but with self-confidence increased by its ties to Raynham, it could look to the future with much greater optimism. Many doubts remained concerning the unity of the assembly and its relationship with external authorities, but it had proved itself an effective leader through the manifold difficulties of William's reign. The ensuing twenty years proved equally testing as the responsibility for local stability and recovery continued to rest heavily on the corporators' shoulders.

Yarmouth's travails since 1688 demonstrate that during the reign of William III the nation faced huge challenges, whose impact had important repercussions for the political development of the provinces. Even as the state set about extracting maximum resources from the realm, enterprising local governors were seizing opportunities to gain advantages from an annually sitting Parliament. Such mutual interest, particularly during a time of general hardship, helped to dampen factionalism and to fix allegiance to the Williamite regime. This process was particularly important, for the Revolutionary settlement was quickly perceived to have compromised on many issues, most notably over the question of religion. The nation's rulers had all but declined to tackle such controversial issues as the borough charters, thereby causing much uncertainty and conflict. However, legislation such as the Toleration and Triennial Acts had a decisive influence on provincial politics, changing the tempo and objectives of local politicians. Divisions remained, but it is also important to acknowledge that the bitter memories of the 1680s counselled caution to the generation which had lived through those difficult times, ensuring that many local politicians reached a working accommodation with former rivals. The next great war would continue to condition the development of local political groupings, as renewed conflict tested the willingness of the provincial leaders to maintain the compromises of the Revolution in the interest of national unity.

[114] Y/C19/10, ff. 2v, 4.

7
The Townshend Triumph: 1702–22

THIS chapter essentially sets out to examine the successful establishment of a parliamentary 'interest' in an urban constituency. Yarmouth, in common with the vast majority of the country's leading towns, experienced all the symptoms of what has been termed as the 'rage of party' of early eighteenth-century England. Having undergone three elections in the period 1701–2, the freemen had six more opportunities to cast votes over the next thirteen years, during which time the borough saw two further contested polls in a burst of almost continual campaigning between 1708 and 1710.[1] However, the decisive outcome of this intensive electioneering only became clear at the poll of 1722, when the town's two seats fell to members of the Townshend and Walpole families. Thereafter the constituency was seemingly relegated to the status of a dependent borough, as a pattern of electoral behaviour was established which lasted for over fifty years. Yarmouth's political development would certainly appear to accord with traditional accounts of the electoral 'coma' to which the country succumbed in the wake of the Whig ascendancy; a triumph of party facilitated by the success of those same Norfolk families at the early Hanoverian court.[2]

However, such an impression fails to portray the difficulties encountered by these great patrons in subduing even a middle-sized electorate, nor does it accurately represent the interests involved in those frequent contests. Closer inspection of the borough's development through this testing time suggests that although local politicians were decisively

---

[1] See W. Speck, *Tory and Whig: The Struggle in the Constituencies, 1701–15* (London, 1970). His appendix, pp. 124–31, indicates that forty-four boroughs experienced more contests than Yarmouth in the period 1701–15, ranging from London's 7,500-strong electorate to the twenty-five corporators of Bewdley. A further thirty-two boroughs had an equal number of contests as Yarmouth.

[2] For surveys of the extensive literature in the field of Augustan politics, see J. V. Beckett, 'Introduction: Stability in Politics and Society, 1680–1750', in C. Jones (ed.), *Britain in the First Age of Party, 1680–1750* (London, 1987), 1–18; G. S. Holmes's introduction to the second edition of his *British Politics in The Age of Anne* (London, 1987). For a recent challenge to the existence of an electoral coma in English politics after 1715, particularly by reference to the experience of the nation's big towns, see N. Rogers, *Whigs and Cities: Popular Politics in the Age of Walpole and Pitt* (Oxford, 1989).

affected by the frequency of elections in the early eighteenth century, it would be wrong to interpret this burst of electoral activity as evidence of a 'divided society' of Whigs and Tories. The great issues of religion and the war against France undoubtedly preoccupied Yarmouth minds as much as anywhere else, but the local response to such matters was far more complex than that suggested by the basic dichotomy of party slogan. For example, the period actually saw a greater accommodation within the town over certain key matters such as religion. Recent research has indeed paid tribute to the potential sophistication of the Augustan electorate, most significantly Gary De Krey's study of London, which demonstrates that even in the capital Tory and Whig campaign managers were influenced by cross-currents threatening to undermine their partisan stance. Of course, such work highlights the problems faced by patrons who sought to control the boroughs, and at Yarmouth the Townshend triumph can be shown to have been a victory for patience and diligence, rather than for aristocratic might. The employment of patronage and electoral bribery undoubtedly had a part to play in bringing the freemen round, but credit must also be paid to the Townshends' provision of services for the general benefit of the town. If a broader conception of 'political' activity is adopted, and allowance is made for the capacity of the provinces for self-determination, then a different picture of early eighteenth-century politics emerges.[3]

Although much work still remains to be completed on the provincial politics of early eighteenth-century England, several local studies have already appeared to question traditional accounts of the triumph of Whig oligarchy. For instance, Brooks concluded from his study of Lord Ashburnham and the excise commission that patronage was a difficult weapon for the noble magnate to master, and that his client would have to display competence for holding office. In addition, Triffit has shown for the towns of the South-West that the relationship between borough and patron was a complex tie of reciprocal obligations, where compliance on the former's part was not as assured as many historians have implied. Jenkins's study of Monmouthshire has further broadened our understanding of the forces underpinning oligarchic rule in the early Hanoverian period by suggesting that demographic factors may have played a key role by diminishing the number of gentry families able to contest for control of the county. Poll book analysis has also helped to refine our understanding of the independence of the localities, and thus it was particularly

---

[3] G. S. De Krey, *Fractured Society: The Politics of London in the First Age of Party* (Oxford, 1985).

frustrating to have no such records for Yarmouth in our period. Nevertheless, Yarmouth can fully illuminate the difficulties inherent in the management of a parliamentary borough, especially as a port which had powerful economic interests to serve.[4]

The corporation's susceptibility to influence and politicking at the beginning of Anne's reign suggested that Viscount Townshend had every right to hope for the advancement of his interest over the forthcoming years. He had already established contacts with several leading townsmen, and the assembly had embraced him with an alacrity which must have satisfied the young peer. However, at this juncture the corporation chose to seek a renewal of its charter, the enduring symbol of its independence. Although distracted by the upheaval of renewed warfare, by February 1703 the assembly had prevailed in this task, having expended over £400 to secure royal consent. The most radical change incorporated in the new charter was a reversion to the mayoralty and fifty-four-man assembly previously in operation in 1684–8, a reform motivated by the corporation's difficulties in finding a sufficient number of able and committed councillors. Moreover, the new grant revealed the assembly's frustration with its supposed external allies, most notably the ineffectual Earl of Yarmouth, for the tenure of the office of high steward was altered from being a life appointment to one held at the pleasure of the corporation. However, given recent concern over James's proclamation of 1688, and the assembly's stubborn defence against the High Court of Admiralty and Joseph Haddock, the charter was most readily welcomed as a vindication of existing corporate rights. Thus, far from being the politicized event which has been ascribed to the charters subsequently gained by London, Norwich, and Bewdley, the Yarmouth charter signalled its independence from any would-be patron or rival.[5] Although borough charters

---

[4] C. Brooks, 'Interest, Patronage, and Professionalism: John, 1st Baron Ashburnham, Hastings, and the Revenue Services', in *Southern History*, 9 (1987), 51–70; J. Triffit, 'Politics and the Urban Community: Parliamentary Boroughs in the South-West of England, 1710–30', Oxford D.Phil. 1985; P. Jenkins, 'Party Conflict and Political Stability in Monmouthshire, 1690–1740', in *HJ* 29 (1986), 557–75; N. Landau, 'Independence, Deference, and Voter Participation: The Behaviour of the Electorate in Early Eighteenth-Century Kent', in *HJ* 22 (1979), 561–83; S. Baskerville *et al.* 'The Dynamics of Lordship Influence in English County Elections, 1701–34: The Evidence of Cheshire', in *Parliamentary History*, 12 (1993), 126–42.

[5] For example, the new charter was soon taken to Beccles 'to vindicate our Southtown jurisdiction'—Y/C27/3; Y/C19/10, ff. 19–23, 32. For other charter studies, see H. Horwitz, 'Party in a Civic Contest: London from the Exclusion Crisis to the Fall of Walpole', in Jones (ed.), *Britain in the First Age of Party*, 173–95; Rogers, *Whigs and Cities*, ch. 9, esp. 319–24; P. Styles, 'The Corporation of Bewdley under the Later Stuarts', in *University of Birmingham Journal*, 1 (1947–8), 92–134.

continued to be used by factions for political ends after 1689, even creating rival assemblies within towns such as Devizes, Dunwich, and Orford, many towns sought new grants, as Nottingham did in 1692, as a means 'to remove divers doubts, questions, and controversies'. The uncertainties of the 1680s had to be overcome for local government to function with any confidence, and in the absence of any act of general confirmation, Yarmouth and other towns were prepared to invest time and money to obtain such assurances.[6]

The corporation's treatment of the Earl of Yarmouth could be interpreted as an inexorable step towards submission to the Townshends, but the relationship between town and viscount remained somewhat equivocal. When the corporation sought to obtain an act of Parliament to confirm receipt of its haven duty under its new mayoral title, Townshend played a prominent role, helping to ensure a smooth passage by acting as chairman of the Lords' committee which reviewed the bill. However, for the more important task of presenting the original petition for the renewal of the charter to the Queen in December 1702, the corporation had appointed the town's MPs, thereby revealing a continued sensitivity over its rights. This decision may not have been intended as a snub to the viscount, but it was a significant change in assembly policy considering his two recent appearances at court on Yarmouth business. The corporation emerged from this process of reform a stronger and more confident institution, and if Townshend was to establish himself as the town's political master, an absolute precondition would have to be the achievement of control over the assembly's leadership.[7]

Recent divisions within the town only compounded the viscount's potential difficulties, forcing him to use extreme caution if he hoped to establish a permanent influence there. Significantly, he had learnt from local sources that the most dynamic force within the Yarmouth electorate, as revealed by the election of July 1702, was the rise of a 'Tory' Church party, whose leaders would obviously pay great attention to the subsequent debates on the occasional conformity bills.[8] Local reaction to such bitter party measures revealed the continued sensitivity of religious issues at Yarmouth, for even the town's clerical leaders were divided

[6] History of Parliament, 1690–1715 section, unpublished constituency articles; *Recs. of the Borough of Nottingham*, v. 85–97. There is no evidence that the assembly attempted to revert to the exclusive parliamentary franchise which had been in force between 1684 and 1688.   [7] *LJ*, xvii. 249; Y/C19/10, f. 23.

[8] For the national impact of the occasional conformity bills, see G. Bennet, *The Tory Crisis in Church and State, 1688–1730* (Oxford, 1975), 63–80.

over the great political matter of the day. In April 1703, in the wake of the defeat of the first occasional conformity bill, lecturer William Lyng preached a controversial sermon at Norwich Cathedral, challenging Nonconformists to show Queen Anne 'more honesty and simple-mindedness than they did her father', and ascribing recent disputes to their needless encouragement of ecclesiological speculation. Amid these very sharp reflections, the more conciliatory message contained in his dedication to its published version—in which he confessed to 'a tenderness to such as conscientiously dissent from the terms of our constitution'—was scarcely audible.[9] However, his senior colleague, curate Barry Love, displayed a much less militant approach to the town's religious settlement, concentrating as he did on the catechizing campaign which he had begun in the previous reign. In October 1703 he made his first contact with the Society for Promoting Christian Knowledge, and less than three months later proposed the erection of a charity school at Yarmouth. His influence would certainly help to mitigate the impact of Lyng's clumsy and aggressive call for a religious peace, and it was Love's brand of constructive reform in Church affairs which would be more readily welcomed by the generality of the town as it once more faced wartime hardship. Townshend may have already gained the support of several 'Whig' leaders in the borough, but he would find it difficult to build a basis of support at Yarmouth solely on the strength of his defence of Dissenters' rights in Parliament, for local leaders were working to combat a return to factionalism.[10]

For its own part, the corporation was prepared to give solid backing to Love's campaign for local religious settlement. Encouraging conciliation in the minds of the town's lay leadership was the fact that the actual threat posed by a strict enforcement of religious tests in the Yarmouth assembly was not a serious one, for only a handful of members with Dissenting links had managed to gain re-election since the packed assembly of 1688. The real secular power of Yarmouth Nonconformity lay with the Congregational board of trustees, whose wealth and economic status would be the most effective obstacle to a persecution of its brethren.

---

[9] W. Lyng, *A Sermon . . . Concerning the Causes, Mischiefs, and Cures of National Divisions* [1703]. Significantly, the dedication is addressed to the Norwich corporation, which had asked Lyng to publish it. Lyng's epitaph testified to the permanent target of his militant spirituality—'*fidem Catholicam intrepidus propugnavit*'—Swinden, *History of Great Yarmouth*, 870.

[10] E. McClure (ed.), *A Chapter in English Church History* (London, 1888), 239, 242, 248, 261. See also W. M. Jacob, 'Clergy and Society in Norfolk, 1707–1806', Exeter Ph.D. 1982, pp. 373–4.

Thus, unlike the predicament facing the corporations of Coventry, Bristol, and London, the occasional conformity measures did not threaten to transform at a stroke the municipal balance of power.[11] Moreover, despite the electoral division of 1701–2, there was a sufficient number of Anglican assemblymen sympathetic to the cause of local Dissent to moderate the corporation's public pronouncements on religious issues, which concentrated on the constructive benefits of Anne's leadership of the Anglican Church. Its address to the Queen in April 1702 had indeed praised the new sovereign's 'known and experienced zeal for our Church as by law established', but its generalized tone only suggested concern for a lack of spiritual authority at a national level since 1688. The corporation's next address, of November 1704, was more forthright, as befitting the stormy month when controversy over the Tack dominated English politics, attributing recent allied military victories to Anne's 'exemplary piety and fervent zeal for our Established Church, and your late unparalleled bounty for the supporting its poorer clergy'. However, even though these expressions of loyalty imitated the High Tory tone of other addresses, in its internal reforms the assembly revealed more pragmatic objectives at heart, principal among which was the encouragement of worship throughout local society.[12]

In August 1703 the assembly made its most decisive intervention in Church affairs since the Revolution, taking the opportunity offered by an alderman's bequest to establish a parish vestry to reorganize lay observance. The vestry's first task was to oversee both the construction and arrangement of pews of a new gallery at St Nicholas's church, using money provided by the legacy. If the Established Church was to flourish at Yarmouth, an increased seating capacity was essential, and the rapid acquisition of the new pews by local parishioners suggested that the townspeople were responsive to the assembly's leadership in religious affairs.[13] Moreover, by that time the assembly had completed its Fisherman's Hospital for retired mariners at a cost of £630, an outlay that underlined the importance which it attached to the provision of comfortable living quarters for elderly sailors of good character.[14] Other charitable schemes had more direct spiritual objectives, for the assembly donated

---

[11] J. Hurwich, 'A Fanatick Town: The Political Influence of Dissenters in Coventry, 1660–1720', in *Midland History*, 4 (1977), 15–47; Holmes, *The Trial of Dr Sacheverell* (London, 1973), 270.

[12] *London Gazette*, 4–7 Dec. 1704; Y/C19/10, ff. 8v, 65v. Yarmouth's MP Benjamin England, usually cited as a Tory, did not vote for the Tack.

[13] Y/C19/10, ff. 37, 39, 49, 53. The allocation of the pews can be found in the vestry book—Y/C40/1.   [14] Y/C19/10, ff. 4, 31v, 47v.

£50 towards the building of an Anglican church at Rotterdam, and launched a subscription to reopen its own Dutch church for the reading of daily prayers. Having taken the lead in this religious revival, the assembly proceeded to encourage the participation of others by publishing a record of local benefactors to both lay and spiritual works, trusting that this would promote wider concern for the moral and physical fabric of the town. All these actions give a more sensitive understanding of Yarmouth 'Toryism' in the immediate aftermath of the 1701–2 elections, for those contests had only served to remind local leaders of the destructive effect of religious militancy. After 1702 both Anglican and Dissenting congregations looked to put their own houses in order to recover lost ground, rather than seeking to discredit each other's cause.[15]

Reorganization and renewal, the major themes of the new charter, had thus been employed to effect in the assembly's religious policy as well, but these initiatives would require a period of consolidation before their impact was really felt. The war, of course, would not help the corporation to build on such progress, though the hostilities undoubtedly motivated its members to attend to governing responsibilities with even greater diligence. Recent experience of sustained military conflict left them with few illusions of the hardships ahead, but the assembly still found its responsibilities for securing prisoners, maintaining fortifications, and obtaining convoys both arduous and frustrating.[16] However, as early as June 1702 there were indications that the corporation's tasks were beginning to be considerably eased by contact with Viscount Townshend, for in that month Townshend's political ally Robert Walpole had to soothe the anger of his King's Lynn constituents over Yarmouth's success in obtaining a convoy ahead of them. Although the Whig patrons wielded more influence at King's Lynn than at Yarmouth, the latter's goodwill was clearly becoming a major objective for them, and as their influence at Whitehall and Westminster grew so they could provide this kind of service with ever greater ease.[17]

Despite these promising signs of advancing interest, Walpole's and Townshend's plans were being undermined by the corporation's continuing

[15] Y/C19/10, ff. 44, 53; *HMC Exeter*, 230; Swinden, *History of Great Yarmouth*, 872–3. Most of the entries in both the Congregational and Baptist church books revolve around disciplinary matters, demonstrating their determination to cultivate a godly community even if it caused (as it probably did) a fall in their active membership—Y/FC31/1; Doctor Williams Lib. mss 38. 109; also see M. R. Watts, *The Dissenters* (Oxford, 1978), 327–8.

[16] Between June 1702 and February 1703, the number of POWs at Yarmouth rose from seventeen to seventy-seven—Y/C19/10, ff. 9v–10, 34v; *CSPD* 1702–3, p. 596.

[17] CUL, Cholmondeley (Houghton) mss 233.

process of reform. Their hopes were most directly affected by the assembly's review of the administration of the freedom in late 1703, which aimed to crack down on abuses and to reassert compulsory residence for all freemen. This move was a natural corollary to the charter's concern to maximize the efficiency of local government, and indeed mirrored the recent campaign of the Norwich corporation to curb the activities of non-freemen. Unfortunately for Townshend, this initiative also had an obvious political importance, for it confined Yarmouth's parliamentary electorate to local townsmen. However, the assembly crack-down should not be interpreted as a calculated rebuke to the Raynham interest, for the spur to this clamp-down was more evidently the Haddock case of 1696–7, than the contests of 1701–2, where there had been no evidence of the creation of 'paper freemen' to swamp the poll.[18] Moreover, the assembly soon had renewed cause to fear for its economic privileges, for at the end of 1704 it was plunged into another major dispute over freeman rights, despite their recent confirmation by the new charter. Such was the significance of this contest that it eventually brought into question the continuing viability of the Yarmouth corporation. The configuration of the competing interests would also establish it as a vital stage in the town's political development, providing Townshend with his most problematic test of management so far.

On 29 November 1704 the counties of Bedfordshire and Huntingdonshire petitioned the Commons for an investigation into the privileges of the corporation of King's Lynn, in particular its custom of foreign bought and sold, which was charged with raising coal prices to unacceptable levels. It was an opportune offensive, for in the first session of the 1702 Parliament the Commons had passed motions condemning the 'combination' of Newcastle pit-owners and London merchants, who were blamed for inflating the price of a vital commodity during wartime. Within weeks, petitions from the city of Norwich and the county of Norfolk were sent to the House, attacking the rights of Yarmouth freemen in a similar vein.[19] The four petitions represented a very powerful interest

[18] In November 1703 the corporation ordered the compilation of a 'case' of questions and answers concerning the administration of the town's freedom. Unfortunately a record of the inquiry's findings does not survive, but the strictness with which the assembly enforced its residence requirement during the following year suggests that absentee freemen may have been its major target—Y/C19/10, ff. 44v, 57; *NNAS* 9 (1910), 138. In 1701 and 1703 the Norwich corporation actually sought a parliamentary bill to curb the activities of non-freeman traders—NRO, Case 16c, book 7, f. 120v; *CJ*, xiv. 238.
[19] *CJ*, xiv. 10, 19, 63, 91, 244, 438, 451, 463. The total revenue which Yarmouth's corporation derived from the coal duty was, so its representatives claimed, only some £64

against freeman privileges, but, as had proved of great aid in the Haddock case, the Yarmouth assembly had the support of the town of King's Lynn to try the matter. The general issue at stake was soon recognized by the King's Lynn representatives, who thought that 'in all corporations in England there is some difference made between freemen and strangers', and this tie of self-interest would bind the two corporate ports in their present adversity.[20] Having once survived a contest in the courts through the employment of dubious methods, the Yarmouth assembly would now have to redouble its efforts if it was emerge successful from the more public arena of Parliament. As Yarmouth's leaders explained when postponing the consideration of all other corporate business to a later date, no other matter could be attended to with 'the county of Norfolk and the city of Norwich having set upon our community on a sudden grave matter'.[21]

Both Yarmouth and King's Lynn based their defence on the threat which the proposed abolition of freeman privileges posed to the structure of their local societies. They both could bring forward archival evidence to prove that the custom of foreign bought and sold was of ancient origin, as well as to substantiate the levying of other port tolls. However, beyond their prescriptive right to collect these duties, in the current wartime situation there was a great onus on the two corporations to display the actual benefit derived from these impositions, which might compensate for their adverse effect on the price of basic commodities. For six weeks the parties thrashed out their differences at the committee for the investigation of coal monopolies, and the contentiousness of the matter saw each side employ every artifice to discredit the reputation of its rivals. Yarmouth's opponents had taken care to inform themselves of the corporation's recent activities, citing the Haddock case as proof of its bullying attitude towards the individual trader, and using the Fisherman's Hospital as evidence of the wealth gained by the assembly at the expense of visiting merchants. In response, the corporation did not attempt to answer every charge against its fiscal management, but widened the scope of the issue at hand, defending its customs as the foundations of

---

p.a.—ibid. 511–12. Although the Queen's speech of November 1703 had alluded to abuses in the coal trade, no statutory regulation would be made until 1710 —*Statutes of the Realm*, ix. 497. See J. U. Nef, *The Rise of the British Coal Industry* (London, 1932), 300–15.

[20] Y/C19/10, f. 66; Cholmondeley (Houghton) mss 404. The King's Lynn MP, Sir Charles Turner, had worked closely with the Yarmouth Members earlier in the Parliament when acting as the chairman of the committee on the Yarmouth haven bill—*CJ*, xiv. 114.

[21] NRO, DCN 115/12.

local government. Without the distinction of freeman privileges, its agents argued, no townsman would ever wish to take up the freedom, let alone an assembly seat, 'for it is a great charge to the freemen to bear the offices of the town'. Moreover, they concluded that without the income derived from strangers, 'the corporation could not subsist'. By throwing the very existence of the corporation at the mercy of the Commons' committee, its representatives obviously hoped to earn its sympathy. However, the seriousness of the threat to corporate control within the town *was* real, for the freedom's importance at the core of the town's economy and government could not be disputed.[22]

Despite such warnings, the Commons' committee ruled that the custom of foreign bought and sold, as practised in both towns, was an 'oppression' and should be abolished. These verdicts were reported to the House on 3 February 1705, but subsequent events on that day revealed that the stubborn defence of the two towns had not been in vain.[23] Rather than agreeing with the committee's report, the Commons proceeded to uphold the freeman privileges of both towns in two closely contested motions: King's Lynn carrying it by 54 votes to 44, Yarmouth by 46 to 39. Unfortunately, there is little evidence to reveal why the House sided with two Norfolk ports, although it can be safely assumed that there was much politicking on their behalf prior to the crucial votes. However, whatever influence they may have been able to muster, they could not override the House's concern for an apparently widespread regional grievance, and immediately after the votes had been counted, their opponents prevailed over the House to order the preparation of a bill for 'the free importation and vending of coals'.[24] The bill did not pass that session, but King's Lynn and Yarmouth were prepared to give some leeway over the sensitive issue of coal prices, subsequently agreeing to negotiate an amicable settlement whereby their rights would be protected in exchange for the levy of 'some certain duty' on coals shipped through their ports. A compromise was the best outcome the corporations could have hoped for after their rebuff at the Commons' committee, but they could take heart

---

[22] *CJ*, xiv. 510–13.

[23] *CJ*, xiv. 513. The committee condemned King's Lynn for the illegal activities of its coal merchants, and for delaying the unloading of colliers at its quayside. The House upheld these charges before it turned to discuss the more fundamental issue of foreign bought and sold, which was debated with reference to both ports.

[24] The only possible overt role played by either Townshend or Walpole was a tellership by the latter to back his King's Lynn constituency. The new bill was introduced by Edward Carteret, MP for Bedford, who was aided in its drafting by a committee of four, three of whom represented constituencies in opposition to the two ports—*CJ*, xiv. 517.

from their success in defending the essential distinction of their freemen within their own locality.[25]

The resolution of a dispute involving the three major towns of the county would also be welcomed by the politician who stood to lose most from prolonged conflict taking root in his natural powerbase: Viscount Townshend. The airing of these regional tensions in the parliamentary arena was a major test of his ability to act as the point of contact between centre and locality, particularly given the alignment of Norfolk interests in this affair. On the eve of the contest he acknowledged his general responsibility to act for his shire when he wrote to Robert Walpole in London, begging him to 'let me hear from you, for tho' I am extremely fond of the county, yet I cannot keep my thoughts entirely from Westminster'.[26] Walpole himself needed little reminding of the duties of borough management, having been earlier advised by one of his electoral allies at King's Lynn that 'it is easy for those that wish us ill to say that they are made properties of, and tools only to serve a turn'. However, the configuration of interests in this dispute gave the Whig patrons an unmistakable opportunity to advance their cause. Henry Horwitz has rightly observed that 'much of the time of the House was taken up by private and local bills which were not often treated as party questions', but patrons clearly could benefit from such parliamentary initiatives, and more work is needed to assess the advantages which politicians at Westminster gained by intervening in such complex regional matters.[27]

Within three weeks of the Commons' divisions Norfolk leaders were eagerly plotting to reap maximum advantage from the freeman dispute. Sir John Turner, Whig Member for King's Lynn, quickly spotted an opportunity to distance Yarmouth MP Benjamin England from the Tory representative for Norfolk, Sir Jacob Astley, who had acted as one of the

[25] Y/C19/10, f. 71v. The Yarmouth audit book triumphantly records that £113 was spent when 'we obtained a vote in our favour'—Y/C27/3, Mich. 1704/5. The distractions of the Aylesbury affair postponed the passage of the Coal Act until the next Parliament, but in February 1707 an act was finally passed which gave Yarmouth permission to levy a duty on non-freemen's coal shipments, and recognized in full the rights of the freemen of the port. Townshend acted as chairman of the Lords' committee which reviewed it—*CJ*, xv. 99, 103–4, 106, 254; *LJ*, x. 206, 268; *Statutes of the Realm*, viii. 564–6.

[26] Cholmondeley (Houghton) mss 364. J. M. Rosenheim notes that eight of the shire's twelve seats were in Tory hands in the 1702 Parliament, thereby highlighting the potential limitations of Townshend's influence at that time—'An Examination of Oligarchy: The Gentry of Restoration Norfolk, 1660–1720', Princeton Ph.D. 1981, pp. 332–7.

[27] History of Parliament, 1690–1715 section, King's Lynn draft constituency article; H. Horwitz, 'The Structure of Parliamentary Politics', in G. S. Holmes (ed.), *Britain after the Glorious Revolution* (London, 1969), 106.

tellers in opposition to England on 3 February. Mindful of the forthcoming general election, Turner argued that England could easily be turned
against Astley 'for endeavouring to take the liberties of his town away',
and, displaying a sensitive understanding of the self-interestedness of
Yarmouth's electors, reasoned that they could hardly be expected to 'vest
that man with power who they are sure will make use of it to their
own destruction'. Most significantly, he outlined the political value of
Yarmouth by stressing how cost-effective it was to bring its electors to
Norwich to vote in the shire election. In comparison, the more difficult
journey from Lynn to Norwich rendered his own constituents 'the heavy
cannon which is never brought up unless the fort will not surrender'.
Yarmouth had clearly become a major objective for the rising Whig
interest in the shire, and though there is no evidence of a *rapprochement*
between England and that party, Astley did lose his seat in the subsequent county election. However, given the importance which Turner
attached to the freeman dispute in his plans, it may well have played a
part in the demise of the Tory interest in Norfolk.[28]

Although control over the Yarmouth electorate had become an urgent
priority for the Whig politicians of Norfolk, many difficulties lay ahead of
them. The ambiguous political sentiments expressed in the assembly's
address of November 1704, which earmarked support for both Marlborough's land campaigns and Rooke's endeavours at sea, would not
have encouraged its presenter Townshend. Moreover, the unopposed re-
election of Nicholson and England at the general election of May 1705 suggested that the town was broadly behind its local representatives, who had
offered such stubborn resistance to the city of Norwich and the county
of Norfolk.[29] Townshend admitted these limitations to Robert Walpole
the following October, informing him that he could not induce Benjamin
England to support the Whig candidate for the Speakership of the Commons because 'I have no reason to think that I have any influence over
him'. He also noted that England's 'nephew and all his friends are very
zealous another way', identifying the powerful inner circle of assemblymen which had established control of the constituency in the aftermath of
the religious divisions of 1701–2.[30] Their supremacy was built upon the

[28] Cholmondeley (Houghton) mss 405. The politicking of the King's Lynn MPs may be
attributed to the ambition of Robert Walpole, a factor yet to influence the Yarmouth
leadership directly—see J. H. Plumb, *Sir Robert Walpole* (London, 1956), i. 102–4.
[29] Y/C19/10, f. 65v. The corporation actually spent £6 on erecting three 'booths' at
election time, probably in expectation of a contested election. The only other occasions
when such payments were made (1702 and 1710) contests did occur.
[30] Cholmondeley (Houghton) mss 443. Robert Walpole was one of Godolphin's agents

accommodation which had emerged to limit the damage caused by religious bigotry, and thus they were unlikely to welcome the spectre of party. The assembly continued to give evidence of its non-partisan priorities by attending to the town's moral fabric, restricting the number of alehouses to remove their 'mischiefs', and taking steps to remedy the 'low condition' of the local grammar school. Curate Love was still at the forefront of this campaign, issuing a third edition of his catechism by 1706, in which he prided himself that 'I have studiously waved all nice speculations and needless controversies'. Townshend would have to be more flexible in his management of the borough than trusting to the workings of party, for the recognizable unity of its leaders recommended that he employ more subtle agencies of currying favour.[31]

Despite the limitations of his influence in the borough, as lord-lieutenant Townshend was in an ideal position from which to assess Yarmouth's political situation, for the assembly continued to employ him as presenter of its addresses at court. As in the previous reign, local reaction towards the war proved the most sensitive guide to the town's political development. From the time of its refutation of the claims of the Old Pretender in October 1701, the corporation dutifully followed the example of the rest of the country by advocating the destruction of French power to preserve 'the liberties of Europe'. In marked contrast to the bitter rumblings over the loss of its trade in the previous war, there was a real jingoism evident in the corporation's address to congratulate Anne over the victory at Blenheim. This enthusiasm persisted until June 1706 when the next address lauded the 'astonishing victory' at Ramillies, and the corporation even went to the expense of supplying roast beef and beer for the populace to celebrate in a true patriotic fashion, climaxing the day with a mass toast to the Queen in the market-place. However, amid these festivities the assembly did make its first subtle overture for peace in the address, expressing hope that Ramillies would bring about the European peace 'you labour for'. Only ten months later this sense of muted grievance flared up into undisguised discontent when Townshend conveyed Yarmouth's congratulations to the crown for the Act of Union with Scotland. The address reaffirmed support for the war, but the assembly stressed

---

for engineering the election of John Smith, the Whig candidate. The Yarmouth MPs both backed their rival, William Bromley—see W. Speck, 'The Choice of the Speaker in 1705', in *BIHR* 37 (1964), 20–46.

[31] Y/C19/10, ff. 80v, 81. Love hoped to increase the school roll from sixty to one-hundred pupils—SPCK RO, minute book 1698–1706, p. 381; J. Whitehead, *A History of Great Yarmouth Grammar School* (Yarmouth, 1951), 43.

that the intended consequence of the armed struggle was 'a safe and durable peace as may effectually secure [a] balance of power and both recover and increase the trade of your kingdoms'. Such impatience demonstrated once again that patriotism could only hold temporary sway in the port as long as it did not clash with more firmly-rooted mercantile interests.[32]

Evidence of wartime hardship in Yarmouth after 1702 was not as apparent as during the previous reign, and this relative good fortune can partly explain the corporation's initial satisfaction with the course of the campaigns. However, during the parliamentary hearing over its freeman dues in early 1705 its representatives had claimed that coal imports—which accounted for the lion's share of its trade at that time—had fallen by nearly half their peacetime level when war intervened. Within a few years there was renewed local concern over the extent of tidal blockage at the havenmouth, a problem which threatened to destroy the port completely. Such was the importance of this issue that the assembly was even divided over the projects put forward to rectify the build-up of sand at the entrance to the port.[33] Townshend had helped to confirm the Haven Act in 1703, but there was little he could do in the longer term to ease local apprehension over the matter. On the other hand, he could hope to aid his interest at Yarmouth and the plight of the townsmen by addressing the port's customary need for protective convoys. In June 1705 his ally Robert Walpole had been appointed to the council of the Lord High Admiral, a position from which he could easily attract the interest of the Norfolk ports. The Whig leaders were evidently quick to press home this advantage, for in October 1706 Townshend reported to Walpole, no doubt with some satisfaction, that two leading Yarmouth officials, alderman Richard Ferrier and understeward Francis Long, were vying with each other to portray themselves as Walpole's local contact. 'I fancy Ferrier suspected Long's design and is resolved to have the merit of the convoy wholly to himself,' Townshend observed, displaying awareness of the kind of service required to secure support in the town. Patronage

---

[32] Y/C19/10, ff. 2v, 65v, 74, 91v, 120. The assembly's support for the Anglo-Scottish Union was not unconditional, however, for in April 1714 it petitioned Parliament over article eight of the Union, which denied local merchants access to cheap Scottish salt—*CJ*, xvii. 537.

[33] *CJ*, xiv. 512. The construction of a jetty at the havenmouth in 1704 was the catalyst for this controversy, for only three years after its erection it was charged with worsening the sandbar. The see-saw career of its engineer Issac Waters—who was fired, reinstated four years later, and then rewarded with a pay rise—reflected the divisiveness of an issue so dear to an anxious mercantile community—Y/C19/10, ff. 122v, 129, 223.

was not simply a matter of personal reward, but also a demonstration of influence with authorities whose powers could decisively affect the locality's future. The hardship of war soon clouded most issues in local minds, and the town's merchants would always prefer a practical response to their urgent problems rather than high principles and rhetoric.[34]

Although the assembly had betrayed growing misgivings over the war from mid-1706, the town's political course was most decisively altered by the threat of an imminent Jacobite invasion in February 1708. On the 18th of that month reports from Rotterdam reached the corporation that the Pretender was organizing a force to attack the British mainland, taking advantage of the commitment of allied forces on the Continent. This intelligence was an accurate forecast of James Stuart's abortive invasion attempt of 9 March, and the seriousness of the threat caused the assembly to issue a succession of emergency orders. The scare passed without any contact with the enemy, but the episode effectively silenced local critics of the fighting in Europe. Yet another loyal address was issued soon afterwards, and the assembly used the opportunity to castigate all those who 'create mistrust of your faithful ministers at home' for following its present war policy. There was even an expression of support for the next of Marlborough's increasingly attritional campaigns. Townshend, as its presenter once again, could not have failed to notice the altered countenance of the corporation towards the current ministry. Moreover, having also acted in close co-operation with the assembly during the emergency in his capacity as lord-lieutenant, he was sufficiently confident of his local popularity to make the first test of his electoral interest at Yarmouth at the incipient general election. His successful political career had been recently highlighted by his elevation to the Privy Council in November 1707, but the May poll of 1708 would reveal just how far the Yarmouth electorate was prepared to forgo its preference for men of local standing in pursuit of favour at court.[35]

Townshend himself made the most significant impact on the pre-election campaign by putting forward the strongest candidate he could have mustered—his own brother Roger, who had actually served as representative for Norfolk for the previous three years. This choice highlighted the importance which the viscount attached to an electoral success

---

[34] Cholmondeley (Houghton) mss 530, 540.

[35] Y/C19/10, ff. 135v, 139v. G. S. Holmes notes the opportunism of Whig politicians in London in 1708, who were prepared to shelve plans for circumventing the Triennial Act in order to go to the polls when public opinion swung back in favour of the war—*British Politics in the Age of Anne*, 219.

at Yarmouth, but even though Roger had been awarded the freedom of the town over six years before, it was unlikely that the intervention of an outsider would be uncritically welcomed by the borough electorate.[36] Therefore, in order to assuage local sentiment, one of the Fuller family was chosen to be Townshend's running-mate.[37] This strong combination of local and central interests, however, was not enough to dispel all lingering doubts towards Raynham, and a rival Yarmouth-based platform emerged. Its candidates were the familiar figure of the town's current MP Benjamin England, whose support Townshend had failed to win after the 1705 election, and Richard Ferrier, the alderman whose self-promoting schemes the viscount had noted only two years before.[38] These two candidates represented the broad Anglican consensus which had dominated the assembly since 1702, and Townshend's only real hope of overcoming such opposition lay with the detachment of civic notables such as the Fullers. Yet the poll revealed that the viscount's strategy had only met with mixed success:

Richard Ferrier	269
Roger Townshend	265
Samuel Fuller	251
Benjamin England	240

Considering the closeness of the contest, and the fact that neither side gained a clear majority, it is all the more frustrating that the poll book does not survive. One observer indeed described it as 'a very laboured election', and the respective total of votes gained by each candidate suggests that cross-voting had an important influence on the outcome. However, the clearest lesson of the election was that for all the promising signs of local favour in the recent past, Townshend had only managed to secure a seat by playing one of his political trump cards. Even though it was some achievement to have established a foothold in the borough, Ferrier's overall victory was a sore reminder of the corporation's potentially obstructive influence. Only four months later a Norfolk observer

---

[36] Y/C19/9, f. 361. Roger Townshend's willingness to stand for the less prestigious seat of Yarmouth was possibly linked to recent ill-health—see History of Parliament, 1690–1715 section, draft biography article.

[37] Ambiguity surrounds the identity of the 'Samuel Fuller' who contested the election. From the evidence of a letter of 1719, in which Fuller senior was said to have 'once set up his son in his room [as MP]', it may possibly be concluded that it was the son who stood in 1708. However, the younger Fuller was also mooted as a candidate in the following year—PRO, SP35/9, f. 409.

[38] Ferrier had actually voted for the Townshend interest at the county election of 1702, but his ambitions had evidently grown since that time—*NRS* (1935), 49.

optimistically boasted of Townshend's supremacy 'not only in the county, but in all the corporations', but it was certainly difficult for the viscount to have drawn that conclusion from the evidence of the Yarmouth election.[39]

As if to remind Townshend of the limitations of his electoral interest at Yarmouth, in the course of the new Parliament the assembly revealed no change in countenance towards its MPs, continuing to make them work hard for the general benefit of the borough. Motivated by the recent invasion scare to make a full review of its defences, it ordered both MPs to attend the Ordnance Office in London to defend the town's rights over part of the local armoury. This was a long-running dispute over a matter of seemingly minor importance, but the assembly directed Townshend and Ferrier to bring it to the Queen's notice if no satisfaction was forthcoming at the appropriate authorities. More importantly, in March 1709 the MPs were ordered to petition Parliament for a ban on the naturalization of vessels built overseas, the assembly citing this practice as a major threat to the nation's ship-building industry. During the difficult times which the Yarmouth merchants had experienced since the 1680s ship-construction had played a saviour's role for the local economy alongside its coal and grain trades, an importance reflected by the election of an increasing number of shipbuilders to the assembly. Despite having the support of the ports of the South-West for their campaign, the Yarmouth Members could not prevail upon Parliament to assuage mercantile grievance on this issue. However, Roger Townshend's preparedness to represent the town on this occasion demonstrated that even landed gentlemen were expected to follow the example of their predecessors in office. Unfortunately for both town and patron, Roger's sudden death in May 1709 only permitted the assembly to make use of his contacts for one session of Parliament, and forced his family to face another test of its interest before the Yarmouth electorate. Five months of intensive electioneering preceded the ensuing by-election, during which time the viscount found that his growing status at court was insufficient to overwhelm the borough's leaders.[40]

At the time of his brother's death, Townshend's attention was more

---

[39] *Norwich Post*, 1–8 May 1708; Ballard mss 4, ff. 89–90; *Camden Society*, NS 15 (1875), 200. A later report cited Roger Townshend's criticism of his local campaign managers, who were blamed for undermining his position at Yarmouth—NRO, Bradfer Lawrence mss VIa [ii], Ashe Windham to Visct. Townshend, 14 June 1709.
[40] Y/C19/10, ff. 147v, 156; *CJ*, xvi. 150–1. For a discussion of the problems of the ship-building industry at this time, see R. Davis, *The Rise of the English Shipping Industry* (Newton Abbot, 1972), 56–7; A. Michel, 'Port and Town of Great Yarmouth . . . 1550–1714', Cambridge Ph.D. 1978, table 6.2.

than a little distracted by his recent appointment as ambassador at the Hague, charged with the heavy responsibility of negotiating a peace treaty with the French. However, this office did not preclude his leadership of a vigorous campaign to find an electoral replacement amenable to his control, nor did his absence prevent his agents in the town from advising him on the most prudent tactics to adopt. On 27 May, the elder Samuel Fuller conveyed his condolences to Townshend, and immediately begged for the viscount's active participation in the quest for a suitable candidate, warning him that 'I can't think anything can safely be done without your lordship's advice therein'. Fuller's initial choice was Horace Walpole, Robert's younger brother, who could boast the same central connections as the previously successful Roger Townshend. However, although the alderman was confident that 'by your Lordship's favour, the interest will be made very successful', he did suggest that Walpole could not rely completely on the Townshend name to sway the electorate, and that borough interests would have to be appeased. Thus, even though Townshend was deeply entrenched in delicate peace talks on the fate of Europe, Fuller passed on a list of Yarmouth's mercantile grievances against the French for direct representation at the Hague! Most significantly, he ended his account by adding, 'I say nothing of our woollen manufacture . . . proper interests will speak for them'. In reply, an undoubtedly wary Townshend promised to raise such issues with the French 'if a fitting opportunity should offer', and acknowledged Fuller's initiatives with the complimentary observation that 'I am infinitely obliged to you for the regard you show to my own interest, which I shall always use for the good of Yarmouth'. This exchange indicated that a tough contest lay ahead, and highlighted the key role which the provision of influence had played in Townshend's success to date.[41]

From his other political contacts Townshend received detailed reports of the current balance of power within Yarmouth's hierarchy, which was perceived as having a vital influence on his election campaign. Ashe Windham, one of the recently elected Whig knights of the shire, informed Townshend on 7 June that their political adversaries had already moved to unite the town against any candidate which Townshend might put forward. Identifying the importance of the three leading local families who had each put forward a candidate at the previous election, Windham

---

[41] NRO, Sotheby's Purchase S 154 D, Samuel Fuller to Visct. Townshend, 27 May 1709, Townshend to Fuller, 18 May 1709. J. M. Rosenheim credits Townshend's failure to persuade the French to reduce their tolls on imported fish as a cause of the viscount's rebuff at the Yarmouth election of 1709—*Townshends of Raynham* (Middletown, 1989), 215–16.

observed that there had already been 'overtures between England's, Ferrier's, and Fuller's friends to keep up the Tory interest and reconcile the two jarring families'. Therefore, the courting of the elder Samuel Fuller by the Whig managers, which had played a key part in breaking the assembly's accommodation prior to the election of 1708, would have to be intensified if Townshend was to maintain a foothold in the town. Windham initially proposed that the elder Fuller be flattered with a seat at this by-election, as long as he agreed 'that he should be under promise of joining the next [election] with whom you shall recommend'.[42] Only a week later political developments had proceeded at such a pace that he could not hold out much hope for any member of the Fuller family, or for Horace Walpole. He even charged Samuel Fuller with duplicity, alleging that his support for Walpole was merely a ruse, masking his real desire to see his own son stand for the borough. Fuller's chances were not rated highly against the combined forces of Ferrier and England, 'who will always be on the spot, sparing no pains or money'. Likewise, Walpole's chances of standing successfully without the backing of Fuller were rated as equally poor, and Windham actually suggested that Horace was more likely to win a contest before the Commons election committee, rather than carry the poll itself. 'Their coolness and the remoteness of the place, the competitors being on the spot, and Mr W. not having one fit to be a manager there . . . will make it the surest game in the world for England', Windham concluded gloomily. His most perceptive comments could not have been glad news for Townshend as he struggled with the complex issue of European settlement.[43]

However, only four days after Windham's revelations, Horace Walpole informed the elder Fuller of his willingness to stand for the vacant seat. As the brother of the recently appointed secretary of war, Walpole evidently hoped to make much political capital out of his family connections, playing down his unfamiliarity with the borough, and promising that he would 'make it my utmost endeavour to promote on all occasions the interests of Yarmouth'.[44] Walpole's declaration may have had a decisive impact on the contest, for, by dashing the immediate hopes of the Fuller family for preferment, it may possibly have aided a *rapprochement*

[42] NRO, Bradfer Lawrence mss VIa [ii], Ashe Windham to Visct. Townshend, 7 June 1709.

[43] NRO, Bradfer Lawrence mss VIa [ii], Windham to Visct. Townshend, 14 June 1709.

[44] NRO, Sotheby's purchase S154D, Horace Walpole to Samuel Fuller, 18 May 1709; *HMC Townshend*, 334–5. Horace, already an under-secretary of state, was willing to spend up to £100 to become a Member, having failed in 1708 to gain a seat at Bishop's Castle, Shropshire.

between the Fullers and other Yarmouth leaders. With the by-election due to take place in November, there was plenty of time for mediators within the town—among whom Windham had identified the two local ministers—to mend the divisions apparent at the 1708 poll. The success of such efforts can be gauged by the tactics subsequently employed by Townshend's agents, who strove to accumulate support by dispensing patronage to local figures. The elder Fuller was still prepared to campaign for the Raynham interest in mid-October, and he suggested that secretary Robert Walpole should secure the command of Yarmouth's fort for a local Whig supporter. In the run-up to the election it was an opportune patronage coup, highlighting Walpole's influence in the capital, but it also indicated increasing apprehension in the Townshend camp as the townsmen rallied against external intervention. Despite the advantages of office enjoyed by Walpole and Townshend, they still could not bulldoze opposition without considering the wishes of the Yarmouth electorate, even when there was no other contest to distract them.[45]

The victory of former assemblyman Nathaniel Symonds at the November poll was a triumph for the town interest over the Whig patrons. Although Symonds had not figured in the electoral calculations of Townshend's agents, his candidacy clearly signified local dissatisfaction with Raynham, and had probably been engineered as a compromise solution to win over the support of Fuller's allies within Yarmouth. By refraining from putting forward a member of their own households, the Englands and Ferriers had prudently removed the obstacle of familial pride from the path towards local settlement, thereby undermining Townshend's closest link to the inner hierarchy of the corporation. Symonds's career certainly suggested that he was well suited to fulfil the hopes placed in him by local leaders, for he had acted as a champion of borough interests against royal intervention in 1682–3, and had provided firm support for the Church party's initiatives since the beginning of Anne's reign.[46] His close friend Curate Love later observed that he was 'not forward to engage himself in public affairs', and the political expediency of his candidacy was revealed by his subsequent decision not to attend Parliament. His local standing could not be matched by Horace

---

[45] *HMC Townshend*, 336. This letter reveals Whig efforts to establish influential Yarmouth contacts *outside* of their rivals' corporate circle. Its author, Atwood, was one of the largest Norwich coal importers to use the port, and he cited discussions that he had had with William Luson, a leading Yarmouth Dissenter and merchant.

[46] Symonds was, most probably, the anonymous donor of a series of £10 gifts to the SPCK—SPCK RO, minute books 1698–1706, pp. 351, 414; 1706–9, p. 51.

Walpole, or even by the young Samuel Fuller, who had refused to take up
a seat in the assembly, a decision which could only weaken his reputation
in town society.[47] Townshend's rivals had proved themselves most astute
in the arts of political management, taking advantage of local suspicion
towards external interference, and appreciating the need to appease influential figures within their own community. Their achievement remains
all the more impressive given the apparent paucity, and general ineffec-
tiveness, of urban electoral pacts during the 'rage of party'.[48]

In the aftermath of the election local divisions were of a mercantile,
rather than political, nature. Two months before Symonds's victory the
assembly had taken firm action against eight Yarmouth freemen who had
failed to conform to the town's 'heyning' custom, which required all
merchants to sell their herring catches under the corporation's supervision so that it could collect a duty from this market. It was a familiar
offence, but the extent of recent evasion, and the leadership of the rebel
merchants by alderman John Andrews, escalated the dispute. Inquorate
assemblies followed, and by the summer of 1710 Andrews had been
blamed for 'several persons of this assembly having absented themselves'.[49]
In significant contrast, town records have left little trace of Yarmouth's
reaction to the great religious storm of the Sacheverell affair. Richard
Ferrier was heralded in the Tory Norfolk press for his support of the
Church's champion in Parliament, but his constituency saw none of the
rioting which marked the impact of the controversy in Bristol, Oxford,
and Shrewsbury.[50] For a town with a bitter history of anti-Nonconformist
agitation, the absence of religious extremism speaks volumes for the tolerance of town leaders, whose non-factional objectives had been apparent
since the beginning of the reign. Further proof of the assembly's spiritual
priorities came in August 1710, when it set about the regulation of the
Yarmouth workhouse, and proposed the erection of a second institution
to aid the reformation of the town's poor. Town MP Nathaniel Symonds

---

[47] B. Love, *A Sermon Preached at the Funeral of Nathaniel Symonds esq. of Great Yarmouth* [1721]; Y/C19/10, f. 86v. The Yarmouth audit book for the year 1709/10 records
that Symonds refused to receive his £15 gratuity as town MP following 'his not going up
to Parliament'—Y/C27/4.

[48] From Speck's general survey, it would seem that this type of informal pact was a rare
occurrence, and still rarer for its efficacy in 1709. However, anti-factional initiatives were
taken at Chichester and Shaftesbury, and further research may furnish other examples—see
Speck, *Tory and Whig*, 57–8.

[49] Y/C19/10, ff. 160v–166v, 177. As recently as 1704 an alderman had been fined £10
for a similar offence, but had been pardoned on submission to the assembly—Y/C19/10,
ff. 47v, 54v.

[50] *Norwich Gazette*, 7–14 Oct. 1710; Holmes, *Trial of Doctor Sacheverell*, 233–5.

epitomized such religious concern, and as the borough faced the prospect of yet another parliamentary election in the autumn of 1710, he and his Church party supporters would obviously have a crucial influence on the town's political future.[51]

Previous analysis of this election at Yarmouth has largely ignored the contention surrounding it, presupposing an ineluctable Tory victory as a logical consequence of the party's national victory and the unmistakable trend of the town's allegiance throughout Anne's reign.[52] However, it was a keenly fought affair, and proved in decisive terms that the Townshend interest had yet to be securely fixed in the town. In the run-up to the election the viscount's prospects were clearly impaired by the fall of Godolphin and other Whig leaders, and his continued residence overseas only further curtailed his influence at home. A Norfolk Tory could enthuse in mid-August that his party had 'good reason' to believe that they could take eight of the county's twelve seats, including the two at Yarmouth.[53] However, only a month later the elder Samuel Fuller reported to Townshend that the town's current political situation was unlikely to resolve itself in party terms so conveniently. His principal revelation was that 'we are at an accommodation', the three great families having agreed that the sitting MP Richard Ferrier, George England (nephew of ex-MP Benjamin), and Fuller's own son Richard 'shall take their lot' to decide which two of them would represent the borough. Even though Fuller himself continued to express support for the Townshend interest, he had clearly shifted his political position. Significantly, he still harboured resentments against the 'jocular' Ferrier, but his willingness to have 'good hopes' of George England indicated that he was prepared to put past divisions behind him in the cause of a local accord. Such unanimity was all the more surprising in the wake of the Andrews affair, but it was an understandable response to recent upheaval, particularly as town leaders faced their third parliamentary election in as many years.[54]

The accommodation, of course, clashed with the viscount's own plans, for from as early as June Townshend's agents had been discussing the possibility of running Horatio Townshend, the viscount's youngest brother, alongside one of the Fullers. As a London merchant, Horatio was more

---

[51] Y/C19/10, ff. 179, 181. Note that in August 1709 the assembly permitted a local Quaker to become a freeman by making a solemn affirmation to uphold its ordinances, rather than have him swear the more contentious corporate oath—Y/C19/10, f. 158.

[52] See Rosenheim, 'An Examination of Oligarchy', 342–3, 416; Plumb, *Sir Robert Walpole*, i. 163–4. For the Tory triumph in the shire, see Holmes *British Politics in the Age of Anne*, 231.   [53] *HMC Portland*, iv. 561.

[54] Add. mss 38501, f. 98.

likely to appeal to the Yarmouth electorate, and Ashe Windham advised Townshend that only £300 or £400 would be necessary to persuade his brother to stand, assuring him that 'if your Lordship has a mind to have him appear, 'twill be very easy to reconcile him to it'.[55] The town's accord clearly threw these preparations off course, but only two weeks after breaking such news, Fuller was already noting signs of friction within the Yarmouth élite. Predictably, the contention centred on Fuller's relations with Ferrier, the latter blaming Fuller for blocking the grant of a land tax commissionship to one of Ferrier's fellow militia officers. This patronage squabble suggested that Fuller's observed consensus was breaking down as election day drew nearer, a development which must have encouraged Townshend to contest the poll.[56] The viscount clearly regarded Fuller with some mistrust, for his campaign managers eventually plumped for another town aldermen, Anthony Ellys, to run alongside Horatio Townshend. This was a reversion to the formula which had achieved some success at the 1708 election, a combination which emphasized the viscount's wish both to flatter and reassure the electorate. Despite this prudent choice of candidates, the October poll proved the Townshend interest's most humiliating defeat to date, with the votes cast as follows:

Richard Ferrier	278
George England	269
Horatio Townshend	231
Anthony Ellys	173

The Yarmouth electorate had thus delivered another decisive blow to Townshend's hopes of controlling the town, but his failure on this occasion defies any simple explanation.[57] The part which religious issues played in the defeat of his interest is especially hard to assess, even though the Tory press might glory in characterizing the election as the victory of 'the Honest Church Party' against 'the undermining tricks usual to the W[hi]gs'. The contest was far from being a straightforward party split along religious lines, and the candidacy of Anthony Ellys, in

[55] NRO, Bradfer Lawrence mss VIa [ii], Ashe Windham to Visct. Townshend, 8 June 1710. Horatio Townshend's experience as a London trader would obviously earn the respect of the Yarmouth electorate, but Horace Walpole was not optimistic of his chances, warning brother Robert that Horatio was 'a little impracticable' in campaign matters—Wolterton mss, Horace Walpole to Robert Walpole, 24 June, 4 July 1710; Sedgwick, *House of Commons, 1715–54*, ii. 473.

[56] Add. mss. 38501, f. 128. Only a month before this incident, Horace Walpole had lamented that 'I am afraid that nothing can be done for Yarmouth'—Wolterton mss, Horace Walpole to Robert Walpole, 18 Aug. 1710.

[57] C. J. Palmer, *Perlustration of Great Yarmouth* (Great Yarmouth, 1872–5), i. 238.

particular, exemplifies the complex influences working on the Yarmouth electorate. Ellys had close ties to the Congregational Church in the town, and may well have been put forward to secure the votes of Dissenters alarmed by the widespread militancy of High Churchmen since the trial of Dr Sacheverell. On the other hand, Ellys was also closely linked with Churchmen such as the Ferriers, and it was unlikely that he would have attempted to make an issue of their treatment at that particular juncture. For over a year the town's Congregational Church had been internally divided over the choice of its pastor, leading its minister to describe its problems as 'incurable' shortly before the election, and only a few months later it was reported that the meeting was 'supported by such weak hands and so few of them'. Of course, this decline might not have directly affected their support among the laity, particularly the hearers who attended their meetings, but the Dissenting cause could not have recommended itself as a strong platform from which to launch a campaign at Yarmouth in 1710.[58] Equally importantly, the conciliatory attitude of Yarmouth's Anglican leaders towards Dissent had helped to suppress division within the constituency since 1702, and if Townshend had expected to capitalize on Ellys's religious connections, he was taking a major gamble. Ferrier and England were obviously in an ideal position to benefit from the tide of Anglican support sweeping the country after the Sacheverell trial, but the development of a Yarmouth Church party prior to 1710 suggested that such euphoria was merely an aid, rather than the catalyst, of their success. Furthermore, their triumph was facilitated by more practical considerations, such as the shortcomings of their opponents, whose campaign was frustrated by the inadequacies of Horatio Townshend as an electioneer, as well as by the temporary detachment of the Fullers from the Raynham interest. If any clear lesson could be drawn from the result, it was that the accommodation of the Yarmouth élite had proved too great an obstacle for the viscount to overcome, and he would now have to wait several years before he could restore his local reputation at the polls.[59]

In the months following the election of 1710 town leaders pragmatically reviewed Townshend's utility as their patron. His political eclipse

[58] *Norwich Gazette*, 7–14 Oct. 1710; Y/FC31/1, 30 Aug. 1710, 7 Feb. 1711. Ellys had been baptized as a Congregationalist in 1661, but had close ties to leading Yarmouth Tories, such as his brother-in-law Richard Ferrier. Since 1707 the Congregationalists had been undergoing a major review of their admission procedures, and looked increasingly to neighbouring parishes to fill up their numbers—PRO, RG4/1973.

[59] See Plumb, *Sir Robert Walpole*, i. 164.

under the Harley administration inevitably had an adverse effect on his standing in his shire, and at Yarmouth his fall from royal favour prompted the corporation to suspend all contacts with Raynham. Public business requiring the mobilization of influential support once again became the responsibility of the town's MPs, who, as representatives with a vested interest in their constituency, readily submitted to the corporation's wishes. The assembly had given an early vote of confidence in Ferrier and England by agreeing to pay the expenses of the election booths used on the day of their victory, and England and Fuller were not slow to repay such loyalty.[60] Rather than give their support to controversial Tory measures such as the Occasional Conformity Act of 1711, the corporation and its two parliamentary representatives channelled their energies into a more introspective, yet purposeful, drive towards urban improvement. Accordingly, Parliament was seen as an agency to improve town facilities, rather than as an arena in which to settle old scores. The first fruit of this constructive campaign was an act for the construction of a causeway to improve the town's communications, passed in January 1712. The Earl of Yarmouth demonstrated his eagerness to be involved with the town's affairs by acting as the chairman for the Lords' committee on that bill, but the assembly made no attempt to close ties with its high steward. Town leaders were understandably wary of courting new patrons at that time, and knew that if any peer was to be approached as a likely contact in the future, Viscount Townshend still promised to be the most prudent long-term choice.[61]

The assembly had good cause to be wary of outside influence, for several of its opponents were quick to take advantage of Townshend's fall to press their claims against the corporation. Chief amongst these opponents was the High Court of Admiralty, who made menacing overtures in October 1711, but there were also other jurisdictions enshrined in the 1703 charter which required protection, particularly the town's rights over the incorporated hamlet of Southtown. All these encroaching authorities were met with characteristic firmness, as the assembly displayed its determination not to return to the constitutional uncertainties of the

[60] Y/C19/10, f. 185v.

[61] *CJ*, xvii. 5–6, 75; *LJ*, xix. 366. The earl was too impoverished to play a forceful role in either the shire or the capital. Furniture auctions at Oxnead in October 1703 and October 1709 highlighted his penury, and he soon became one of the 'necessitous Lords' under Harley's patronage, taking a £400 annual pension in return for his consistent support for the ministry between 1710 and 1714—CUL, Buxton mss 4; PRO, C111/119, piece 7; C. Jones (ed.), *Party and Management in Parliament, 1660–1784* (Leicester, 1984), 129, 159, 166.

1690s.[62] However, John Andrews's stand against the heyning custom remained a major source of anxiety, for the corporation could not suffer the administration of the locality to be subverted by any factional interest. Division within the assembly was never a welcome intrusion for its debilitating effect on its efficiency, and for one of its own members to question a corporate privilege was a very serious matter. Sustained efforts at effecting a settlement with the rebel alderman had achieved some success by January 1712, but in the course of the dispute the assembly received an unexpected setback when a judge of the Norfolk assizes refused to recognize the legality of the fines levied to bring recalcitrant councillors to heel.[63] The Andrews affair did not permit the assembly to enjoy a respite from factionalism during the lull in parliamentary electioneering. Andrews might not pose a direct threat to the borough accommodation, but he did endanger the more fundamental basis of its constitutional structure, and his challenge to borough custom had to be met. Significantly, Peter Clark has observed similar priorities among the corporators of Gloucester, who, even in a time of party strife, would not permit any faction to undermine the routine of local government.[64]

A further cause of the assembly's continued discomfort after 1710 was the prolongation of European conflict. Yarmouth ship-owners clearly suffered in the last three years of the War of the Spanish Succession, losing over fifty vessels to the value of some £25,000, and such hardship suggests that local enthusiasm for 'no peace without Spain' had been exhausted.[65] The speed with which the assembly issued an address to mark the suspension of hostilities in Flanders in June 1712 betrayed an overwhelming sense of relief, which in all probability reflected the views of the generality of the town. Although the address firmly reasserted the town's support for the Hanoverian Succession and the Protestant religion, the assembly's call for 'a just and honourable peace' could not disguise its desperate wish for a restoration of European commerce. In

[62] Y/C19/10, ff. 187, 209. In December 1710 permission was granted to the Southtown constables to take the town's 1668 charter to the Beccles quarter-sessions, following an attempt by Suffolk officials to make the inhabitants of Southtown pay quarterage. The assembly even agreed to pay their costs in January 1713—Y/C19/10, f. 238.

[63] Y/C19/10, ff. 212v, 223. The particular objection raised by the assize judge against Yarmouth's corporate fines was that the assembly could ultimately disenfranchise its own freemen, a judgement which reflected greatly on the controversial nature of the freedom in the wake of the Aylesbury affair. The Bristol assembly suffered similar anxieties in this period—R. C. Latham (ed.), 'Bristol Charters, 1509–1899', in *Bristol Rec. Soc. Publs.* 12 (1947), 58–60.

[64] P. Clark (ed.), *The Transformation of English Provincial Towns* (London, 1984), 327–8.

[65] Add. mss 28331, f. 5.

particular, much joy was expressed over the recent seizure of Dunkirk, testifying to bitter resentment within the Yarmouth mercantile community. 'An immense treasure' was said to have been taken by the privateers based at Dunkirk, and local merchants wished to make it known that 'the trade of this town has had a very feeling share'. Furthermore, there was no gushing compliment for the ministry's religious initiatives, and the valedictory wish was the far from militant objective of allowing all subjects 'the quiet enjoyment' of their rights. Therefore, the assembly's decision to request its MPs to present the address at court was clearly based on a prudent assessment of Viscount Townshend's political isolation, rather than on party-based conviction. The town had had enough of war, but even in the first raptures of peace the assembly had to review its long-term interests with a cool head and not opt for the most proximate route to recovery.[66]

In contrast to the caution which it displayed towards its political contacts, at the end of the war the assembly stepped up its campaign of self-improvement. The confidence of Yarmouth's leaders was not completely misplaced, for since the turn of the century local traders had managed to improve their markets, defying to some extent the perils of wartime. Coal and corn were the basis for an era of prosperity which was to last for some decades, and the removal of the burdens of war permitted local leaders to manifest their wealth in a series of projects aimed at the general benefit of the town.[67] As early as August 1712, in the first assembly since the order for the thankful address for the end of the war, MP Richard Ferrier rose at the Tolhouse to deliver an impassioned speech arguing for the erection of a new chapel of ease to aid the spread of the gospel at Yarmouth. This proposal obviously reflected his experience of the efforts of Manchester, Birmingham, and London to advance the Anglican cause by application to Parliament, but his support for this project was not rooted in militant High Toryism. He expressed regret at the 'unhappy schism' of Yarmouth's past, but rather than blame local Dissenters for such contention, he identified the incapacity of St Nicholas's Church to accommodate all its parishioners as the town's fundamental religious problem. Ferrier had highlighted a basic difficulty facing Anglican clerics and magistrates since

---

[66] Y/C19/10, f. 228. For the impact of the Dunkirk privateers, see P. Crowhurst, *The Defence of British Trade* (Folkestone, 1977).

[67] See A. Michel, 'Port and Town of Great Yarmouth . . . 1550–1714', Cambridge Ph.D. 1978, pp. 45–8. C. Wilson makes a direct correlation between the advance of Norfolk agriculture in the course of the seventeenth century and the erection of fine merchant houses in King's Lynn and Yarmouth—*England's Apprenticeship, 1603–1763* (London, 1984), 146–7.

the passage of the Toleration Act, and the assembly quickly approved his motion.[68] In contrast, its next meeting saw the negative influence of the Tory government's religious policy, when common councillor Robert Ward was discharged for a failure to take the Anglican sacrament. However, Ward was the only casualty of the radical Tory campaign of the final Stuart years, and in marked contrast to previous religious purges, his lone dismissal had no apparent ramifications. Significantly, a study of the impact of the Occasional Conformity Act on the Coventry assembly, which in contrast to Yarmouth boasted a strong Dissenting presence, has demonstrated its limited value to local Tory activists, only serving to gain them a temporary advantage at the cost of great local opprobrium.[69]

Considering the challenges facing the Yarmouth corporation, which had to repair the damage inflicted by over twenty years of almost continual warfare, this reluctance to penalize religious belief can be viewed as a sensible policy of putting the needs of the present before the dissensions of the past. Freed from the cares of wartime, in the remainder of Anne's reign town leaders tackled many pressing problems, ranging from the revival of the local fishing industry to a substantial review of the assembly's committee structure. Lacking the aid of a patron in the highest circles of power, they were now forced to rely on domestic resources of man-power and influence, a predicament which promoted further reform of their modes of government. The assembly's growing confidence in tackling these issues was demonstrated in May 1713, when, in the wake of a major overhaul of corporate finances, the go-ahead was given for the erection of a new civic hall 'for the entertainment of the mayor and gentlemen of the corporation upon the public feasts'. Alongside the arrangements under way for the new church, it signalled an end to the uncertainties of the war years, and bespoke a confidence in the future of both town and corporation.[70] Further evidence of local revival was provided by a scheme over which the assembly boasted no direct control, for in December 1713 Curate Love's long-cherished desire for the establishment of a charity school at Yarmouth was finally fulfilled, after local

---

[68] Y/C19/10, f. 228v. The bishop's licence for the erection of the new gallery in 1704 had specifically alluded to the lack of seating at St Nicholas's as a major concern for local Anglicans—Y/C40/1 ff. 3–4. For the Church's response to the problems of accommodating urban populations, see C. W. Chalklin, 'The Financing of Church-Building in the Provincial Towns of Eighteenth-Century England', in Clark (ed.), *Transformation of English Provincial Towns*, 284–310; Holmes, *Trial of Doctor Sacheverell*, 28.

[69] *Midland History*, 4 (1977), 30.

[70] Y/C19/10, f. 243v. For a list of other civic halls built in this period, see P. Borsay's most helpful appendices in his *The English Urban Renaissance* (Oxford, 1989), 325–8.

townsmen had raised an annual subscription of £110 to fund it. Its objective of providing a Christian education for the borough's poorest children
was very much in keeping with the corporation's own religious policy,
and thus it was no surprise to see councillors dominate the list of subscribers. Moreover, from the evidence of their voting record just fourteen
months later, both Whig and Tory supporters were prepared to back the
project, thereby re-emphasizing their non-partisan approach to religious
matters.[71] Yarmouth's governors were now championing the interests
of the community as a whole, and the scale of the tasks at hand would
subdue the fires of faction within the town, even though they might
burn brightly at a national stage.

It was the ability of Richard Ferrier and George England to act as
the industrious exemplars of this corporate campaign for local regeneration which earned them an unopposed victory at the general election of
August 1713.[72] The Norfolk Whigs were clearly in no position to challenge their local influence, Viscount Townshend having lost the lord-
lieutenancy of the shire in April of that year to undermine his standing
still further. Moreover, only a few months before the election Robert
Harley had paid indirect testimony to Ferrier's concern for the advancement of trade, by taking steps to forestall the Yarmouth Member's vote
against the ministry on the controversial French commerce bill. The
price of Ferrier's support on this occasion was a waitership in the port
of London for his son, which was granted only a week before the key
vote on the bill.[73] However, even though Ferrier may have been swayed
by personal considerations to vote against his conscience in that division,
he certainly did not neglect the views of Yarmouth merchants. Indeed, in

[71] Y/ED 269; SPCK RO, CR1/5, letter 3833. Of the initial forty-eight subscribers,
twenty-two were current assemblymen and three were former councillors. Thirty-three
subscribers voted at the 1715 election: seventeen Tories, fifteen Whigs, and one freeholder
who split his votes—NRO, Hare mss 6372/1–5.

[72] The parliamentary voting record of England, in particular, does not recommend the
pigeon-holing of Yarmouth's MPs into Whig or Tory camps. G. S. Holmes cites him as
a Whimsical or Hanoverian Tory, who became increasingly distanced from the Harley
ministry in the course of 1714—*British Politics in the Age of Anne*, 281, 501. Ferrier was
more consistent in his support of the ministry—History of Parliament, 1690–1715 section,
unpublished biography.

[73] NRO, NRS 27276; *CTB* 1713, pp. 244, 255. The mass of petitions to Parliament
against the French commerce treaty in the summer of 1713 demonstrated that trade issues
could dominate political debate at Westminster, and even force ministers to respect the
views of provincial merchants. For a commendable attempt to integrate political and economic history, see D. C. Coleman, 'Politics and Economics in the Age of Anne: The Case
of the Anglo-French Trade Treaty', in D. C. Coleman and A. H. John (eds.), *Trade,
Government, and Economy in Pre-Industrial England* (London, 1976), 187–211. Some locals

the wake of their re-election both MPs were made *ex-officio* members of the corporation's own trade committee, which was set up in October 1713 to promote the general interests of the port. Even a foreign visitor to the town could recognize their tie to their constituency, observing that 'as in Holland, the present Members are both merchants and inhabitants in the place'. Significantly, his account also noted signs of economic recovery at Yarmouth, and went on to report the sad state of the rival port of Ipswich, thereby identifying the urgent motivation behind the corporation's present industriousness.[74]

Even though the civic hall and church schemes suggested an upturn in Yarmouth's fortunes, there were still plenty of worries to cloud the corporate horizon. For example, the months preceding the 1713 election had been dominated by a renewed challenge to the town's admiralty court from the lord-lieutenant of Suffolk, the Duke of Grafton. Grafton chose to back down after the case had been aired in court, but the assembly took the precaution of appointing deputies in every coastal village within its admiralty jurisdiction in order to broadcast its intention to protect its privilege.[75] Past controversy also counselled caution with respect to the new church scheme, for having resolved that an act to levy a duty on the town's coal imports would be needed to fund the project, the assembly was very careful to direct its Members to assure Parliament that the toll would only be levied on fuel used at Yarmouth itself. Opposition to Yarmouth's port dues in the 1702 Parliament was too fresh a memory, and the assembly did not wish to risk the success of the church scheme by inviting renewed controversy. Once again Ferrier gained the principal credit as manager of the requisite act, which received the royal assent in May 1714 after a very smooth passage through both Houses.[76] Alongside other maritime representatives, he did not prove as successful when trying to turn Parliament's expressed concern for the fishing industry into legislative action, but his prominent activity in the Commons over

---

never forgave Ferrier for his support of that measure, for on his death in 1728 a satirical epitaph was written which made a direct reference to the issue:

His acquaintance this vouch for his politic skill,
We refer to his votes on the French Commerce Bill.

Camden Miscellany, 9 (1894), 11–12.

[74] J. Macky, *A Journey through England* [1713], i. 2–3, 5–6. For Ipswich's hardships, see M. Reed, in P. Clark (ed.), *Country Towns in Pre-Industrial England* (Leicester, 1981), 87–141.
[75] Y/C19/10, ff. 237, 245v. Grafton was the son of the military commander Henry Fitzroy, who owed his dukedom to his natural father, Charles II. The second duke had become lord-lieutenant of Suffolk in 1705.   [76] Y/C19/10, f. 253v; *CJ*, xvii. 477, 626.

the issue would undoubtedly earn him the thanks and respect of his constituents.[77]

The death of Queen Anne certainly did not appear to pose any immediate threat to this fruitful partnership between centre and locality, for the assembly's frequent protestations of support for the Hanoverian succession had demonstrated its loyalty to her royal successor. However, the ministerial changes which accompanied the arrival of George I would give the assembly more food for thought, especially the new monarch's attachment to Viscount Townshend. Having been appointed one of the Regents charged with making preparations for the King's arrival, Townshend found himself catapulted to new heights of favour in September 1714 when appointed a secretary of state.[78] He was immediately presented with an opportunity to impress the Yarmouth corporation, for he was able to use his re-found influence to secure one of the town's customs posts for common councillor John Negus. More importantly, such a demonstration of power would have been appreciated not only by the assembly but also by Negus's godfather, MP George England.[79] With his reinstatement as lord-lieutenant of Norfolk following only weeks later, Townshend could remind Yarmouth's other MP of his personal authority in a similarly direct manner, for Richard Ferrier had recently been appointed major of the town's militia by Townshend's predecessor, the Duke of Ormond. The viscount actually sought to reconcile Ferrier at this stage, allowing him to keep his commission while ruthlessly purging the rest of the county's militia. Such demonstrations of interest at the new court were sufficient to convince the assembly of the need to repair relations with Raynham, and this *rapprochement* between town and patron was marked in October by Townshend's presentation of a Yarmouth address to the new King. However, the general election scheduled for the new year promised to provide a more precise yardstick of the political impact of these rapid changes.[80]

[77] *CJ*, xvii. 565. Ferrier was one of five Members chosen on 14 April 1714 to prepare a bill to ban the import of fresh fish by foreigners. However, it was to be rejected after its third reading. A month earlier, Yarmouth had partaken in a major survey of the industry ordered by the Board of Trade—*Journal of the Commissioners for Trade and Plantations 1709–15*, pp. 501, 509, 517.

[78] R. Hatton attributes Townshend's rise to his pro-Hanoverian stance over the Barrier and Succession Treaty of 1709—*George I: Elector and King* (London, 1978), 121.

[79] *CTB* 1714–15, pp. 12, 70; *Calendar of Treasury Papers 1714–19*, p. 43. The surveyorship, at £50 p.a., was the port's second most lucrative post. However, there was no widespread purge of customs officials in the port in 1714–15—see Y/S6/13–15.

[80] NRS 27276; Y/C19/10, f. 274. Rosenheim notes that Townshend purged half of his senior militia officers on his reinstatement, though showing greater lenience towards local Tory JPs—'An Examination of Oligarchy', 350–1, 357–9.

The outcome of the January election, where George England was returned unopposed alongside the viscount's brother Horatio, was a somewhat predictable affair in the light of recent events. Yarmouth's leadership evidently wished to court the interest of Raynham, and was willing to waive its influence over one of the borough's two seats in order to appease the reinstated master of the shire. An honorary freedom was conferred upon Horatio some three weeks before election day, indicating the corporation's approval of his candidacy well in advance of the poll.[81] However, while paying tribute to Townshend's familial prestige, town leaders were not prepared to sacrifice electoral independence either cheaply or meekly. Over a year later Richard Ferrier informed Robert Walpole that an electoral compact *had* influenced the Yarmouth return of 1715, and boasted of 'having, in solemn agreement with all our people, my option of the next turn for this town to Parliament'.[82] Considering Ferrier's outstanding service to his constituency over the previous five years, it was extremely unlikely that the Townshends could have avoided a contest without accommodating his wishes. If any further evidence was needed of the contingent strength of the Raynham interest in the town, the participation of Yarmouth freeholders in the ensuing county election provided it. Four hundred and twelve of them travelled to Norwich to register their votes at the Norfolk poll, serving to demonstrate the political value of the borough to the Townshends. However, these Yarmouth men did not come to back the Whig candidates in unison as the viscount might have wished, for 171 of them voted Tory. Most worryingly for him, twenty-one of the thirty-eight assemblymen who cast their votes were in favour of the Tories, and over the next two years the corporation elected mayors sympathetic to his county rivals. The potential volatility of the electorate and the accommodation existing within the town élite were thus serious limitations on Townshend's control over Yarmouth.[83]

Furthermore, at the outset of the new reign the corporation continued to tighten its firm grip over the locality, intensifying its campaign to eliminate any perceived weakness. At the first assembly of the Hanoverian period three councillors were expelled for persistent non-attendance,

[81] Y/C19/10, f. 577v. The corporation's local control at this time is attested by N. Rogers, who noted that Yarmouth was one of only two major towns not to suffer political disorder between 1714 and 1719—*Whigs and Cities*, 366.

[82] Cholmondeley (Houghton) mss 718.

[83] NRO, Hare mss 6372/1–5 509x1. Of the 412 freeholders from Yarmouth, only 194 held the freedom of the borough. Thus, the county election can be seen as an opportunity for a wider spectrum of the town population to influence the political process. The freemen showed a marked preference for the Whig candidates, for only about a third of them voted Tory.

including the controversial figure of John Andrews. As a preliminary move before a full review and confirmation of the corporation's ordinances, this action left the remaining councillors in no doubt of the commitment expected from them. The assembly was then fortunate to recruit several key local figures to boost its prestige, including MP George England, the younger Samuel Fuller, and William Pacy, a receiver of taxes for the shire.[84] The success of these initiatives both strengthened the assembly's resolve to tackle local problems, and bolstered its defence against the encroachments of outsiders. In November 1714 the town's admiralty registrar was sent into Suffolk to seize wrecked cargoes taken up illegally within Yarmouth's jurisdiction, as yet another act in the long-running saga surrounding this corporate privilege unfolded. Even the ineffectual Earl of Yarmouth came under the scrutiny of the assembly, in the course of a reassessment of its most senior officials.[85] Townshend had been the obvious benefactor of the town's search for allies under the new dynasty, but he could see for himself that the corporation was not slavish in its relations with the nobility of the region. In December 1715 the assembly had ample opportunity to demonstrate its civic pride during the town's extensive celebrations for the consecration of the newly completed St George's Chapel. As a project conceived in response to a specific local need, and substantially funded by the advancement of local credit, it permitted town leaders to indulge in more than a little self-congratulation. Yarmouth's curate Barry Love articulated this sense of achievement when he addressed the corporation, expressing his sincere wish that 'your town may long flourish and be like a city at unity with itself'. However, by highlighting the general unanimity and prosperity of the urban community, he alluded to the potential obstacles which remained in the path of the Townshends in their quest for the control of the town.[86]

Townshend's next decisive move against the borough came in the wake of the Jacobite rebellion in Scotland. In a manner which recalled the town's reaction to the invasion scare of 1708, the 'Fifteen provoked a frantic response from Yarmouth's leaders, who rushed to bring the town's defences up to scratch, and in August contacted Townshend to present a

[84] Y/C19/10, f. 266.

[85] Y/C19/10, ff. 272v, 276v. The Earl of Yarmouth made a strenuous attempt to improve his position at the new court, backing the Whigs in April 1716 over the septennial bill, and later voting for the repeal of the Occasional Conformity and Schism Acts—see *HMC Stuart*, ii. 122; L. Colley, *In Defiance of Oligarchy* (Cambridge, 1982), 62.

[86] B. Love, *A Sermon preached at the Consecration of St. George's Chapel at Great Yarmouth* [1716], dedication of 4 January 1716. Perhaps significantly, Townshend did not attend the consecration—NRO, DCN 59/44/1.

loyal address at court. Most significantly, the address actually blamed the
'feigned zeal' of High Tory mobs for encouraging the revolt, although
Anglican supporters subsequently endeavoured to exonerate themselves
and their co-religionists by reserving greatest venom for 'papists, nonjurors,
and others falsely pretending to be of the Church of England'. Townshend
would obviously gain credit in the town, not to mention at court, for
fulfilling this request, and his ties with the assembly were further strengthened in December when he secured the repayment of expenses incurred
by the town when quartering Dutch troops during the emergency. His
identification with the town's anti-Jacobite initiatives increased as the
crisis developed, for the assembly resolved later in that month to organize
a mass association in support of the Hanoverian regime, and entrusted
the viscount with its presentation at court. The spontaneity of this loyal
response could only reflect favourably on both borough and patron when
the latter handed the association to King George in January 1716.[87]

Another who thought that the town's reaction to the crisis merited
recognition from the government was Richard Ferrier, although he did
so for more personal reasons. Only two months after the presentation of
the association, he sent an account of his role in suppressing rebellion at
Yarmouth to Robert Walpole, recently appointed first lord of the Treasury and chancellor of the Exchequer, hoping thereby to save his son's
waitership in the port of London, which was rumoured to be under
threat. Ferrier knew that his opposition to the Townshend–Walpole interest in the past would not endear him to the first lord, but felt that he
still had something to attract the ministry's favour, claiming to have an
'option' to take one of the town's seats at the next general election. The
manner in which the town's élite had frustrated Whig hopes at Yarmouth
since 1709 made this a tempting bait for Walpole, but, having presumably
taken Townshend's counsel in the matter, he felt able to refuse the offer.
Even as the delicate patronage move was being deliberated in Whitehall,
events in Westminster were rapidly undermining the strength of Ferrier's
position, for the passage of the controversial Septennial Act countered his
boast that he would "ere long' have the chance to demonstrate the value
of his interest at the next general election. Three days before that act
received the royal assent, Ferrier's son lost his post as the Whig ministers
sent out a clear warning that they were no longer seeking reconciliation
with their opponents in Yarmouth.[88] However, it would be six years

---

[87] Y/C19/10, ff. 589v, 606, 609v.

[88] Cholmondeley (Houghton) mss 718; *CTB* 1716, p. 215. Ferrier's son had been confirmed in office in December 1714, which again demonstrates Townshend's initial lenience
towards the Yarmouth Tories—*CTB* 1714–15, p. 206.

before the next parliamentary contest provided Townshend and Walpole with an opportunity to challenge their local adversaries, and the intervening period would demonstrate how difficult it was for them to maintain pressure on the locality.

Of course, the dismissal of young Ferrier did not mean that the town was prepared to surrender its political independence, even when confronted with clear evidence of the standing of Walpole and Townshend in London. Moreover, just as Richard Ferrier had miscalculated by banking on a general election in 1718, so the instability of ministerial office would, once again, decisively affect Townshend's plans. Divisions within the Whig administration had appeared well before the end of 1716, and the rivalry between the Townshend–Walpole camp and that of Sunderland and Stanhope was already threatening to jeopardize the conclusive victory which their party had scored over the Tories at court and in Parliament. The spring of 1717 saw Townshend dramatically turned out of office, followed quickly by Walpole and other acolytes.[89] This upheaval created difficulties not only for those involved in the world of London politics, but also for the provincial supporters of the Whigs 'outs'. Within a few months of Townshend's dismissal, Sunderland's emissaries were already seeking to undermine the viscount's strength in the country, not surprisingly directing their attack towards Townshend's and Walpole's home county. Just as Townshend had scored political points by securing a customs post for John Negus in 1714, so in September 1717 Sunderland endeavoured to vaunt his authority via a similar exercise of patronage.

A vacancy for the consulship of the Italian port of Leghorn was brought to Sunderland's attention by the Bishop of Norwich, who quickly recognized its value as a means to detach one of Townshend's more reliable allies at Yarmouth, the elder Samuel Fuller. The Fullers had been active participants in Mediterranean trade for many years, and thus the proposal to make Fuller's son, John, consul had practical merit to recommend it.[90] However, as the bishop opined to Secretary Addison, the real argument in favour of Fuller's candidacy was that 'it would be of some use to his Majesty in Norfolk'.[91] The task of securing Fuller's appointment at the Board of Trade was entrusted to Sir Edward Gould, who succinctly underlined the importance of the scheme by observing that 'Mr Fuller's father is a very rich man and the head of the town, and makes what

[89] Hatton, *George I*, 193–210.
[90] The elder Samuel Fuller had exported lead and herrings to the Italian states since the 1690s, and had traded via Leghorn itself—PRO, E190, 513/6, 529/13.
[91] PRO, SP35/9, f. 338.

Member of Parliament he pleases, and has a good interest in the county of Norfolk.' This assessment certainly exaggerated the family's electoral strength at Yarmouth, but there is no doubt that the loss of the Fullers would be a major blow to Townshend's interest there. However, even though the elder Samuel Fuller was eager for his son's advancement, his response to this politicking was still somewhat guarded. Indeed, he had warned Gould that 'our discarded countrymen will do their utmost against the ministry in sure revenge', and had stressed his loyalty to the crown rather than to party, declaring that 'I hold myself obliged by all the means and influence I can have to support his Majesty in his present ministry, who, I am satisfied, have the good of the realm at heart'. His son did gain the consulship, but Fuller's *rapprochement* with the ministry did not undermine Townshend's position at Yarmouth. Moreover, even though the elder Fuller's professed support for the Sunderland ministry had undoubtedly been qualified by his links with Raynham, his views also spoke for the town's enduring independence from magnate control, and the rival Whig politicians would have to respect such sentiment.[92]

A lack of patronage was not the only disadvantage from which Townshend suffered while exiled from court. As Secretary of State for the Northern Department, he had shared the anxieties of Yarmouth's merchants over the economic and political development of Europe, and had been in a fine position from which to aid the town's exhaustive efforts to improve trade. With his dismissal from office, he could no longer play such a dynamic role, thereby robbing the town of an important ally at a time when it was eager to take full advantage of the opportunities of peacetime. Under Sunderland, the Yarmouth corporation did not cease its campaign, paying particular attention to the revival of the ailing local fishing industry, which in recent years had received little encouragement from central government.[93] In February 1718 the Earl of Yarmouth made a notable reappearance in public life as a petitioner to the Board of Trade for a review of the nation's fisheries, well knowing that such a stance would gain him credit at Yarmouth. Fortunately for both the earl and

[92] PRO, SP35/9, f. 409. Fuller's opinions are quoted at length in Gould's letter. Gould became the Board of Trade's adviser on Mediterranean commerce over the next few years—*Journal of the Commissioners of Trade and Plantations, 1715–18*, pp. 427–8, 434–5; 1718–22, p. 52.

[93] In August 1715 the ports of the South-East had successfully led a campaign to ban the import of fresh fish by foreigners. However, this was the only encouragement which Parliament had given to the fishing industry since the Queen's speech of April 1713 had earmarked its revival as a matter of national concern—*Statutes at Large*, v. 34–37; *CJ*, xvii. 278.

the town, Parliament responded to such grievances with the passage of the Fishery Act of 1719. The very satisfaction of actually seeing something done in the name of Britain's fishermen would do much to appease local feeling towards the Whig ministry, even if its ranks did not boast the reassuring presence of Norfolk politicians.[94]

The responsibility for upholding the good name of Raynham within Yarmouth inevitably fell on the shoulders of the town's MP, Horatio Townshend. On the eve of his brother's dismissal, he had demonstrated his value to the assembly by obtaining a remission of £160 from the Excise office for the town's 'fishery' beer. This task was routine in nature, but Horatio's efficiency again suggested that his family's electoral success at Yarmouth had to be supported by diligent representation of the town's interests. The Fishery Act was another feather in Horatio's cap, for he had given the assembly early warning of its introduction, and subsequently helped to incorporate some of the town's proposals into the final statute.[95] The necessity for the gentlemen of Raynham and Houghton to be acquainted with trading matters would be repeatedly hammered home to them. In December 1719 Robert Walpole received a long lecture from Richard Ferrier concerning the assessment and levy of malt and salt duties, after rumours reached the town that the Treasury was about to reform its methods of collection. Walpole was not even in office at the time, and thus Ferrier's approach speaks volumes for his reputation as a financial spokesman in the Lower House. Displaying great temerity, Ferrier even tried to goad him into attacking the Treasury proposals, observing that they could have only been framed by 'those who know little of trade, and much less of how little profit merchants often adventure'. Yarmouth's merchant lobby could certainly learn to respect a man of Walpole's competence in trading matters, but if the Walpole–Townshend interest was to benefit from any personal attachment to the former first lord, continued attention would have to be paid to the town's specific grievances. Their rival Stanhope clearly understood this

---

[94] *Journal of the Board of Trade and Plantations, 1715–18*, pp. 344, 387, 395. The main aim of the petitioners was for the establishment of a new chartered fishing company, but the project had little success—see W. R. Scott, *The Constitution and Finance of English, Scottish, and Irish Joint Stock Companies* (Cambridge, 1910–12), ii. 361–76. Parliament's response was to waive all duties on salt used in the preparation of exported fish—*Statutes at Large*, v. 136–42.

[95] Y/C19/10, ff. 636v, 672; *CJ*, xix. 101. Yarmouth's proposals concerned the levy of salt duties, and the assembly was prepared to spend £102 'about the Salt Act'—Y/C27/5, Mich. 1718/19. Horatio, as a director of the South Sea Company, was evidently familiar with City affairs, and he eventually became an excise commissioner in 1735—Sedgwick, *House of Commons, 1715–54*, ii. 473.

requirement, for in October 1720 he endeavoured to use his diplomatic contacts to prevent the Danes from imposing a levy on the town's valuable corn exports.[96]

The assembly could therefore draw encouragement from the attentiveness of the Sunderland–Stanhope ministry to commercial affairs, but it still experienced many local difficulties. Although a series of prestige projects was completed at this time, such as the new civic hall, a new guildhall, and an impressive residence for the town's faithful servant Barry Love, most of the assembly's time was taken up with expensive and dilatory lawsuits.[97] Renewed proceedings against the Duke of Grafton over the town's admiralty jurisdiction, and against John Andrews for his refusal to pay heyning dues, dominated corporate debates in 1719 and 1720. Both opponents were rebuffed once more, the Duke of Grafton decisively so, but such distractions were an unwelcome drain on resources, and bred uncertainty in assembly ranks. Equally worryingly, a serious breach between the two houses of the corporation rendered it more vulnerable to attack. For five months in 1719 assembly business ground to a complete halt as an open rift appeared between the aldermen and the common councillors over voting procedures, with the latter refuting claims that the upper house had power to veto their wishes. Frustratingly, the civic records give no clue as to the deeper roots of this controversy, even though the matter was not finally resolved until July 1721, when the constitutional balance of power between the two houses was reaffirmed. However, as a demonstration of the underlying tensions which could surface within a close-knit corporation, where the dominance of the few could cause resentment within an already-oligarchic institution, this dispute is highly significant, particularly as it mirrored the development of municipal government in other towns such as Warwick and Northampton. Although the confrontation had no decisive long-term consequences, it seriously delayed the assembly's agenda at a time when urban improvement was a major priority, throwing an unforeseen obstacle in its ambitious path. By the time Townshend and Walpole had returned to national office in February 1721, the corporation must have

---

[96] Cholmondeley (Houghton) mss 780; *HMC Polwarth*, ii. 638–9. Walpole clearly understood the mercantile mind, judging by his comment that in contrast to his handling of sheep-like country gentlemen, he had only to touch 'a bristle of the hog of trade, and he is sure to squeal and bite till all his neighbours believe him ill treated, whether in reality he is or not'—Rogers, *Whigs and Cities*, 395–6.

[97] The £3,500 spent on these three schemes serves as sufficient testament to the town's general recovery since the turn of the century.

been hoping for a similar upturn in fortune to mirror that of the county magnates.[98]

On returning to royal favour, Townshend had good reason to believe that his interest at Yarmouth would be quickly re-established. Horatio Townshend continued to serve his constituency with diligence, leading a successful campaign in the early months of 1721 to obtain an extension of the coal duty currently subsidizing the building of St George's Chapel.[99] By way of response, one of the Fullers paid his respects to the viscount's eldest son, thereby confirming the altered countenance of town leaders towards Raynham. Although this exchange was occasioned by the death of the elder Samuel Fuller, the Townshends' closest ally at Yarmouth over the previous 20 years, it was no doubt encouraging for the viscount to receive acknowledgement of 'the very great obligations' owed to Raynham by one of the town's most influential families. In August the assembly finally made its first direct overture to the viscount in over four years, significantly concerning yet another fishing matter.[100] Importantly for his interest, the ensuing parliamentary session was again productive in the eyes of the port, for an act was passed to regulate the duties levied on salt used in the preparation of red herrings. Members of the Walpole and Townshend families were conspicuous by their presence on the drafting committee for the bill, well aware that such activity would pay dividends at the forthcoming general election. However, despite clear signs that the town was conducive to Raynham's influence, bitter past experience had taught Viscount Townshend to show no complacency when attempting to turn such amenability into success at the polls.[101]

---

[98] Y/C19/11, folio 2 and ff. The scale of the disruption caused by this dispute rivalled that of the Great Plague of 1665–6. Seven inquorate assemblies occurred in the twelve months following April 1719, after only two had been recorded in the whole of the previous decade. See above, Ch. 1, sect. i.

[99] *CJ*, xix. 412, 419, 462, 464, 672. The second Chapel Act also provided funds for the installation of street-lighting.

[100] PRO, SP35/26, f. 182; Y/C19/11, f. 41. Yarmouth's entreaty to Townshend echoed a very traditional concern over the encroachment of Dutch fishermen in local waters. Interestingly, the Earl of Yarmouth was the recipient of a gift from the assembly in September 1721, though the reason for such generosity was unspecified and it remained a one-off reward—Y/C19/11, f. 39.

[101] *CJ*, xix. 475, 664, 669, 742–3. The Salt Duty Act replaced the toll on salt used in the curing of domestically consumed red herrings with a proportional duty levied on sales of fish in the home market—*Statutes at Large*, v. 252–4. In addition, during that session a petition from the town's merchants helped to obstruct a bill to maintain Scarborough harbour, which threatened to impose additional tolls on the coals carried by Yarmouth vessels from the North-East—*CJ*, xix. 730.

The importance of the Yarmouth election of 1722 in establishing the interest of the Walpoles and Townshends is all too evident, since it set the town's electoral pattern for the succeeding fifty years. Moreover, the crushing victory enjoyed by the Whig patrons on this occasion suggests that after twenty years of struggle the magnates had scored an irresistible triumph:

Charles Townshend	456
Horace Walpole	440
Sir John Holland	94
George England	77

However, the apparent ease with which the successful candidates stormed the poll belies the many obstacles which they had to overcome during their pre-election campaign. In particular, the poor showing by George England, the town's native representative for the previous twelve years, should not be interpreted as evidence of the demise of the corporation's influence. The result accurately reflected the strength of the shire patrons at that time, but the long-term significance of the borough-mongers' victory should not be exaggerated. The first double return of non-resident MPs at Yarmouth since 1685 could not have been achieved without the support of the corporation, and, in that regard, the town's politics had changed little. Fortunately, the survival of the viscount's own election expenses allows a more realistic impression of his campaign, with all its attendant difficulties, to be formed. Even though the uniqueness of the 1722 election should be recognized, this source will also cast light on his previous tactics, as well as on the problems he failed to surmount on earlier occasions.[102]

Electioneering began several months before the poll, for in course of 1721 no less than seventy-five freedoms were granted, the highest number in any one year since James II's controversial campaign to 'pack' Parliament in 1687.[103] Townshend's expenses prove that he did encourage local residents to take up their freedoms for monetary reward, but they also show that this corrupt practice was not a decisive agency in engineering his eventual victory. He clearly refrained from creating vast numbers of 'paper freemen' to swamp the electorate, probably out of fear of antagonizing the corporation, rather than as a result of the prohibitive costs

---

[102] Sedgwick, *House of Commons, 1715–54*, i. 20; Raynham Hall archive, box 120.

[103] *NNAS* 10 (1910), 120–3, 154–6. Freeman admissions suggest that there had been no significant attempt to flood the electorate with mass creations prior to any election between 1687 and 1722.

involved.[104] Instead of seeking confrontation, the viscount endeavoured to win over town leaders, seeing this strategy as a means to gain a permanent advantage. Past experience had taught him that his major obstacle remained the extensive control exercised by the corporation, whose supremacy was personified by the town's leading three families. He could at least rely on the support of the Fullers after their recent expressions of loyalty, even though their standing had been weakened by deaths in the family. Therefore, his main targets remained the Englands and Ferriers, and in circumventing their possible opposition he proved a skilful opportunist. He found little difficulty in overcoming the former, for financial hardship initially prevented the town's current MP from mounting a campaign for re-election. The Ferriers alone remained to be dealt with, and in a notable change of heart, Townshend preferred to accommodate their interest rather than challenge it. The value of this reconciliation became clear only six days before the election, when the corporation acknowledged Charles Townshend and Horace Walpole as the town's new MPs, and granted them both a gift of the town freedom.[105]

Having achieved the consent of the assembly, Townshend could have been forgiven for thinking that the two seats were now his. However, the opposition which he met at the poll revealed that his influence was still not universally welcomed in the borough. The candidacy of his eldest son alongside the influential figure of diplomat Horace Walpole was prudently designed to flatter the corporation and satisfy its desire for political clout in London, but these choices had evidently not pleased all their future constituents.[106] Townshend, for one, was certainly expecting a challenge, judging by the extent of his preparations for election day. In particular, his enlistment of town notables as his principal election managers was evidently designed to assuage local feeling against outside interference. Aldermen Richard Ferrier and William Pacy played a key role in bringing the freemen round to the Townshend–Walpole camp, with the former compiling a list of 124 'carriers' for their interest. Pacy was the overall

[104] Raynham Hall archive, box 120. Two lists survive which record individual payments to Yarmouth freemen. Only twenty-seven of the 141 townsmen named therein received their freedoms in 1721, but it would seem that this minority were induced by Townshend's agents to petition for their freedoms. The standard bribe was 10s. 6d.; these new freemen received up to £2 each.

[105] Y/C19/11, ff. 49, 52. George England had been warned by his uncle Benjamin, an MP himself, to curb excessive expenditures, especially 'gaming or extravagant living'— PROB 11, 1711, f. 127.

[106] Walpole currently held the office of secretary to the Treasury, and although re-elected by his constituency of East Looe in Cornwall in 1722, he chose to sit for Yarmouth instead—Sedgwick, *House of Commons, 1715–1754*, ii. 509–10.

mastermind, arranging for the transportation of freemen from other parts of East Anglia, and even from London. He also paid the hefty bills for the provision of entertainment and bribes for local residents, the principal items of expenditure in a campaign costing £820. However, he displayed an understandable sensitivity over his role, asking Viscount Townshend to destroy any record of his transactions once the accounts had been settled.[107] The thoroughness of this assault on the electorate could never be matched by an opposition whose most likely leaders had been skilfully detached by their ministerial rivals, and their platform offered no more than token resistance. The candidacy of Sir John Holland, a once influential supporter of the Townshends, was a particularly surprising move, for he had little connection with the town. George England was obviously put forward to attract local voters, but he did so reluctantly when burdened with severe financial difficulties. These choices only suggested desperation on the part of the viscount's opponents, and electoral disaster duly followed, with the Tory Norfolk press simply recording that they polled for 'about an hour, and then left off'. At last Townshend had scored clear-cut victory over his Yarmouth rivals, but it had not been won without considerable cost and effort.[108]

While there was certainly much for Townshend to savour in this result, it was clear that he would have to maintain close supervision of the borough if the two seats were to be retained. The landslide victory did not mean that the new MPs could ignore the duties expected of their predecessors, and even before the year was out, they had been employed by the assembly to present an address to the King condemning the Atterbury conspiracy.[109] However, their greatest responsibility lay with the renewal of the Haven Act. Ever since the expiration of the previous Act in July 1720, the assembly had shown immense concern over the issue, and Townshend may well have used the promise of a new act as a bargaining-

---

[107] Raynham Hall archive, box 120. The first election payment—for £8 of beef distributed to 'several houses' in Yarmouth—came on 14 March, two days before the assembly's recognition of Townshend and Walpole as MPs. A list of forty-four Yarmouth freemen living in London and its environs also survives, dated 1722—NRO, Bradfer Lawrence mss Ic.

[108] *Norwich Gazette*, 17–24, 24–31 Mar. 1722. Sir John Holland had once been one of the Norfolk 'squadron' which G. S. Holmes identified as a powerful force in the 1708 Parliament. However, he had broken with the hard-line Whigs in the wake of the Sacheverell affair, following his refusal to present a virulently anti-Tory address to the Queen, which would have jeopardized his position as Comptroller of the Royal Household—Holmes, *British Politics in the Reign of Anne*, 229–34; Rosenheim, 'An Examination of Oligarchy', 343–6.

[109] Y/C19/11, f. 59v. A loyal association was drawn up in the wake of the plot, and 1,234 subscriptions were taken between 19 September and 24 December 1723. However, unlike the Association of 1696, over a quarter of the subscribers were women—Y/S7/1.

counter in his pre-election campaign. For certain, the successful passage of the sixth Haven Act in May 1723 further secured the Townshend–Walpole interest in the town, for the townsmen could expect no more dutiful, or as important, a service from any local resident.[110] A month later the Townshends' success in a uncontested by-election at Yarmouth confirmed their local standing, when the recently ennobled Charles was replaced by his brother William. Their father received the welcoming news that 'there was no other contest in the town than who should show the greatest respect to your lordship', but this overwhelming victory had only been secured after respecting the town's interests. Even as the assembly voted to make their new MP a freeman of the town, it revealed a more traditional inflexibility towards outsiders, banning the 'purchase' of freedoms for seven years to suppress the 'great commotions' which had been caused by this practice. The Townshends and Walpoles may have appeared outstanding patrons, but Yarmouth's leaders were not prepared to allow the constitutional basis of the corporation to be subverted, and their stance on the freeman issue would be adopted by the corporators of towns such as Coventry and Hull in the course of the eighteenth century. It would be this kind of lesson in municipal self-interest that the Norfolk magnates would be taught time and again over the ensuing decades.[111]

Yarmouth's conditional 'surrender' to two of the most powerful families in early eighteenth-century England supports the findings of scholars such as Nicholas Rogers, who have demonstrated the continuing vitality of urban politics after 1715.[112] For two decades a borough of less than 800 constituents had withstood concerted attempts from its county patrons to force it into electoral compliance, and local leaders would continue to limit their control. Contested elections occurred at Yarmouth in 1727, 1730, 1734, and 1741, all of which featured a local challenge to the Walpole–Townshend ticket. None would be successful, but even the agents for the Whig magnates admitted that their successes had only been achieved

---

[110] *CJ*, xx. 111–12, 128, 160, 177.

[111] PRO, SP35/43, f. 313; Y/C19/11, f. 71v; S. and B. Webb, *English Local Government: The Manor and the Borough* (London, 1924, 2nd edn.), 438–9; G. Jackson, *Hull in the Eighteenth Century* (Oxford, 1972), 303–5. The assembly's reference to freedom 'purchases' obviously alluded to Townshend's corrupt practices, for the actual number of freedoms sold by the corporation had declined dramatically since the start of the century—see App. 3.

[112] Rogers, *Whigs and Cities*, 5–7, 390–1. Also, see Triffit's account of the difficulties experienced by the Duke of Chandos, Sir John Rogers, and George Treby in their respective political associations with the smaller towns of Bridgwater, Plymouth, and Totnes—'Politics and the Urban Community', Oxford D.Phil. 1985, pp. 203–22.

after 'much art, difficulty, and expense'.[113] The principal 'art' required of the borough patrons was that of respecting the town's particular interests, and representing them effectively in the capital. This essential task had always been expected of native and non-native MPs alike, and, in this regard, the victory of Raynham in 1722 had seen no revolutionary change in the priorities of the Yarmouth electorate. Thereafter the corporation would continue to play a leading role in determining the port's future, and its influence over every aspect of local life could not be ignored, even by the Turnip and the Great Man.

By highlighting the difficulties which lay behind the Townshend triumph, this chapter demonstrates the need for intensive research into other seemingly dependent towns. If politicians of the stature of Walpole and Townshend discovered such problems in their own backyard, then there is much still to be learnt about the influence of local interests. More specifically, Yarmouth's experience suggests that more work is needed to illuminate certain key areas of political activity. For example, the contest over freeman dues in the parliamentary session of 1704–5 clearly demonstrates that local economic issues could have a political impact, and that such controversies have to be placed in a regional context. In addition, the poll of 1722 suggests that more analysis is needed of the identity of electoral agents, and of their management of the localities. Most importantly, there has been little concern to study the provision of legislative influence at Westminster, particularly as a means to gain electoral subservience in the provinces. Yarmouth was only one of many boroughs to benefit from the increase in local legislation after 1689, and it was this kind of patronage which promised a surer return on the patron's efforts than a judicious appointment to a government post. The establishment of this type of 'interest' was undoubtedly difficult to achieve, and personal associations, or even out-and-out bribery, would be required to maintain it. However, with patience and hard work, even truculent localities such as Yarmouth could be tamed if magnates could reassure their leaders that the political system was working to their general advantage. Students of 'political stability' can thus learn much from the interaction of locality and centre, as long as due attention is paid to the vital brokerage of the regional patron.

[113] Sedgwick, *House of Commons, 1715–54*, i. 290. The Fuller family, once the Townshend's most dependable local ally, led the town's challenge in these contests. In 1727 such was the strength of the opposition to the Norfolk magnates that John Fuller, a defeated candidate at Yarmouth, was actually bought off with another seat at Plympton Earle in Devon—ibid. ii. 55. In addition, note the strength of political unrest at Yarmouth during the Excise crisis— P. Langford, *The Excise Crisis* (Oxford, 1975), 120–1.

CONCLUSION

THE volume of work currently being produced on late Stuart and early Hanoverian politics reflects the growing importance which has been attached to the period, as new generations of historians seek to till a field of scholarship once bestrode by the colossi of Macaulay and Trevelyan. Of late, even the national press has sought to re-evaluate the importance of the age, prompted by the tricentenary of the Glorious Revolution to examine the responsiveness of the constitution to modern times. In contrast, academic interest has centred on themes of great significance for the history of eighteenth-century England, most notably the consolidation of parliamentary sovereignty, the expansion of the state apparatus, and the country's response to the financial and commercial revolutions. Amid such historiographic ferment consensus is rarely to be found, but even though some historians would question the profundity of political and social change before the 1720s, the challenges of the Augustan age have been widely acknowledged.[1] Despite this outpouring of research, however, the perspective of the provincial town has remained neglected, and this study of Yarmouth has sought to remedy that deficiency. The most important agencies of innovation may have been located in London and Westminster, but scholars should not ignore the contribution of the localities, for their study can illuminate both cause and consequence of national development.

My primary concern when embarking on this work was to analyse the local political process, taking my cue from some of the most exciting work produced on the period in the last thirty years. Attracted by the frequent elections of the reigns of William and Anne, historians have focused attention on the growth of political groupings from the 1680s onwards, seeking to delineate the contribution of the 'rage of party' to the evolution of Georgian politics. In particular, scholars such as Plumb, Holmes, and Speck have identified the parliamentary borough as a key arena of party conflict, highlighting the role played by the nation's towns as initiators and mediators of change. However, despite the fact that the boroughs returned over three-quarters of the Members of the Lower House, few town studies have appeared to test their findings, and intensive analysis of

---

[1] See G. S. Holmes, *Augustan England* (London, 1982), pp. ix–x.

a single constituency shows that many areas of political activity have yet to receive due attention. Most importantly, Yarmouth's example suggests that our understanding of provincial 'politics' be widened to encompass a broader range of issues than psephology and patronage. Parliamentary elections may appear in conventional accounts of the period as the principal fascination, indeed the sole attraction, of urban life, but they did not dominate local society to the exclusion of other, more permanent concerns. Indeed, the necessity of considering the local economy and familial rivalries in the same breadth as the great issues of the day indicates that provincial politics was not exclusively dominated by the ideology of Whig and Tory. Campaign managers had to compete with a host of other interests when the poll approached, and the role of the corporation in crystallizing local opinion has been overlooked. Office-holding in this period has rarely been considered in any other light than as a tool of patronage, but recognition of the impact of self-government on the outlook of a local élite is long overdue. Clearly, analysts striving to account for the relative 'political stability' of eighteenth-century England could benefit from the study of municipal administration, especially as an agency for both continuity and change.

The centrality of the Yarmouth assembly in this work simply reflects its crucial role in local politics. The early modern corporation has seldom been depicted as a dynamic institution, and the opening chapters sought to restore its tarnished image by examining how it could act as the principal forum for urban society. Fortunately, Yarmouth's excellent corporate archive permitted the intricate workings of the assembly to be explored in detail, casting light on the onerous duties of the local governor. Rather than appearing as a ruling caste with little concern for their fellow townsmen, the assemblymen were shown to have borne great responsibilities for the future of the borough. Moreover, the structure of corporate government ensured that the assembly decisively influenced all walks of urban life, and politics was no exception. Corporate debates were of key importance, broaching topics of widespread importance such as trade, religion, sanitation, and poor relief. The regular meetings of the assembly gave the corporators a ready platform from which to promulgate their views on the issues of the moment, thereby ensuring vigorous political discussion. Faction could thrive in the assembly, spurred on by the often divisive nature of the matters raised there, and by the annual round of civic elections, but their office also directed councillors to pursue apolitical ends, particularly with regard to economic issues. For certain, the most urgent and recurrent problem for Yarmouth's leaders in the period was haven blockage, and they had to employ every 'political' advantage at their disposal to tackle that issue. Judging by the travails of the assembly between 1660 and 1720, it may be concluded that, in general, local government demanded pragmatism rather than principle from its hard-pressed administrators.

Helping to remind Yarmouth's rulers of the onus of office was the freeman body, which, although with few opportunities to participate in corporate activity, played a key role within town life. As a fundamental distinction within urban society, and as the first step on the civic ladder, the freedom bound the corporation and a very significant proportion of the local populace in a pact of mutual dependence. Although often dismissed as a pawn of the borough-monger, at Yarmouth the freedom maintained its economic value throughout our period, and the assembly was quick to defend freeman privileges on all occasions, even using its political connections at Westminster to uphold its rights. In return, successive generations of freemen were content for the corporation to act as the town's mouthpiece, and many of their number were prepared to undertake the considerable burden of assembly duty. Frustratingly, local sources were less revealing about the responsiveness of corporate leaders to the views of the unenfranchised majority of townsmen, but the reciprocal concern of ruler and ruled for the general prosperity of the borough ensured in practice that the interests of the lower orders were represented in assembly debate.

The patrons who sought to gain control of Yarmouth's parliamentary seats probably occupied the best vantage-point from which to appreciate the breadth of corporate responsibility. However, despite their elevated status, the Townshend and Paston families could not expect to win automatic loyalty from the borough, for their authority was largely interpreted by corporate leaders as a possible source of influence for attaining their own objectives. There were undoubtedly townsmen who benefited in a more personal manner from their association with these peers, but it was the general service of the town which promised to secure the port's allegiance to outsiders. Even though party issues undoubtedly had a major influence on the locality, their impact has to be assessed in the light of the borough's past experience, for Yarmouth voters did not mindlessly adopt the rhetoric of national politicians. It is clear that the pace of local politics was often forced by initiatives taken in London, or by regional power-brokers such as the Pastons and Townshends, but in the longer term it was the townsmen themselves who had the greatest say in determining the borough's political complexion. The allegiance of the larger towns did not come without strings and commitments attached, and patrons had to pay very close attention to the changing moods of the local electorate, and act accordingly. Not surprisingly, the degree of self-government ceded by the centre to the localities imbued local leaders with an autonomous spirit, which often worked to undermine the authority of the deputies delegated by Whitehall to administer the provinces.[2]

As a bulwark against gentry interference, the corporation could have a vital influence on the course of local politics. However, although much recent work has investigated the importance of oligarchy in determining the particular character of Hanoverian England, studies of the eighteenth-century corporation are still scarce. This remains a somewhat puzzling omission, for the rule of the few had been established in most English towns from medieval times, and represented a pole of order for urban society through the upheavals of the seventeenth and early eighteenth centuries. Furthermore, neither the assault of the crown in the 1660s and 1680s, nor the distractions of the rage of party, could ultimately undermine the importance of the corporations as engines of urban development. As a sign of this, the Webbs could take 1688 as their starting point for their survey of municipal government, safe in the knowledge that it had assumed the essential form which would endure into the 1830s. However, as historians are coming to recognize, the provincial assemblies did not stagnate, nor did the corporators rest content with the simple preservation of their power. The increase in urban improvement Acts from the 1690s onwards has belatedly become a focus of scholarly interest, and Peter Borsay's putative urban 'renaissance' has challenged any notion that provincial town life was incurably introspective. In turn, urban governors have been portrayed as energetic and ambitious, even while retaining the superficial air of an unchanging local élite, comfortably secure in their privileged and leisured world. As bastions of tradition, the corporations did not welcome all the new winds of change, but their perspective only serves to make them a sensitive barometer of Augustan advance.[3]

The most cursory comparison of the Yarmouth of 1660 with that of

---

[2] Ironically, the analyst who has most aptly summarized the reciprocity inherent in Hanoverian 'paternalism' is J. C. D. Clark, a historian who conceives of eighteenth-century English society as an hierarchical 'ancien regime'—*English Society, 1688–1832: Ideology, Social Structure, and Political Practice during the Ancien Regime* (Cambridge, 1985), 78–9.

[3] See E. L. Jones and M. E. Falkus, 'Urban Improvement and the English Economy in the Seventeenth and Eighteenth Centuries', in P. Borsay (ed.), *The Eighteenth-Century Town: A Reader in English Urban History, 1688–1820* (London, 1990), 116–58; P. Borsay, *The English Urban Renaissance* (London, 1989).

1720 suggests that local society had undergone a subtle, though significant, transformation. As an institution, the assembly was now an even more oligarchic body than it had been at the Restoration, but this development should not be seen as a triumph for introspection and self-interest. Particularly since 1700, the corporation had proved an ever resourceful and dynamic leader of the locality, righting its own finances and celebrating such fiscal stability with a series of public works. In order to attain solvency, its members had been prepared to undergo a complete overhaul of its committee structure, and to engage in the treacherous activities of City investment and Westminster politicking. The Haven Acts and St George's Chapel were the rewards for its courage and commitment, but such successes were not won without cost. The growth of corporate responsibilities put increasing pressure on its personnel, and the favour it required in the capital to achieve such objectives had important repercussions for the political orientation of the borough. Moreover, while vigorously leading this campaign for improvement, the assembly was faced by several new adversaries, who continued to test its authority, and placed increasing pressures upon corporate privileges. These challenges, both old and new, would demand the corporation's continued vigilance even as the town experienced an era of prosperity it had not known for nearly half a century.

The corporators themselves, upon whom the whole edifice of local government relied, naturally reflected the assembly's changing perspective. The merchant body still predominated, as a testament to the continuing source of wealth and influence within the borough, but the increasing number of professionals within assembly ranks had broadened the corporate outlook. Similarly, although most townsmen still regarded the assembly as the outlet for personal ambition, geographical and social mobility was not denied to sons of civic leaders, and some Yarmouth men succeeded on the national stage. This tension between traditional practice and the opportunities of the future would be obvious to any visitor to the town. As the classical orders appeared amidst the Dutch gables, and the hawkers started to sell *The Yarmouth Gazette* and *The Yarmouth Post*, so a more genteel environment slowly arrived at the mouth of the Yare. Defoe, writing after many trips to Yarmouth, was evidently very taken with the port, and though espying little cultural advance there, pronounced it a 'beautiful town'. The borough could never be styled a Bath or Tunbridge Wells, but it had assimilated many of the trappings of a refined national culture, which symbolized the potential openness of the corporate élite, even as it became more oligarchic in form. A flexibility of approach, akin to that displayed by these local governors, should be adopted by historians when attempting to chart social and political change in the eighteenth century.[4]

A fitting guide to the contrasts offered by Yarmouth's development is the Corbridge Map of 1725, a prospect of the town surrounded by elevations of notable public and private buildings. The corporation readily supported the subscription for the map, regarding it as an opportunity to publicize its achievements since the turn of the century. Accordingly, St George's Chapel, the new town hall, the Fisherman's Hospital, and the charity school all featured to symbolize the assembly's beneficent administration. Even more significantly, of the twenty-one private subscribers who paid to have their properties depicted, no less than fifteen served in the assembly at one stage in their career, thereby demonstrating the corporation's continuing success in attracting the service of influential members of local society. However, a reminder of the leadership's susceptibility to division was represented by the inclusion of the residence of rebel alderman John Andrews, who in about 1720 had provocatively built a great mansion at the very centre of the quay. Moreover, at least two of the subscribers without assembly ties can be identified as Nonconformists, their homes testifying to the wealth which had enabled their brethren to weather the persecution of previous generations. Corbridge thus succeeded in providing a sensitive portrait of a prosperous and proud urban hierarchy, most satisfyingly with its warts and all.[5]

Even an outsider such as Corbridge recognized that the assembly could not be portrayed as the cosy ideal of a community in harmony. However, by 1720 the cause of local settlement had been significantly advanced, particularly with regard to religion. A division of churches was the bitterest legacy of the Civil War and Interregnum, for it struck at the very heart of town life, causing rifts between neighbours, robbing many of a civic career, and, in the high spirits of the 1680s, even threatening the livelihoods of freemen. Between 1660 and 1689 it certainly 'politicized' more

---

[4] D. Defoe, *A Tour through the Whole Island of Great Britain*, (eds.) D. Browning and G. D. H. Cole (London, 1962), i. 65–71. Yarmouth's limited gentrification would be a good case-study to further current debate over the urban 'renaissance'. Despite Defoe's reservations concerning the extent of cultured pursuits in the town, cited by Borsay himself, the Norfolk press reveals that race meetings, assemblies, and concerts all took place there in the 1720s. However, the Earl of Oxford could still be very amused by the town's efforts to turn a trolley cart into a coach suitable for gentle visitors. There is a great deal of material which could be used to examine such subtle social developments—see P. Borsay and A. McInnes, 'Debate: The Emergence of a Leisure Town, or an Urban Renaissance?', in *Past and Present*, 126 (1990), 189–202; *Norwich Gazette, passim*; *HMC Portland*, vi. 153–5.

[5] Y/PP3; Y/C19/11, f. 107v.

townsmen than any other issue, such was its capacity to divide. However, despite the compromises of the Toleration Act of 1689, and continuing concern among Nonconformists at the activities of their High Church rivals, the reigns of William and Anne were generally a period of healing and settling for Yarmouth's religious groups. There were undoubtedly moments when unhappy visions of the past were revived, such as in 1701–2, and perhaps in 1710, but these tensions could not disguise the fact that local leaders had generally reached a working accommodation. The tolerance exhibited by the corporate group spearheading an Anglican revival in the town must be recognized as a most significant influence, and it suggests that local politicians were not incurably factious. Yarmouth was clearly more fortunate than towns such as Coventry and Oxford, where anti-Dissenter feeling manifested itself into open violence, and credit must be given to the moderation of Yarmouth 'Toryism'. It probably would have taken little more than a firebrand of Luke Milbourne's calibre to stir up local passions once more, but under the charitable direction of curate Barry Love the town was given new spiritual priorities. More than any other single issue, religion demonstrates the overwhelming importance of local circumstances for the political development of the provinces.

The career of a single corporator may serve to emphasize the progress which Yarmouth society had made towards a more stable polity. John Spendlove, a local attorney, had been baptized in the Congregationalist church under the Protectorate, and had experienced the vicissitudes of 1687–8 from the assembly benches. However, by the time he came to write his will in 1726, having served another term as a common councillor between 1696 and 1714, he had embraced the Anglican creed. Yet, as if to testify to the momentous changes which he had witnessed in his own neighbourhood, he proudly boasted that he had always shown 'a prudent and Christian temper and moderation to those who were so unhappy as to dissent'. Moreover, having resigned from the assembly over the Andrews affair in 1714, he still could look favourably on 'the worthy corporation of Great Yarmouth, long may it flourish'. Significantly, his views were even endorsed by a Dissenting teacher at Yarmouth, who in 1721 lamented the difficulties of 'this fine and well-governed corporation'. From such testimony, the advantages of a prosopographic approach become particularly apparent, especially for the facility with which a researcher can move from an individual to a collective perspective. The career of John Spendlove also warns against pigeon-holing local figures with convenient party labels, for councillors were imbued with sufficient political sophistication to alter their views over time. In common with the great men of the age, provincial leaders lived through the watersheds of 1660, 1688, and 1714, and had to adjust to successive changes of regime. Therefore, when trying to ascertain the nature of political change in the late Stuart age, it is essential to appreciate the importance of generational experience. In Yarmouth's case, such an approach clearly demonstrates that the accommodation of religious pluralism after 1660 proved the most exacting test facing the town's corporate community.[6]

The ensuing century would provide many more challenges for the Yarmouth assembly, and for the rest of the nation's corporations. Certain problems had already been identified and would continue to weaken corporate control, most notably the growing opposition to customary borough tolls, and the increasing pressure put on the freedom by inter-loping traders and rapacious borough-mongers. Moreover, from the mid-century onwards rival sources of local authority were created by a massive increase in the number of improvement commissions, as many boroughs struggled to adapt to rapid urban growth. However, the ultimate fate of the corporations in 1835 should not lead researchers to dismiss their capacity to accommodate earlier change.[7] From this study of a provincial corporation already in the throes of great difficulty, it appears that despite the inadequacies of an archaic system of urban government, local leaders could face the future with some confidence and no little skill. In one important respect the corporations were actually in a stronger position in 1720 than they had been sixty years before, for the threat of arbitrary regulation by the crown had been largely neutralized, thanks to wide-spread condemnation of the remodellings of the 1680s. More studies of the corporate response to the demands of the late Stuart and Hanoverian periods are evidently needed, if only to redress the balance of research away from party politics and the London perspective.

Yarmouth's experience was not unique amongst English provincial towns; neither should its development be represented as a model for the period. The town suffered from difficulties peculiar to its size and loca-tion, just as it gained advantages from its influence as a major centre of wealth and population. As the Webbs found, a forbidding list of urban

[6] NAC wills 1731, f. 220; Wellcome Institute of Medicine mss 5313, letterbook of Thomas King 1719–25, Thomas King to his father, 9 Oct. 1721.

[7] Significantly, Paul Langford has recently concluded that no automatic rift was created between the corporations and the improvement commissions—*Public Life and the Propertied Englishman, 1689–1798* (Oxford, 1991), 226–32. Moreover, the corporations have been credited by one scholar as 'nearly always' the instigator of the new commissions—B. Keith-Lucas, *The Unreformed Local Government System* (London, 1980), 33.

variables could be compiled to daunt the most confident of generalizations.[8] However, by exploring the mechanisms and structures of Yarmouth's corporate life, I hope to have shown that the interplay of urban politics, society, and economy merits greater investigation. Not every town had a corporation to run its affairs, but the presence of the institution in the vast majority of English boroughs should promote its study as a vantage-point from which to analyse urban development across all disciplines. Even the most tedious of town hall agendas can cast light on the real concerns of the nation's local governors, and with sufficient research our impression of urban politics might not be as dramatic as some scholars would have us believe. The study of the provincial town between 1660 and 1720 promises to correct several of the assumptions we hold about English society and politics during a tempestuous age, enlightening many of the still dark corners of the realm. Only when these monographs appear will there be 'a general satisfaction' between historians of locality and centre, to mirror that which Robert Paston reached with the leaders of Yarmouth on a long-forgotten day in the autumn of 1675.

[8] S. and B. Webb, *English Local Government: the Manor and the Borough* (London, 1924, 2nd edn.), 381–3.

APPENDIX 1

Survey of Yarmouth Corporate Finances:
1660–1720

THE complexities of borough finance make any attempt to chart its development a difficult enterprise, as testified by the most authoritative study in this field, E. Dawson's mammoth 'Finance and the Unreformed Borough', Hull Ph.D. 1978. In Yarmouth's case, the sheer diversity of its sources of income and its items of expenditure would make any detailed analysis of its fiscal workings a basis for confusion rather than clarity. Therefore, in order to provide some guidance in this vital area, all the major town accounts are listed here as they were presented at the Black Friday audit, followed by a breakdown of the key chamberlains' account.

When using these tables, some important features should be noted. All the accounts listed are running accounts, and therefore income and expenditure within each of them may include sums held over from the year before or kept for the succeeding one. The fiscal year ran from Michaelmas, and the sums recorded here are given to the nearest pound. Accounts were abandoned and new ones created during the assembly's reforming drives, a frequent occurrence which does not help to clarify the overall financial picture, but serves to highlight the fluidity of the corporation's fiscal management. Particularly after 1700, when the assembly became increasingly interested in national stocks, a year-by-year study is needed—see A. Michel, 'Port and Town of Great Yarmouth . . . 1550–1714', Cambridge Ph.D. 1978, pp. 244–59. Thus the tables simply provide a general guide to corporate finance, the unpredictability of which is most readily represented by the bumper yield from sea wrecks in the chamberlains' account for 1700.

Account	1660 In./Ex.		1670 In./Ex.		1680 In./Ex.		1690 In./Ex.		1700 In./Ex.		1710 In./Ex.		1720 In./Ex.	
Chamberlains	4615	2659	3392	2406	4207	2510	2008	1774	8935	5453	3467	1807	2885	2462
Ballast Master	586	560	496	498	534	534	401	401	364	364	386	386	unrecorded	
Half-Doles	436	148	203	108	197	116	54	52	30	30	56	56	16	16
Churchwardens	307	145	587	494	143	171	unrecorded		451	432	100	145	152	161
Muringers	72	5	41	45	9	53	8	23	5	6	9	32	4	23
Pier Act Duty					978	978	1341	1341	1611	1611	1366	1366	2630	2360
Captive Stock							42	42	269	0	590	441	terminated	
Town Stock							525	0	191	0	terminated			
Haven Paymaster									1646	1825	1407	1623	1803	1823
Fishery Excise											218	207	199	146
Workhouse											1471	1422	866	694
Waterbailiff office											237	237	4534	4534
Chapel Duty											445	42	2218	1692

Chamberlains' Account 1660–1720

INCOME	1660	1670	1680	1690	1700	1710	1720
Balance	2603	1186	2201	0	3410	1997	637
Waterbailiff	192	187	103	54	43	96	196
Heyning Dues	970	470	614	51	368	574	277
Town Rental	256	257	214	195	104	102	81
Tonnage	53	86	82	58	67	59	85
New ships	0	0	7	30	19	45	37
Sea Wrecks	3	2	0	13	1125	4	46
Freemen Fees	33	120	14	74	8	4	6
Borough court	7	12	18	10	12	7	10
Butchers Stalls	21	22	0	18	21	123	55
Bridge Toll	4	29	28	22	15	28	29
Miscellaneous	473	1021	926	1483	3743	268	1426

EXPENDITURE	1660	1670	1680	1690	1700	1710	1720
Haven works	400	695	722	354	account moved		
House Repairs	128	286	169	81	66	137	15
Legal Affairs	92	23	197	60	52	25	179
Bailiffs/Mayor	86	91	91	91	91	91	91
Other Officials	55	58	57	58	70	88	148
Freeschool	31	143	194	222	264	241	63
Remittances	623	114	2	0	0	0	0
Loans	866	143	540	163	4	5	12
Miscellaneous	378	853	538	745	4906	1220	1954

APPENDIX 2

Distribution of Wealth through the Ward System: 1660–1720

Ward	1661 %	1678 %	1689 %	1694 %	1719 %
1st N	5.4	8.2	9.9	9.9	10.8
2nd N	6.8	14.3	12.7	12.2	12.9
1st NW	20.6	13.8	17.4	15.6	10.9
2nd NW	11.8	10.7	9.8	10.2	13.6
2nd SM	19.2	11.1	12.5	11.8	13.4
1st SM	11.3	13.0	10.1	11.9	10.0
2nd S	12.4	12.6	17.3	18.2	14.4
1st S	11.6	15.7	10.4	9.9	13.7
Yield (£)	355	515	1668	2820	2115

Note: The 1661 Free Gift return records the actual sums collected, while the other columns are based on tax assessments. As basis for comparison, the rating system of each levy is provided here:

Levy	Rating	PRO Reference
1661 Free gift (13 C.II c.4)	None Set	E179/253/40
1678 Poll Tax (29/30 C.II c.1)	1s. in the £	E179/154/698
1689 Land Tax (1 W + M s.2, c.1)	3s. in the £	E182/686
1694 Land Tax (5 W + M c.1)	4s. in the £	E182/686
1719 Land Tax (5 Geo I c.1)	3s. in the £	E182/690

APPENDIX 3

Admission of Freemen by Yarmouth Corporation: 1620–1740

Decade	Birth	Apprentice	Purchase	Gift	Unknown	Total
1620–9	18	96	18	0	2	134
1630–9	72	122	26	0	0	220
1640–9	97	141	46	3	0	287
1650–9	66	143	51	5	0	265
1660–9	125	153	64	8	2	352
1670–9	145	163	33	6	0	347
1680–9	133	163	31	6	3	336
1690–9	110	107	26	4	1	248
1700–9	135	112	8	4	0	259
1710–9	167	107	7	2	4	287
1720–9	184	141	3	5	0	333
1730–9	145	156	0	4	0	305

Analysis of Admissions: 1660–1720

	Birth	Apprentice	Purchase	Gift	Unknown	Total
1660–89	403 (38.9%)	479 (46.3%)	128 (12.3%)	20 (1.9%)	5 (0.5%)	1035
1690–1719	412 (51.9%)	326 (41.1%)	41 (5.2%)	10 (1.3%)	5 (0.6%)	794
Overall	815 (44.6%)	805 (44.0%)	169 (9.2%)	30 (1.6%)	10 (0.6%)	1829

A Mercantile Élite: The England Dynasty

Careers

Name	Civic Career	Other Distinctions
William Burton I	1641–60	MP 1656, 1659. 'The late great rebel'
John Burton	1684–8	MP 1701–2; Indpt. trustee 1689
John Carter I	1625–62	
John Carter II	1688	
Nathaniel Carter	1688	Indpt. trustee 1689
Anthony Ellys I	1688–1709	Indpt. trustee 1689
Anthony Ellys II	1688–1736	Unsuccessful candidate, Yarmouth 1710
Anthony Ellys III	—	Bishop of St Davids 1752–61
John Ellys II	—	Knighted 1705; Vice-Chancellor, Camb.
John Ellys III	—	Fellow at Caius, Camb. 1690–1716
Thomas Ellys	Refused, 1688	Indpt. trustee 1689
Benjamin England	1668–84, 1688–1711	MP 1702–8
George England I	1641–9, 1657–77	Knighted 1671
George England II	—	MP 1681, 1689–1701; town recorder.
George England III	1714–25	MP 1710–22
George England IV	—	Rector of Alby, Norfolk
Joseph England	1672–4	
Thomas England I	1666–84, 1684–94	
Benjamin Ferrier	1709–15	Expelled for 'evil behaviour'
Richard Ferrier I	1673–6, 1688–95	
Richard Ferrier II	1690–1728	MP 1708–15
Richard Ferrier III	1718–38	Town clerk
Robert Ferrier I	1630–48	
Robert Ferrier II	1658–62	
Samuel Fuller	1673–76	
Thomas Lovell	1699–1711	
Edmund Thaxter	1647–9, 1660–84, 1688–90	

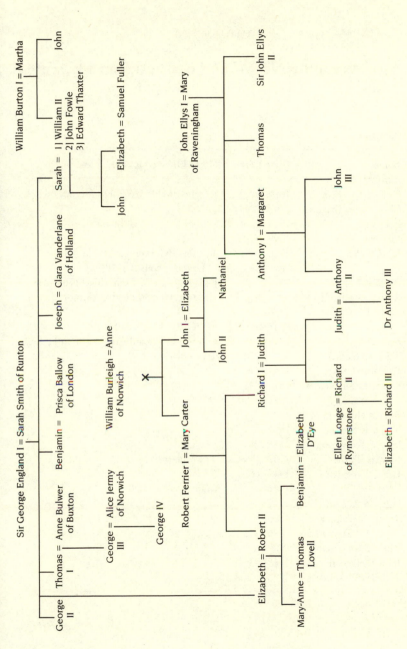

FIG. 1 The England Dynasty

APPENDIX 5

An Assembly Network: The Wakeman Dynasty

Careers

Name	Civic Career	Other Distinctions
Richard Brightin	1689–92	Expelled by the assembly for absenteeism
Christopher Brightin	1695–1747	
Benjamin Engle	1688–1714	
Richard Engle	1699–1707	
John Fuller	1728	MP for Plympton Erle 1728–34; Leghorn consul 1718–22
Richard Fuller I	—	Fellow at Caius, Cambridge 1704–26
Richard Fuller II	—	Unsuccessful candidate, Yarmouth, 1741
Samuel Fuller I	1674–84, 1688–1721	MP 1689–98, 1701–2
Samuel Fuller II	1715–20	Unsuccessful candidate, Yarmouth, 1708
Thomas Godfrey	1679–1704	Town clerk
William Harmer	1649–60	
Richard Huntington	1649–84, 1688–90	MP 1679–81
Robert Huntington	1681–87	
Nicholas Spilman	1651–62	
Henry Thompson	1636–49	
Francis Turner	1707–20	Town clerk
Giles Wakeman I	1649–60, 1688	Indpt. trustee 1689
Giles Wakeman II	1741	
Robert Wakeman	1625–45	
Samuel Wakeman I	1690–1720	
Samuel Wakeman II	1729–49	
John Wakeman	1648–60	
Thomas Wakeman	1723	

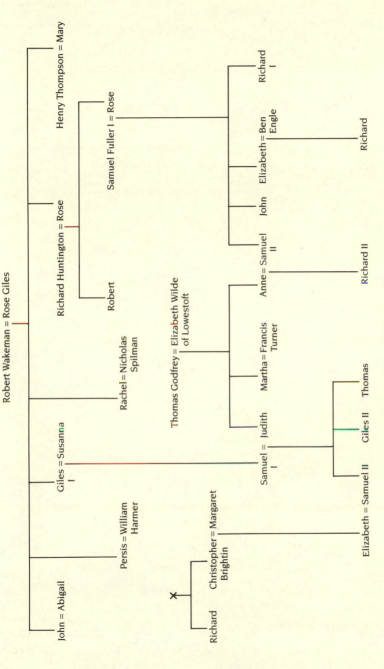

Fig. 2   The Wakeman Dynasty

BIBLIOGRAPHY

This bibliography lists all major sources consulted, though some items might not have appeared in the footnotes. In particular, the listing of manuscript material has been confined to those collections which have provided extensive or especially pertinent information, even if only one piece. The secondary sources include those works which have been found to have been of most use.

MANUSCRIPT SOURCES
1. ARUNDEL CASTLE, SUSSEX
A735, Aylward letters 1699
MD 010, Norfolk survey 1694
MD1012, Haven survey 1686
Norfolk House document, packet 27

2. BANK OF ENGLAND, LONDON
Subscription Registers 1694, 1697

3. BODLEIAN LIBRARY, OXFORD
Ballard mss 4
Carte mss 78, 103
Clarendon mss 80, 83, 104
Gough mss, Norfolk 1–2, 19, 27, 33, 40
Rawlinson mss A. 180, A. 182, A. 185
Tanner mss 27, 29, 31, 100, 133–5, 137–8, 239, 311
Willis mss 85

4. BRITISH LIBRARY, LONDON
Additional mss
23012, 23023, 23049–52, 23062, 23739–42, 27967 (Turner collection)
27447–8, 28261, 36540, 36988, 39220 (Paston correspondence)
28880 (Ellis papers)
38501 (Townshend papers)
41804 (Middleton papers)

Egerton mss
2719 (Le Neve collection)
3328–9, 3338 (Danby correspondence)
Harleian mss 6762 (Yarmouth inscriptions)
Lansdowne mss 923 (Warburton papers)
Sloane mss 1028

5. CAMBRIDGE UNIVERSITY LIBRARY
Add. 4356, Hannot sermons
Add. 6968, Paston genealogy
Cholmondeley (Houghton) mss, Walpole correspondence
Dd. 11. 57, Aglionby papers
Oo. 6. 115, Jackson notebook

6. GUILDHALL LIBRARY, LONDON
Mss 6428, Clayton/Morris account ledgers 1669–80

7. HASTINGS ART MUSEUM AND GALLERY, SUSSEX
Section A/H [a] 15–18, Yarmouth Herring Fair books

8. NORFOLK RECORD OFFICE, NORWICH
Civic Records:

Assembly books 1625–1737	C19/6–11
Admiralty court book	C16/1
Book of oaths and ordinances	C18/1
Liber Juramentorum	C18/2
Liber Ordinum	C18/3
Book of charters	C18/4
Book of entries	C18/6
Hutch book	C20/1
Haven book	C20/2
Breeds (attendance records)	C21/1
Audit books	C27/2–5
Custumal	C36/14
St George's Chapel book	C38/2
Churchwardens' accounts	C39/2–3
Vestry book	C40/1
Sessions books	S1 /3–4
Test rolls	S6 /1–18

Correspondence/Papers:

Archive list 1612	C1 /1
Admiralty court papers	C16/6
St George's Chapel papers	C34/9, 13
Lowestoft disputes	C36/7
Haven Act papers	C36/6
Corporation Act purges	C36/12
MP correspondence 1696–7	C36/15–16
Admiralty Court papers	C36/17
Association rolls 1723	S 7/1

Personal Collections:
Ferrier genealogy   MC 44/119
Paston letters 1660–88   Bradfer Lawrence Ic
Paston finances   NRS 4004–4029 13F7
Prideaux papers   DCN 115/10, 12
Townshend papers   Sotheby's Purchase S154D
Windham papers   Bradfer Lawrence VIa [ii]

Diocesan Records:
Archdeaconry Court wills   NAC Wills
Consistory Court wills   NCC Wills
Archdeaconry Court inventories   ANW 23
Consistory Court inventories   INV
1677 Visitation   Vis 7/3

Maps:
Admiralty jurisdiction   PP 3
Yarmouth 1734   PP 23
Swinden Map 1753   PP 4

Miscellaneous:
Haven survey   BUL 14/9 619x6
Meeting-house licences   Dis 1/1
Charity school book   ED 269
Independent Church book   FC 31/1
Workhouse register   L 3/4
1715 Poll book   Hare 6372/1–509x1
Hindle sermon 1692   MC 117/1
Annotated copy of Manship   4593 T138E
Fort inspections 1699–1701   MS 11408/29 A2
Lord-Lieutenancy book 1701–15   NRS 27276
Parish registers   PD 28/3–5
Quaker baptisms, etc.   SF 42–44
Quaker meetings   SF 53–54
Quaker trust deeds   SF 259

9. PUBLIC RECORD OFFICE, LONDON
Norfolk assizes   ASSI 16
Chancery cases   C5
Chancery Masters exhibits   C111/120
Association rolls 1696   C213
Exchequer depositions   E134
Exchequer commissions   E178
Taxation records   E179

Taxation records   E181–2
Port books   E190
Privy Council registers   PC2/54–73
Inventories   PROB 4
Wills   PROB 11
Nonconformist registers   RG4
State papers   SP18, 29, 35
Yarmouth maps   WO78

10. RAYNHAM HOUSE, NORFOLK
Box 65
Box 120, Townshend election expenses 1722
Boxfile 74, Misc. papers
Boxfile, 1st Visct. Townshend misc. corresp. 1650s–1687
Boxfile, Lord-Lieutenancy proceedings 1662–9

11. ROYAL BANK OF SCOTLAND, LONDON
Child and co. accounts, Earl of Yarmouth 1687–8

12. SOCIETY FOR PROMOTING CHRISTIAN KNOWLEDGE, LONDON
Minute books, vols. 1–4
Abstract letter books 1709–21

13. WELCOME INSTITUTE OF MEDICINE, LONDON
Mss 5313, Thomas King's letterbook 1719–25

14. DR WILLIAMS LIBRARY, LONDON
38. 109, Yarmouth Baptist Church book
Ms. 34. 4, Evans List

PRINTED PRIMARY MATERIAL

1. NATIONAL GOVERNMENT SERIES:
Calendar of the Committee for Compounding
Calendar of the Committee for Trade and Plantations
Calendar of the State Papers, Domestic
Calendar of the State Papers, Venetian
Calendar of Treasury Books
Calendar of Treasury Papers
Historical Manuscripts Commission Reports:
6th Report, Ingilby mss
7th Report, Frere mss

Bath
Devonshire I
Downshire I
Egmont II
Exeter
Hastings II
Lindsey
Polwarth II
Portland II, IV, VI
Stuart II
Townshend
Westmoreland
Journal of the House of Commons
Journal of the House of Lords
Statutes of the Realm
Statutes at Large

2. OTHER PRINTED PRIMARY SOURCES:

[a] *Printed tracts*
BENNITT, W., *The Work and Mercy of God Conduceth to his Praise* (1669).
BRIDGE, W., *The Works of the Rev. William Bridge, M. A.* (London, 1845) 5 vols.
BRINSLEY, J., *Two Treatises: i) A Groan for Israel; ii) The Spiritual Vertigo* (London, 1655).
——*Gospel Marrow* (London, 1659).
The Case of Great Yarmouth . . . against Southtown concerning a Bill for Confirming an Alleged Privilege of Lading and Unlading Goods (1665).
The Case of Great Yarmouth and Lowestoft in relation to the Bill for Making Billingsgate a Free Market for Fish.
The Case of Southtown, alias Little Yarmouth, . . . concerning their Fishery and Merchandise (London, 1665).
Encouragements to Builders and Planters of Little Yarmouth (London, 1668).
HILDEYARD, J., *A Sermon Preached at the Funeral of the Rt. Hon. Robert, Earl and Viscount Yarmouth* (London, 1683).
LOVE, B., *The Catechism of the Church Resolved into Short and Easy Questions and Answers* (London, 1699, 2nd edn.), (Norwich, 1706, 3rd edn.).
——*A Sermon Preached at the Consecration of St. George's Chapel in Great Yarmouth* (Norwich, 1716).
——*A Sermon Preached at the Funeral of Nathaniel Symonds esq.* (London, 1721).
LYNG, W., *A Sermon Preached in the Cathedral Church of Norwich concerning the Causes, Mischiefs, and Cures of National Divisions* (London, 1703).
——*A Discourse on the Usefulness, Antiquity, and Dedication of Churches* (Cambridge, 1716).

MILBOURNE, L., *Original of Rebellion: Or the Ends of Separation* (London, 1683).
——*Samaritism Revived* (London, 1683).
——*A Short Defence of the Orders of the Church of England* (London, 1688).
——*Mysteries in Religion Vindicated* (London, 1692).
Proposals relating to Little Yarmouth: The Manner of the Situation of Great Yarmouth, and of its Trade and Buildings etc. (London, 1672).
A True Relation of the Firing of the Steeple of the Great Church at Yarmouth (London, 1683).

[b] *Other printed primary materials*
The First Hall Book of the Borough of New Windsor, ed. S. Bond (Windsor, 1968).
BRADY, R., *An Historical Treatise of Cities and Burghs or Boroughs* (London, 1690).
BROME, J., *Travels over England, Scotland and Wales* (London, 1700).
The Memoirs of Sir John Reresby, ed. A. Browning (London, 1991, 2nd edn.).
CAMDEN, W., *Britannia* (London, 1586).
'East Anglian Pedigrees', ed. A. Campling, *NRS* 13 (1940).
'The Journal of the Very Reverend Rowland Davies', ed. W. R. Caulfield, *Camden Society*, 68 (1857).
The Records of the Borough of Leicester, 1689–1835, ed. G. A. Chinnery (Leicester, 1965).
'Letters Addressed from London to Sir Joseph Williamson, 1673–4', ed. W. D. Christie, *Camden Society*, NS 8–9 (1874).
'The 1664 Visitation of Norfolk', eds. A. Clarke and A. Campling, *NRS* 4–5 (1934).
The Records of the Borough of Northampton, ed. J. C. Cox (London, 1898).
COX, T., *Magna Britannica et Hibernia* (London, 1720–31), 6 vols.
'Old Meeting House, Norwich, and Great Yarmouth Independent Church', ed. B. Cozens-Hardy, *NRS* 22 (1951).
'Norfolk Lieutenancy Journal, 1676–1701', ed. B. Cozens-Hardy, *NRS* 30 (1961).
'Calendar of the Freemen of Great Yarmouth, 1429–1800', B. De Chair, *NNAS* 9 (1910).
DEFOE, D., *A Tour through the Whole Island of Great Britain*, eds. G. Cole and D. Browning (London, 1962), 2 vols.
'Norfolk Lieutenancy Journal, 1660–76', ed. R. M. Dunn, *NRS* 45 (1977).
'The Journal of Major Richard Ferrier, MP', eds. R. F. E. and J. A. H. Ferrier, *Camden Miscellany*, 9 (1895).
'The Norfolk Hearth Tax Assessment, Michaelmas 1664', eds. M. Frankel and R. Seaman, *Norfolk Genealogy*, 15 (1983).
GENTLEMAN, T., *England's Way to Win Wealth* (London, 1614).
Joannis Lelandi . . . De Rebus Britannicus Collectanea, ed. T. Hearne (Oxford, 1715), 6 vols.
'The Correspondence of Thomas Corie, Town Clerk of Norwich, 1664–87', ed. R. H. Hill, *NRS* 27 (1956).

'The Port Books of Boston, 1601–40', ed. R. Hinton, *Lincoln Record Society*, 50 (1956).

The Book of Fines of the Pontefract Corporation, 1653–1726, ed. R. Holmes (Pontefract, 1882).

The Parliamentary Diary of Narcissus Luttrell, 1691–3, ed. H. Horwitz (Oxford, 1972).

The Autobiography of Roger North, ed. A. Jessop (London, 1887).

'Register of Passengers from Great Yarmouth to Holland and New England, 1637–9', ed. C. Jewson, *NRS* 25 (1954).

'Bristol Borough Charters, 1509–1899', ed. R. Latham, *Bristol Record Society Publications*, 12 (1947).

LUTTRELL, N., *A Brief Historical Relation of State Affairs from September 1678 to April 1714* (Oxford, 1857), 6 vols.

MACKY, J., *A Journey through England* (London, 1713–23), 3 vols.

MADOX, T., *Firma Burgi* (London, 1726).

'Le Neve's Pedigrees of the Knights', ed. G. W. Marshall, *Harleian Society*, 8 (1873).

The Journeys of Celia Fiennes, ed. C. Morris (London, 1947).

NASH, T., *Nashes Lenten Stuffe, with the Praise of the Red Herring* (London, 1599).

Norwich Post 1707–12.

Norwich Gazette 1706–33.

Henry Manship's History of Great Yarmouth, ed. C. J. Palmer (Great Yarmouth, 1854).

A Booke of the Foundacion and Antiquitye of the Towne of Greate Yermouthe, ed. C. J. Palmer (Great Yarmouth, 1847).

'Yarmouth Letters', ed. F. D. Palmer, *The East Anglian*, NS 4–5 (1891–4).

The City of Liverpool: Selections from the Municipal Archives and Records from the Thirteenth to the Seventeenth Centuries, ed. J. A. Picton (Liverpool, 1883).

PRIMATT, S., *The City and Country Purchaser and Builder* (London, 1668, 1st edn.), (London, 1680, 2nd edn.).

The Records of the Borough of Nottingham (London, 1900).

Markets and Merchants of the Late Seventeenth Century, ed. H. Roseveare (Oxford, 1987).

Sources of English Constitutional History, eds. C. Stephens and F. G. Marcham (London, 1938).

STEVENSON, M., *Norfolk Drollery* (London, 1673).

'The Correspondence of the Family of Haddock, 1657–1719', ed. E. M. Thompson, *Camden Miscellany*, 8 (1883).

'The Letters of Humphrey Prideaux to John Ellis, 1674–1722', ed. E. M. Thompson, *Camden Society*, NS 15 (1875).

Original Records of Early Nonconformity, ed. C. Turner (London, 1911).

The English Travels of Sir John Perceval and William Bird II, ed. M. Wenger (Missouri, 1989).

The Compton Census, ed. A. O. Whiteman (Oxford, 1986).

SELECTED SECONDARY WORKS

ABRAMS, P., and WRIGLEY, E. (eds.) *Towns in Societies* (Cambridge, 1978).

APPLEBY, J., *Economic Thought and Ideology in Seventeenth-Century England* (Princeton, 1978).

ASHTON, R., *Financial and Commercial Policy under the Cromwellian Protectorate* (London, 1934).

AUSTIN, R., 'The City of Gloucester and the Regulation of Corporations, 1662–3', *Transactions of the Bristol and Gloucestershire Archaeological Society*, 58 (1936), 257–74.

BARRET, H., *The Great Yarmouth Corporation* (London, 1834).

BARRY, J. (ed.), *The Tudor and Stuart Town: A Reader in English Urban History, 1530–1688* (London, 1990).

BASKERVILLE, S. *et al.*, 'The Dynamics of Lordship Influence in English County Elections, 1701–34: The Evidence of Cheshire', *Parliamentary History*, 12 (1993), 126–42.

BECKETT, J. V., *Coal and Tobacco* (Cambridge, 1991).

BEDDARD, R., *A Kingdom without A King* (Oxford, 1988).

——(ed.) *The Revolutions of 1688* (Oxford, 1991).

BEIER, A., CANNADINE, D., and ROSENHEIM, J. M. (eds.), *The First Modern Society* (Cambridge, 1989).

BELL, C. and R., *City Fathers* (London, 1969).

BENNET, G., *The Tory Crisis in Church and State, 1688–1730* (Oxford, 1975).

BESSE, J., *A Collection of the Sufferings of the People Called Quakers* (London 1753), 2 vols.

BLOMEFIELD, F., and PARKIN, C., *Essay Towards a Topographical History of the County of Norfolk* (London, 1805–10), 11 vols.

BONFIELD, L., SMITH, R., and WRIGHTSON, K. (eds.), *The World We Have Gained* (Oxford, 1986).

BORSAY, P., *The English Urban Renaissance* (Oxford, 1989).

——(ed.), *The Georgian Town: A Reader in English Urban History, 1688–1820* (London, 1990).

BORSAY, P., and McINNES, A., 'Debate: The Emergence of a Leisure Town, or an Urban Renaissance', *Past and Present*, 126 (1990), 189–202.

BREWER, J., *Sinews of Power: Money and the State, 1688–1760* (London, 1989).

BROOKS, C., 'Interest, Patronage, and Professionalism: John, First Baron Ashburnham, Hastings, and the Revenue Services' in *Southern History*, 9 (1987), 51–70.

BROWNE, J., *A History of Congregationalism . . . in Norfolk and Suffolk* (London, 1877).

BROWNING, A., *Thomas Osborne, Earl of Danby* (Glasgow, 1944–51), 3 vols.

BURKE, P., *Venice and Amsterdam* (London, 1974).

BURTON, I., RILEY, P., and ROWLANDS, E., 'Political Parties in the Reigns of

William III and Anne: the Evidence of Division Lists', *BIHR*, Special Supplement 7 (1968).

CANNADINE, D., and REEDER, D. (eds.), *Exploring the Urban Past* (Cambridge, 1982).

CARRUTHERS, S. W., 'Norfolk Presbyterianism in the Seventeenth Century', *Norfolk Archaeology*, 30 (1952), 89–100.

CHALKLIN, C., *The Provincial Towns of Georgian England* (London, 1974).

——and HAVINDEN, M. (eds.), *Rural Change and Urban Growth, 1500–1800* (London, 1974).

——and WORDIE, J. R. (eds.), *Town and Countryside* (London, 1989).

CHARNOCK, J., *Biographia Navalis* (London, 1794–98), 6 vols.

CLARK, J. D. C., *English Society, 1688–1832: Ideology, Social Structure, and Political Practice during the Ancien Regime* (Cambridge, 1985).

CLARK, P. (ed.), *The Early Modern Town: A Reader* (London, 1976).

——(ed.) *Country Towns in Pre-Industrial England* (Leicester, 1981).

——(ed.) *The Transformation of English Provincial Towns* (London, 1984).

——and SLACK, P. (eds.), *Crisis and Order in English Towns, 1500–1700* (London, 1972).

—————— (eds.), *English Towns in Transition* (London, 1976).

COCKBURN, A. J. E., *The Corporations of England and Wales* (London, 1835).

COLEBY, A., *Central Government and the Localities: Hampshire, 1649–89* (Cambridge, 1987).

COLEMAN, D. C., 'London Scriveners and the Estate Market in the Later Seventeenth Century', *Economic History Review*, 2nd ser. 4 (1951–2), 221–30.

——and JOHN, A. (eds.), *Trade, Government, and the Economy in Pre-Industrial England* (London, 1976).

COLLEY, L., *In Defiance of Oligarchy* (Cambridge, 1982).

CORFIELD, P., *The Impact of English Towns, 1700–1800* (Oxford, 1982).

COLVIN, H., *A Biographical Dictionary of British Architects, 1600–1800* (London, 1978).

COSTIN, W. C., and WATSON, J. S. (eds.), *The Law and Working of the Constitution* (London, 1961), 2 vols.

COWAN, A., 'Urban Elites in Early Modern Europe: An Endangered Species?', *BIHR* 64 (1991), 121–37.

CRANFIELD, G. A., *The Development of the Provincial Newspaper, 1700–60* (Oxford, 1962).

CROWHURST, P., *The Defence of British Trade* (Folkestone, 1977).

CRUIKSHANKS, E., *By Force or By Default? The Revolution of 1688–89* (Edinburgh, 1989).

CUST, R., 'Anti-Puritanism and Urban Politics: Charles I and Great Yarmouth', *HJ* 35 (1992), 1–26.

——'Parliamentary Elections in the 1620s: The Case of Great Yarmouth', *Parliamentary History*, 11 (1992), 179–91.

DAVIS, R. H. C., *The Rise of the English Shipping Industry* (Newton Abbot, 1972).

DAVISON, L., HITCHCOCK, T., KEIRN, T., and SHOEMAKER, R. (eds.), *Stilling the Grumbling Hive: The Response to Social and Economic Problems in England, 1689–1750* (Stroud, 1992).

DEAN, D., 'Parliament, Privy Council, and Local Politics in Elizabethan England: the Yarmouth-Lowestoft Fishing Dispute', *Albion*, 22 (1990), 39–64.

DE KREY, G. S., *A Fractured Society: The Politics of London in the First Age of Party, 1688–1715* (Oxford, 1985).

Dictionary of National Biography (London, 1885–1900), 63 vols.

DE VRIES, J., *European Urbanisation, 1500–1800* (London, 1984).

DICKSON, P. G. M., *The Financial Revolution in England* (London, 1967).

DRUERY, J., *Historical and Topographical Notices of Great Yarmouth* (London, 1826).

DUCKETT, C., *Penal Laws and Test Act* (London, 1882).

DYOS, J. (ed.), *The Study of Urban History* (London, 1968).

EARLE, P., *The Making of the English Middle Classes* (London, 1989).

ECCLESTONE, A. W. L. and J. L., *The Rise of Great Yarmouth* (Norwich, 1959).

EVANS, J. T., 'The Decline of Oligarchy in Seventeenth-Century Norwich', *JBS* 14 (1974), 46–76.

——*Seventeenth-Century Norwich: Politics, Religion, and Government, 1620–90* (Oxford, 1979).

EVERITT, A., *The Community of Kent and the Great Rebellion, 1640–60* (Leicester, 1966).

——*Change in the Provinces: The Seventeenth Century* (Leicester, 1969).

——(ed.), *Perspectives in English Urban History* (London, 1973).

——(ed.), *Landscape and Community* (London, 1985).

FINBERG, H. P. R., *Local History in the University* (Leicester, 1964).

FLETCHER, A., *Reform in the Provinces* (New Haven, 1986).

——'The Enforcement of the Conventicle Acts', *Studies in Church History*, 21 (1984), 235–46.

FORSTER, G., 'Government in Provincial England under the Later Stuarts', in *TRHS* 5th ser. 33 (1983), 29–48.

——'Hull in the Sixteenth and Seventeenth Centuries', in *VCH Yorkshire, East Riding*, 1 (London, 1969).

FRASER, D., and SUTCLIFFE, A. (eds.), *The Pursuit of Urban History* (London, 1983).

GEORGE, R. H., 'The Charters granted to English Parliamentary Corporations in 1688', *EHR* 55 (1940), 47–56.

GLASSEY, L., *Politics and the Appointment of the Justices of the Peace, 1675–1720* (Oxford, 1979).

——'The Origins of Political Parties in Late Seventeenth-Century Lancashire', *Transactions of Historical Society of Lancashire and Cheshire*, 136 (1986), 39–58.

GOLDIE, M., 'James II and the Dissenters' Revenge: The Commission of Enquiry of 1688', *BIHR* 66 (1993), 53–88.

GORDAN, A. (ed.), *Freedom after Ejection* (Manchester, 1917).

GRASSBY, R., 'The Personal Wealth of the Business Community in Seventeenth-Century England' in *Economic History Review*, 2nd ser. 23 (1970), 220–34.

—— 'Social Mobility and Business Enterprise in Seventeenth-Century England', Kennington, D., and Thomas, K. (eds.), *Puritans and Revolutionaries* (Oxford, 1978).

GREAVES, R., *The Corporation of Leicester, 1689–1836* (Leicester, 1970, 2nd edn.).

GREAVES, R. L., *Deliver Us from Evil* (Oxford, 1986).

—— and ZALLER, R. (eds.), *Biographical Dictionary of British Radicals* (Brighton, 1972), 3 vols.

GRELL, O. P., ISRAEL, J. I., and TYACKE, N. (eds.), *From Persecution to Toleration* (Oxford, 1991).

HALEY, K. H. D., *The British and the Dutch* (London, 1988).

HANDLEY, S., 'Local Legislative Initiatives for Economic and Social Development in Lancashire, 1689–1731', *Parliamentary History*, 9 (1990), 231–49.

HARRIS, T., *London Crowds in the Reign of Charles II* (Cambridge, 1987).

—— *Politics under the Later Stuarts: Party Conflict in a Divided Society, 1660–1715* (London, 1993).

HARRIS, T., SEAWARD, P., and GOLDIE, M. (eds.), *The Politics of Religion in Restoration England* (Oxford, 1990).

HATTON, R., *George I: Elector and King* (London, 1978).

HAVINDEN, M., and CHALKLIN, C. (eds.), *Rural Change and Urban Growth, 1500–1800* (London, 1974).

HEAL, F., *Hospitality in Early Modern England* (Oxford, 1990).

HENDERSON, B. 'The Commonwealth Charters', *TRHS* 3rd ser. 6 (1912), 129–62.

HENNING, B. (ed.), *The History of Parliament: The House of Commons, 1660–1690* (London, 1983), 3 vols.

HEY, D., *The Fiery Blades of Hallamshire: Sheffield and its Neighbourhood, 1660–1740* (Leicester, 1991).

HILL, F., *Tudor and Stuart Lincoln* (Cambridge, 1956).

—— *Georgian Lincoln* (Cambridge, 1966).

HIRST, D., *The Representative of the People?* (Cambridge, 1975).

HOLMES, C., *The Eastern Association in the English Civil War* (Cambridge, 1974).

—— 'The County Community in Stuart Historiography', *JBS* 19 (1980), 54–73.

—— *Seventeenth-Century Lincolnshire* (Lincoln, 1980).

HOLMES, G. S. (ed.), *Britain after the Glorious Revolution* (London, 1969).

—— *The Trial of Doctor Sacheverell* (London, 1973).

—— *Augustan England* (London, 1982).

—— *British Politics in the Age of Anne* (London, 1987, 2nd edn.).

—— *The Making of A Great Power* (London, 1993).

HORLE, C. W., *The Quakers and the English Legal System, 1660–88* (Philadelphia, 1988).

HORWITZ, H., *Parliament, Politics, and Policy in the Reign of William III* (Manchester, 1977).

HOSKINS, W. G., *Industry, Trade, and People in Exeter, 1688–1800* (Manchester, 1935).

——*Local History in England* (London, 1959).

——*Provincial England* (London, 1963).

——*English Local History: The Past and the Future* (Leicester, 1966).

HOWELL, R., *Newcastle-upon-Tyne and the Puritan Revolution* (Oxford, 1967).

——'Neutralism, Conservatism, and Political Alignment in the English Revolution: the Case of the Towns, 1642–9', in Morrill, J. (ed.), *Reactions to the English Civil War, 1642–9* (Oxford, 1982).

——*Puritans and Radicals in Northern England: Essays on the English Revolution* (London, 1984).

HURWICH, J., 'A Fanatick Town: The Political Influence of Dissenters in Coventry, 1660–1720', *Midland History*, 4 (1977), 15–47.

HUTTON, R., *The Restoration* (Oxford, 1985).

——*Charles II, King of England, Scotland, and Ireland* (Oxford, 1989).

——*The English Republic, 1649–60* (London, 1990).

ISRAEL, J., *The Anglo-Dutch Moment* (Cambridge, 1991).

JACKSON, G., *Hull in the Eighteenth Century* (Oxford, 1972).

JENKINS, P., *The Making of a Ruling Class: The Glamorgan Gentry, 1640–1790* (Cambridge, 1983).

——'Tory Industrialism and Town Politics: Swansea in the Eighteenth Century', *HJ* 28 (1985), 103–23.

——'Party Conflict and Political Stability in Monmouthshire, 1690–1740', *HJ* 29 (1986), 557–75.

JEWSON, C., 'Norfolk Baptists up to 1700', *Baptist Quarterly*, 18 (1959–60), 308–15, 363–9.

JOHNSTON, J., 'Worcestershire Probate Inventories, 1699–1716', *Midland History*, 4 (1978), 191–211.

JOHNSTON, J. A., 'Parliament and the Protection of Trade, 1689–94', *Mariner's Mirror*, 57 (1971), 399–413.

JONES, A., 'Great Plague in Yarmouth', *Notes and Queries*, 202 (1957), 108–112.

JONES, C. (ed.), *Britain in the First Age of Party, 1680–1750* (London, 1987).

——(ed.), *Party and Management in Parliament, 1660–1784* (Leicester, 1984).

JONES, D. W., *War and Economy* (Oxford, 1988).

JONES, J. R., 'The First Whig Party in Norfolk', *Durham University Journal*, 46 (1953–4), 13–21.

——*The First Whigs* (Oxford, 1961).

——*The Revolution of 1688* (London, 1972).

——(ed.), *The Restored Monarchy, 1660–88* (London, 1979).

——*Charles II: Royal Politician* (London, 1987).

——(ed.), *Liberty Secured: Britain before and after 1688* (Stanford, 1992).

KEITH-LUCAS, B., *The Unreformed Local Government System* (London, 1980).

KETTON-CREMER, B., *Norfolk Portraits* (London, 1944).

——*Norfolk Assembly* (London, 1957).

KIRBY, J., 'Restoration Leeds and the Aldermen of the Corporation, 1661–1700', *Northern History*, 22 (1986), 123–74.

KISHLANSKY, M., *Parliamentary Selection* (Cambridge, 1986).

KUYPER, *Dutch Classicist Architecture 1625–1700* (Delft, 1980).

LACEY, D., *Dissent and Parliamentary Politics in England, 1661–89* (New Brunswick, 1969).

LANDAU, N., *The Justices of the Peace, 1679–1760* (Berkeley, 1984).

——'Independence, Deference, and Voter Participation: The Behaviour of the Electorate in Early Eighteenth-Century Kent', *HJ* 22 (1979), 561–83.

LANGFORD, P., *The Excise Crisis* (Oxford, 1975).

——*Public Life and the Propertied Englishman* (Oxford, 1991).

LEE, C., 'Fanatic Magistrates: Religious and Political Conflict in Three Kent Boroughs, 1680–4', *HJ* 35 (1992), 43–61.

LEVIN, J., *The Charter Controversy in the City of London, 1660–88, and its Consequences* (London, 1969).

LILLYWHITE, B., *London Coffee Houses* (London, 1963).

MACCAFFREY, W. T., *Exeter, 1540–1640* (Cambridge, Mass., 1958).

MACCLURE, E. (ed.), *A Chapter in English Church History* (London, 1888).

MACFARLANE, J., *Reconstructing Historical Communities* (Cambridge, 1977).

MACGRATH, P., *The Merchant Venturers of Bristol* (Bristol, 1975).

MACINNES, A., *The English Town, 1660–1720* (London,1980).

——'The Emergence of a Leisure Town: Shrewsbury, 1660–1760', *Past and Present*, 120 (1988), 53–87.

MCKENDRICK, N., BREWER, J., and PLUMB, J. (eds.), *The Birth of A Consumer Society: The Commercialisation of Eighteenth-Century England* (London, 1982).

MCKENDRICK, N., and OUTHWAITE, R. (eds.), *Business Life and Public Policy* (Cambridge, 1986).

MANDLEBAUM, S. J., 'H. J. Dyos and British Urban History', *Economic History Review*, 2nd ser. 37 (1985), 437–47.

MARTIN, G., and MACINTYRE, S. (eds.), *A Bibliography of British and Irish Municipal History* (Leicester, 1971).

MATTHEWS, A. G., *Calamy Revised* (Oxford, 1934).

MELTON, F. T., 'Sir Robert Clayton's Building Projects in London, 1666–72', *Guildhall Studies in London History*, 3 (1977), 37–42.

MILLER, J., *Popery and Politics in England, 1660–88* (Cambridge, 1973).

——'The Crown and the Borough Charters in the Reign of Charles II', *EHR* 100 (1985), 53–84.

——*Charles II* (London, 1991).

MULLETT, M., 'The Politics of Liverpool, 1660–88', *Transactions of the Historical Society of Lancashire and Cheshire*, 124 (1972), 31–56.

——'Deprived of Our Former Place: The Internal Politics of Bedford, 1660–88', *Bedfordshire Historical Record Society*, 59 (1980), 1–42.

—— 'Conflict, Politics, and Elections in Lancaster, 1660–88', *Northern History*, 19 (1983), 61–86.

—— 'Men of Known Loyalty: The Politics of the Lancashire Borough of Clitheroe, 1660–89', *Northern History*, 21 (1985), 108–36.

MURRELL, P., 'Bury St Edmunds and the Campaign to Pack Parliament, 1687–8', *BIHR* 54 (1981), 188–206.

NEF, J. U., *The Rise of the British Coal Industry* (London, 1932).

NEWTON, R., *Eighteenth-Century Exeter* (Exeter, 1984).

NORREY, P. J., 'The Restoration Regime in Action: The Relationship between Central and Local Government in Dorset, Somerset and Wiltshire, 1660–78', *HJ* 31 (1988), 789–812.

O'DAY, R., SLACK, P., CORFIELD, P., PHYTHIAN-ADAMS, P. (eds.), *The Traditional Community Under Stress* (Milton Keynes, 1977).

O'NEIL, B., 'Some Seventeenth-Century Houses in Great Yarmouth', *Archaeologia*, 95 (1953), 141–80.

PALLISER, D., 'Civic Mentality and the Environment in Tudor York', *Northern History*, 18 (1982), 78–115.

PALMER, C. J., *A History of Great Yarmouth, Designed as a Continuation of Manship's History of that Town* (Great Yarmouth, 1856).

—— *The Perlustration of Great Yarmouth with Gorlestone and Southtown* (Great Yarmouth, 1872–5), 3 vols.

PARSLOE, C., 'The Corporation of Bedford, 1647–64', *TRHS* 4th ser. 29 (1947), 151–65.

PATTEN, J., *English Towns, 1500–1700* (Folkestone, 1978).

PATTERSON, A. T., *A History of Southampton*, vol. 1 (Southampton, 1966).

PEARL, V., *London and the Outbreak of the Puritan Revolution* (Oxford, 1961).

PHYTHIAN-ADAMS, C., *Desolation of a City: Coventry and the Urban Crisis of the Late Middle Ages* (Cambridge, 1979).

—— *Rethinking English Local History* (Leicester, 1987).

PLUMB, J. H., *Sir Robert Walpole* (London, 1956–60), 2 vols.

—— *The Growth of Political Stability in England, 1675–1725* (London, 1967).

POCOCK, J. G. A., 'Robert Brady, 1627–1700: A Cambridge Historian of the Restoration', *Cambridge Historical Journal*, 10 (1951), 186–204.

POUND, J. F., 'The Social and Trade Structure of Norwich, 1525–75', *Past and Present*, 34 (1966), 49–69.

PREST, W. R. (ed.), *The Professions in Early Modern England* (London, 1987).

REDDAWAY, T., *Rebuilding London after the Great Fire* (London, 1940).

REYNOLDS, S., *An Introduction to the History of English Medieval Towns* (Oxford, 1977).

RICHARDSON, R. C. (ed.), *Town and Countryside in the English Revolution* (Manchester, 1992).

RIDEN, P. (ed.), *Probate Records and the Local Community* (Gloucester, 1985).

RIGBY, S., 'Urban Oligarchy in Late Medieval England', in Thomson, J. A. F. (ed.), *Towns and Townspeople in Late Medieval England* (Gloucester, 1988).

ROBERTS, S. K., *Recovery and Restoration in an English County: Devon Local Administration, 1646–70* (Exeter, 1985).

——'Public or Private? Revenge and Recovery at the Restoration of Charles II', *BIHR* 59 (1986), 172–88.

ROGERS, N., *Whigs and Cities: Popular Politics in the Age of Walpole and Pitt* (Oxford, 1989).

ROSCOE, E. J., *Admiralty Jurisdiction and the Practice of the High Court of Justice* (London, 1920).

——*Studies in the History of the Admiralty and Prize Courts* (London, 1932).

ROSENHEIM, J. M., 'Party Organisation at the Local Level: The Norfolk Sheriff's Subscription of 1676', *HJ* 29 (1986), 713–22.

——*The Townshends of Raynham* (Middleton, 1989).

RUBINI, D., *Court and Country* (London, 1967).

RUPP, G., *Religion in England, 1689–1791* (Oxford, 1986).

RUTLEDGE, P., 'Thomas Damet and the Historiography of Great Yarmouth', *Norfolk Archaeology*, 33 (1963), 119–30; and 34 (1968), 332–4.

——'Archive Management at Great Yarmouth since 1540', *Journal of the Society of Archivists*, 3 (1965), 89–91.

——'Great Yarmouth Assembly Minutes, 1538–1545', *NRS* 39 (1970), 1–80.

RYE, W., *Norfolk Families* (Norwich, 1913) 2 vols.

SACKS, D. H., *Trade, Society, and Politics in Bristol, 1540–1640* (New York, 1985), 2 vols.

——'The Corporate Town and the English State: Bristol's Little Businesses, 1625–41', *Past and Present*, 110 (1986), 69–105.

——*The Widening Gate: Bristol and the Atlantic Economy, 1650–1700* (Berkeley, 1991).

SACRET, J. H., 'The Restoration Government and Municipal Corporations', *EHR* 45 (1930), 232–59.

SCHWOERER, L., *The Declaration of Rights* (Baltimore, 1981).

——*The Revolution of 1688–9: Changing Perspectives* (Cambridge, 1992).

SCOTT, J., *Algernon Sidney and the Restoration Crisis, 1677–83* (Cambridge, 1991).

SCOTT, W. R., *The Constitution and Finance of English, Scottish, and Irish Joint Stock Companies* (Cambridge, 1910–12), 3 vols.

SEAWARD, P., *The Cavalier Parliament and the Reconstruction of the Old Regime, 1661–7* (Cambridge, 1989).

SEDGWICK, R. (ed.), *The History of Parliament: House of Commons, 1715–54* (London, 1970), 2 vols.

SLATER, V., 'Continuity and Change in English Provincial Politics: Robert Paston in Norfolk, 1675–83', *Albion*, 25 (1993), 193–216.

SMITH, A. H., *County and Court* (Oxford, 1974).

SOUDEN, D., and CLARK, P. (eds.), *Migration and Society in Early Modern England* (London, 1987).

SPECK, W., 'The Choice of the Speaker in 1705', *BIHR* 37 (1964), 20–46.

——*Tory and Whig: The Struggle in the Constituencies, 1701–15* (London, 1970).

—— 'Brackley: A Study in the Growth of Oligarchy', *Midland History*, 3 (1975–6), 30–41.

—— *Reluctant Revolutionaries* (Oxford, 1988).

SPUFFORD, M., *Contrasting Communities* (Cambridge, 1974).

SPURR, J., 'The Church of England, Comprehension, and the Toleration Act of 1689', *EHR* 104 (1989), 927–46.

STONE, L., 'Prosopography', *Daedalus*, 100 (1971), 46–79.

STYLES, P., *The Corporation of Warwick, 1660–1835* (Oxford, 1938).

—— 'The Corporation of Bewdley under the Later Stuarts', in *University of Birmingham Journal*, 1 (1947–8), 92–134.

SUCKLING, A., *The History and Antiquities of Suffolk* (London, 1846), 2 vols.

SWINDEN, H., *The History and Antiquities of the Ancient Burgh of Great Yarmouth* (Norwich, 1772).

TAIT, J., 'The Common Council of the Borough', *EHR* 46 (1931), 1–29.

THOMSON, M. A., *The Secretaries of State, 1681–1782* (Oxford, 1932).

—— *A Constitutional History of England, 1642–1801* (London, 1938).

TITLER, R., *Architecture and Power: The Town Hall and the English Urban Community, c.1500–1640* (Oxford, 1991).

TURNER, D., *A Sketch of the History of Caister Castle* (London, 1842).

—— *Sepulchral Reminiscences* (Great, Yarmouth, 1848).

VENN, J., *Gonville and Caius College* (Cambridge, 1897–1901), 3 vols.

—— *Alumni Canterbrigienses* (Cambridge, 1922), 4 vols.

WATTS, M. R., *The Dissenters* (Oxford, 1978).

WEBB, S. and B., *English Local Government: The Manor and the Borough* (London, 1924, 2nd edn.), 2 vols.

WEINBAUM, M., *British Borough Charters, 1307–1660* (Cambridge, 1943).

WESTERN, J. R., *Monarchy and Revolution* (London, 1972).

—— *The English Militia in the Eighteenth Century* (London, 1965).

WHITEHEAD, J., *A History of Great Yarmouth Grammar School* (Great Yarmouth, 1951).

WHITING, C. E., *Studies in English Puritanism, 1660–88* (London, 1931).

WILLIAMS, N. J., *The Maritime Trade of the East Anglian Ports, 1550–1590* (Oxford, 1988).

WILSON, C., *England's Apprenticeship, 1603–1763* (London, 1984, 2nd edn.).

WILSON, R., *Gentlemen Merchants* (Manchester, 1971).

—— 'Merchants and Land: The Ibbetsons of Leeds, 1650–1850', *Northern History*, 24 (1988), 75–100.

WORDEN, B., 'Toleration and the Cromwellian Protectorate', *Studies in Church History*, 21 (1984), 199–234.

WORSHIP, F., 'On the Crowther Monument, Yarmouth Church', *NNAS* 2 (1849), 35–42.

WRIGHT, S. (ed.), *Parish, Church, and People* (London, 1988).

WRIGHTSON, K., *English Society, 1580–1680* (London, 1982).

WRIGLEY, E. A., 'Urban Growth and Agricultural Change', *Journal of Inter-Disciplinary History*, 15 (1984–5), 683–728.

UNPUBLISHED THESES

DAWSON, E. J., 'Finance and the Unreformed Borough', Hull Ph.D. 1978.

DOOLITTLE, I., 'The Government of the City of London, 1694–1767', Oxford D.Phil. 1979.

JACOB, W. M., 'Clergy and Society in Norfolk, 1707–1806', Exeter Ph.D. 1982.

LEE, J. M., 'Stamford and the Cecils, 1700–1835: A Study in Political Control', Oxford B.Litt. 1957.

KNIGHTS, M., 'Politics and Opinion during the Exclusion Crisis, 1678–81', Oxford D.Phil. 1989.

METTERS, G., 'The Rulers and Merchants of King's Lynn in the Early Seventeenth Century', UEA Ph.D. 1982.

MICHEL, A. R., 'Port and Town of Great Yarmouth and its Economic and Social Relationships with its Neighbours on Both Sides of the Seas, 1550–1714', Cambridge Ph.D. 1978.

MURPHY, J. D., 'The Town and Trade of Great Yarmouth, 1740–1850', UEA Ph.D. 1979.

PICKAVANCE, R., 'The English Boroughs and the King's Government: A Study of the Tory Reaction, 1681–5', Oxford D.Phil. 1976.

ROSENHEIM, J. M., 'An Examination of Oligarchy: The Gentry of Restoration Norfolk, 1660–1720', Princetown Ph.D. 1981.

SAUL, A. R., 'Great Yarmouth in the Fourteenth Century: A Study in Trade, Politics, and Society', Oxford D.Phil. 1975.

TRIFFIT, J., 'Politics and the Urban Community: Parliamentary Boroughs in the South-West, 1710–1730', Oxford D.Phil. 1985.

INDEX

Abingdon 90, 104
Addison, Joseph 245
Admiralty, High Court of 191, 192 n.,
    200, 205, 213, 235
Ailesbury, Earl of, *see* Bruce, Thomas
Aldeburgh 23, 187 n.
Andrews, John 39 n., 81, 231, 232, 236,
    243, 248, 260, 261
Anne, Queen 216
Appleby 193
Arlington, Lord, *see* Bennet, Henry
Arran, Lord, *see* Butler, Richard
Arundel, Earl of, *see* Howard, Thomas
Ashburnham, Lord John 212
Associations 190–1, 193, 244, 252 n.
Astley, Sir Jacob 221–2
Atterbury, Francis 252
Atwood, Robert 83, 230 n.

Bacon, Nathaniel 37
Baldock, Sir Robert 148
Bank of England 205
Barry, J. 7
Baskerville, Sir Thomas 72
Bath, Earl of, *see* Granville, John
Beau, Dr 196
Beccles 213 n.
Bedford 46, 104, 162, 167 n., 172
Bendish, Thomas 124
Bennet, Henry, Lord Arlington 122
Bertie, Montagu, Earl of Lindsey 115
Berwick 91, 104
Betts, Richard 44
Bewdley 211 n., 213
Birch, John 52
Birmingham 237
Bishop's Castle 229 n.
Blenheim, battle of 223
borough regulation:
    (1660s) 63–4, 87, 101–2, 103, 108 n., 110
    (1680s) 15, 63–5, 151–2, 154–5, 165,
        172–3, 230
Borsay, P. 7, 258
Bower, Richard 104, 106, 122, 123, 127,
    130, 133, 136–9, 141–2, 143, 146,
    149 n., 153, 156, 183, 197 n.

Brady, Robert 180
Breda, Declaration of 103
Bridge, William 89, 90, 91, 122
Bridlington 199
Brightin, Richard 77 n.
Brinsley, John 89, 90
Bristol 4, 7, 55, 78, 90, 104, 110, 159 n.,
    168, 179 n., 193, 231, 236 n.
Brooks, C. 212
Bruce, Thomas, Earl of Ailesbury 173 n.
Bure, River 36
Burgh Castle 93
Burton family 71
Burton, John 207–8
Burton, William 103
Bury St Edmunds 147, 172, 180 n., 193
Butler, James, Duke of Ormonde 241
Butler, Richard, Lord Arran 115

Caister 36 n., 53, 131
Caius College, Cambridge 96
Camden, William 53
Canterbury 155
Carteret, Edward 220 n.
Castel family 93
Castel, Abraham 168
Castel, John 96
Catholicism, Roman 134 n., 172
Caulier, Peter 65–6, 157
Charles II 100, 101, 110, 115, 116, 121–2,
    123, 129, 137, 153, 162
Chester 52, 104, 154, 161 n., 180, 193
Churchill, John, Duke of Marlborough
    222, 225
Cinque Ports 37, 53–4
Clark, P. 5, 16, 37, 59, 65, 236
Clarendon, Earl of, *see* Hyde, Edward
Clitheroe 141 n.
Colby, Samuel 67
Colchester 180 n.
Compton census 133
Cook, Sir William 163, 164 n., 166, 204
Cooper family 93
Corbet, Miles 51 n.
Corbridge map 260
Cousens, Christopher 95

Cousens, Henry 95
Coventry 78, 90, 100 n., 104, 238, 253, 261
Coventry, William 111, 146, 147
Cromwell, Henry 105 n.
Cromwell, Oliver 17, 100
Cromwell, Richard 103
Cutting family 69

Danby, Lord, *see* Osborne, Thomas
Damet, Thomas 37
Dartmouth, Earl of, *see* Legge, George
Davies, Rowland 36–7, 51, 181–2
Davison, John 203 n.
Dawson, John 134
Declarations of Indulgence:
    (1672) 127, 169 n.
    (1687) 166
    (1688) 168, 169 n.
Defoe, Daniel 71, 259
De Gomme, Sir Bernard 119
De Krey, G. S. 212
Devizes 214
Dickenson, William 125
Dissenters, *see* Nonconformity
Dorset, Earl of, *see* Sackville, Richard
Dover 199 n., 204 n.
D'Oyly, Sir William 104–6, 109, 127, 130, 137, 141
Duncon, Edmund 108
Dunkirk 237
Dunster, Giles 137
Dunwich 176, 180 n., 202 n., 214
Dutch, relationship with the 92, 111, 113–14, 124, 125, 249 n.
Dyos, H. J. 5, 6

Earle, P. 75
Edward III 37
Ellys family 95
Ellys, Anthony I 182
Ellys, Anthony II 189–90, 191, 200, 201 n., 233–4
Ellys, Sir John 189–90
Ellys, Thomas 77
England family 69, 71–2, 136, 139, 270–1
England, Benjamin 157, 170, 201, 208–9, 221–2, 226, 229–30, 232
England, Sir George 71, 72, 86, 97 n., 103, 106, 122, 123, 130, 132, 136
England, George I 96, 144, 145, 147, 149, 155, 164, 170, 171 n., 177, 178–9, 180, 185, 186–7, 194, 195, 196, 199, 202, 203, 204, 207, 208

England, George II 232, 235, 239–40, 241, 242, 243, 250–2
England, Sarah 71–2
England, Thomas 154
Evans, J. T. 16, 59
Everitt, A. 3, 4, 70
Exclusion 129–30, 145–50
Exeter 33, 37, 43, 52, 173
Eye 180 n.

Fal, River 121
Ferrier family 69, 72–3
Ferrier, Richard I 73 n.
Ferrier, Richard II 43 n., 66, 196–7, 198, 224, 226, 227, 229–30, 231, 232–4, 235, 237, 239–41, 242, 244, 251
Ferrier, Richard III 73, 239, 244–5
Ferrier, Robert 72
Fiennes, Celia 94 n.
Fitch, Sir Thomas 132
Fitzroy, Charles, Duke of Grafton 240, 248
Fletcher, A. 122
Fowey 180 n.
Fowle, John 71
free trade 195, 204
Friend, John 163, 164 n., 166, 171 n., 185, 254 n.
Fuller family 69, 73, 74, 95, 251, 254 n.
Fuller, John 245–6
Fuller, Richard 232
Fuller, Samuel I 73, 96, 177, 178–9, 180, 186–7, 194, 195, 196–7, 199, 203, 207–8, 209, 226, 228–30, 232, 245–6, 249
Fuller, Samuel II 226, 231, 243

Gatford, Lionel 108–9
Gayford, John 170
Glassey, L. 192
Gloucester 52, 57, 70, 78, 94 n., 104
Godfrey, Thomas 74, 147, 159, 160, 168, 197, 198
Gooch family 95
Gooch, Thomas 159, 160, 167, 183
Goose, Benjamin 67
Gould, Sir Edward 245–6
government departments:
    Admiralty Board 187, 188, 194, 196–7, 203, 204
    Customs House 137
    Office of Sick and Wounded 197 n., 198–9
    Ordnance 187, 227

Grafton, Duke of, *see* Fitzroy, Charles
Granville, John, Earl of Bath 173
Greenwich 1, 206

Haddock, Joseph 194, 197–8, 213, 218, 219
Hannot, James 169, 183, 207 n.
Harley, Robert 239
Harwich 189 n.
Henshawe, Thomas 119
Heraldic visitation 97
Hereford 87
Hindle, Nathaniel 183
Hirst, D. 45
Hobart, Sir John 94, 127 n.
Hobbes, Thomas 15, 55
Holland, Sir John, 1st Bt. 114
Holland, Sir John, 2nd Bt. 250, 252
Holmes, G. 10, 255
Holt, Sir John 170, 197
Hooker, John 37, 43
Horth, Thomas 83 n.
Horwitz, H. 10, 179, 221
Hoskins, W. G. 5
Howard, Thomas, Earl of Arundel and
    Duke of Norfolk 157, 158 n., 164,
    184–5, 187 n., 193, 201 n., 206
Hull 26 n., 28 n., 52, 57, 81, 89 n., 104,
    154, 162, 172
Huntington, Richard 73, 103, 122, 135,
    136, 138, 139, 141, 143, 144, 145, 147,
    154, 157, 158 n., 164, 171 n., 183
Huntington, Rose 91
Hunton, Edmund 34
Hyde, Edward, Earl of Clarendon 102 n.,
    105, 108–9, 114 n., 120, 126

invasions 225, 243
Ipswich 37, 55 n., 75, 240
Ives, John 13

Jackson, William 145 n.
James II 101, 129, 154, 163, 165, 171–3
Jenkins, Sir Leoline 153, 158, 161
Jenkins, P. 212
Johnson family 69
Johnson, Sir James 123, 140 n., 144, 145,
    149, 153, 167, 169, 170, 183
Johnson, Thomas 35
Jones, D. 186

King, Thomas 125
King's Lynn 18, 29 n., 46, 52, 80, 94,
    142, 195, 217, 218–22, 237 n.

Kirby, J. 16, 59
Kirkley Road 31, 112
Kishlansky, M. 24–5

Lancaster 172
Leeds 35, 39, 44 n., 70, 92, 110
Legge, George, Lord Dartmouth 169 n.
Leghorn 245
Leicester 18, 26, 29, 41 n., 55 n., 110,
    140 n.
Lincoln 27 n., 34, 41 n., 55
Lindsey, Earl of, *see* Bertie, Montagu
Liverpool 24, 33, 52, 110, 115, 157,
    180 n., 193
Lloyd, William, Bishop of Norwich 167 n.,
    168 n.
London 51, 119
    corporation 28 n., 40, 57, 70, 104,
        124 n., 155, 202 n., 204, 213
    influence 92, 118–9, 205–6
    politics 179, 201, 211 n., 212
Long, Francis 224
Lothingland, Lords of 53
Love, Barry 188, 202, 207, 209, 215, 223,
    230, 238, 243, 248, 261
Lowestoft 37, 53, 55, 112, 161, 204
Lowther, Sir John 119
Ludlow 176, 180 n.
Luson, William 202 n., 230 n.
Lyng, William 215

MacCaffrey, W. 4
Magdalene College, Oxford 165
Malmesbury 180 n.
Manchester 237
mandamus 117, 159
Manship, Henry 37, 53–4
Marlborough, Duke of, *see* Churchill, John
Medowe family 69
Medowe Sir Thomas 86, 97 n., 106–7,
    113 n., 122, 135, 137 n., 141–7, 153,
    154, 155–7, 158–9, 160, 167, 170, 183
Meen, Joshua 176 n.
Michel, A. 65, 81
Milbourne, Luke 147, 150, 158, 161, 182,
    183, 261
Miller, J. 110
Monmouth Rebellion 164
Montagu, William 138
Mullett, M. 157, 172
Municipal Reform 8, 15, 19 n., 57, 68–9,
    98, 262
Murrell, P. 172

Negus, John 241, 245
Newcastle-under-Lyme 55 n.
Newcastle-upon-Tyne 4, 25 n., 39, 41, 46, 78, 81
newspapers 259
Newton, William 119
Nicholson, John 202–3, 204, 207, 222
Nonconformity 137, 156, 158, 165, 166–7, 171, 180–3, 214–16, 237
  Baptists 127 n., 134 n., 166 n., 182 n., 217 n.
  Congregationalists/Independents 46–7, 89–90, 102–3, 107, 123 n., 127 n., 169, 181–2, 183, 217 n.
  numbers 133, 136, 182 n.
  persecution 63, 70 n., 106–7, 122–3, 127, 153, 154, 164, 202
  political impact 104, 105–6, 129–30, 142, 143–4, 148–9, 150, 152, 157, 207–9, 234, 260–2
  Presbyterians 46–7, 89–90, 103, 107, 127 n., 183n.
  Quakers 88, 89–90, 107 n., 134 n., 166 n., 181 n., 182, 232 n.
  Separatists 89
  social impact 11, 90–1, 101
non-jurors 181, 191
Norfolk, Duke of, *see* Howard, Thomas
Norfolk elections:
  (1702) 208
  (1715) 242
Northampton 26, 159, 193, 248
Northey, Edward 195
Norwich 4, 27 n., 57, 92, 119, 132, 157
  corporation 40, 70, 80 n., 91 n., 93, 97 n., 110, 120, 140, 155, 158 n., 167 n., 186, 213, 218–19, 222
  Dean and Chapter 107–8, 183 n.
  politics 142, 143 n., 159
  trade 85
Nottingham 27–8, 33, 41 n., 155, 180 n., 214

Orford 176, 214
Ormesby St Margaret 93
Ormonde, Duke of, *see* Butler, James
Osborne, Leonard 86
Osborne, Thomas, Lord Danby 52, 126 n., 134, 135, 142
Owner, Edward 52 n.
Oxford 41 n., 231, 261
Oxnead 121–2, 134

Pacy, William 243, 251–2
Parish, Robert 67
Parliament:
  Acts: Billingsgate (1699) 204; Causeway (1712) 235; Conventicle (1670) 122–3; Corporation (1661) 101–2, 104 n., 105, 108, 154, 169 n.; Fishery (1719) 246–7; Haven (1670) 117, 120–1, 123; Haven (1677) 140, 160; Haven (1685) 163, 164, 177; Haven (1689) 177, 186; Haven (1699) 203–4; Haven (1703) 214; Haven (1723) 252–3; Herring (1663) 111; London Charter Confirmation (1690) 179–80; New Chapel (1714) 240; New Chapel (1721) 249; Occasional Conformity (1711) 235, 238; Septennial (1716) 244; Southtown (1664) 114–16, 124; Test (1673) 127, 169 n.; Toleration (1690) 180–1, 182, 210, 238, 261; Triennial (1694) 210; Uniformity (1662) 107
  bills: corporation (1689–91) 177–9, 180; French commerce (1713) 239; occasional conformity (1702–4) 214–16
  elections: (1654) 46; (1660) 46–7, 102, 104, 105 n.; (1661) 104, 111; (1678) 141–3; (1679(1)) 145–7, 150 n.; (1679(2)) 147, 150 n.; (1681) 148–9, 150 n.; (1685) 163–4; (1689) 176–7; (1690) 179; (1695) 189; (1698) 201–3; (1701(1)) 207; (1701(2)) 207–8; (1702) 208–9, 214, 222 n.; (1705) 222; (1708) 225–7; (1709) 227–31; (1710) 222 n., 232–4; (1713) 239; (1715) 242; (1722) 250–2; (1723) 253
  franchise 45–7, 162
  instructions 51
  Members' responsibilities 45–6, 50–3, 149, 179, 192–4, 199
  payments to Members 185
Paston, Robert, 1st Earl of Yarmouth 1–2, 52, 94, 112–50, 152–4, 157–8, 198, 263
  economic schemes 112–13, 117–20, 123–6, 131–2, 134–6, 138, 139–40, 141, 144–5, 147–8
  family debts 112 n., 126, 131 n.
  politics 143, 144, 146, 147–8, 152–3, 153–4, 157 n.
  royal favour 117, 125–6, 133, 147

Paston, Robert 165
Paston, Thomas 165
Paston, Sir William 112 n., 113 n., 131 n.
Paston, William, 2nd Earl of Yarmouth
    122 n., 157–65, 168, 206, 213, 214
  Jacobitism 171–2, 183–4, 246–7
  as patron 195–6, 201 n., 235, 246–7
Paterson, John, Archbishop of Glasgow
    191
Pearl, V. 4
Pepys, Samuel 169 n.
Perceval, Sir John 209
Phythian-Adams, C. 5
plague 27, 117, 159
Plumb, J. 10, 255
Plymouth 90, 180 n., 193
political affiliations and groupings:
  accommodations 176, 212, 222–3,
    228–30, 239, 261
  commonwealthsmen 137, 152
  fanatics/faction 143–4, 148–9, 152,
    157, 159 n.
  Jacobites 187, 191
  loyalists 106, 113 n., 143–4, 148–9,
    149–50, 152, 159 n.
  moderates/neutrals 159–60
  Tories 129, 152, 172–3, 207 n., 208–9,
    212, 214–15, 217, 233–4, 256, 261
  Whigs 129, 152, 157, 172–3, 207 n.,
    212, 214–15, 233–4, 256
Pollexfen, Henry 170
Pontefract 23, 29
Poole 154, 180 n.
Popish Plot 143, 145
Portsmouth 55
Preston 51–2
Primatt, Stephen 118, 119 n., 163
Privy Council 34, 107, 112, 122, 137, 138,
    139, 141, 155, 156, 168, 188 n.

quo warranto 20, 109, 154, 159, 160, 172

Ramillies, battle of 223
Revolution of 1688 170–2, 174–5, 177,
    210, 255
Reynolds, Edward, Bishop of Norwich
    108–9
Rich, Sir Robert 196
riot and disorder 156, 164, 171, 189–90,
    242 n.
Ripon 162
Robinson, Sir William 194
Rogers, N. 253

Rooke, Sir George 222
Rotterdam, Anglican church at 216–17
Rye House Plot 158
Ryswick, Treaty of 199, 201

Sacheverell, Henry 231, 234
Sackville, Richard, Earl of Dorset 115
Sancroft, William, Archbishop of
    Canterbury 166
Scarborough 249 n.
Sheers, Sir Henry 164, 169
Shrewsbury 27, 231
Slack P. 5
Sluys, battle of 38
Smith, John 202 n.
Smyrna convoy 187–8
Society for Promoting Christian
    Knowledge 215
Southampton 41, 55, 151 n., 155
Southern, James 187
Southtown, *see* Yarmouth, Little
Sparrow, Anthony, Bishop of Norwich
    153–4, 155
Speck, W. A. 10, 255
Speed, John 53
Spencer, Charles, Earl of Sunderland
    245–6
Spencer, Robert, Earl of Sunderland 166
Spendlove, John 261
Springall, Matthew 42 n.
Stafford 155
Stamford 124 n., 141 n.
Stanhope, James 247–8
Steadman, Thomas 66
Stevenson, Matthew 123
Stone, L. 59
Sunderland, Earls of, *see* Spencer, Charles
    and Robert
Swinden, Henry 120
Symonds, Nathaniel 155–7, 160, 161,
    230–2

taxation and customs:
  coal duties 199, 220, 221 n., 240
  land tax 188–9, 205
  malt duties 199, 247
  salt duties 188, 199, 247, 249
Tewkesbury 155, 180 n.
Thaxter, Edmund 72, 103, 122, 131,
    135, 136, 139, 143, 154, 157, 158 n.,
    183
Thetford 121, 132, 143, 176, 197
Thursby, William 136

Townshend, Charles, 2nd Viscount 10, 52, 206, 208–14, 217, 218, 221–5, 237, 239, 243–4, 246, 249
  political management 221, 225–7, 228–31, 232–5, 241–2, 244–5, 250–4, 257
Townshend, Charles 250, 251, 253
Townshend, Horatio, 1st Viscount 105–6, 108–9, 111, 120–1, 122, 126–7, 137 n., 140
Townshend, Horatio 232–4, 242, 247, 249
Townshend, Roger 225–6, 228
Townshend, William 253
Tregony 121
Trevanion, Charles 121
Triffit, J. 212
Trimnell, Charles, Bishop of Norwich 245
Turner, Sir Charles 219 n.
Turner, Francis 74
Turner, Sir John 221
Turnor, Sir Edward 114

Union, Anglo-Scottish 223–4
Urwen, John 168

Wakeman family 73, 74, 272–3
Wakeman, Giles 74 n.
Wakeman, Robert 73
Walpole, Horace 228–9, 233 n., 250–1
Walpole, Robert 211, 217, 221, 224, 228, 230, 244–5, 247, 248–9, 253–4
Ward family 69 n.
Ward, Benjamin 201
Ward, George 159, 162, 167
Ward, Robert 238
wars, impact of:
  (1665–7) 113–14, 117
  (1672–4) 125
  (1689–97) 44, 68, 185–6, 187–90, 198–9, 201
  (1702–13) 44, 68, 209–10, 223–5, 236–7
Warwick 26, 29, 180 n., 248
Waters, Issac 224
Waveney, River 36
Webb, S. and B. 8, 15, 17, 18, 175, 258, 262
Western, J. 173
Whitby 199 n.
Whitehaven 119
Wigan 110, 155 n.

William III 170–1, 187
Williamson, Sir Joseph 104, 121, 125, 136, 138, 139, 141, 143–4, 146, 149 n.
Wilson, C. 204
Wilson, R. 75, 92
Windham, Ashe 228–9, 233
Windsor, New 24
Woodroffe, John 76, 103, 104 n., 122, 144, 147, 157, 159
Worcester 27 n.
Wren, Sir Christopher 1

Yare, River 36
Yarmouth, Earls of, *see* Paston, Robert and William
Yarmouth, Great:
  buildings and places: Breydon Water 36; charity school 215, 238–9, 260; Deneside 141, 145, 161; Dutch chapel 70 n., 125 n., 217; Fisherman's Hospital 206, 216, 219, 260; Guildhall 21, 41 n., 248; haven fort 156, 171, 187, 209 n., 230; haven 164, 190, 201 n., 224, 256–7; marketplace 39; St George's chapel 237–8, 243, 259, 260; St Nicholas's church 30, 35, 67, 89 n., 156, 237, 238 n.; South Quay 39, 118; Tolhouse 21 n.; town hall 238, 248, 260
  corporation: officers and members: aldermen 22, 28 n., 64–5, 67–8, 248; attorney 50; bailiffs 22, 28–9; ballastmaster 30; chamberlain 29–30; churchwardens 30; common councillors 22, 28 n., 64–5, 67–8, 248; constables 42; freemen 40–8, 61–3, 65–7, 171 n., 257, 260, 262, economic privileges 178, 194–5, 197–8, 218–21, numbers 18, 242 n., 269, political influences on 166–7, 250–2, 253, political tests 144, 160; half-dole collectors 30; herring-tellers 30; high steward 49, 50, 109, 126, 157–8; jurats 22; justices of the peace 22; mayor 28–9, 161; muragers 30; recorder 49–50, 109, 158; swordbearer 28, 162; town clerk 50, 109; understeward 162
  corporation: structures: admiralty court 20, 192, 194, 196, 200, 205, 240, 243; assembly meetings 26 n.,

115, 198 n.; charters 19–21, 27, 109–10, 124 n., (1684) 154, 156, 157, 158–62, 168, (1688 reversion) 170, 173, 175 n., 176 n., 180, 213, (1703) 212–14; committees 31–2, 205, 238, 240; elections 24–5; finances 29–31, 121, 186, 198–9, 205, 265–7; Guild of Merchants 21, 37; militia 106, 107, 122, 133, 135–6, 153–4, 191, 233; parish structure 38–9; quarter sessions 22; scarlet days 35, 165, 187; tolls 30, 31 n., 42, 81, 83, 231, 236, 248; vestry 216; ward system 39, 190 n., 268; Water Feast 36–7

corporation: themes: absenteeism 26–8; corruption 34, 169; defence of trade 78–84, 111, 187–8, 217, 224–5, 227–8; entertainments 1–2, 35, 71, 94, 123, 131–2, 206, 223; kinship 68–77; landholding 93–4; oaths 33, 42; occupations 79–81; oligarchic trends 61–2, 81–2, 98, 248, 259; order and discipline 23–6, 187–8; patronage 34; poor relief 54–5, 188, 190, 231; professions 74–5, 80, 87, 95–6, 97, 259; recruitment and promotion 22–3, 60–8; ritual and history 32–3, 35, 36–8; secrecy 33–4; status and wealth 32–3, 59, 84–7, 95–7, 268; voting 25–6

Yarmouth, Little (alias Southtown) 161, 213, 235, 236 n.

development scheme 112–13, 117–22, 123–6, 131–2, 134, 136, 139–40, 141, 144–5, 147–8, 153, 163

Yarmouth Tragedy 94–5

York 23 n., 27 n., 41 n., 52, 80, 142, 159 n., 194